BREAKING the IMPASSE in the WAR ON DRUGS

Recent Titles in
Contributions in Political Science
Series Editor: Bernard K. Johnpoll

The Politics of Developed Socialism: The Soviet Union as a Postindustrial State
Donald R. Kelley

Harry S. Truman: The Man from Independence
William F. Levantrosser, editor

News from Somewhere: Connecting Health and Freedom at the Workplace
Gary A. Lewis

"Pursuing the Just Cause of Their People": A Study of Contemporary Armenian Terrorism
Michael M. Gunter

When Marxists Do Research
Pauline Marie Vaillancourt

Government Violence and Repression: An Agenda for Research
Michael Stohl and George A. Lopez, editors

Rural Public Administration: Problems and Prospects
Jim Seroka, editor

Hidden Power: The Seniority System and Other Customs of Congress
Maurice B. Tobin

The Sino-Indian Border Dispute: A Legal Study
Chih H. Lu

The Primordial Challenge: Ethnicity in the Contemporary World
John F. Stack, Jr., editor

Strangers or Friends: Principles for a New Alien Admission Policy
Mark Gibney

Intergovernmental Relations and Public Policy
J. Edwin Benton and David R. Morgan, editors

BREAKING the IMPASSE in the WAR ON DRUGS

STEVEN WISOTSKY

Foreword by Thomas Szasz

CONTRIBUTIONS IN POLITICAL SCIENCE, NUMBER 159

GREENWOOD PRESS
New York • Westport, Connecticut • London

Library of Congress Cataloging-in-Publication Data

Wisotsky, Steven.
Breaking the impasse in the war on drugs.

(Contributions in political science, ISSN 0147-1066 ; no. 159)
Bibliography: p.
Includes index.
1. Narcotics, Control of—United States. 2. Drug abuse—United States. 3. Cocaine habit—United States. I. Title. II. Series.
HV5825.W55 1986 363.4'5'0973 86–7574
ISBN 0–313–24266–6 (lib. bdg. : alk. paper)

Library of Congress Catalog Card Number: 86–7574
ISBN: 0–313–24266–6
ISSN: 0147–1066

First published in 1986

Greenwood Press, Inc.
88 Post Road West, Westport, Connecticut 06881

Printed in the United States of America

The paper used in this book complies with the Permanent Paper Standard issued by the National Information Standards Organization (Z39.48–1984).

10 9 8 7 6 5 4 3 2 1

Copyright Acknowledgments

Permission to reproduce materials from the following sources is gratefully acknowledged.

Pico Iyer, "Fighting the Cocaine Wars," *Time* Magazine, February 25, 1985. Copyright 1985 Time Inc. All rights reserved. Reprinted by permission from *Time*.

Jim McGee and Carl Hiaasen, "A Nation for Sale," *Miami Herald*, September 23, 1984. Reprinted with permission of the *Miami Herald*.

David F. Musto, *The American Disease: Origins of Narcotic Control*. New Haven, Conn.: Yale University Press. Copyright © 1973 by David F. Musto.

Thomas Szasz, *Ceremonial Chemistry: The Ritual Persecution of Drugs, Addicts, and Pushers*. Garden City, New York: Anchor Press/Doubleday. Copyright © 1974 by Thomas Szasz. Reprinted by permission of McIntosh and Otis, Inc.

Craig Van Dyke and Robert Byck, *Drugs in American Society*. The H.W. Wilson Company, New York, 1986. Reprinted by permission of the authors.

To the memory of my father,
To the future of my children.

Contents

Figures and Tables xiii

Foreword *by Thomas Szasz* xv

Preface xvii

Acknowledgments xxi

Acronyms xxiii

PART ONE
LOSING THE WAR ON DRUGS

Introduction: Declaring War on Drugs (Again) 3

1. The Black Market in Cocaine 9

The Rise and Fall and Rise of Cocaine in the United States 9
Measuring the Black Market in Cocaine 12
The "Effects" of Cocaine 17

2. The Economics of the Black Market in Cocaine 31

3. The Structure of the Cocaine Industry 37

Production in Latin America 37
Importation and Distribution 41

Money Laundering 47

4. International Law Enforcement: The Futile Quest for Control of Coca and Cocaine at the Source 49

5. The Federal Drug Police: The U.S. Law Enforcement System 61

Interdicting Cocaine 61
Busting the Trafficker 65
Financial Controls 78

6. Escalating the War on Drugs: No Light at the End of the Tunnel 91

The Interdiction Network: From Miami Task Force to National Narcotics Border Interdiction System 91
The Organized Crime Drug Enforcement Task Force Program 99

7. The Pathology of the War on Drugs: The Assault on Justice and Civil Liberties 117

The Assault on Justice 118
The Growth of Big Brotherism 126

8. The Pathology of the War on Drugs: Corruption and Violence in the Black Market 141

Tax Evasion 141
Corrosion of the Work Ethic 142
Corruption of Public Officials 145
Violence 150
Disrespect for the Law 153

9. The International Pathology of the War on Drugs: Corruption, Instability, and Narco-Terrorism 155

Corruption and Narco-Destabilization 156
Narco-Terrorism 162

PART TWO
BREAKING THE IMPASSE IN THE WAR ON DRUGS

10. Sources of the Impasse 173

11. Beyond the War on Drugs: Creating a New Context 197

12. Drugs in the Future 217

Notes 223

Appendix 1. The War on Drugs (Cocaine)—An Overview 245

Appendix 2. Chronology of Milestones in the War on Drugs 249

Afterword: An Agenda for Study and Action 257

Bibliography 263

Index 273

Figures and Tables

FIGURES

1. Effects of "Criminalization Tax" on Quantity and Price of Cocaine 35
2. Probable Sources of Cocaine Available in the United States, 1984 41
3. Cocaine Seizures from Various Smuggling Conveyances, 1984 44
4. Effects of Law Enforcement on Cultivation of Coca Leaf in New Growing Areas 60
5. Effects of Increased Interdiction Rates on Quantity and Price of Cocaine 96
6. Task Force Cases, Indictments, Convictions, and Estimated Potential Defendants in 1983 102
7. Effects of the War on Drugs on Cocaine Production Costs 114

TABLES

1. Theoretical Maximum Cocaine Available from Coca Leaf Produced in Peru and Bolivia 13
2. Estimate of Illicit Cocaine Entering the United States, 1981 14
3. Narcotics Intelligence Estimate Based on Assumed Consumption Patterns 15
4. NIDA Prevalence Estimates and Population Projections (1982) 16

5. Cocaine Use and Trafficking Indicators, 1981–1984 16
6. Species of Coca and Their Characteristics 38
7. Representative Prices for One Kilogram of Cocaine at Successive Stages of Trafficking, 1980 42
8. Federal Drug Law Enforcement—Summary 62
9. Seizures in South Florida by Miami Task Force and Other Federal Agencies (Through September 30, 1983) 97
10. Drugs, Cash, and Property Seized and Fines Levied in OCDE Task Force Cases in 1983 103

Foreword

For seven decades, the American Government has been waging a War on Drugs. Seemingly, this war has received the enthusiastic support of the American people who have chosen to vote into office politicians promising to prosecute it vigorously. However, inasmuch as drugs on a shelf are inert substances, the War on Drugs cannot, in fact, be directed against drugs; it can only be directed against those persons who sell, buy, or consume the officially forbidden chemicals. In that case, of course, the War on Drugs becomes an exercise similar to Prohibition or the Comstock Laws, wherein a democratic people choose to abolish the free market in a product or service which they intensely crave. Obviously, such a prohibitionist effort cannot succeed unless draconian measures are used to enforce it—measures rarely employed by democratic governments. Not very surprisingly, the effort fails, or more precisely, *seems* to fail. Again, I say *seems,* because if a person simultaneously seeks and avoids an act or object, he may be said to fail or succeed regardless of whether or not he obtains the object of his desired aversion.

In this exhaustively, indeed masterfully, documented study, Professor Steven Wisotsky demonstrates the failure, on a truly gigantic scale, of the American people's effort to deprive themselves of the drugs so many of them want. His hope—which I share, but about which I am considerably less confident than he—is that by documenting this massive failure, those who prosecute the War on Drugs might be persuaded to lay down their arms.

What makes me temper my hopes about such a rationalistic perspective on the War on Drugs is that it neglects certain key elements in America's effort to become "drug-free." Briefly put, in the United States, the Judeo-Christian (and especially Puritan) struggle against temptation, combined with the passion for the immediate satisfaction of "needs," have generated an unusually intense ambivalence about a host of pleasure-producing acts and objects, illicit drugs being but one. In addition, perhaps because of our diversity as a people, it is difficult for us to find a stable basis for "congregating" as a nation, a circumstance that amplifies our collective craving for moral crusades against scapegoats bearing heavy loads of imaginary dangers. These considerations support and underscore the importance of Kenneth Burke's wise observation that "The sacrificial principle of victimage (the 'scapegoat') is intrinsic to human congregation." This principle explains why it is such a sad truism that, as Friedrich von Hayek puts it, "It is indeed probable that more harm and misery have been caused by men determined to use coercion to stamp out a moral evil than by men intent on doing evil." In my opinion, this is not just probable, it is quite certain.

In short, we must not underestimate the demagogic appeal which the prospect of stamping out evil by suitably dramatic means has always exercised, and will continue to exercise, on the minds of men and women. The Romans, barbarians that they were, had circuses where they watched gladiators kill each other. Our circuses—splashed across the front pages of newspapers and magazines, and flashed unceasingly on television screens—entertain us with our own civilized, and of course scientific, spectacles: we are shown how "bad" illicit drugs—ingested, injected, and inhaled by persons who want to use them—injure and kill their victims; and how "good" psychiatric drugs—forced on persons who do not want to use them—cure them of their nonexistent mental illnesses. At the same time, we are expected not to measure the putative harm caused by illegal substances such as marijuana against the proven harm caused by legal substances such as tobacco or to compare the putative dangers of using prohibited drugs with the proven dangers of enforcing their prohibition. Finally, to top off this absurd spectacle, we are subjected to the public prayers of the wives of presidents, beseeching their deity to save us, not from temptation, but from the dread disease of drug abuse—a travesty on both religion and science neither theologians nor scientists dare to ridicule. Professor Wisotsky's book is a heroic attempt to stem the tide of this crowd madness.

Thomas Szasz

Preface

Cocaine is here to stay. What, if anything, should we do about that? The answer begins by rejecting the question thus posed. Cocaine is not the issue. No progress can be made from that false formulation.

When I started the research that culminated in the writing of this book, I began with the conception that locates cocaine and its effects at the center of inquiry. I held the opinion that cocaine was a relatively benign drug; that its reputation as a dangerous drug resulted primarily from an outrageous U.S. Government propaganda campaign, aided by sensationalism in the broadcast and print media; and that regardless of the properties and effects of cocaine, the Government's efforts to suppress it were not only predestined to fail, but enormously destructive in their own right.

After some years of research during the period of the greatest cocaine boom in history, my judgment on the adverse consequences of drug law enforcement hardened, while my attitude about cocaine became more cautious. The rapid proliferation of casualties of freebase smoking demonstrated the remarkable psychic "pull" of what many users regard as the most euphoric drug experience of them all. The dangers of intravenous cocaine use, often combined with heroin in a "speedball" injection, also gave me pause. Nevertheless, I concluded that the Government has grossly distorted the actual risks of taking cocaine by a campaign of scare tactics. Millions of Americans consume billions of lines (or puffs) of cocaine every year, with little or no long-term damage to their physical or emotional well-being. Legitimate health concerns do revolve around a minority of users of cocaine who fall into the trap of chronic, compulsive use, especially by injection or smoking. For them, the drug experience often ends in disaster.

While this information is true in a superficial sense, it is nonetheless misleading insofar as it uncritically assumes that the drug is the active force or cause of problems in the life of the cocaine user. Cocaine (or any other drug) as "the problem" is no more than metaphor. The nearly universal belief that cocaine has caused the undoing of tens of thousands of victims who succumbed to its seductive/addictive charms reflects a dubious and simplistic conception of human behavior that must not be allowed to go unchallenged. The conceptual error lies in the conventional preoccupation with objective "causes" of cocaine dependency (neurotransmitters, dopamine deficiency, and so forth). This focus on what the drug "does" to the subject ignores the critical qualities that distinguish human beings from caged laboratory animals with catheters stuck in their veins to deliver unlimited quantities of cocaine. Under conditions of unlimited access to cocaine, monkeys or rats will frequently dose themselves to death. Researchers then infer that cocaine has a powerful, addicting quality. In this Cartesian reduction of the human being to a physical entity, there is no scope for intelligence, restraint, responsibility, or moral choice. Rather, man becomes a mere object, a machine or mass of tissue, waiting to be acted upon by an outside force. Under this distorted stimulus-response model of reality, cocaine *is* addictive. Indeed, some researchers have asserted that it is the most addictive drug of all.

But the facts lend themselves more sensibly to a competing interpretation in which human volition rather than the pharmacology of the drug plays the dominant role. Neither cocaine nor any other drug "is" addicting under this model simply because the overwhelming majority of people do not *permit* themselves to become "addicted." The decision to take a drug, the frequency, amount, occasion, and place all control its "effects" and undermine the validity of "scientific" model of "addiction." Thus, the standard loosely estimated claim that about 10–20 percent of those using cocaine sooner or later become addicted obviously means that the remaining 80 percent do not become addicted. Clearly, the effects of the drug do not cause any single or inevitable pattern of human behavior. Does it make sense to call cocaine addictive when 80 percent of those who use it do *not* become addicted?

Yet that is precisely the position of the Government and its reason for classifying cocaine as a narcotic. The claim seems as silly to me as the logically parallel claim that food must be "addictive" because X percent of the population is clinically obese and cannot stop overeating. Food "causes" obesity, does it not? Similarly, we could conclude that compulsive fingernail biters are "addicted" to the chemical properties of fingernails, which reinforce the compulsion. This conception exactly reverses cause and effect, mistaking the mere object of desire for its cause.

Focusing on the properties of cocaine (or any other drug), labeling it as a dangerous or addictive drug, and attacking its supply as a way of controlling drug abuse is as foolish as focusing on the chemical properties of food and its supply as a way of controlling obesity. While the dieter needs accurate information about nutrition (fat, protein, calories, carbohydrates, and the like), everyone understands or should understand that informed self-regulation is the path to weight control. Researchers can theorize endlessly about fat cells and basal metabolism; and recent studies claim to have confirmed a strong genetic "predisposition" toward childhood obesity. Such arguments simply reflect the researchers' materialist conception of human behavior, i.e., one that prefers "objective" and deterministic explanations to immeasurable "unscientific" truths about volition and self-control. Yet are there any "genetically predisposed" fat people in the famine-stricken areas of Ethiopia? Under less extreme conditions, is it possible *not* to lose weight on a fast?

Under this competing anti-materialist, ethical conception, what we call drug abuse is not a function of "addicting drugs" but of human failure or preference. Drugs are not the issue and should receive relatively little attention per se. The emphasis belongs instead on encouraging responsible behavior to avoid impairment, not on preventive checking of the content of the blood or urine. No drug is "addictive" if avoided in the first place or taken in moderation. The study and control of "addiction" thus belong primarily to the realm of moral philosophy and psychology, with biology and pharmacology playing no more than secondary roles. Under this ethical model, a war on drugs would make no more sense than a war on any other inanimate object. Drugs would instead be understood by the public to belong to a very large category of ordinary things having a potential for mischief when ignorantly mishandled, like butcher knives, roach poison, aspirin, hammers, chain saws, motorcycles, and firearms. In the management of these "dangerous" objects, knowledge and responsibility would be required, and maybe appropriate legal regulation (including protection of minors), but not a "war."

Wars are destructive by definition, and the Reagan Administration's War on Drugs is no exception. Not only has it failed to suppress the U.S. supply of cocaine, which nearly trebled from 1980 to 1985 to exceed 100 metric tons, but in the process of trying it has inflicted major damage on the political and economic institutions of the United States and its allies. Through the black market that it perpetuates, intensified enforcement has nurtured the growth of a vicious international trafficking parasite. Governed by the laws of supply and demand the alchemy of prohibition transforms a $50 ounce of pharmaceutical cocaine into $2,000 or $3,000 worth of contraband with total sales of $30 billion or so. This black market cocaine money circulates in a vast underground drug economy of $80-$100 billion per year. These narco-billions corrupt public officials, pay for drug "hits" or ripoffs, and finance "narco-terrorism" and subversion in Latin America. The War on Drugs thus yields the worst of both worlds: a steadily rising tide of illegal drugs and a burgeoning syndrome of pathologies inevitably called forth when millions of people systematically defy the law.

Logic teaches that false premises lead to false conclusions. The War on Drugs has produced such poor results—futility and destruction—precisely because it was conceived in error and confusion. If ever we are to make any progress in breaking away from what the editors of *Consumer Reports* perceptively described in a 1970 study as the "drug problem problem," we must begin with a fundamental conceptual reorientation. We must move beyond the very idea of the War on Drugs, repudiating its obsessive preoccupation with the control of drugs as dangerous objects and replacing it with controls that acknowledge the centrality of individual responsibility. It's a big challenge, no doubt. But the reversal of the premise that drug taking controls human behavior is the only moral and political principle appropriate to an understanding of human beings as responsible moral agents rather than caged rhesus monkeys with catheters fixed in their veins.

Acknowledgments

Few will be surprised to read that I relied on the support of many people in the course of researching and writing this book, my first. What may be a bit unusual is the extent to which faculty, staff, and students of the Nova University Law Center provided indispensable support for my work, creating rich layers of opportunity over a period of years. Drug law and social policy is not a conventional course offering at law schools, yet the Nova faculty readily accepted my proposal in 1981 to teach a Drug Enforcement Seminar, which I have taught every year since. Nova law students responded energetically to the seminar, and challenging interchanges with sharp-witted law students played an important role in the evolution of my ideas by forcing me to refine my thinking.

Former Dean Ovid Lewis gave me a gentle starting nudge and propped up my motivation whenever it faltered. He also selected my book proposal in a competition for a summer research grant, liberating me from the financial necessity of teaching summer school to pay the mortgage. That support conferred upon me an exceptional opportunity to read and think about my subject free of mundane distractions.

Outside the Nova Law Center, the editorial board of the *University of Wisconsin Law Review* deserves mention for publishing an early version of what later evolved into Part One of this book. The *Wisconsin* editors responded with enthusiasm, running my lengthy piece as the lead article of the issue (1983, number 6) in which it appeared. Of equal importance were their academic contributions. Corey Ayling in particular subjected my economic analysis of the black market in cocaine to helpful criticism.

The process of producing lengthy typescripts rife with footnotes, tables, charts, and graphs turned out to be far more demanding than I had anticipated. The word processing staff at the Nova Law Center, supervised by the efficient Paula Sabino, performed with exceptional skill. Jesse Monteagudo and Nancy Kelly Sanguigni produced countless drafts and revisions of article and book typescripts with dazzling speed and impressive accuracy. My loyal secretary Lillian Sartell took care of the necessary correspondence and did an esthetically pleasing job of producing tables and figures.

Before the writing, of course, came the research. Because much of it falls under the rubric of either pharmacology or sociology, you will not find the literature of drug enforcement and drug policy on the shelves at most law school libraries. Nova Law Library Director Carol Roehrenbeck and her staff did an outstanding job of acquiring the necessary books and materials. Pat Harris and Nikki Singleton, who have since advanced to positions of higher responsibility at other institutions, guided me through the maze of government documents in print and microfiche. Other materials, especially books out of print, they tracked down by computer and retrieved for me through interlibrary loans. Carol and her staff also searched computerized data banks to ensure the comprehensiveness of my research. Finally, exercising the prerogative of Nova faculty members to recommend books for acquisition, I worked with Ron Stroud to purchase dozens of new titles for our shelves. The Nova University Law Library now has an extensive collection of books, monographs, medical journals, and other materials on drug law enforcement.

My work benefitted from the generosity of former and present Nova faculty members who took the time to make suggestions, to bring data to my attention, or simply to offer a word of encouragement when one was needed. Nearly everyone contributed in some fashion. Art Miller, retired to Key West, tutored me in the techniques of academic publishing. Peter Nimkoff, who departed for the federal bench, frequently contributed information on new developments in law enforcement. Marty Feinrider gave generously of his time, serving as a sounding board for ideas and criticizing an early version of my work. Mike Masinter lent his expertise in economic analysis to my questions about elasticity of supply and the like.

Former student and good friend Sandy Karlan waded through a rough manuscript with a sharp pencil. Jean Kneale, my Goodwin Research Assistant, performed the essential tasks of proofreading the ever-changing typescript, compiling the bibliography, and assisting with research and source checking. Gil Pastoriza compiled a fine index.

Finally, my wife, Marcia Cypen, should be acknowledged for her role in bringing the book to completion. Not only did she read and edit a draft, but the tone of her frequent rhetorical inquiry about the incomplete state of the book had its intended stimulative effect. Completion is a very satisfying experience.

Acronyms

ABA	American Bar Association
ACLU	American Civil Liberties Union
AID	Agency for International Development
AMA	American Medical Association
BATF	Bureau of Alcohol, Tobacco and Firearms
BNDD	Bureau of Narcotics and Dangerous Drugs
BSA	Bank Secrecy Act
CAMP	California Antimarijuana Project
CCC Act	Comprehensive Crime Control Act
CCE	Continuing Criminal Enterprise
CI	Confidential Informant
CIA	Central Intelligence Agency
CID	Criminal Investigation Division
CMIR	Currency and Monetary Instrument Report
CTR	Currency Transaction Report
DAWN	Drug Abuse Warning Network
DEA	Drug Enforcement Administration
DOD	Department of Defense
DOJ	Department of Justice
FAA	Federal Aviation Administation
FARC	Colombian Revolutionary Armed Forces
FBAR	Foreign Bank Account Report
FBI	Federal Bureau of Investigation

FBN	Federal Bureau of Narcotics
FCC	Federal Communications Commission
FDA	Food and Drug Administration
FLEC	Financial Law Enforcement Center
GAO	General Accounting Office
GDEP	Geographic Drug Enforcement Program
GEP	General Enforcement Program
IBRD	International Bank for Reconstruction and Development
IDA	International Development Association
IICC	Intelligence Information Command Center
IOIC	Inderdiction Operations Intelligence Center
INM	(Bureau of) International Narcotics Matters
INS	Immigration and Naturalization Service
IRS	Internal Revenue Service
NADDIS	Narcotics and Dangerous Drug Information System
NIDA	National Institute on Drug Abuse
NIE	Narcotics Intelligence Estimate
NNBIS	National Narcotics Border Interdiction System
NNICC	National Narcotics Intelligence Consumers Committee
NORML	National Organization for the Reform of Marijuana Laws
OCDETF	Organized Crime Drug Enforcement Task Force
ODALE	Office of Drug Abuse Law Enforcement
ONNI	Office of National Narcotics Intelligence
RICO	Racketeer Influenced Corrupt Organization
SEP	Special Enforcement Program
STARS	Small Tethered Aerostat Relocatable System

PART ONE

Losing the War on Drugs

The world we have made as a result of the level of thinking we have done thus far creates problems we cannot solve at the same level at which we created them.

—Albert Einstein

The chief cause of problems is solutions.

—Eric Sevareid

Introduction: Declaring War on Drugs (Again)

On October 14, 1982, President Ronald Reagan delivered a speech at the Department of Justice, declaring war on crime and pledging an "unshakable" commitment "to do what is necessary to end the drug menace" and "to cripple the power of the mob in America."[1] This was not the first time a President had declared war on drugs. A decade before, in a message to Congress on June 17, 1971, Richard Nixon had portrayed drug abuse as "a national emergency," labeling it "public enemy number one" and calling for "a total offensive."[2]

Both Presidents reacted to the rapid proliferation of recreational drug use, which rippled outward in concentric social circles. Under Nixon, it spread from the beatniks and the bohemian avant garde of the 1950s to the hippies, yippies, and straight youth of the 1960s. In the 1970s and 1980s, the use of marijuana, cocaine, and other drugs spread to the yuppies, the upper middle class, and then to the very mainstream of society: 24 million admitted marijuana smokers and 12 million users of cocaine turned up in the 1982 *National Household Survey on Drug Abuse.*[3]

To counteract this perceived drug menace, both drug wars began with major build-ups of personnel and reorganizations of the drug enforcement agencies. President Nixon succeeded in doubling the manpower of the Bureau of Narcotics and Dangerous Drugs (to 1,500 agents), later consolidating prime federal drug enforcement power in the newly created Drug Enforcement Administration (DEA). The Reagan Administration likewise built up and reorganized the anti-drug bureaucracy, but went far beyond Nixon in mobilizing virtually the entire federal government, including the military, in the War on Drugs. The scale of this enterprise perfectly reflected the Administration's attitude toward the drug issue, as conveyed in this Presidential statement of October 2, 1982: "The mood towards drugs is changing in this country and the momentum is with us. We're making no excuses for drugs, hard, soft or otherwise. Drugs are bad and we're going after them."[4] And the Administration did just that.

The President's speech of October 14 called for and got more of everything: (1) more personnel—1,020 law enforcement agents for the DEA, Federal Bureau of Investigation (FBI), and other agencies, 200 Assistant United States Attorneys, and 340 clerical staff; (2) more aggressive law enforcement—creating 12 (later 13) regional prosecutorial task forces across the nation "to identify, investigate, and prosecute members of high-level drug trafficking enterprises, and to destroy the operations of those organizations;" (3) more money—$127.5 million in *additional* funding, and a substantial re-allocation of the existing $702.8 million budget away from prevention, treatment, and research programs to law enforcement programs; (4) more prison bed space—the addition of 1,260 beds at 11 federal prisons to accommodate the increase in drug offenders to be incarcerated; (5) more stringent laws—a "legislative offensive designed to win approval of reforms" with respect to bail, sentencing, criminal forfeiture, and the exclusionary rule; (6) more (better) inter-agency coordination, bringing together all federal law enforcement agencies in "a comprehensive attack on drug trafficking and organized crime" under a Cabinet-level committee chaired by the Attorney General; and (7) improved federal-state coordination, including federal assisting state agencies by training their agents.[5]

The President's perception about the mood of the country seemed accurate. His anti-drug initiative was not imposed from above upon an indifferent public but drew energy from a broad base of political support. Before his October 14 speech, for example, the Attorney General's Task Force on Violent Crime had recommended "an unequivocal commitment to combatting international and domestic drug traffic."[6] In the Senate, 28 Senators had banded together in the Drug Enforcement Caucus in order to "establish drug enforcement as a Senate priority."[7] And the House Select Committee on Narcotics Abuse and Control had urged the President to "declare war on drugs."[8]

Congress itself soon became a beehive of activity in support of the War on Drugs. First, the Administration persuaded Congress to enact all of its "legislative offensive" toughening the laws governing bail, sentencing, criminal forfeiture, and the exclusionary rule. Second, Congress was called upon to finance the war, and it responded in the first year of the war with a special appropriation that gave the Administration 100 percent of what it had requested in addition to the regular fiscal 1983 drug enforcement budget.[9]

This political cohesion between the Administration and Congress for the War on Drugs seemed to reflect a growing social consensus that illegal drug use had gotten out of hand. The backlash took many forms: schools adopted programs of drug-detector dog sniffing and surprise searches for drugs in student lockers. State highway patrols implemented surprise roadblocks at which cars were subjected to drug-sniffing dogs. In the media, editorials condemning drug abuse became a staple item. Television began to take a leading role during 1982 and 1983; the national television networks broadcast news or documentary programs of at least one hour in length, including "Pleasure Drugs: The Great American High" (NBC) and "The Cocaine Cartel" (ABC). NBC embellished its drug awareness with the melodrama "Cocaine—One Man's Seduction." Weekly news magazines were particularly active purveyors of drugs-on-the-American-scene reportage. *Time* magazine did three cover stories on cocaine: "Cocaine: Middle Class High" (1981), "Crashing on Cocaine" (1983), and "Fighting the Cocaine Wars" (1985). *Newsweek* also ran three covers on drugs: "Guns, Grass and Money" (1982), "Drugs on the Job" (1983), and "Getting Straight" (1984). The tone of these stories left no doubt about the attitude of the writers or editors—this was bad news.

The anti-drug backlash gained momentum with the rapid proliferation of over 4,000 parents' groups under the umbrella of the National Federation of Parents for Drug-Free Youth. Later, it spread to alcohol abuse, as demonstrated by the sudden emergence of Mothers Against Drunk Driving (MADD) as a political force: in just two years about half the states adopted stricter drunk-driving laws.

Energized by this hardening attitude toward alcohol and illegal drugs, the Administration acted aggressively, hiring hundreds more agents for the DEA, FBI, and other enforcement agencies and mobilizing an impressive array of federal bureaucracies and resources in a coordinated (although futile) attack on the drug supply. The roles of the FBI and the Internal Revenue Service (IRS) in drug enforcement were significantly expanded. The Administration created a national network of Organized Crime Drug Enforcement Task Forces (OCDETFs) spread across 13 core cities in the United States. The Central Intelligence Agency (CIA) was recruited for aerial surveillance and other intelligence on foreign drug supplies and suppliers. The State Department pursued crop control programs in drug-producing nations. Emboldened by the "unqualified success" of the Special Task Force on Crime in South Florida, the Administration created the National Narcotics Border Interdiction System (NNBIS), designed to stop the flow of drugs at the border.

Reagan also succeeded in literally militarizing what had previously been a rhetorical war by deploying the military forces of the United States in drug enforcement operations. The Department of Defense (DOD) provided pursuit planes, helicopters, and other equipment to civilian enforcement agencies, while Navy "hawkeye" radar planes patrolled the coastal skies in search of smuggling aircraft and ships. The Coast Guard intensified its customary task of interdicting drug-carrying vessels at sea; and for the first time in American history Navy ships, including a nuclear-powered anti-aircraft carrier, interdicted—and in one case fired upon—drug-smuggling ships in international waters.

As the sales leader in the black market in drugs, cocaine became the principal target of the War on Drugs. Until 1975 or so, cocaine had been fourth on the Government's list of drug enforcement priorities. Later it elevated cocaine to a second enforcement priority behind heroin. But in response to the spectacular growth of the black market in cocaine in the 1980s, the Reagan Administration made cocaine its top priority drug, allocating 55 percent of its investigative energies to cocaine trafficking.[10]

In view of the predominance of the Government commitment to suppress the cocaine traffic, its seems reasonable to assess the War on Drugs primarily in terms of its effect on its primary target. The other principal targets in the War on Drugs—marijuana and heroin—are so thoroughly institutionalized in American life that the War on Drugs cannot seriously propose to make a dent in their supply, whatever the symbolism intended by initiatives such as the California Antimarijuana Project (CAMP). With heroin, the consuming population includes a significant percentage of addicts who are strongly committed to buying the drug at almost any price. Seven decades of relentless efforts to suppress it since enactment of the Harrison Narcotics Act of 1914 have proved that the supply of heroin always finds its way to the consumer demand, albeit at very high prices. Recent evidence also points to a growing level of episodic, recreational use among progeny of the wealthy and the middle class.[11] In this domain, the War on Drugs might make sense as a containment policy, struggling to keep the lid on further growth in heroin's "market share" for non-addicted users. But rationing consumption by "taxing" heroin to extraordinary price levels has the *least* chance of success with affluent consumers. Heroin is here to stay.

With marijuana, the attack on supply approaches the absurd. In contrast to the opium poppy, which grows primarily in Mexico, Turkey, the Far East, and Southwest Asia, and must accordingly be smuggled into the United States, marijuana is grown and can be grown virtually anywhere in the world, including all 50 states of the United States. Thus, a large-scale American marijuana industry has emerged to fill the gap in foreign supply produced by intensive interdiction of marijuana freighters in Caribbean and Atlantic waters. As a result of this "successful" interdiction of marijuana from abroad, we now have extensive, and still burgeoning, cultivation of high potency marijuana in the United States. In one three-day "sweep" during 1985, DEA agents sighted 3,010 illegal plots of marijuana. The National Organization for the Reform of Marijuana Laws (NORML) estimates that marijuana is now America's third largest cash crop, worth nearly $14 billion per year.[12] Notably, prices of commercial grade marijuana at $40–60 an ounce are lower, after correcting for inflation, than they were

15–20 years ago. Domestic cultivation of marijuana ranges so far and wide that a technical "fix" such as intensive aerial spraying of paraquat (putting aside concerns about its impact on the environment and on human health) is impractical and very costly. Inaccessible fields and indoor cultivation of marijuana in warehouses equipped with heat lamps would still remain beyond the reach of an intensive paraquat program.

Apart from the relative immunity of supply, demand emanates from a solid base of some 24 million smokers. And despite the growing backlash against drugs, a substantial minority of adults believes that possession of marijuana should not be a crime. It was not long ago—during the 1970s—that important mainstream organizations like the American Medical Association (AMA), the American Bar Association (ABA), the American Public Health Association, the National Council of Churches, the National Commission on Marihuana and Drug Abuse, and others went on record in favor of decriminalization, as did President Jimmy Carter. Whatever the backlash, the pendulum has not reversed course far enough to delegitimize the acceptance that marijuana has gained in American life.

So, if the War on Drugs has any chance of success at all, it will have to be against cocaine, a relative newcomer to the American scene. Cocaine was, after all, effectively suppressed once before, in the 1920s, when enforcement of the Harrison Narcotics Act put an end to the almost free availability of the drug during the two decades of the "golden age" of patent medicines. If it was effectively suppressed then, perhaps it can be done again. One might argue that more than 20 million people have tried it but only 6.75 million reported having used it within the past month. Perhaps, as the government hopes, it is a passing fad, like speed was in the sixties. The pharmacology of cocaine as a "non-addictive" stimulant also encourages this line of wistful speculation. Also, the national weaning process, if it should occur, would not cause any significant pain or discomfort to the great bulk of recreational users. Even habitual users would not experience the intense physiological symptoms and craving characteristic of heroin withdrawal.

On the supply side of the equation, moreover, the production of coca leaves for conversion to cocaine is concentrated overwhelmingly in just two countries, Peru and Bolivia. This concentration holds open the possibility that crop control might be achieved, an impossibility with marijuana. Trafficking patterns also are highly concentrated, with an estimated 75–80 percent of the supply of finished cocaine or cocaine base coming from Colombia. Again, the intense concentration of supply lines offers some encouragement to enforcement authorities about the prospects for effective political controls and interdiction of the product at its source before it reaches market. While the Government's attempt to suppress marijuana and heroin might be compared to King Canute's command to roll back the tide, the war against cocaine offers these potential handholds on supply. For this reason, and because of its sudden prominence, it will be the ultimate battleground for the war against drugs.

But the war against cocaine inevitably is a losing proposition. The laws of supply and demand guarantee that. It is precisely the fact of its illegality that makes trafficking in cocaine so extraordinarily lucrative, perhaps the most lucrative trade in the world. Law enforcement only inflates the price, providing the incentive that perpetuates the cycle. Even if intensified enforcement somehow succeeded in reducing supply, it would also succeed, as long as demand holds, in raising prices and the revenues received by drug traffickers. This in turn would exacerbate the pathologies of the black market, inflicting further social, political, and economic wounds on American society and destabilizing our allies in Latin America.

The paramilitary pounding away at the production and distribution of cocaine props up its high price in the black market, thereby creating a vast underground economy of billions. The black market feeds the growth of powerful crime syndicates willing to commit murder and to corrupt public officials and indeed whole governments; it promotes international terrorism and subversion by funding unholy alliances between drug traffickers and terrorists or guerrillas; it broadens police powers and destroys the civil rights of citizens through its incessant demands for more power over daily life; and it debases the rule of law through a gradual but obvious result-oriented queezing of the criminal justice system designed to "get" drug traffickers. Ultimately, the War on Drugs is not against those inanimate objects called drugs but against American citizens and their values. One way or another, no matter what the War on Drugs does to supply, the black market in cocaine will play its trump: it thrives on enforcement, depends on it. There is no escape from the drug supply or from the effects of drug enforcement.

The blind failure of federal policy makers to acknowledge this truth and to confront it in some realistic, constructive way presents an easy target for critics of the status quo. Yet, the criticisms are not only fair, they spring from a moral imperative. The federal drug enforcement machinery is a system out of control, unaccountable, irresponsible, and mindlessly stuck to a course of action that has made things worse and will inevitably continue to do so in the future. This situation challenges the ability of our society to engage in critical thinking on a difficult subject. The need is to precipitate a breakthrough, a turning point, a transformation of the social context so that the destructive machinery of the War on Drugs ceases to be the only conceivable response to the problems created by illegal drug use. A dose of reality seems the logical starting point.

1

The Black Market in Cocaine

THE RISE AND FALL AND RISE OF COCAINE IN THE UNITED STATES

In July, 1884, Sigmund Freud, then an impoverished twenty-seven-year-old Viennese physician struggling for the professional success that would provide him with enough money to marry his fiancee, published "Uber Coca," the first of his five medical papers on cocaine.[1] Freud regarded cocaine as a panacea, and in the article he recommended it for a variety of therapeutic purposes, including treatment of poor health, as a cure for morphine addiction, as a stimulant, for relief of digestive disorders, for asthma, and as an aphrodisiac.

Freud first took an oral dose of 1/20 gram of cocaine dissolved in water on April 30, 1884, and experienced euphoria. He was so impressed with the euphoric and therapeutic effects of what he termed this "magical drug" that he not only became a regular user himself, but pressed it on his friends, colleagues, sisters, and fiancee.[2] Freud's personal enthusiasm and published work generated great interest in the drug in medical circles. In 1885, Freud's colleague, Carl Koller, used cocaine as a topical anesthetic and successfully performed cataract surgery on Freud's father, thereby establishing the enduring role of cocaine in modern surgery.[3]

In addition to Freud, several American doctors advocated various cocaine therapies for the cure of alcoholism and morphinism. Chief among them was W. H. Bentley. Bentley, along with Theodor Aschenbrandt in Europe, had published on cocaine, stimulating Freud's interest.[4] The use of coca preparations and tonics received wide endorsement, including formal endorsement by over 3,000 doctors and numerous celebrities:

> Cocaine achieved popularity in the United States as a general tonic, for sinusitis and hay fever, and as a cure for the opium, morphine, and alcohol habits. Learned

journals published accounts which just avoided advising unlimited intake of cocaine. . . . In the United States the exhilarating properties of cocaine made it a favorite ingredient of medicine, soda pop, wines, and so on. The Parke Davis Company, an exceptionally enthusiastic producer of cocaine, even sold coca-leaf cigarettes and coca cheroots to accompany their other products, which provided cocaine in a variety of media and routes such as a liqueurlike alcohol mixture called Coca Cordial, tablets, hypodermic injections, ointments, and sprays.[5]

Cocaine proved not to be a panacea, however. In addition to its therapeutic powers, it showed a dark side, and reports of cocaine psychosis and addiction began circulating as early as 1886. By 1887, Dr. A. Erlenmeyer, a leading figure in the medical profession, had denounced cocaine as "the third scourge of mankind," after morphine and alcohol, and Freud was forced to retract his advocacy of curing morphine addiction with cocaine. In his defensive response to Erlenmeyer's charges, Freud called them "pathological" labeling and disingenuously denied having made the earlier recommendation to administer cocaine by injection.[6]

The counterattack on cocaine was much larger in scale than a contest of egos. In the same year as Erlenmeyer's denunciation, Oregon became the first of several states to restrict over-the-counter sales of cocaine by requiring a doctor's prescription. By 1900, seven other states had adopted such laws.[7] Nevertheless, these statutes did not apply to the often high concentrations of cocaine contained in patent medicines and other cheap tonic-type remedies, and national consumption of cocaine continued to rise until passage of the Pure Food and Drug Act of 1906.[8] The act's required disclosure of the contents of medicines shipped in commerce tended to discourage the use of cocaine in patent remedies because of growing suspicion and criticism of the drug. Thus, it is probably not a coincidence that national cocaine consumption peaked in 1906 at 21,000 pounds, a figure unsurpassed on a per capita basis until the mid–1970s.[9]

Direct federal suppression of both cocaine and opiate drugs began in 1914 when Congress passed the Harrison Narcotics Act.[10] Initially, the law relied upon registration and revenue provisions, permitting doctors to dispense cocaine and other drugs upon the filing of the required forms and payment of the required fees. By 1922, a series of restrictive amendments to the statute seemed to outlaw the dispensing of cocaine to patients.[11] Some doctors continued prescribing cocaine for addicted patients under the apparent authority of the Harrison Act, which allowed a physician to dispense the drug "in the course of his professional practice." But pressure by federal agents quickly cut off the practice of addiction maintenance. The dominance of enforcement agents over the authority of addict-treating physicians was vindicated by a compliant Supreme Court. By the mid–1920s, the addiction maintenance clinics had been shut down. Medical use of cocaine in the United States was thereafter restricted to surgical anesthesia or the "treatment" of terminal cancer patients with the pain-killing "Brompton's cocktail." Thus, the licit supply of cocaine in the United States to patients (rather than doctors) was abolished.

The moral condemnation and the often hysterical fears that had motivated the passage of the Harrison Narcotics Act of 1914 succeeded, by the 1930s, in driving cocaine underground. Social history tells us that its use was confined to a relatively small black market. Clearly, it was available to musicians and sophisticates of cafe society, judging by the era's films and popular music, such as the Cole Porter song "I Get a Kick out of You" ("I get no kick from cocaine").

Some authorities argue that the introduction in 1932 of amphetamine, a drug with strikingly similar stimulant effects, diverted consumer attention from cocaine.[12] With a cheap and legal alternative stimulant available, the argument goes, the attraction of cocaine was substantially diminished. By the same logic, some writers have argued that the current consumer interest in cocaine stems at least in part from federal enforcement actions that in the late 1960s restricted both the legal and illegal supplies of amphetamines.[13] Of course, other factors were also at work, such as easier access to cocaine supplies in South America through Cuban immigrants who came to the United States in the 1960s. In addition, more tolerant social attitudes toward illegal drug abuse and the advent of the disco culture of the 1970s also played important roles in the proliferation of the use of cocaine in middle-class society.

Whatever the reasons for its spread, the renascence of cocaine in the United States began with vigor in the 1960s. It was reflected in a variety of ways. Seizures of the drug by the United States Customs Service rose gradually during the 1960s and then sharply in the 1970s.[14] References to the drug in the pop culture of the period became commonplace in films like *Easy Rider* and *Superfly* and songs like the Grateful Dead's "Casey Jones" and J. J. Cale's "Cocaine."

The mass media quickly seized upon the development. For example, from 1962 through 1970, the *Readers' Guide to Periodical Literature* lists only one article on cocaine. In 1979 alone there were 25. The adoption of cocaine by the middle classes was evidently considered hot copy by the media, which reported on it incessantly and often sensationally. The cover of *Time* magazine in July, 1981, may have nevertheless captured the essence of the phenomenon with its image of a martini glass filled with white powder, topped by an olive, to symbolize the accompanying cover story, "Middle Class High." Less than two years later, *Time* ran yet another cocaine cover with a more ominous story, "Crashing on Cocaine." The article emphasized the dangers of cocaine and the risks of injury and dependency. For the second time in the twentieth century, the glamor of cocaine had been superceded by its dark side, replicating in cultural terms the odyssey of cocaine through the legal system nearly seven decades before.

MEASURING THE BLACK MARKET IN COCAINE

Everyone agrees that the black market in cocaine is very, very big. But no one knows for sure how much cocaine Americans buy and consume. The Government relies on the educated guesses of the National Narcotics Intelligence Consumers Committee (NNICC), an inter-agency committee composed of representatives from the Coast Guard, Customs Service, DEA, FBI, Immigration and Naturalization Service (INS), IRS, National Institute on Drug Abuse (NIDA), and State Department and chaired by the Director of Official Intelligence of DEA. Annually it publishes an estimate of the size of the black market in cocaine and other illicit drugs. This Narcotics Intelligence Estimate (NIE) consists of two separate figures, one based on production and one on consumption.

The NIE derives its estimate of cocaine production from satellite surveillance of land under coca cultivation in the primary growing areas of Peru, Bolivia, and, to a much smaller extent in Colombia. The NIE estimate represents the net quantity of cocaine that can be converted from the coca leaf that is harvested and shipped to markets in the United States, Canada, and Europe. Using this technique (illustrated in Tables 1 and 2 for 1981), the estimated supply of cocaine to the United States market rose from a range of 14 to 19 metric tons in 1976, to 40–65 metric tons in 1982, to 71–137 tons in 1984.[15]

A different methodology makes use of a set of assumptions about consumption patterns. With this technique, illustrated for 1981 by Table 3, the estimates range from 45–54 metric tons for 1982 to 55–76 tons for 1984.[16] Unfortunately for the cause of consistency, the Attorney General's report for 1984 comes out with a non-corresponding figure—74–90 metric tons exported to the United States. By any technique, however, one thing is clear: the black market in cocaine has expanded dramatically since the mid–1970s.

The consumption-based measurement technique is derived from the National Institute on Drug Abuse (NIDA) *National Household Survey*. Rather than hypothesizing estimated rates of consumption, NIDA measures the prevalence of drug abuse by asking respondents about past and present use of legal and illegal drugs. The 1979 NIDA survey showed roughly a two-and-one-half to threefold increase over the 1977 survey in the percentage of respondents who had used cocaine (1) within the past month, (2) within the past year, or (3) at any time in the past. In absolute terms, the 1979 survey estimated that 4.4 million people had used cocaine within the past 30 days, 9.7 million had used it at least once within the past year, and 15.1 million had used it at least once.[17] The NIDA estimates (Table 4) for 1982 ran higher except for the past-month category: 4.1, 11.9, and 21.6 million, respectively.[18] These figures are probably low because of the tendency of respondents to withhold admission of a felony and because the survey

Table 1
Theoretical Maximum Cocaine Available from Coca Leaf Produced in Peru and Bolivia

PERU	BOLIVIA
1. Annual Production:	
50,000 Hectares Under Cultivation × 1,000 Kilos per Hectare 50,000,000 Kilos of Leaf	35,000 Hectares Under Cultivation × 1,500 Kilos per Hectare 55,000,000 Kilos of Leaf (rounded)
2. Accountable Stocks:	
12,000,000 Kilos for Chewing + 2,000,000 Kilos Exported Worldwide and Domestic Ind/Med. Use 14,000,000 Kilos Accountable	15,530,000 Kilos for Chewing 2,000,000 Kilos Exported Wor dwide + Unknown 16,000,000 Kilos Annually Accountable (rounded)
3. Potential Unaccountable Stocks:	
50,000,000 Kilos of Leaf -14,000,000 Kilos Accountable 36,000,000 Kilos Potentially Unaccountable	55,000,000 Kilos of Leaf -16,000,000 Kilos Accountable 39,000,000 Kilos Potentially Unaccountable
4. Reduction to Cocaine Hydrochloride:	
A. Coca Leaf to Coca Paste: Reduction Factor—200:1 36,000,000 Kilos of Leaf—180,000 Kilos of Paste—39,000,000 Kilos of Leaf—195,000 Kilos of Paste B. Paste to Cocaine Hydrochloride: Reduction Factor—2.5:1 180,000 Kilos of Paste—72,000 Kilos of Cocaine 195,000 Kilos of Paste—78,000 Kilos of Cocaine 72 M.T. + 78 M.T. = 150 M.T. Cocaine HCL 150 M.T. + 6 M.T. HCl from Colombian Leaf—156 M.T.	
5. Allowing ten percent margin of error each way, the 156 M.T. theoretical maximum of cocaine hydrochloride available from coca leaf produced in Peru and Bolivia produces a range of 140 to 170 M.T.	

Source: National Narcotics Intelligence Consumers Committee, *The Supply of Drugs to the U.S. Illicit Market From Foreign and Domestic Sources in 1981*, Fig. 8, p. 44.

excluded respondents from "group quarters" (e.g., college dorms and military bases) who probably take drugs at greater than average rates. For this reason, the NIE regards the NIDA data as too conservative and in its own projections for 1981 (Table 3) came up with 15 million annual users and

Table 2
Estimate of Illicit Cocaine Entering the United States, 1981

Estimated maximum illicit cocaine hydrochloride theoretically available for world use	140–170 tons
Less cocaine hydrochloride not converted because of inefficient production methods, crop loss, excessive cultivation, spoilage, loss in transit, pilferage, including loss through eradication and seizure of prime materials	90 tons
SUBTOTAL	50–80 tons
Less amount seized worldwide	8 tons
SUBTOTAL	42-72 tons
Less cocaine hydrochloride exported to third countries (Europe, Canada, and Latin America).	12 tons
TOTAL	30–60 tons

Source: National Narcotics Intelligence Consumers Committee, *The Supply of Drugs to the U.S. Illicit Market From Foreign and Domestic Sources in 1981*, Fig. 9, p. 45.

6.75 million past-month users (half of them having used cocaine on five or more days that month). Conservative or not, the NIDA data confirm the rapid expansion of national experience with cocaine. And since 1981 the market penetration of cocaine has undoubtedly set new records.

Further confirming the proliferation of cocaine in American society during the 1980s, health problems resulting from the use of cocaine increased significantly, according to the main monitoring criteria used by NIDA. Overdose deaths approximately tripled from 1977 to 1980. Nonfatal overdoses treated in Drug Abuse Warning Network (DAWN) emergency rooms (hospitals located in selected Standard Metropolitan Statistical Areas) more than doubled during the same period.[19] Table 5 presents the data for the 1980s.

However crude these measurements may be, cocaine unquestionably has secured a large and still-rising share of the American market. Sale of cocaine constitutes very big business; its dollar value must be estimated with even less certainty than its volume. The DEA used to measure its value by multiplying the NIE estimate of quantity by its "street value." Its formula for 1980 assumed the dilution of cocaine at retail to an average gram purity of 12.5 percent, at an average price of $100, yielding a price of $800 per pure gram and a street value of $800,000 per kilogram.[20] Actual (wholesale)

Table 3
Narcotics Intelligence Estimate Based on Assumed Consumption Patterns

CONSUMPTION ESTIMATE			ESTIMATED CONSUMPTION	
TYPE OF USE: (FREQUENCY OF USE)	% OF USERS	NUMBER OF ANNUAL USERS X AMOUNT CONSUMED @ 100% PER SESSION X AVERAGE NUMBER OF SESSIONS PER PERSON PER YEAR =	METRIC TONS	%
HEAVY USE: (5 or More Days Per Month)	6.9%	50 mg. × 4 administrations × 0.45 purity 1,030,500 × 90.0 mg. × 234.0 =	21,702,300,000 mg. @ 100 % purity 21.7 metric tons	63%
REGULAR USE: (5 or More Days Per Month)	8.1%	50 mg. × 3 administrations × 0.30 purity 1,219,500 × 45.0 mg. × 84.0 =	4,609,710,000 mg. @ 100% purity 4.6 metric tons	13%
REGULAR USE: (1-4 Days Per Month)	30%	50 mg. × 3 administrations × 0.30 purity 4,500,000 × 45.0 mg. × 30.0 =	6,075,000,000 mg. @ 100% purity 6.1 metric tons	18%
REGULAR USE: (Past Year But Not Past Month)	55%	50 mg. × 3 administrations × 0.30 purity 8,250,000 × 45.0 mg. × 5.5 =	2,041,875,000 mg. @ 100% purity 2.0 metric tons	6%
TOTAL	100%	15,000,000 ANNUAL COCAINE USERS	34,428,915,000 mg. @ 100% purity 34.4 metric tons	100%

Source: National Narcotics Intelligence Consumers Committee, *The Supply of Drugs to the U.S. Illicit Market From Foreign and Domestic Sources in 1981*, Table B-4, p. 107.

kilo prices at that time, however, were only $50,000. (In addition, the street value formula neglects to account for cocaine transactions in units larger than grams at discounted prices). But enforcement agency press releases typically ignore the wholesale value and report the value of a seizure at the street value. A 100-kilo seizure thus becomes valued at $80 million rather than $5 million (only $3 million in 1985). Street value, moreover, continues to find acceptance in some uncritical reports of drug seizures by the media.

A second source of overstatement in the DEA's computation arose from sampling techniques that produced unrealistically low purity figures. The DEA subsequently revised its purity-of-gram estimates upward to 25–30

Table 4
NIDA Prevalence Estimates and Population Projections (1982)

	Ever Tried	12 Months	Past Month
Youth 12-17 (1581 respondents)	1,490,000 (6.5%)	940,000 (4.1%)	380,000 (1.6%)
Younger Adults 18-25 (1283 respondents)	9,260,000 (28.3%)	6,150,000 (18.8%)	2,230,000 (6.8%)
Adults 26+ (2760 respondents)	10,820,000 (8.5%)	4,810,000 (3.8%)	1,550,000 (1.2%)
Older Adult Age Groups			
26-34	7,060,000 (21.7%)	3,510,000 (10.8%)	1,080,000 (3.3%)
35+	3,760,000 (4.0%)	1,300,000 (1.4%)	470,000 (0.5%)
Totals	21,570,000	11,900,000	4,160,000

Source: National Institute on Drug Abuse, *Cocaine Use in America: Epidemiologic and Clinical Perspectives*, p. 37, Table 2.

Table 5
Cocaine Use and Trafficking Indicators, 1981–1984

	1981	1982	1983	1984
Hospital Emergencies Reported Through the DAWN System	3,251	4,269	5,636	8,510
Cocaine-Related Deaths (Less New York City)	194	202	328	579
Cocaine Retail Purity (%)	25-30	30-35	35	35
Laboratories Seized	5	6	11	21

Source: National Narcotics Intelligence Consumers Committee, *Narcotics Intelligence Estimate 1984*, Fig. 10, p. 24.

percent purity for 1980, and 35 percent for 1983 and 1984 (Table 5). At that figure, a pure gram yields only three street grams instead of eight, so the street value of a seized kilo must be cut by that ratio. Despite these inaccuracies and uncertainties, there is little doubt that the black market in cocaine generates vast revenues. Using the low purity assumptions then prevailing, the NIE estimate of gross sales rose from the range of $12.6–14.72 billion in 1977 to $26.80–32.16 billion in 1980 out of a total black market in drugs of $80 billion. Viewing the entire cocaine industry as one corporation, it would rank seventh in sales among the Fortune 500.[21] Effective for 1981, the NIE abandoned its previous practice of making dollar estimates of the black market in cocaine. Nevertheless, the House Select Committee on Narcotics Abuse and Control asserted (without citing a source) that the "estimated retail value" of all black market drugs reached $100 billion in 1984.[22] Cocaine is the sales leader in that market.

THE "EFFECTS" OF COCAINE

> Give cocaine to a man already wise, schooled to the world, morally forceful, a man of intelligence and self-control. If he be really master of himself, it will do him no harm. But give it to the clod, to the self-indulgent, to the blasé—to the average man, in a word—and he is lost.
>
> —Aleister Crowley, *Cocaine*, 1918

The physical and behavioral effects of cocaine have received a great deal of attention from the Government and the mass media. That emphasis is unwise because it tends to conflate the question of the validity of the War on Drugs as national policy with the very different question of whether cocaine is an addictive or otherwise dangerous drug. Even if cocaine be regarded as "addictive" or "dangerous," it does not follow that a war on cocaine is necessary or desirable. The law or policy chosen in response to problems of drug abuse is inescapably a normative judgment, to be informed by moral values and political principles. Focusing on the psychopharmacology of drugs obscures those issues by casting them as medical questions. What is worse, to call a drug "addictive" or "dangerous" presupposes a conception that falsely objectifies the drug taker (as victim) and anthropomorphizes the drug (as the active force). Public discourse has been thoroughly debased by this "scientific" terminology, which uncritically uses scary labels to portray cocaine (and other drugs) as a demonic force that takes charge of the user, reducing him or her to helplessness. The true roles of sentient being and inanimate object thus become reversed, making clear thinking and sound policy choices about drug control impossible. Indeed, if drugs are dangerous or addictive, the sensible thing is to make war on them. Our historic predicament arises from this erroneous conception.

Intelligent control of drugs of course requires knowledge of the characteristics of those drugs. Still, to concentrate on "the effects" of taking cocaine (or any other drug) distorts reality in at least three ways. First, the approach misleadingly frames the inquiry as though the physical or psychic effects of the drug determine the "cause" of drug abuse. Thinking so falls into the same conceptual error as studying the physiology of food consumption as a means of understanding and controlling obesity, or the metabolism of digesting fingernails as a means of understanding and controlling compulsive fingernail biting. A focus on physiology, chemistry, metabolism, or other aspects of biology completely obscures the centrality of individual motivation and responsibility for controlling drug (or food or fingernail) intake to avoid impairment and maintain health.

The physiology and chemistry of alcohol, for example, have been studied *ad nauseum.* This knowledge does not increase our ability to prevent or control alcoholism precisely because problem drinking does not arise from the physiology of alcohol intake. Even if the theory that promotes a genetic etiology of alcoholism is ultimately validated, the "prescription" for the "victim" of that genetic deficiency would be the same as for a genetically "normal" individual: moderation or abstention. These ethical prescriptions, however, offer no (illusory) prospect of cures, unlike biological theories; and one doubts whether the Government would give grant money to a professor proposing to prevent drug abuse by ethical training and self discipline rather than medical research. The bias in favor of "objective" or "scientific" causes is very great, and the laboratory rather than the library as a research venue receives overwhelming preference.

The second source of confusion that arises from emphasizing the effects of cocaine or any other drug is that it assumes a standardization of human response to psychoactive drugs. In reality, a great range of responses prevails. While certain physical responses are predictable, for example, cocaine elevates the heart rate, the individual's *behavioral* response cannot be extrapolated from the physiological action. Indeed, there may not be any such response. True, one can predict that an individual stimulated by cocaine is less likely to go to sleep, but on important issues—aggressiveness, physical and mental performance, and so on—meaningful predictions are impossible. This is especially true for long-term behavior patterns, for example, the meeting of professional or family commitments.

The same uncertainty holds true for the ability of science to capture the *experience* of the drug taker. For one thing, most social drug taking involves mixing of drugs: cocaine usually goes with alcohol, marijuana, or sedatives, or all three. Additionally, set and setting become critically important to the drug taker's experience of the drug's "effects." Results obtained in the relatively unstimulating environment of a hospital room or clinic may not reveal much about human behavior "in the wild." They ignore the individual's prior drug experience, his mental state, degree of stress, and qualities of personality. The role of set and setting—of mind and environment—in producing a "high" (or low) means that psychopharmacology cannot measure or describe the experience of drug taking. Response to a drug is not a singular, objectively verifiable phenomenon.

Consider, for example, the observable behavioral "effects" of alcohol.

At a cocktail party, four 30-year-old persons of similar body weight and physical condition each have two glasses of wine in the course of an hour. One becomes animated and gregarious in his conversation, reacting positively to the pleasant buzz of the alcohol in his brain. A second becomes morose and depressed and leaves feeling alienated in his "high" state. A third develops a pounding headache "from" the alcohol. A fourth becomes boisterous and aggressive, showing open hostility to others at the party. In each case, the physical effects of the alcohol are the same. Can we attribute each drinker's mood and behavior to the alcohol? If not, what meaning does it have to say that alcohol (or another drug) "causes" a given response?

Despite the great diversity of human response to drugs, the prevailing model of scientific inquiry attempts to objectify the drug experience by relying on the scientific model of reproducible experiments in the clinic or laboratory. But as Dr. Norman Zinberg has observed, the more controlled an experiment, the less likely it is to reveal truths about actual drug use. The lay writer Richard Ashley has criticized the scientific bias against crediting the "subjective" reports of drug users, the single most important source of information about the experience.

> Why then, to return to our old questions, have pharmacologists and other medical researchers generally written as if what happens to a few individuals on cocaine (and other psychoactive drugs for that matter) holds true for all or most individuals? And in so doing promulgated a vast body of cocaine mythology? The reason, I have suggested, is that they have refused to give proper weight to the accounts of users. And they have refused to do so chiefly because they have insisted on applying a scientific model which views subjective evidence with great suspicion.[23]

The split between the "subjective," experiential knowledge of drugs obtained by users and the "objective," cognitive understanding that prevails among medical researchers forms a central theme of Andrew Weil's *The Natural Mind.* As a doctor and experienced drug user, he criticizes the standard scientific approach as manifesting attachment to the ego-sensory system for obtaining information about the world. By rejecting the validity of knowledge obtained through intuition and direct experience, he argues, scientific research limits its capacity for full appreciation of the phenomenon under study and perpetuates a false way of thinking about drugs and drug use.

Another way of describing the rationalistic bias of this research method is to see it as anti-holistic, i.e., a captive of the Cartesian division between mind and body, analyzing the sum of the parts to learn about the whole without considering the interaction of the parts and possible synergistic effects. The bias against "experiential" models of drug effects reflects a conceptual reductionism of human beings to mere components or parts (body or mind) reacting like machines to drug stimuli in standardized fashion. As a result of ignoring the interaction of mind and body (in a particular social setting), this "objective" model cannot capture the truth of the drug-taking experience. Indeed, the model distorts reality by identifying the drug as the exclusive source or cause of the user's experience when in fact people have to learn how to "read" or experience a drug. This phenomenon is most apparent in first-time drug takers, who often report no "effects" from a drug because they have not yet learned to interpret them. Similarly, physical tolerance plays a role. The first cigarette or first beer often produces nausea; the neophyte drug user has yet to screen out, or develop tolerance to, the "bad" effects of those drugs while concentrating on the "good" effects.

Having made these conceptual caveats, the conventional study of the physical and psychological effects of cocaine begins with acknowledgment of the self-imposed ignorance surrounding the subject. The effects of cocaine have not been adequately studied because of the historically repressive approach of the federal government. NIDA did not even begin to fund research on cocaine until 1974. As a result of what leading researcher Dr. Robert Byck has called a "complete lack of responsible experimentation," there is much we do not know about cocaine, including the possibility of additional therapeutic uses in medical practice.[24]

Of course, in recent years a lot of clinical data has been generated by casualties of the cocaine boom. But people seeking treatment are by definition problem cases, and their difficulties obviously do not and cannot typify the "ordinary" experience. As Dr. Jerome Jaffe of NIDA put the matter:

> [W]e still need an estimate of the proportion of the [cocaine] using population who have experienced problems due to their drug use. In contrast, clinicians often see the problem users but may not collect sufficient drug histories so that risk may be assessed and have no contact with users who are not experiencing problems.[25]

In short, we know almost nothing about the real-world situations of people taking cocaine and thriving on it or at least not experiencing serious problems. Moreover, so long as law and social stigma make it risky for such people to come out of the closet, we are not likely to learn much about them. In short, the laws against possession, which are unnecessary to the legal attack on supply, have the predictable effect of maintaining ignorance of phenomena that might cause us to question the very thing of which we are ignorant. The law thus neatly serves as prescription both for ignorance and for maintenance of the status quo.

What we do know about the physiology of cocaine tends not to be very informative. Without attempting a systematic statement, it stimulates the central nervous system, by blocking the re-uptake of norepinephrine. It affects the cardiovascular system by raising the heart rate. Its action as a vasoconstrictor causes a rise in blood pressure. At low to moderate doses, cocaine is a "relatively benign" drug in these effects on the human body.

> In laboratory studies, an increase of 30 to 50 percent in heart rate accompanies use, together with a 10 to 15 percent increase in blood pressure during the contractile phase of the heart (systolic blood pressure). Such changes are no greater than might be expected under conditions of mild physical exertion and in a healthy individual are not likely to be hazardous.[26]

The problem with such technical descriptions is their contingency. At higher doses, for example, cocaine can be toxic, and overdose can produce cardiovascular collapse or grand mal seizures. Less dramatic, and more common, adverse physical effects include sleep problems, fatigue, headaches, nasal sores, nausea, and so on.

In addition, effective dosage turns on the method of administration. Other things being equal, cocaine taken by injection or smoking freebase delivers a far higher blood plasma level than nasal inhalation, the most common method of administration. Blood plasma levels, or *changes* in those levels, bear a rough correlation to the subjective experience of euphoria in laboratory tests. The stimulant effect of cocaine diminishes rapidly because it has a short half-life in the blood, one to two hours. It is metabolized in the liver. As the blood level falls, the subjective stimulant effect of a 50 milligram dose tends to dissipate in 10 to 30 minutes. (This rapid recovery from the stimulant effects of the drug is a desirable quality in a "recreational" drug.)

These subjective or psychological effects illustrate an even deeper area of ambiguity. According to the World Health Committee on Addiction-Producing Drugs, cocaine is the "prototype of the stimulant drugs capable of inducing euphoric excitement." This statement echoes Freud's classic description:

> The psychic effect [of cocaine] in doses of 0.05–0.10 g. consists of exhilaration and lasting euphoria, which does not differ in any way from the normal euphoria of a healthy person. The feeling of excitement which accompanies stimulus by alcohol is completely lacking; the characteristic urge for immediate activity which alcohol produces is also absent. One senses an increase of self-control and feels more vigorous and more capable of work. . . . One is simply normal and soon finds it difficult to believe that one is under the influence of any drug at all.[27]

But Freud, always the astute observer, qualified his attribution of his experience to the drug to take account of idiosyncratic effects: "[T]he individual disposition plays a major role in the effects of cocaine, perhaps a more important role than with other alkaloids. The subjective phenomena after the ingestion of cocaine differ from person to person, and only a few persons experience, like myself, a pure euphoria without alteration."[28] In other words, other persons do experience the negative aspects of cocaine. Dr. Louis Lewin in 1924 wrote of the "frightful symptoms due to the craving for cocaine," but Freud never had such problems. Which, then is the "truth" about cocaine? Or isn't the question misleading in looking to the properties of cocaine rather than the character of the user?

Cocaine is thus a drug of antinomies. Crowley's quote makes that clear. As a result, almost any statement beginning "Cocaine is . . . " or "Cocaine causes . . . " is false because incomplete. It "produces" a range of subjective phenomena, which varies with dosage, frequency, and method of administration, from euphoria to dysphoria. Its dualistic character cannot be captured by the bureaucratic prose of DEA fact sheets on cocaine, or even by NIDA research monographs. Given its subtleties, a novelist is more likely to capture the truth about cocaine than a scientist.

Within the scientific world, some of the most realistic and informative studies have been done by Dr. Ronald Siegel of UCLA.[29] In a long-term (longitudinal) study, Dr. Siegel followed the lives of 99 cocaine users (85 males, and 14 females, ages 21–38) commencing in 1974. His subjects engaged in "social-recreational use of cocaine hydrochloride by the intranasal route," averaging three grams of 53 percent cocaine per month. The social recreational subjects reported long-term positive effects of euphoria and stimulation, increased energy, garrulousness, diminished appetite and weight loss, and sexual stimulation. Long-term negative effects included restlessness, anxiety, irritability, fatigue, and nasal problems. Most subjects "titrated [regulated] their dosages in order to circumvent negative effects." The study concluded that "these long term negative effects were consistently overshadowed by the long term positive effects."[30]

In a follow-up paper, Siegel characterized the first four years of the study as ones in which the social-recreational pattern of use appeared "relatively stable." Although three-quarters of the subjects engaged in more intensified patterns, and most indulged in occasional binges or "runs" lasting a period of hours, most of "the subjects returned to social-recreational use as their primary pattern."[31]

"Social-recreational use" forms one of five categories in Siegel's typology of drug abuse, patterned after that of the National Commission on Marihuana and Drug Abuse:

1. Experimental Use

   . . . short-term, nonpatterned trials of cocaine with varying intensity and with a maximum lifetime frequency of 10 times (or a total intake of less than 1 gram). These users were primarily motivated by curiosity about cocaine and a desire to experience the anticipated drug effects of euphoria, stimulation, and enhanced sexual motivation. Experimental use was generally social and among close friends.

2. Social-Recreational Use

> The most common pattern was social-recreational . . . friends or acquaintances who wished to share an experience perceived by them as acceptable and pleasurable. Use tended to occur in weekly or biweekly episodes and continued primarily for three reasons: (1) cocaine was viewed as a social drug which facilitated social behavior; (2) cocaine was viewed as "ideal" and "safe" in terms of convenience of use, minimal bulk, rapid onset, minimal duration, and few side effects and after effects; and (3) cocaine was viewed as appealing in terms of sociocultural images.
>
> 3. Circumstantial-Situational Use
> Circumstantial-situational use was defined as a task-specific, self-limited use which was variably patterned, differing in frequency, intensity, and duration. This use was motivated by a perceived need or desire to achieve a known and anticipated drug effect deemed desirable to cope with a specific condition or situation. Use tended to occur in four or five episodes per week. Motivation cited by users included the enhancement of performance or mood at work and play.
>
> 4. Intensified Use
> Intensified use was defined as long-term patterned use at least once a day. Such use was motivated chiefly by a perceived need to achieve relief from a persistent problem or stressful situation or a desire to maintain a certain self-prescribed level of performance.
>
> 5. Compulsive Use
> Compulsive use was defined as high-frequency and high-intensity levels of relatively long duration, producing some degree of psychological dependency. The dependence is such that the individual user cannot discontinue such use without experiencing physiological discomfort or psychological disruption. The compulsive patterns are usually associated with preoccupation with cocaine-seeking and cocaine-using behavior to the relative exclusion of other behaviors. The motivation to continue compulsive levels of use was primarily related to a need to elicit the euphoria and stimulation of cocaine in the wake of increasing tolerance and incipient withdrawallike effects.[32]

In the next phase of the study (1978–1983), Siegel found that "the patterns of use among continuing users began to change." First, they were using more cocaine: 1–3 grams per week from 1978 to 1983, compared to 3 grams per month during the initial phase. Furthermore, half the users still in the study (N = 50) remained social-recreational users (averaging 1 gram per week), but 32 percent (N = 16) became circumstantial situational users (2 grams per week); 8 percent (N = 4) became intensified users (3 grams per week); and 10 percent (N = 5) became compulsive users.[33] The compulsive users averaged 1.5 grams per day. They all smoked cocaine freebase and frequently binged over periods of time ranging from 1 to 96 hours. Forty-three percent of Siegel's respondents used methaqualone or diazepam (Valium) to "come down" from the cocaine high.

In a 1984 paper for NIDA *(Research Monograph 50),* Siegel retrospectively concluded that the "hypothesis that long term use of cocaine is inevitably associated with an escalating dependency marked by more frequent patterns of use is not supported by these findings." Instead, he found that "social recreational users maintained relatively stable patterns of use" in the face of ready supplies and increased income as they aged. This undermines the view that cocaine is inherently addictive. Still, some users do become compulsive and end up as clinical cases. A study from Lima reported a classic pattern of abuse by a 29-year-old businessman. The Lima subject used 5–8 grams of cocaine per day by nasal aspiration. Over a five-year period, he experienced three psychotic, paranoid episodes requiring hospitalization. During those episodes, he was "dangerous due to his ideas of persecution," accompanied by hallucinations and a tendency to become aggressive. In one incident, he climbed up on the roof of his house, almost nude, with a carbine in order to "defend his life."[34]

The Lima case typifies the "cocaine psychosis" that arises in cases of truly excessive dosages consumed repetitively over a long period of time. At the turn of the century, the hysterical rumors circulating about "cocaine fiends" had as a kernel of truth that kind of paranoid reaction, and it did much to motivate passage of the Harrison Narcotics Act. Contemporary public fears continue to feed off similar images of human wreckage purveyed by sensationalized media accounts of entertainment-world disasters, such as John Belushi's speedball (heroin/cocaine) overdose death and Richard Pryor's brush with death from an explosion and fire while freebasing. David Kennedy also died from a polydrug overdose involving cocaine. Apart from superstar catastrophes, celebrity confessionals, and professional sports scandals, media reports of the extremes of cocaine abuse also appear with regularity. Some include genuinely scary accounts of cocaine psychosis, such as the middle-aged businessman who freebased several hundred thousand dollars worth of cocaine in less than a year and ended up barricaded in his bathroom with an automatic rifle pointed at imaginary enemies out to get him. The role of the media in portraying these extremes as *the* reality, instead of one of the antinomies, is discussed in Chapter Ten.

Another aspect of the preoccupation with death and destruction comes from researchers who have conducted animal experiments with cocaine. These experiments typically lead researchers to conclude that cocaine is the most "reinforcing" drug of all. In the design of such experiments, caged laboratory animals, by pressing a lever, can obtain doses of cocaine through a catheter inserted in a vein. Under conditions of unlimited access, some percentage of "naive untrained" rhesus monkeys will forsake food and self-administer cocaine (or amphetamines) to the point of respiratory collapse and death.[35] In one experiment, the test animals preferred cocaine to all other drugs and reached a higher mortality rate with cocaine than with heroin.

The headlines garnered by such studies obliterate from the public perception all subtleties, not only of the importance of set and setting in human response, but of the greater stability in *animal* responses under more realistic conditions of limited drug access. "Under these limited access conditions, animals regulate their drug intake. After animals are conditioned, they show remarkable stability in their daily intake of cocaine over periods of months."[36]

The tension between studies with limited access to drugs, which more closely resemble the real-world constraints imposed by family, work, and other social commitments, and those with unlimited access to drugs precisely parallels the structure of the argument in Chapter Ten. There I pit the conventional assumption of drug taker as slave of desire (or physiological mechanisms) against a view of drug taking as a controlled exercise of autonomy and the innate drive to alter consciousness. The unlimited-access animal studies represent the triumph of the Cartesian split between mind and body, adopting a machine-like model of human behavior that completely ignores human values, volition, and social restraints. Within that artificial world, animal studies provide an important piece of the "evidence" that cocaine is addicting.

A currently popular hypothesis for cocaine addiction traces it to dopamine depletion in the brain (the cocaine "crash"), which stimulates the taking of more cocaine to temporarily increase the brain's concentration of dopamine, followed by depletion, *ad infinitum* in a hopeless roller coaster ride culminating in addiction. Dr. Mark S. Gold, founder of the cocaine hot line, is a proponent of this theory.[37] The press has quoted his unqualified public assertion that cocaine is "the" most addicting of all drugs. The Associated Press reported that Gold's "national survey among cocaine users has confirmed that cocaine is addictive, and almost one out of four people who use the drug admit they steal to support their dependency."[38] The survey itself was conducted with 500 cocaine users from 42 states selected at random from among the first 50,000 people who called the free (800) cocaine hot line (1–800-COCAINE). Half of them were daily users; the average was 5.7 days a week. Sixty-six percent felt addicted; 75 percent said they had lost control; and over 90 percent reported negative physical, psychological, social, or financial consequences. Since the cocaine hot line provides help to troubled cocaine users who want to stop, these calls by definition represent problem cases. The much greater number of "non-addicted" users had no occasion to call and become part of the survey.

Similarly, the cocaine hot line at the drug abuse unit of the Fair Oaks Psychiatric Hospital reports receiving 1,000 calls a day.[39] That datum has itself been cited as evidence of the addictive nature of cocaine. But, as Dr. Jaffe points out, such data reveal nothing about the number of non-addicted users. The self-selection of callers means that the survey could not possibly "confirm" that cocaine is addictive. Conceptually, moreover, the high number of calls for help, rather than reflecting widespread victimization by the drug, can be viewed with equal justification as showing a powerful inner drive to achieve stability and health. Indeed, the very belief that addiction can be broken argues in favor of a non-biological basis for behavior that is now called "addiction." Otherwise, how would it be possible to stop a pattern that is biologically compelled?

Whatever the true etiology, the traditional view of addiction focuses on technical criteria of tolerance and withdrawal. Dr. Robert Byck applies those criteria to cocaine with ambiguous results:

> Is cocaine addictive? The question appears to call for a simple answer, but a yes or no reply does not do justice to the tangle of medical definition, folk wisdom, legal classification and social recrimination that is summarized by the word "addictive." One longstanding medically accepted definition of the term is derived from the description of opiate effects. For a drug to be considered addictive a person must develop tolerance for it, in the sense that repeating the same dose causes a diminishing response. Moreover, the drug must lead to physical dependence, so that repeated doses are required to prevent the onset of a withdrawal syndrome.
>
> According to this restrictive definition, cocaine may be addictive. While cocaine users can take the same dose every day and get the same effect, accute tolerance to cocaine effects has now been shown. . . .
>
> There are withdrawal signs detectable on the electroencephalogram and in sleep patterns, but they are quite undramatic when compared with the withdrawal syndromes associated with opiates, barbiturates or alcohol.
>
> On the other hand, cocaine certainly is addicting within the broader sense of the term that is accepted by most authorities. In this context the chronic consumption of cocaine through the nose is similar only in some respects to its regular injection and free-base smoking. Dependence on intranasal cocaine manifests itself in a pattern of continued use while supplies are available and in simple abstention when supplies are lacking. Increased availability has made this less likely and some intranasal users become "addicts."
>
> In contrast, the smoking or injection of cocaine almost always leads to continual consumption and drug-seeking behavior, destructive to personal competence and productivity. Free-base smoking is probably also dangerous to the respiratory system because it constricts the blood vessels of the lungs. The high price of street cocaine, together with the relatively large amounts of the substance necessary for injections or free-base smoking, undoubtedly function to limit the damage people might otherwise inflict on themselves.[40]

Dr. Byck's statement, reasonable in tone, represents the consensus of medical knowledge about cocaine. It is objectionable, however, in failing to acknowledge that the very concept of an addicting drug is highly debatable. As I will argue in Chapter 11, a question like "Is cocaine addictive?" (or even habit forming) misstates the fundamental issue because it obscures the critical role of human volition and ethical choice in drug taking—abstention or self-regulation. The very concept of "addictive" or "habit forming" presupposes a lack of choice, which is contradicted by the Siegel Study. Even with heroin, long thought to be *the* classically addicting drug, yet researchers like Dr. Norman Zinberg and others have demonstrated the fact that most heroin consumption is episodic rather than chronic or compulsive. The experience of United States soldiers who consumed high potency heroin on a daily or frequent basis while in Vietnam also provides strong refutation to the idea of heroin as an addicting drug. Follow-up studies showed that better than 90 percent of the heroin-using soldiers ceased their habit upon return to the United States. How could that occur if heroin *is* addictive?

"Addiction" conveys some rough conception of enslavement to a drug by a mechanism (biological, psychological, or otherwise) so powerful that freeing oneself is impossible or exceptionally difficult. Only the clinical cases fit that paradigm. Most others do not. In the final analysis, to call cocaine or any other drug "addicting" requires both blindness to evidence and the adoption of a conceptual apparatus of victimization. That in turn does violence to the predicate of our legal and political systems—the fundamental assumption that human beings are morally responsible agents having the capacity to control their conduct.

Even if science could transcend its methodological limitations and produce perfectly reliable and unambiguous data about the physical, psychological, and behavioral effects of a drug on human beings, that alone could never control the outcome of a policy debate. In making sound law, many factors must be balanced—considerations of enforcement feasibility, of benefits and detriments from prohibiting or regulating the activity or leaving it alone, and, most of all, normative decisions about the relations between state power and individual freedom. Drug regulation thus belongs to the realm of moral and political discourse, not to science or medicine. Only the prestige of modern medicine, its aura of scientific objectivity, keeps it so prominently placed in a field where it has no real authority or competence. Indeed, the very conceptual model of drug research is detrimental to intelligent drug policy because of its focus on chemistry and physical effects rather than on questions of behavior and responsibility.

To his credit, Byck notes that "[a] considerable bureaucratic constituency depends for its existence on the public belief that cocaine is unequivocally pernicious."[41] Government propaganda reflects that bias, and the media uncritically transmit it, without questioning its premises, its accuracy, or its completeness. As a result, even within the conceptual framework that focuses on drug effects, a considerable body of evidence suggesting positive effects and expanded therapeutic applications for cocaine has been almost completely ignored.

Among the most important data neglected by this negative consensus on cocaine are Freud's own studies suggesting that as a stimulant of the central nervous system (CNS), cocaine in moderate doses can improve physical and mental performance. For example, Freud's self-experiments with cocaine showed some improvement in eye, ear, and hand coordination in his tests with a neuroamoebimeter, a device that emits a tone and measures the time it takes for a subject to react to stop the tone. After taking a tenth of a gram of cocaine, Freud's reaction times were usually shorter and more uniform than before taking the drug.[42] This suggests a potential application where alertness is important, perhaps to drivers and other operators of machinery, although excessive stimulation might well impair concentration and judgment. Whatever the actual results might be, the critical factor is that an important research agenda goes unfulfilled because of legal and political hostility to cocaine.

In addition to improved reaction times, Freud found that taking cocaine generally caused his physical strength, as measured with a hand dynamometer, to increase.[43] Freud's findings have been rediscovered by contemporary athletes. According to media reports, many professional athletes, especially football and baseball players, have used cocaine during the playing season, and sometimes amphetamines during the games themselves. Some of these players turned in brilliant performances, suggesting that the consumption of cocaine, like amphetamines, may be beneficial for speed and strength, at least in the short run. In a sports "scandal," the Commissioner of the National Football League suspended four players for four games of the 1983 season "because of their involvement with cocaine." One of the four, defensive end Ross Browner, had set a Super Bowl record of 10 unassisted tackles. Another, running back Pete Johnson, was the all-time leading rusher for the Cincinnati Bengals. A third, a rookie, finished third in team tackles. It seems doubtful that cocaine hurt their playing.

Of course, some players, like Hollywood Henderson or Carl Eller, developed a debilitating dependency that required clinical treatment. Some never regained their peak form. Here again, it is necessary to distinguish between short-run and long-run, moderate and excessive use in making judgments about ambiguous evidence on the "effects" of cocaine. Science cannot, however, tell us which is the "real" cocaine story, the Super Bowl record or the hospital case, because of the human factor. According to Dr. Lester Grinspoon, "[I]f we just consider people who use it intranasally two or three times a week, I am unable to persuade myself that they are very much at risk."[44] On the other hand, Byck is especially concerned about freebase: "There is a hook in smoked cocaine. People become compulsive users."[45] The intense euphoria of the first hit of the pipe seems to set up a pattern of repeated, nonstop smoking in the futile attempt to recapture the initial high to avoid coming down. In the hot line survey described above, three-quarters of the freebasers stated that they preferred freebase to food, family, job, or sex. Byck maintains, nevertheless, that cocaine use has been "treated with . . . unnecessary fear and often inappropriate regulation . . . cocaine has a far worse reputation than its pharmacology indicates and so, as with marijuana, it would be unwise to represent falsely the health dangers of its use."[46]

The real challenge in controlling cocaine, as with any drug, is to maintain moderation in dose and frequency and appropriate limits on time and place. The tendency of some, loosely estimated at 10–20 percent, to move through progressive stages in the Siegel typology, from social-recreational use to compulsive, chronic use, provides the strongest (although not conclusive) argument against the unrestricted availability of cocaine to the general public. In Byck's view, "[M]aking it freely available would be medically and socially unwise. Even though it is a relatively benign drug pharmacologically, cocaine is often abused."[47]

Still, as Byck himself concedes, there is "no such thing as a 'bad' drug" and the reputation of cocaine as a dangerous and addictive drug has been grossly exaggerated out of proportion to the actual experience of people who have used it without wretched excesses of dosage, injection, or free-basing. One method of gaining insight into the "risk factor" of using cocaine comes from viewing the total "casualty" list in relation to the size of the population at risk. In 1981, for example, the United States consumed 34 metric tons or 34 million grams of cocaine *before* dilution or cutting.[48] Since the national average purity of cocaine for 1981 was estimated by the DEA at a (revised) figure of 25 percent,[49] the precut number must be multiplied by a factor of four to yield a theoretical maximum quantity of roughly 136 million grams consumed in the United States. At an average estimated intranasal dose of 25 milligrams, each gram yields 40 doses (lines), for a grand total in excess of 5 billion lines of cocaine in 1981. The 5 billion doses were consumed by 11.9 million Americans who used cocaine at least once that year.[50] Measured against this staggering volume, the adverse health consequences of cocaine in 1981 seem almost trivial: 4,777 overdoses reported to the Drug Abuse Warning System (DAWN) emergency rooms; 14,354 admissions to federally funded treatment centers; and 326 overdose deaths "involving" cocaine.[51] The 1984 and 1985 data will show higher casualties in all categories, but also a doubling (or more) of the amount consumed and an expansion of the using population. The "risk factor" thus appears roughly the same.

The data lead to one conclusion: even allowing for legitimate concerns about the health consequences of cocaine and fears about the spread of cocaine dependency, the legal prohibition of cocaine and its severe penalties cannot be justified solely on grounds of public health. At the very least, the health and death toll of legal drugs—cigarettes and alcohol—runs far higher. Cocaine, by contrast, does not "represent an acute or chronic health hazard of any significance."[52] But for that 10–20 percent minority, especially those who freebase it or inject it, a destructive, accelerating pattern of compulsive use can develop over time. Approximately the same percentage fall "victim" to alcoholism or heroin addiction. Does it make any sense, to return to the opening theme of this section, to focus on the chemical properties of the drugs which "cause" the addiction or dependency? Isn't the question whether cocaine is "dangerous" or "addictive" fundamentally misleading? Isn't it more meaningful and more useful to ask why 80–90 percent can regulate their intake, avoiding needles or excessive dosages? Shouldn't we focus our attention instead on issues of human motiviation and responsibility? These questions frame the inquiry in Part Two.

2

The Economics of the Black Market in Cocaine

If the threat of criminal penalties (and related civil sanctions) worked to achieve a high level of deterrence, the distribution and consumption of controlled substances would remain largely confined to lawful medical channels. But as Professor Herbert Packer demonstrated in his classic work, *The Limits of the Criminal Sanction*, such control lies beyond the effective reach of criminal law.[1] As a result, law enforcement officials must settle for a strategy that merely contains the illegal supply of drugs. The basic objective of this supply reduction strategy is to make drugs in the black market inconvenient, expensive, and risky to exchange.[2] The concept is simple: apply legal pressures to the transportation and distribution of drugs, thereby limiting the volume that would circulate in the absence of legal coercion. This strategy works—up to a point.

With powder drugs like cocaine and heroin, law enforcement officials measure the effectiveness of enforcement in terms of the availability of a drug, its cost, and its purity at street level sales. By keeping drugs relatively scarce and driving up their prices on the black market, law enforcement officials do restrict the consumption of illegal drugs. High price serves as a rationing mechanism. Maintaining the price of illicit cocaine at artificially high levels is thus a central goal of law enforcement. As one member of Congress put it, "[I]f you legalized it and brought it down to the price of the pharmacies, then it would be murder in the streets because the thing that keeps people away from it now is the exorbitant price."[3] We shall consider later the validity of this reasoning. For now, it is sufficient to note that the law intentionally promotes the extraordinary price differential between the average black market gram, which after price declines in the 1980s retailed for about $60-$100 (at perhaps 25–35 percent purity), and the legal, pharmaceutical product used for surgery, which retailed in 1982 for $50/ounce, or about $1.80 per *pure* gram.

Therein lies a paradoxical tale. The "success" of law enforcement in maintaining high prices is also its Achilles heel, creating extraordinary opportunities for extraordinary profits, thereby attracting entrepreneurs whom the law seeks to discourage by enforcement of the very law(s) which created profitable markets and attracted the entrepreneurs in the first place. Catch 22, if ever there was one.

An economist would put the matter more analytically, following the elegant model of classical micro-economics. Under conditions of perfect competition (many buyers and sellers, perfect knowledge, and no transaction costs), cocaine, like any other product, would trade at an equilibrium market price determined by the intersection of the supply and demand schedules.[4] Adoption of a criminal prohibition shows up in the marketplace as a "tax" on producers, who shy away from the legal risk and as a group become less willing to bring their product to market, thus restricting supply and raising market price.

History tends to validate this analysis. Something close to a free market in cocaine and cocaine products existed in the United States at the turn of the century. Cocaine was pure, cheap, and widely distributed over the counter.[5] For example, Coca Bola, a patent remedy, contained 3/4 gram of cocaine and sold for 50 cents a box. In 1914 Congress adopted a regime of legal restriction under the Harrison Narcotics Act, followed in the 1920s by total prohibition. Banning cocaine affected both the demand and supply schedules. It choked off demand to some extent by reducing the number of buyers and the amount they consumed, as former users stopped or reduced consumption and potential new consumers forbore starting. Deterred by fear of arrest and prosecution or by simple respect for the mandate of the law, aggregate demand declined. Current demand likewise must be lower than it would be in a free market.

But prohibition cannot completely destroy consumer demand. First, the consumer faces very small risks of detection and punishment. Several hundred million cocaine transactions take place every year, yet the DEA managed to arrest only 4,393 people for cocaine-related violations in 1982.[6] On the state level, a larger but unknown number of arrests takes its toll; Florida, the only state to keep separate figures for cocaine arrests, tallied 3,100 in 1982.[7] Under the War on Drugs, arrests of drug users remain *de minimis* because law enforcement agencies place priority on catching importers and sellers rather than buyers. As a result, arrests for possession rarely occur purposefully; on the contrary, consumers tend to be caught adventitiously, typically in connection with a traffic stop or some indiscreet public display.

Moreover, if a consumer is caught, the maximum penalties imposed by law for possession of a "personal use" amount are relatively light. For example, the maximum federal penalty upon conviction for a first offense of possession is one year in prison and a fine of $5,000,[8] and most federal prosecutors would probably decline to prosecute such a case. A first-time offender in most states can expect a suspended sentence or some form of pretrial diversion. The primary "cost" of such an arrest comes from the embarrassment it imposes, the inconvenience of attending court, and expenses for defense counsel, court costs, and fines.

Other factors moderate the tendency of prohibition to reduce the aggregate demand schedule for cocaine. Some consumers disdain the law as an infringement of personal autonomy. Still others derive satisfaction from defying the law, from partaking of forbidden fruit. As Dr. Thomas Szasz has written, "[C]oercion stimulates resistance, prohibition engenders desire."[9] Yet, some level of compliance with the law, whether out of fear or respect, necessarily reduces the total number of buyers and the quantity of their purchases. Thus, a regime of prohibition drives demand down to a level below what would prevail under free market conditions. In this respect, the Government can claim some success for its policy: fewer consumers of cocaine, with less purchasing power in the face of high prices.

Nevertheless, legal prohibition directs its primary force toward sellers. If they decide to violate the law, they face much greater risks, both legal and nonlegal, than do buyers. First, the law authorizes far more severe maximum penalties for drug distribution offenses. Federal law punishes a first offense of unlawful distribution of cocaine by a maximum term of 20 years in prison and a fine of $250,000.[10] The maximum penalty doubles for a repeat offender. Second, law enforcement policy focuses on importers and major distributors as prime targets of investigation, and the law subjects them to even more severe penalties than lower-level sellers. For example, the so-called federal drug "kingpin" statute (Continuing Criminal Enterprise Act) mandates a minimum of ten years to life in prison upon conviction, plus forfeiture of property.[11] Third, even low-level distributors or transporters, compared to consumers, must make more frequent transactions and possess larger quantities of the drug for longer periods of time. These factors increase both the risk of detection and the gravity of the consequences for the seller, particularly in jurisdictions that provide stricter and/or mandatory prison terms for drug trafficking. In Florida, for example, the law imposes a mandatory minimum term of 15 years without probation or parole for possession or otherwise "trafficking" in as little as 400 grams (less than 1 pound) of cocaine.

The law imposes costs in several other ways. Sellers of cocaine and other illegal drugs command status and inspire envy among habitués of the fast lane. But prevailing social attitudes stigmatize them as "merchants of misery, destruction and death" who, "engulfed by their greed," have wrought "hideous evil" and brought "unimaginable sorrow . . . upon the people of this . . . nation."[12] As a result, drug dealers bear a stigma, an intangible cost of doing business, that must be monetized to the extent that they place value upon the loss of good reputation or entree to respectable society. Staying underground must also take its toll in alienation and stress.

The seller of cocaine also bears substantial monetary costs incident to doing business in the black market. These include the costs of avoidance, concealment, and security strategies (sometimes including bribes); defense costs (lawyers' fees and bail bonds); losses resulting from seizures by Government agents of cash, drugs, and other property; and other underground tariffs, such as tribute to rogue cops or more powerful dealers.

Most of all, the seller of illegal drugs faces risk to his personal safety. Operating outside the protection of the law, he presents an attractive target for murder and robbery of his drugs, cash, or other property. The prominence of Colombians in the drug trade escalates the level of violence; not only does Colombia have one of the highest rates of homicide and street crime in the world, but the Colombian "ethic" of loyalty and enmity embraces execution as a basic tool of discipline. The appellation "cocaine cowboys" is not simply media hype. Even the bureaucratic prose of the DEA remarks upon the "inordinate propensity" of Colombian dealers "to engage in wanton violence"[13] To protect against these dangers requires substantial expenditures of money and psychic energy, but protection never can be complete. One simply lives with these threats and gets paid for accepting them.

Precisely because the risks run so high, the black market provides exceptionally lucrative rewards to those who play the game. Classical economic theory assumes that people act rationally to maximize wealth, undertaking a business or transaction (legal or not) only if they perceive it as profitable.[14] According to this rationalistic model, cocaine entrepreneurs would not assume the risks of doing business unless they receive adequate compensation for the extra tangible and intangible costs of doing business in the black market.

The monetary costs that they impute to the risks of arrest, conviction, and imprisonment depend upon some rough calculation of the penalties imposed by law; the chances of detection; the odds of avoiding imprisonment; prevailing judicial sentences upon conviction; and opportunities available in legitimate endeavors. Ultimately, the subjective valuation of these perceived risks—personal attitudes about money and freedom—determines the price at which an individual is willing to bear them. Whatever dollar values they assign to an illegal transaction, drug dealers must monetize their risks—include them in the final cost of the illicit drug. Because cost includes a reasonable profit, these risks increase the cost of illegal drugs by raising the seller's perception of what is a reasonable profit in such dangerous circumstances.

The risk premium for bearing these threats to a dealer's life, limb, and liberty, along with the out-of-pocket costs of doing business in a black market, results from prohibition and has been analogized to a "crime tariff"[15]

Figure 1
Effects of "Criminalization Tax" on Quantity and Price of Cocaine

The supply curve shifts upward and leftward because at any market price, producers will be willing to supply less as a result of the crime tariff; and to get them to bring any given quantity to market will require a higher price. Graphically, the change may be depicted as follows:

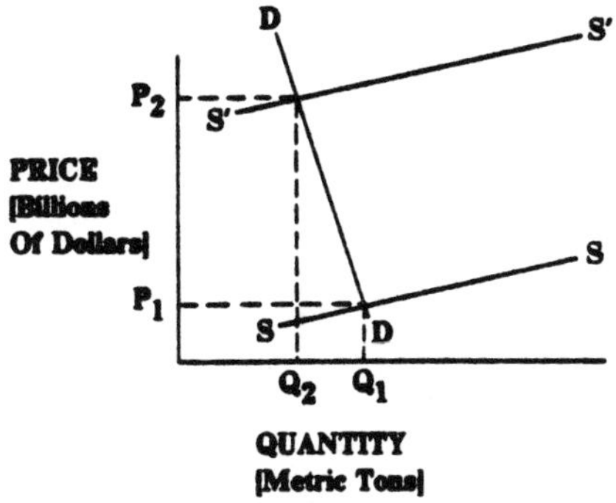

Price rises from P_1 to P_2, and quantity consumed and produced declines from Q_1 to Q_2.

or "criminalization tax."[16] The criminalization tax is the minimum amount of money required by the dealer in order to cancel out the perceived risks imposed directly or indirectly by the law, causing him to view the deal or enterprise as profitable. Deterring some potential sellers completely and raising the risk premium for others, this tax obviously makes cocaine more costly than it would be otherwise. In the aggregate, this tax reduces total supply, thereby inflating the equilibrium market price and restricting the amount sold.[17] In short, enforcement pressures succeed in making cocaine more expensive and less available than it would be in a free market (see Figure 1).

The price differential between pharmaceutical and black market cocaine provides a valid approximation of the amount of the crime tariff. Both products are refined from the coca leaf by similar processes. Legal status is the primary difference between the product of the makeshift field labs and that of the pharmaceutical factories. Federal law authorizes the Attorney General to permit a limited amount of cocaine to be imported for legitimate medical needs (1,482 kilograms in 1979).[18] The price of Merck & Company pharmaceutical cocaine hydrochloride was then about $50 per ounce,[19] or $1.80 per pure gram, compared to the 1980 DEA figure of $100 per gram for street cocaine of only 12.5 percent (±) purity. The criminal law in effect "taxed" cocaine approximately $800 per gram, or $22,350 per ounce. Even after the DEA revised upward its assumption of purity to 25 percent, thus cutting the crime tariff by one-half, there remains by the standards of legitimate business an extraordinary "markup" on black market cocaine.

Yet another example of the crime tariff: In 1981, a sealed, one-ounce bottle of Merck & Company pharmaceutical cocaine cost about $50 through legal channels; when stolen, it commanded $3,200 on the black market.[20] The $3,150 price differential arose *solely* from the difference in legality. This power of the criminal law to create value represents a modern-day version of alchemy, taking a mundane medicinal product and transforming it into a treasure. This is the stubborn paradox of prohibition: by artificially inflating prices, the laws against drug dealing create opportunities for instant wealth. The criminal law thus institutionalizes its own violation, accompanied by a corrosive set of black market pathologies.

In light of these economic forces, it should come as no surprise that the black market in cocaine has been booming. From 1976 to 1985, the volume of cocaine imported into the United States grew by a factor of six or seven. This occurred, moreover, despite substantially increased enforcement—seizures of the drug, arrests of traffickers, and forfeiture of their property. This extraordinary burgeoning of the black market not only confirms Packer's thesis about the limited power of drug law enforcement, it also demonstrates the high political, social, and economic costs of such enforcement of a thriving black market. In order to understand the interdependence of these two structures, we must first examine how the cocaine industry functions, how the drug law enforcement system operates, and how the two interact symbiotically. As we will see, if the cocaine industry commissioned a consultant to design a mechanism to ensure its profitability, it could not have done better than the War on Drugs: just enough pressure to inflate prices from $2 to $100 per gram, but not enough to keep its product from the market.

3

The Structure of the Cocaine Industry

The cocaine industry operates in four basic phases: production, export, distribution, and money processing. The production phase includes the growing and processing of the coca leaf for conversion to cocaine hydrochloride. Export means smuggling the product into the United States (and lesser markets in Europe and Canada). Distribution includes interstate and intercity transportation and delivery to wholesalers and retail sellers. The money processing phase consists of recycling some of the profits to finance future operations while spending, secreting, investing, or "laundering" the rest. Each of these phases calls forth a different law enforcement strategy; and careful analysis of each strategy exposes the incapacity of the drug enforcement system to accomplish more than episodic disruption of normal business operations. Viewed from an industry perspective, the only enduring accomplishment of drug law enforcement is the maintenance of artificially high prices in the black market.

PRODUCTION IN LATIN AMERICA

Cocaine hydrochloride is an alkaloid derived from the leaves of two species of coca bush. Although the coca bush grows in several countries of South America, cultivation is legal only in Peru and Bolivia, where the Andean Indians continue traditional leaf-chewing practices of ancient origin to alleviate hunger, cold, and fatigue.[1] *Erythroxylum coca* (*E. coca)* is the most important commercial species of coca and produces the majority of the world's supply of cocaine. Two varieties of *E. coca* are widespread: *Huanaco* is cultivated primarily on the eastern slopes of the Andes Mountains in Peru and Bolivia, and *Ipadu* grows in the western Amazon region of Brazil, Colombia, and Peru.[2] The second species, *Erythroxylum novograno-*

Table 6
Species of Coca and Their Characteristics

Genus, Species	ERYTHROXYLUM COCA		ERYTHROXYLUM NOVOGRANATENSE	
Varieties	coca	ipadu	novogranatense	truxillense
Origin	montaña region of eastern Andes: Ecuador, Peru, and Bolivia, mainly between 500-1500m	western Amazon of Brazil, Colombia, and Peru	Colombia, Venezuela and Central America, Sierra Nevada de Santa Marta and rugged mountains of Cauca and Hucha	desert coast of Peru and in adjacent arid valley of the Rio Maranon, Truxillo region on the north coast of Peru
Description of plant and/or leaves	pointed leaves, parallel longitudinal lines on leaf undersides	tall, spindly shrub with long weak branches and relatively large elliptical leaves which are blunt or rounded at the apex; flowers have a shorter flusher pedicel and a markedly denticulate staminal tube only short styled morphs	large bush plant with small, narrow, thin, and bright yellow-green leaves which are rounded	up to 3 m tall with multiple trunks reaching 4cm in diameter; branches are dense erect and spread leaves narrowly elliptical to oblong—lanceolate 20-65mm long; medium to light green above pale green to glossy green beneath and midrib fluted with slight medial ridge
Odor	grassy or haylike		wintergreen	wintergreen

Climate	favorable tropical environment with high rainfall, moderate temperatures and well drained mineral rich soils; moist cool	does not like intense heat or poorly drained soils, short-lived	hot, seasonably dry habitat resistant to drought	has been cultivated in arid, desert climate and wet montaña habitat of Colombia; even more tolerant to drought; prefers desert conditions
Adaptability	very little	very little	will survive under a wide range of environmental conditions. Resistant to drought.	
Means of propagation	seeds	cuttings	seeds	seeds
Commercial uses	most important commercial species providing by far the largest supply of coca leaves and cocaine; 95% of Peru's crop	used for chewing	illegal in Colombia; grown illegally for coca chewing and cocaine production	principal variety used in beverage industry owing to its high content of essential oils and flavors—several hundred tons exported to N.Y. for preparation of extracts, used in making Coca-Cola
% Alkaloids	0.5-1.0	unknown	1.0-2.5	1.0-2.5
% Cocaine of total alkaloid content	70-90	very little	20-50	20-50

Source: David Lee, *Cocaine Handbook: An Essential Reference* (Berkeley, Calif.: And/Or Press, 1980), p. 30.

tense, is native to Colombia, Venezuela, and parts of Central America and has two popular varieties. This species has a lower cocaine content than *E. coca* but has greater adaptability to various climates (see Table 6).[3]

For 1980 and 1981, the Narcotics Intelligence Estimate (NIE) projected about 50,000 hectares under cultivation in Peru and about 35,000 hectares in Bolivia. One hectare, (2.471 acres) yields about one metric ton of drug leaf, subject to local variations. NIE estimates that 70 to 80 percent of the leaf goes to produce illicit cocaine.[4] The remainder of the crop goes to fill worldwide needs for production of pharmaceutical cocaine and for traditional forms of coca consumption such as leaf chewing and the brewing of coca tea by the Indians. A small but expanding amount of illicit coca cultivation for cocaine occurs in the Amazonian region of Colombia.[5] Enforcement pressures—governmental eradication of coca at the insistence of the United States—have resulted in the spreading of illicit cultivation to Ecuador, Brazil, and elsewhere.

The coca leaf represents one of Mother Nature's finest adaptations to a hostile environment. Despite the obstacles imposed by high altitudes, steep mountain slopes, and poor soil, the coca bush grows prolifically in the Andes. It produces its first crop of leaves after 18 months. In favorable conditions it yields three to four leaf crops per year and may continue to produce for 30 to 40 years.

After the leaf is harvested and dried, it goes through a three-stage process for the extraction of cocaine. First, in the *pasta* lab, 200 kilos of leaf are immersed in a solution of kerosene, water, caustic soda, and other chemicals to produce 1 kilo of coca paste. Subsequently, base labs convert the coca paste to cocaine base at a ratio of 2.5:1 by adding sulfur and other chemicals. Finally, the "crystal" labs crystallize the base into cocaine hydrochloride at a ratio of roughly 1:1.[6]

In these "kitchens," South American "cooks" produce high-grade cocaine in the 90 percent purity range with relative ease, using crude equipment. Indeed, "all you need to make cocaine is three buckets and two sheets."[7] For this reason, kitchens are easy to set up almost anywhere—in makeshift huts in remote areas, in rural cottages or urban warehouses, etc.—and difficult to detect. *Pasta* labs have proliferated in the coca-growing regions because paste is less bulky to ship than coca leaves. The coca paste is most commonly smuggled into other countries, particularly Colombia, for processing into crystal, followed by export to foreign markets. Although laboratories exist throughout South America, Colombia probably manufactures three-quarters of the tonnage entering the United States;[8] it has the best cooks and the most experienced smugglers. Also, about half (by weight) of the cocaine seized worldwide (and 30 percent of the number of seizures) involves Colombian cocaine (see Figure 2).[9] In recent years, labs converting cocaine base into crystal have sprouted in Miami and elsewhere in the United States. Eleven such labs were seized in 1983. In 1984, authorities busted a

Figure 2
Probable Sources of Cocaine Available in the United States, 1984

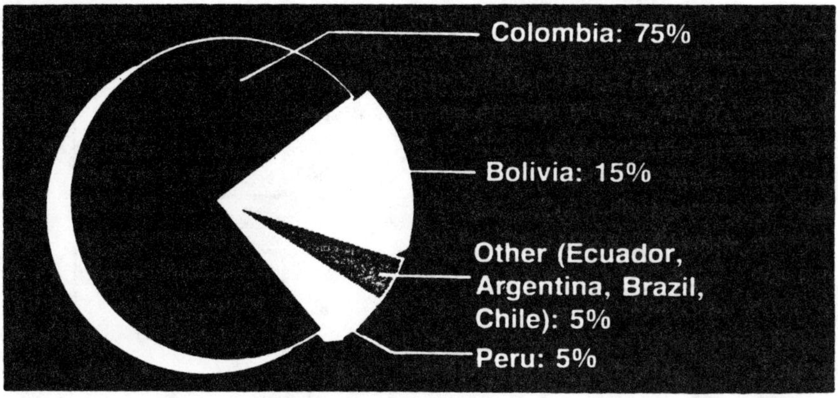

Source: National Narcotics Intelligence Consumers Committee, *Narcotics Intelligence Estimate 1984*, Fig. 13, p. 31.

total of 21 labs, one of them having an exceptionally large production capacity. Reportedly, a Colombian shortage of ether influenced smugglers to bring the cocaine base to Miami for conversion to crystal. Base is also easier to get past Customs' drug detector dogs, who have been trained to respond to the different odor of cocaine.[10]

Coca leaves grow abundantly, and in Peru and Bolivia the economic incentives virtually compel the peasants to sell them to traffickers or to convert them to coca paste for sale to traffickers. Prices paid to farmers vary with market conditions, of course, but coca yields a better return than any other crop. At the same time, coca leaves generally cost the producer or trafficker only a few dollars per kilogram; prevailing prices paid to coca growers in Coripata, Bolivia, in December, 1982, were about $2 a pound. A higher price of $290 for a 23 kilogram drum was reported elsewhere.[11] At every stage of processing the cheap raw material, the value of the product escalates dramatically. Although the 1980 dollar values contained in Table 7 are obsolete, they do capture the magnitude of the markup at each step of production.

The pattern is obvious: as the production process moves closer to completion of the final product, the price escalates. The single largest "value added" step occurs when the product is successfully smuggled into the United States, presumably because the cost (risk) is then at its greatest.

IMPORTATION AND DISTRIBUTION

Cocaine smugglers transport the drug into the United States primarily by air and sea. According to DEA estimates for 1980, only 15 percent was

Table 7
Representative Prices for One Kilogram of Cocaine at Successive Stages of Trafficking, 1980

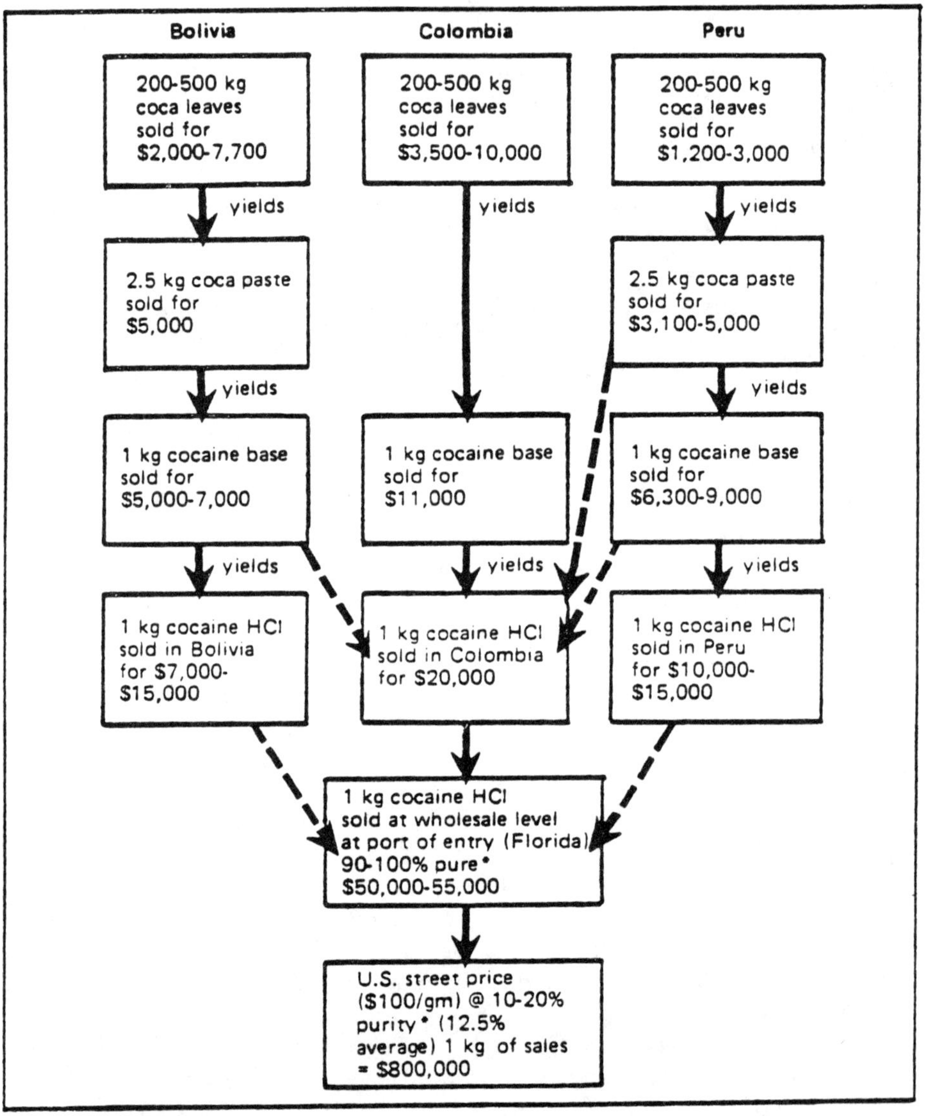

Source: National Narcotics Intelligence Committee, *The Supply of Drugs to the U.S. Illicit Market from Foreign and Domestic Sources in 1980*, Fig. 13, p. 49.

shipped by land (presumably through Mexico and Canada); 50 percent was shipped by air, and 35 percent was shipped by sea, using a variety of clever methods to evade detection by the Customs Service. Air cargo, in which smugglers conceal cocaine in flowers, freezers, foodstuffs, and other goods, has become an increasingly important technique for two reasons—there is relatively low risk of product loss, and even if agents find and seize the cocaine, they can rarely identify a culpable party to arrest. The two largest seizures of cocaine ever made in the United States (3,728 and 1,197 lbs.), did not produce any arrests or even indictments.[12] Figure 3 shows that 62 percent of cocaine seized in 1984 came from general aviation aircraft, and much of that represents air cargo.

The DEA claims that well-financed, well-organized, and powerful Colombian syndicates dominate the cocaine export/import trade. The occasional freelance smuggler may also operate in this market on a minor scale, but cocaine is big (and dangerous) business. As a result, the late 1960s/early 1970s model of adventurer and rogue-hero smuggler, typified by Zachary Swan, the protagonist of the novel *Snowblind*, has largely disappeared. Because of the extraordinary amounts of money involved, the smuggling of cocaine into the United States has become too highly organized and too violent for amateurs and small-scale operators to survive very long. They soon fall prey either to Colombian police or rival smugglers or to United States authorities.

Colombians dominate the import/export trade, according to the NIE, because of their geographic proximity to Florida, and because the "criminal elements in Colombia are the most sophisticated and organized of any in South America. They have the necessary international contacts and expertise to move significant quantities of cocaine to the world market."[13] The Colombians also have a reputation for merciless violence wherever they operate. Accordingly, the NIE opines that Bolivian and Peruvian traffickers are deterred from market entry in part because "the Colombians would put up vicious resistance to encroachment on the sizable share of the United States cocaine market they wrested from the Cuban and organized crime trafficking syndicates."[14] Nevertheless, another empire operates out of Bolivia. According to the DEA, the Roberto Suarez organization of Bolivia is the single largest exporter of cocaine, with output to the United States estimated at 13 to 26 tons per year. The press also speculates that the Suarez organization bought the complicity of the corrupt Garcia Meza government of Bolivia for $50 million to protect and assist its operations.[15]

In the United States, the Colombian network bases its families primarily in the large Colombian communities of Miami or New York City (Jackson Heights), where they have some degree of anonymity among each other and other Hispanics. As company representatives, they arrange for the delivery of multikilo quantities to distribution centers or drop points within the United States. In 1980, the DEA identified the principal ports of entry

Figure 3
Cocaine Seizures from Various Smuggling Conveyances, 1984 (percent of total volume)

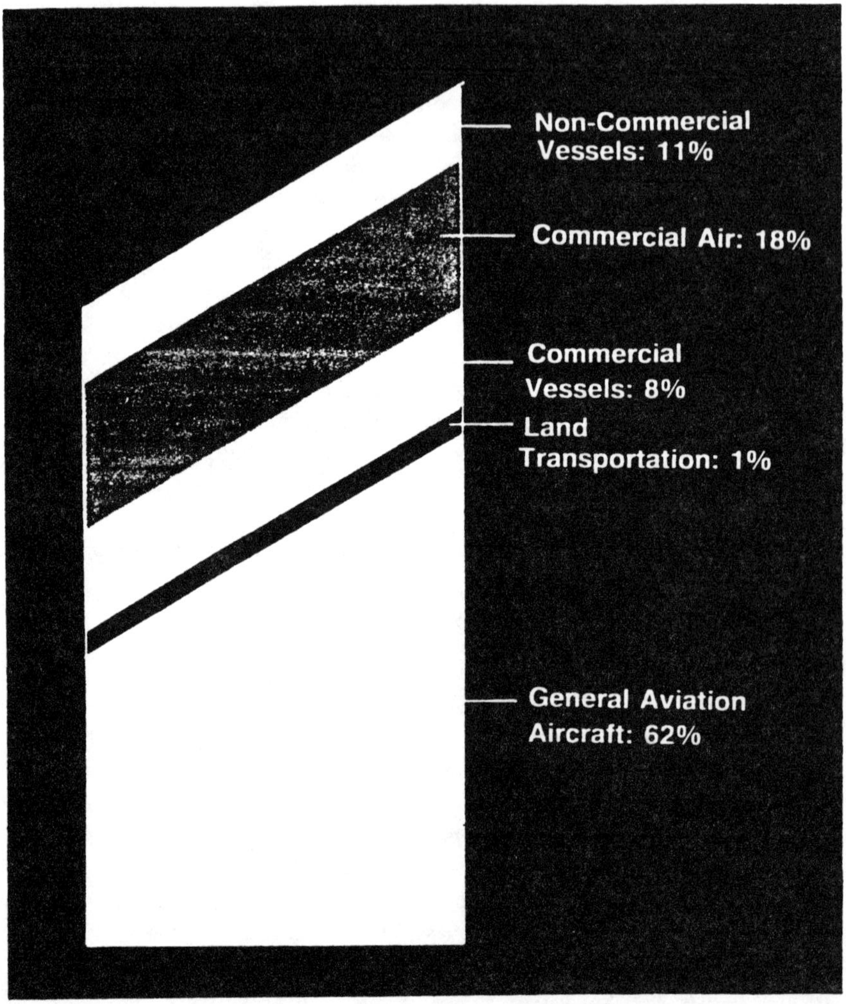

Source: National Narcotics Intelligence Consumers Committee, *Narcotics Intelligence Estimate 1984*, Fig. 14, p. 33.

for cocaine as Miami, Los Angeles, and San Juan.[16] Because of increased law enforcement pressure by the Government and an expanding market, smugglers later diversified their transportation and distribution routes, making increased use of the Bahamas and other Caribbean transshipment stations. Such routes change constantly. Nevertheless, because of their proximity, Miami and other areas along the Florida coast remain the major United States ports of entry.

The Colombian importers sell kilo quantities of cocaine to American distributors for cash, or, in case of a continuing relationship, they may "front" the kilos on credit in the expectation of payment after sale. For national distribution, the DEA claims, Colombian importers collaborate with traditional organized crime syndicates to distribute cocaine in the large cities of the United States.[17] The Mob, of course, has traditionally controlled the importation and distribution of heroin in the United States, so the alliance posited by the DEA makes good business sense.

With or without the Mafia, major distributors play a critical role in transporting cocaine by courier (car, rail, or plane) to other cities for sale to regional wholesalers. They also distribute the product to local wholesalers for resale within their own cities. Wholesalers divide the kilos into pounds for sale to pound dealers, who in turn further divide them into ounces for sale to ounce dealers, and so on down the chain of retail distribution to the ultimate consumer.

At retail, cocaine sells primarily in fractions of an ounce—quarters (7 grams), eighths (3.5 grams), and grams. The gram is probably the most common unit of sale, having the right balance between price ($60-$100) and quantity and providing enough for an evening's entertainment for one or two couples. For a shorter ride at a lower price, sellers of sub-gram $10 and $20 "caps" cater to the youth and low-income markets in many cities. A demographic survey in Miami identified cultural differences in retailing practices among blacks, Latins, and non-Latin whites.[18] The practice of selling in "bags," "caps," and "dimes" was identified most strongly with blacks, though there was some dime selling to very young white users. Other retail practices include drive-through drug markets; and in freebase houses users pay to smoke pipes provided by the proprietors based on the size of the rock. The growing popularity of freebase smoking gave rise to the development of "crack," preprocessed cocaine freebase rocks ready for smoking at a cost of $10 for a pea-sized pellet.

Because of the dynamic and illicit nature of the business, marketing practices vary greatly and change frequently. Still, general patterns prevail. As one descends the pyramid of distribution, increasingly large numbers of transactions occur, involving smaller units sold at lower prices and lesser purity. At the low wholesale and retail levels, the cocaine business resembles a cottage industry in which an informal network of friends (and friends of friends) transports and distributes the product to other sellers and to the ultimate consumer. The profit may be concentrated in a few hands or spread among a number of middlemen who deal in intermediate quantities, such as half or quarter ounces, before the product is broken down to the gram level. The profit is therefore spread thinner among more people, and adulteration or "cutting" occurs in more stages.[19]

Although the dollar amount of these lower-level transactions is necessarily smaller, the rate of return, or profit margin, may be even greater, perhaps as compensation for the extra labor involved in making a larger number of transactions. For example, a kilo bought in 1982 for $50,000 might have been sold in two one-pound transactions for $30,000 each, netting $10,000, a 20 percent profit. But the pound dealer could have realized a much larger profit by cutting his pound to half purity, yielding 32 ounces at perhaps $1,500 each, netting $18,000, a 60 percent profit.

The lowest-level retailers, gram dealers, may do even better on a percentage basis, and they confront the lowest risk of detection because investigative priority attaches to catching importers and large distributors. In addition, the extraordinarily large number of transactions occurring at retail renders the risk of detection for any one sale statistically minimal. For example, ignoring wholesale transactions and assuming for illustrative purposes that all sales to the ultimate consumer occurred in gram units, the 1982 importation of 50 metric tons at average gram purity of 25 percent equals a theoretical maximum of 200 million separate transactions. This rough estimate of 200 million grams sold remains a useful approximation of the *scale* of national cocaine sales, as well as the low level of attendant risks. While the total number of arrests nationwide for the offense of selling cocaine is not known, the combined total of such arrests in 1982 by the state of Florida[20] (one of the most active states) and the United States Government[21] was about 6,000.

In addition to low risk, profits run high in the retail business. Even a gram dealer can earn more money by selling cocaine than at most of the legitimate jobs available to a young person or a worker without skills. For example, a knowledgeable gram dealer in 1981 could have bought (or been fronted) a high-quality ounce for less than $2,000. If it was, for example, 70 percent pure, he could have tripled his salable product by adding 56 grams of inositol, mannitol, or any of a number of cheap diluents, yielding 84 grams to sell (at about 30 percent purity). Gross revenues at $100 per gram would total $8,400, a profit of $6,400 on the "investment" in a relatively short time, less the cost of cocaine kept for personal consumption. This process need only be repeated a few times per year to earn a relatively large, untaxed income. There is little risk of detection if sales are confined to and through friends. The time demands of the business are low enough to permit part-time or even regular employment, maintaining a legitimate source of income to report to the IRS. The high-profit/low-risk nature of retailing cocaine partially accounts for the immunity of the system from law enforcement pressure.

At somewhat higher levels of risk, large sums of money are paid to pilots and seamen to smuggle cocaine into the United States, while "mules" or couriers who transport kilo quantities of cocaine by car or plane from market to market in the United States receive less. At the highest levels of the business, the profits can be Midas-like. For example, in the mid 1970s, the DEA broke a large Mexican-based cocaine and marijuana smuggling organization; one of the principals "possessed two bankbooks, with assets reflecting in excess of $260 million in U.S. currency."[22]

The black market in cocaine is such a dynamic enterprise that details of time, place, and price in the production and distribution process changed rapidly as this book was being written. But these changes are matters of detail rather than structure. By the end of 1985, the black market continued to evolve in response to market forces, including pressures from the War on Drugs; and it continued to thrive and prosper at record levels.

MONEY LAUNDERING

Importers and major dealers at the top level of the pyramid must confront the problem of processing a volume of cash so enormous that it must be counted with the aid of high-speed machines. Lacking high technology, weighing provides the quickest method. At 500 bills of United States currency to the pound, 20 pounds of $100 bills equal $1 million. Or, 100 pounds of $20 bills equal $1 million. Since the ultimate consumer almost always pays in cash, some people claim that "getting rid of the money has become the hardest part of the dope business."[23] The Reagan Administration's emphasis on financial investigations has made that part a bit harder.

In the now-legendary Operation Greenback, a multi-agency anti-drug task force initiated by the Treasury Department in 1980, Isaac Kattan-Kassin was caught depositing cash of $1.612 million, $2.122 million, and $1.066 million at a local bank in an eight-day period.[24] The Greenback task force seized $9.5 million of a total of $19 million laundered by one cocaine organization in Miami in a two-week period. Encouraged by these results, law enforcement officials have investigated and prosecuted drug financiers, bankers, and money launderers with vigor and notable publicity. Despite this added pressure and the indictment of complicit banking officials, the smuggling syndicates have devised a variety of successful stratagems to conceal and launder drug money.

In this connnection, the proximity, friendly business climate, and strict secrecy enjoyed by banks and corporations in tax haven countries play an indispensable role. Indeed, the movement of "dirty money" from the United States to foreign banks and offshore corporations constitutes a highly developed industry in the Bahamas, the Cayman Islands, Panama, and other tax havens.

Tax havens offer sanctuary.[25] They are distinguished by the absence of income taxes and by laws that maintain strict confidentiality as to the identity of bank account holders and corporate principals. As a result, securities or property in the United States may be acquired by offshore corporations owned anonymously by drug dealers and drug financiers. Bank deposits abroad also leave no paper trails. Thus, investigators in the United States generally run into the dead end of anonymity unless they have sufficient evidence to justify an indictment independent of the confidential foreign financial data.

Once the drug money has been exported and deposited in a tax haven, drug financiers can repatriate it to the United States by wire transfer or by drawing checks on the tax haven accounts to people inside the United States. The money is then effectively laundered and can be shown of record as taxable income or as loans from a foreign (anonymously owned) corporation. Alternatively, the money can be wired to foreign bank accounts outside the United States to pay drug suppliers. In either event, the means to finance further imports is secured, and the drug business cycle can repeat itself more or less indefinitely.

4

International Law Enforcement: The Futile Quest for Control of Coca and Cocaine at the Source

Given the structure of the cocaine industry, the law enforcement system has four principal opportunities to implement its supply reduction strategy. It can target the source of production, shipment to the United States, distribution within the United States, and movement or concealment of the money generated by the cocaine traffic.

With respect to the production phase, the law enforcement system of the United States works against the cultivation of coca and its conversion to cocaine, primarily through (1) on-site law enforcement by South American police agencies who have been trained and equipped largely by the DEA, and (2) crop substitution programs funded by the State Department and operated by the Agency for International Development (AID) in cooperation with agencies of the recipient country. The goals are to prevent excess coca planting in the first instance and, failing that, to seize cocaine before it reaches the United States.

The dramatic expansion during the late 1970s and early 1980s in the size of the black market in cocaine demonstrated the relative powerlessness of U.S. law enforcement agencies to squelch the smuggling of cocaine into the country. Drug enforcement officials themselves soon abandoned the "light at the end of the tunnel" braggadocio that once prevailed, making only modest claims about the effectiveness of drug law enforcement within the borders of the United States. Indeed, the Chief of the Cocaine Investigations Section of the DEA issued a disclaimer about the long-term potency of traditional enforcement methods: "The problem will continue until it is ultimately solved on foreign soil through coca eradication."[1] Accordingly, the DEA argues that crop control must be the "first priority,"[2] and the President and Congress agree on the importance of control at the source. As a result, the State Department has responded with expanded or intensified programs intended to suppress cocaine at its source by destroying illegal coca plants and developing substitute crops for the peasant farmers to cultivate. For many good reasons, however, these programs have failed completely in Peru and Bolivia. In fact, the obstacles to suppression of cocaine at the source seem even more insuperable than the barriers to effective drug law enforcement within the United States.

The overseas drug control policy of the United States operates within a framework of international law, United States foreign assistance legislation, and bilateral agreements with coca-producing countries. In the realm of international law, the 1961 Single Convention on Narcotic Drugs obligates signatories, including Peru and Bolivia, to confine cocaine and other scheduled drugs to medical and scientific uses and to participate in "continuous international cooperation and control" toward that end.[3] It establishes a system of production and inventory controls for pharmaceutical cocaine and limits cultivation of coca to the acreage necessary to meet estimated world needs. The production and inventory controls are administered through a statistical return system that reports production of drugs, utilization of drugs for the manufacture of other drugs, consumption of drugs, imports and exports of drugs, seizures of drugs, and stocks of drugs. Excess production is prohibited by the Single Convention, which regulates the cultivation of coca under the model adopted for the opium poppy. The governments are supposed to confine cultivation to designated areas by licensed growers, who are required to deliver their total crop to a designated governmental agency. These governmental monopolies, in turn, are supposed to prevent diversion of coca to the black market.

The Single Convention requires illegal coca bushes and those growing wild to be destroyed.[4] It outlaws coca leaf chewing and other traditional, native uses in South America after 1986. Additionally, it obliges signatories to assist each other against drug trafficking and to adopt domestic criminal legislation appropriate to that end. Thus, each party is required to adopt penal laws against illicit cultivation, production, manufacture, possession, sale, offering for sale, etc., and to follow the United States legal model in outlawing conspiracy, attempts, and financial operations in connection with such offenses. All drugs, substances, and equipment used in or intended for the commission of any of these offenses are subject to seizure and confiscation.

The flaw in this grand design is its sole reliance on exhortation. The administrative agencies established by the Single Convention do not have enforcement powers. They rely instead upon voluntary compliance, research, international cooperation, and moral suasion. As might be expected, absent powers of investigation, inspection, and sanction, the "controls" established by the Single Convention have been historically ineffective. The 1972 Amendment to the Single Convention made no significant change in these respects, although it did authorize the provision of technical and financial assistance to the government of a noncomplying country as incentives to induce compliance.[5]

Invoking the obligations imposed by international law, and applying the leverage afforded by its own foreign assistance legislation, the United States in recent years has intensified its diplomatic and financial pressures upon the governments of Peru and Bolivia to suppress coca production. The carrot-and-stick inducements include the stationing of DEA agents abroad to provide technical and financial assistance to law enforcement agencies of the host country; according "priority consideration" (under the Foreign Assistance Act of 1961) to programs intended to reduce illicit narcotics cultivation by stimulating broader economic development opportunities; and funding of herbicide projects to destroy narcotics-producing plants.

Additional (dis)incentives sharpen the tools of persuasion. The President of the United States may withhold economic or military assistance from a country that fails "to take adequate steps to prevent narcotic drugs . . . from entering the United States unlawfully."[6] In addition to suspension of United States financial aid, under the Rangel Amendment to the Foreign Assistance Act of 1961 the President can block the granting of loans by the International Bank for Reconstruction and Development (IBRD) and the International Development Association (IDA) to a nation that has not taken adequate steps to prevent the flow of illegal drugs to the United States.[7]

Within this framework of international law and domestic legislation, the bilateral programs of the United States with Peru and Bolivia consist of two basic components: providing technical and financial assistance to the source country's law enforcement agencies, and funding long-term projects to develop crops to replace coca. As to the law enforcement component, the DEA trains, equips, and provides intelligence to South American counterparts. Furthermore, DEA agents stationed in source countries conduct cooperative investigations. For example, "cooperative" cocaine seizures for fiscal year 1979 totaled 10,207 pounds, compared to 1,064 pounds seized within the borders of the United States by the DEA.[8] But there is a limit to the powers of DEA agents abroad. Under the Mansfield Amendment, "no officer or employee of the United States may engage or participate in any direct police arrest action in any foreign country with respect to narcotics control efforts."[9] This limitation is intended "to insure that U.S. personnel do not become involved in sensitive, internal law enforcement operations which could adversely affect U.S. relations with that country."[10]

Training and equipping local drug agents to enforce their own laws is not prohibited by the Mansfield Amendment, and the DEA has been very active in that regard.[11] The DEA claims that interdiction of cocaine at the source is more effective, yielding seizures of larger and purer quantities than occur in the United States. The seizure data bear this out. In 1981, Peruvian authorities seized 5,930 kilograms of coca paste, 44 kilograms of cocaine base, 122 kilograms of cocaine hydrochloride, and 26,807 kilograms of coca leaves.[12] Perhaps the single most dramatic demonstration of the power of enforcement close to the source occurred in 1984, when Colombian authorities effected the largest seizure of cocaine in history—almost 14 *tons* at Tranquilandia, a remote jungle "factory" with a capacity to process about 300 tons a year.[13]

But the practical value of these seizures in achieving supply reduction is elusive. A Congressional subcommittee noted that in spite of massive seizures of cocaine in South America (6.7 tons in FY '79 and 8.4 tons in FY '80) there was no shortage in the United States—"no noticeable reduction in availability or increase in price of cocaine."[14] Apparently, production of cocaine was so great that even seizure of about 16 to 20 percent of the total actually delivered to the United States in that period did not pinch supply enough to raise the black market price. Similarly, the massive 1984 Colombian seizure of 14 tons did not precipitate any general shortage of cocaine or major price increase in the United States.

As a result of its inability to seize enough supplies of cocaine at the source to make a difference, the United States has relied increasingly on pursuit of a long-term "solution" to the cocaine problem: displacement of coca cultivation by policies designed to encourage crop substitution. Since the 1970s, the State Department has been funding pilot projects to encourage peasant farmers to plant cash crops other than coca. Because such projects ignore the laws of the marketplace, they have not worked at all.

In 1981, the United States and Peru jointly undertook a major coca substitution program in the Upper Huallaga Valley (Tingo Maria), the largest illicit coca-growing region of Peru. The project targeted an area of 17,000 hectares of coca out of a national total of 40,000 to 60,000 hectares. The program was funded and administered by the State Department's Bureau of International Narcotics Matters (INM) and the Agency for International Development (AID). AID committed $15 million in loans and $3 million in grant money over a five-year period, augmented by an $8.5 million contribution from the Peruvian government.[15]

The goal of Tingo Maria was to serve as an agricultural development project providing a mix of services needed to improve agricultural productivity in the region. That mix included research, training, road maintenance, marketing, potable water, sanitation, and other services. The intention was to develop, over the long term, viable economic alternatives to the production of coca for the black market, rather than simply to destroy illicit production. In this respect, the Tingo Maria project differed, for example, from Operation Green Sea II (1980), a cooperative enforcement effort with the Peruvian government which eradicated nearly 1,500 acres of coca and destroyed 12 million plants and 57 laboratories without lasting effect. "The long term impact of this one-time effort was primarily psychological."[16] Nevertheless, the Tingo Maria project did include law enforcement funding to destroy illegal plants, an aspect of the program necessary to counteract powerful economic incentives to divert coca to the black market. Market realities dictate that no other crop "over the medium and long term will produce as much income to the farmer as coca."[17]

Under Peruvian law, all coca production acreage must be registered and the crops sold exclusively to ENACO, the official purchasing agency. In practice, the Peruvian government cannot enforce its monopoly purchasing system because traffickers pay up to five times the government price for the raw coca leaf. Accordingly, a law enforcement component remains necessary, and INM budgeted $17.5 million over a five-year period for enforcement and eradication of illicit plants.

The United States for years pressed the government of Bolivia to adopt a similar program of coca control. Bolivia responded in the early 1970s with a small pilot project to explore the potential for a crop substitution program. Agreements with Bolivia were signed in 1977 whereby the United States funded expanded research into the feasibility of alternative crops and assistance (to the National Directorate for the Control of Dangerous Substances) for a law enforcement program. The Bolivian government registered coca fields for licit production in 1977 and 1981, confining such cultivation to the departments of La Paz and Cochabamba. Plans to implement a crop substitution and development project on the Tingo Maria model were suspended following the "cocaine coup" of July 17, 1980. In response, the United States cut off all aid except food assistance and a small amount of seed money to PRODES.[18] After several more military governments, the civilian government of Hernan Siles Zuazo acceded to power in 1982. That government, friendly to the United States, agreed in principle in 1983 to bring major portions of Bolivia's illicit coca fields under control by eradication and crop substitution. But because of the Zuazo government's tenuous grip on power, the control program remained largely in limbo, although soldiers in the field made some sporadic eradication forays.

The prospects for this two-pronged attack on the illicit cultivation of coca clearly are not promising in either Peru or Bolivia. In a 1978 review of the drug control effort in South America, the General Accounting Office (GAO) concluded that supplies of cocaine to the United States were increasing and that prospects for limiting coca production in South America were "unfavorable."[19] That report could be regarded as old news. One could argue that the income substitution approach represented by the Tingo Maria project had not been tried prior to 1978; that the United States now spends several millions per year more on its South American drug control program; and that AID now has the benefit of experience in this area. But the negative assessment of the 1978 GAO report remains true because it reflects basic, structural factors, not technical problems to be solved by mere programmatic adjustments or even the commitment of more resources. Rather, the unfavorable prospects for displacement of coca are deeply rooted in the political, economic, and cultural life of the Andean nations.

Effective coca control in today's world is implausible for many reasons. First, coca chewing represents a centuries-old and revered tradition among the Andean Indians. Coca was a sacrament to the Incas; and there is archeological evidence of coca chewing as early as 300 B.C. Daily coca chewing by the masses probably dates from the Spanish conquest of the Incas in the sixteenth century.[20] Currently, some 4 million of the Indians in Bolivia and Peru, and perhaps 8 million worldwide, regularly chew coca. This represents a majority and near-majority of the two countries. The Bolivian population is 55 percent and 25–30 percent mestizo. Peruvians are 45 percent Indian and 37 percent mestizo.[21]

Coca is thoroughly socialized in Bolivian society. It comes close to serving as a panacea, an all-purpose cure. People chew it or drink it as a tea daily, primarily in the workplace, as a mild stimulant and for the relief of cold, fatigue, and hunger. For this reason the agricultural workday contains several breaks for rest and the chewing of coca. Outside the workplace, "many social activities are solemnized by coca."[22] "Coca fills the role of an all-purpose healing herb. . . . It might be said to combine the functions of coffee, tobacco, aspirin and bicarbonate of soda in our society."[23] In addition, coca has nutritional value: 183 calories plus some vitamins and minerals in the average daily intake.[24]

For these reasons, even though the Single Convention outlaws coca chewing after 1986, coca forms such an integral part of Indian culture that abolition in this century is out of the question. In fact, many Bolivians resent the pressures for coca eradication and substitution applied by the *Coloso del Norte*. As a result of this hostile reaction, "the American Embassy felt impelled . . . to send a spokesman around the country to reassure Bolivians that the United States does not want to eradicate all coca crops."[25] This concession—acceptance of traditional coca cultivation while seeking to ban excess coca grown to make cocaine—almost guarantees defeat of United States policy. Once the licit cultivation of coca is accepted as a fact of life, the economics of the black market dictate the planting or diversion of coca for production of cocaine. Total prohibition would in that respect clarify production ambiguities, although it would generate political controversy and universal defiance. What else should we expect?

Bolivia is the poorest nation in South America, with an annual per capita income in 1979 of $390 and the highest overall death rate in the Western Hemisphere. Life expectancy for males is 45.7 years, 47.9 for women. Life for the Indians is not only poor and short, but hard. They live in remote, inhospitable areas under very primitive, unsanitary conditions. Nutrition is poor. Basic governmental services like hospitals are scarce. Infant mortality is 77.3 per 100,000 births. The rate of illiteracy is 65 percent.[26]

Peruvians fare somewhat better on these standard demographic indices, but they confront similar conditions of life. Per capita GNP in Peru in 1979 was $800, ranking it 68th of 145 countries worldwide. The literacy rate was

45 percent. Male life expectancy was 52.59 years, 55.48 for females.[27] The level of hardship appears to be somewhat less onerous than in Bolivia, but Peru is a poor, Third World nation nevertheless.

In both countries, the people who grow and use coca perch on the bottom rung of the social and economic ladder. In meeting the challenge of survival in a subsistence economy, coca is a critical resource, one of the few cash crops that grows well. For many growers, it is the only source of subsistence. Even where there are alternatives, the economics of coca are compelling. In some regions of Bolivia, for example, a hectare crop of coca is worth about $5,000, compared to $500 for a crop of coffee.[28]

> Francisco Berbetty Urguieta, a 55-year-old farmer, says that depending on supply and demand, 50 pounds of coca leaves sell at anywhere from about 350,000 pesos to 700,000 pesos, about $175-$350, at the official exchange rate.
>
> "I get three crops a year from these [coca] plants," Berbetty says. His orange trees, he says, "take eight years to develop, then you get only one crop a year. The banana gives good results, but not as good as coca."[29]

Two years earlier, in Coripata, Bolivia, a center of the coca trade in the Yungas (La Paz) region, the author was told by a leader of the *campesinos'* labor organization that coffee, oranges, or other cash crops do not grow well in the relatively poor soil of the Yungas. By contrast, coca fares well, yielding three crops per year. He said, "Coca is our bread; without coca we die." He emphasized an additional dimension in the proliferation of the coca trade. The *campesinos* felt befriended by the traffickers, who gave them cash advances or loans to tide them over between crops. By contrast, they described themselves as victimized or oppressed by the *narcoticos* who had been enforcing government controls (before the Chulumani massacre of October, 1982).

Public sentiment similarly favors Roberto Suarez, the central figure in the Bolivian cocaine trade, and explains in part his ability to elude his would-be captors. Serving as generous benefactor to his countrymen in the Beni region, he has underwritten education costs for an entire district.[30] As the modern-day Robin Hood of Bolivia, he benefits from the admiration and affection of the populace, who protect him from the government. Carlos Lehder enjoyed similar popularity for a time in Colombia, and the Ochoa family and others continue to do so.

Given these economic and social incentives, the cultivation of coca for the black market has proliferated rapidly, with an estimated 125,000 families in South America earning their livelihood by growing coca. The growth of cultivation in Bolivia has been particularly rapid, estimated by the 1981 NIE at 75 percent from 1977 to 1981.[31] The increase in the vast Chapare region has been even greater, in the range of 183 to 268 percent between 1978 and 1980.[32]

With the first taste of a condition approaching material sufficiency, the *campesinos* of Bolivia have become understandably militant in defense of the coca trade. For example, a mob of 200 coca growers in Chulumani murdered seven Bolivian narcotics agents following a raid by the agents in October, 1982. The government was forced to recall most of its agents from the field because of the danger of further killings.[33] Apart from this violent incident, growers have mounted a general counterattack against government pressures. Thus, in 1982, a small manual and herbicidal eradication project covering 80 to 90 hectares in Yapacani, instigated by the United States, became the subject of extensive criticism in the Bolivian media. A Bolivian television program criticized the eradication project as outside interference with Bolivian concerns.[34] Even the Catholic Church in the city of La Paz denounced the United States "for imposing a policy to liquidate part of our countryside, where the farmer lives exclusively from his products."[35]

Because abuse of cocaine has not (yet) become a serious problem in Bolivian society, the *campesinos* argue that the United States should not force Bolivians to pay the price for solving a Yankee problem. As a result, when the governments of Bolivia and the United States issued a joint communiqué in 1983 announcing an agreement in principle for control of coca by substitution and eradication, a conclave of growers' union representatives denounced the accord.[36] Two years later, hundreds of peasants marched through La Paz to the United States Embassy, shouting, "Long live coca. Death to the Yankees." In short, there is no mandate in Bolivian society for the suppression of coca, their "gift from God."

Given these circumstances, how can the Bolivian government possibly fulfill its agreement to wipe out coca production in excess of traditional, legitimate needs within five years through eradication and crop substitution? The government faces intractable problems. First, the thoroughly corrupt enforcement apparatus inherited from the Garcia Meza regime of "Black Eagles" had to be purged and reconstituted, starting with the shutting down of the special narcotics squad because it had "covered up and participated in the cocaine trafficking."[37] Corruption still runs deep, but it almost doesn't matter in light of a more fundamental barrier to enforcement. The simple truth of the matter is that Bolivia depends on coca. The *campesinos* who grow or carry coca, or otherwise find work as drones in the army of cocaine workers, rely on coca to make the difference between subsistence and poverty. The government, for its part, sinking under the weight of an annual inflation rate that ran close to 3,000 percent in 1985 and a staggering foreign debt of almost $5 billion on which it has defaulted, cannot possibly be eager to shut down its primary source of hard currency.[38] In 1984, coca brought in roughly $2 billion in foreign exchange, at least three times the value of Bolivia's leading (official) export, tin.[39]

As a result of this ambivalence, very little coca has been uprooted since the coca substitution and eradication accord between Bolivia and the United

States was announced in 1983. In August, 1984, President Zuazo ordered 1,200 troops to destroy coca crops in the Chapare region, where nearly a third of Bolivia's coca is grown. Half that number actually took to the field, and some of them gave local growers advance warning of their raid. One general resigned rather than take action against his countrymen. The elite, 130-man Bolivian army unit known as the Leopards, funded by the United States, has seized bundles of harvested leaves from peasants, and some coca paste, but their "enforcement" has been little more than a gesture. Finally, they were ordered in October, 1984, to make a sweep of the remote Beni region where Suarez and other cocaine "lords" operate huge, feudal-style coca plantations and cocaine-processing plants on a huge scale, up to 100,000 acres. Some have private airstrips. Though they raided several ranches, the Leopards failed to find Suarez; and they seized merely 380 kilos of cocaine.[40]

To fully appreciate Bolivia's enforcement climate, it is necessary to consider its chronic political and economic instability. It brought 199 changes of government from 1825 to the election of President Zuazo, who was kidnapped in 1984 and later released. The delicacy of Bolivian political control obviously limits the power of the government to enforce a law that runs counter to the vital economic interests of large numbers of its own citizens. As a result, in the national elections of 1985, no major candidate spoke out against illicit coca cultivation or promised a crackdown on the cocaine traffic.

BOLIVIAN POLS SPEAK NO COKE EVIL
WON'T BITE HAND FEEDING RURAL VOTERS IN DRUG AREA

UCUERENA, Bolivia—Fearful of alienating thousands of peasants who earn their living from coca farming, all 18 presidential candidates in Sunday's elections are avoiding debate on the growing problem of cocaine trafficking to the United States.

"Addressing the subject of coca is like walking on the edge of a sword," Victor Paz Estenssoro, the candidate for the Revolutionary National Movement, said in an interview in this village in southwestern Bolivia.

Alberto Diaz Romero, a coca grower from the nearby Chapare lowlands, put it more bluntly: "Any candidate who goes into the Chapare saying he is going to eradicate coca will not come out alive."[41]

In both Peru and Bolivia, the failure of coca control is not a temporary aberration but a function of culture, tradition, and the weakness and poverty of underdevelopment. These basic social conditions render effective enforcement against coca impossible. Widespread corruption in the enforcement agencies, the judiciary, and elsewhere in government is endemic. Indeed, the central governments do not necessarily control major portions of the coca-growing countryside, where traffickers rule like feudal warlords. As the Bolivians avoid going after Suarez in his fiefdom, so the Peruvian police stay out of the "wild border areas" around Lake Titicaca, where government agents were expelled by force.

Even were it to secure control over the remote coca-growing regions, the government would still confront the surprising technical difficulty of eradicating the coca bush. No paraquat-style aerial spraying technique has yet been developed. Because coca is generally grown near or interspersed with other crops on small plots of a hectare or two, chopping the stalk and manually painting the stump with 2–4-D (diesel oil) is necessary to avoid herbicidal damage to other crops. The labor-intensive process also requires that the coca bushes be uprooted manually. But uprooting worsens an already bad erosion problem on the steep slopes in high rainfall areas.

Additionally, the vastness of the illicit coca-growing regions and the abundance of leaves produced in relation to black market needs make the whole idea of crop control seem hopeless, if not actually silly, in view of U.S. inability to kill off a massive domestic marijuana crop. Satellite surveillance revealed approximately 68,000 acres under cultivation just in the Chapare region of Bolivia, with a projected 1982 yield of 82,000 tons of leaves capable of producing in excess of 200 metric tons of cocaine, four times the United States market at that time.[42] Even after a total "scorched-earth" eradication of the Chapare, the productive capacities of the Yungas region of Bolivia and Peru would remain intact.

Ultimately, the economics of coca and cocaine render programs of eradication and crop substitution little more than pie in the sky. Coca enables a poor nation to accrue enormous amounts of foreign exchange. Bolivia's dependence on coca has already been noted. Peru earns $850 million annually. The dilemma that drug-exporting nations face is suggested by the "immediate, wide and generous amnesty" on all illegal income declared in 1982 by the President of Colombia.[43]

Even in Peru, which is politically more stable than Bolivia and less economically dependent upon the cocaine trade, the government backed down in the face of political pressure from the coca growers, repealing its previous commitment to declare illegal and eradicate all coca in the Upper Huallaga Valley. A 1982 law repealed the 1980 decree of a state of emergency in the Upper Huallaga Valley and modified the total illegality of coca cultivation in the region. Turbulence continued in Tingo Maria, however, and the President responded by declaring another state of emergency in 1984. In November, a band of some 50 traffickers "burst into a jungle campsite and opened fire with automatic weapons," killing 19 Peruvians working on a coca control crop.[44]

Even before that dramatic turn of events, a delegation of the House Select Committee headed by Chairman Charles Rangel made an official visit to Tingo Maria in August, 1983, and found that the illicit cultivation of coca had become "a tidal wave."[45] Representatives of the government of Peru told the delegation that severe economic recession and a combination of disastrous droughts and floods had drained the country's resources so greatly that it could not organize and support the forces needed to effectively destroy the illicit cultivation,[46] estimated at 36,000 metric tons, or supress the trafficking in coca paste and cocaine. (The delegation found similar conditions in Bolivia, where cultivation of coca had "dramatically escalated out of control."[47])

The delegation's suggestion in its report, that "dedicated implementation" of control agreements could "within a few years" bring the coca problem "under control," borders on the fantastic. For the committee to formally recommend that the governments of Peru and Bolivia initiate programs to progressively eliminate the practice of coca leaf chewing by December, 1986, manifests a lack of realism and a disregard of the survival needs of those countries.

Ultimately, the State Department concedes that cultivation of coca "is a social problem that will probably never be solved. Our goal is to make it more manageable."[48] But even that modest goal should be discounted in light of the demonstrated, though unintentional, tendency of agricultural development projects to facilitate expanded cultivation of illicit coca in new areas. For example, United States foreign aid further opened the Chapare region of Bolivia to settlement and development by the building of bridges and roads. With no real markets for other agricultural products, nearly all of the recent settlers in the Chapare grow coca as their main crop.[49] A similar phenomenon occurred in Peru. When an all-weather road from Tingo Maria was built, "it provided easy access to illicit coca plantations for the traffickers."[50]

On the other hand, enforcement in the Tingo Maria area did result in shifting the illicit coca-growing region further into the remote *selva* (jungle). But thousands more square miles of such territory remain available and are rapidly being brought under cultivation. Similarly, brand new acreage in western Brazil has been planted. Thus, new coca cultivation in other countries would undercut whatever success is achieved in Bolivia and Peru. Even if coca were effectively curtailed in *all* of South America, cultivation could shift to other countries, including Indonesia, Madagascar, Guyana, and Sri Lanka (see Figure 4).[51] Coca was in fact grown on a large scale in Java, which until World War II provided much of the coca leaf for the world supply of pharmaceutical cocaine.[52] It doesn't take much, either. A student of mine once calculated that the entire crop of coca leaf necessary to supply the 1980 United States black market would only require about 12 square miles of land.[53] The equivalent figure for 1984 would be about double, not very much considering the vast wilderness areas of the Andes.

In the very long term, of course, it is possible that the development of a modern socioeconomic infrastructure will transform the conditions of life in Andean Peru and Bolivia and thereby facilitate some measure of control of coca and cocaine production. Short of such a transformation, however, neither the United States nor the source countries can realistically expect to achieve significant limitations on the supply of coca for cocaine without

Figure 4
Effects of Law Enforcement on Cultivation of Coca Leaf in New Growing Areas

---

An effective crackdown in Bolivia and Peru would manifest itself in higher prices for coca leaf (P_2). At some point, higher prices would make production in less efficient growing areas in these and other countries profitable. The introduction of new sources of supply (SS") would then ease the pressure on price (P_3) by increasing total production (Q_3).

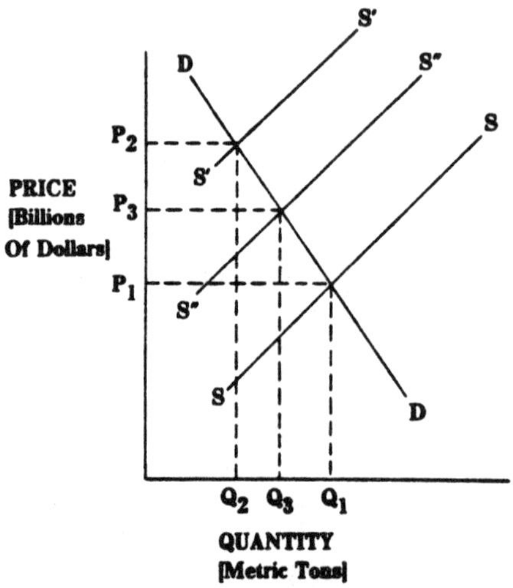

DD = Demand
SS = Original Supply
SS' = Reduced Supply Resulting From South American Crackdown
($P_2 - P_1$) = Resulting Price Rise
($Q_1 - Q_2$) = Resulting Quantity Reduction

SS" = Increased Supply Resulting From New Producers Seeking To Take Advantage Of Higher Prices
($P_2 - P_3$) = Resulting Decline In Price
($Q_3 - Q_2$) = Resulting Increase In Quantity
($Q_1 - Q_3$) = Net Reduction In Quantity Of Cocaine Produced And Consumed

---

resorting to some radical or violent "fix" such as military occupation of the coca-growing regions. Even then, it is doubtful whether the weak governments involved have the political and economic power to sustain such repression over the long term. Peru, for example, confronts a serious terrorist problem in the Maoist-oriented "Shining Path" insurgency. Bolivia struggles merely to govern itself for more than one year per government. The United States Government exhibits incredibly powerful denial mechanisms in holding out crop control as even a palliative for the "cocaine problem."

5

The Federal Drug Police: The U.S. Law Enforcement System

Once the cocaine or cocaine base has been produced in South America and routed to the United States, it becomes the responsibility of the domestic law enforcement system to try to intercept it before it reaches the consumer or, failing that, to administer sanctions after the fact for its distribution. These enforcement efforts seek to promote the policy of supply reduction by pressuring those in the drug business with a variety of threats to freedom and finances. At the same time, those pressures have the effect of maintaining high price levels, thereby perpetuating the profitability of the black market, with all its destructive pathologies (analyzed in Chapters Seven, Eight, and Nine).

With President Nixon's reorganization of drug enforcement agencies in 1973, the Drug Enforcement Administration became the lead drug enforcement agency of the United States Government. Specialized areas of drug authority also belong to the Customs Service, the Coast Guard, the Internal Revenue Service, and since 1981, the Federal Bureau of Investigation. The Central Intelligence Agency and the Department of Defense also play supporting roles. Total funding of the drug law enforcement system for fiscal year 1985 was $1.2 billion, and nearly all of it was spent for the domestic enforcement system.[1] By agency, the federal budget allocated the largest amounts to the DEA ($334.7 million), Customs ($257.3 million), and the Coast Guard ($245.1 million). Only $253 million was allocated for drug abuse prevention and treatment programs (see Table 8).

INTERDICTING COCAINE

The function of interdicting cocaine and other drugs at the borders of the United States belongs primarily to the United States Customs Service.

Table 8
Federal Drug Law Enforcement—Summary

May 7, 1984 (Millions of Dollars)

AGENCY	FY 1981		FY 1982		FY 1983		FY 1984		FY 1985	
	BA	Outlay	BA	Outlay	BA	Outlay	BA	Outlay	BA	Outlay
Department of Justice										
DEA	215.3	216.8	242.7	224.6	283.0	275.9	329.1	320.6	334.7	327.7
FBI	8.3	8.3	40.0	40.0	107.6	107.6	94.5	94.5	93.2	93.2
Criminal Division	1.8	1.8	2.0	2.0	2.2	2.2	1.9	1.9	3.2	3.1
Tax Div.	0.0	0.0	0.0	0.0	1.0	1.0	1.0	1.0	1.8	1.8
US Attorneys	18.8	18.4	19.9	19.5	31.6	31.0	42.5	42.3	48.9	48.7
US Marshals Service	0.0	0.0	0.0	0.0	0.7	0.6	0.6	0.6	0.7	0.7
OCDE TF (Direct)	0.0	0.0	0.0	0.0	0.7	0.2	2.7	2.6	2.8	2.7
INS	2.2	2.2	2.4	2.4	2.4	2.4	2.4	2.4	2.5	2.5
Bureau of Prisons	82.3	81.9	86.2	85.3	99.1	91.2	115.3	106.1	129.8	120.4
Prisons (CAP)	0.0	0.0	0.0	0.0	12.6	1.7	0.0	10.9	0.0	0.0
OJARS	0.0	11.1	0.0	3.6	0.0	0.0	0.0	0.0	0.0	0.0
Treasury Department										
Customs	144.0	142.0	196.0	193.0	245.1	241.5	278.5	278.0	257.3†	251.9†
IRS	34.7	34.7	43.5	43.5	49.4	49.4	55.0	55.0	58.3	58.3
BATF	0.0	0.0	1.5	1.5	4.6	2.9	6.0	6.0	5.2	5.2
Department of State										
INM	35.9	28.4	36.7	42.3	36.7	36.6	41.2	37.7	50.2	42.8
AID (Direct)	0.0	0.0	15.7‡	0.2‡	9.2‡	10.6‡	11.7‡	12.5‡	9.2‡	14.2
Dept. of Transportation										
US Coast Guard	159.1	159.1	194.1	194.1	218.1	218.1	234.7	234.7	245.1	245.1
FAA	0.0	0.0	0.1	0.1	0.1	0.1	0.1	0.1	0.1	0.1
USDA (Research)	1.4	1.4	1.4	1.4	1.4	1.4	1.4	1.4	1.4	1.4
US Forest Service	0.0	0.0	0.0	0.0	1.0	1.0	1.3	1.3	1.2	1.2
FDA	1.4	1.4	0.8	0.8	0.7	0.7	0.7	0.7	0.7	0.7
TOTAL (See Footnotes)	705.3	707.6	883.0	854.3	1107.2	1076.1	1220.6	1210.3	1246.3	1221.7

*Does not include law enforcement support furnished by DOD for border interdiction, estimated at $15.8M in FY84, no estimate available for FY85.
‡Does not include AID projects which provide indirect support in producing countries, estimated in FY82—$7.4M; FY83—$10.0M; FY84—$7.4M; FY85—$5.0M.
†Does not include an FY85 Budget Amendment which restores $15M to the Customs air interdiction program.

Source: Drug Abuse Policy Office, *1984 National Strategy for Prevention of Drug Abuse and Drug Trafficking*, Appendix B-2, p. 122.

The drug enforcement role of the Customs Service is, in legal theory, a corollary of its primary function: to collect revenue and to clear imported merchandise and travelers from abroad. In that domain, the size and scope of Customs' operations are vast. In fiscal year 1981, for example, Customs collected almost $9.2 billion in duties and fees. It processed more than 25 million entries of merchandise, 96.4 million carriers (vessels, aircraft, trucks, buses, cars, and trains), over 314 million passengers, 400 million pieces of luggage, and 84.4 million items of letter class mail.[2]

Given this enormous influx of goods, the 4,500 inspectors of the Customs Service must inspect for drugs and other contraband on a highly selective basis. But the Customs drug interdiction program goes far beyond routine inspections, including (in fiscal year 1981) about 1,000 marine and air patrol officers, 122 detector dog teams, numerous mail examiners,[3] and 25 special cargo enforcement teams deployed at major ports of entry to scrutinize suspicious cargo.[4] In addition to inspections and patrols, Customs maintains a network of informants, contact with foreign customs agencies, and computerized data bases. These provide the intelligence and financial data for Customs to conduct special enforcement operations, investigating specific targets or leads.

Notwithstanding these various interdiction and enforcement programs and the advantage of knowing that Miami is the principal port of entry for illegal cocaine, the Customs Service in 1980 made 1,307 seizures totaling 4,743 pounds of cocaine, or only about 5 percent of the 40 to 48 metric tons imported to the United States.[5] Under the War on Drugs, intensified enforcement pushed this seizure rate to about 10 percent in 1982 and achieved a similar percentage (about 8.9 tons out of 60±) for fiscal year 1983.[6]

This low yield is not surprising in view of the ease with which cocaine can be concealed in an airplane or ship and the infinite diversity of delivery techniques, such as body carriers, body packers, mail, cargo, and air and sea drops. Indeed, the variety of smuggling schemes runs the gamut of human ingenuity. For example, since cocaine can be dissolved and reconstituted, smugglers can dissolve it in alcohol and conceal it in bottles.[7] There are also credible reports of high-tech smuggling schemes involving one-man submarines and radio-controlled, pilotless aircraft. Even without these exotic techniques, touch and go delivery methods—air and sea drops—have proved generally successful. For example, in August, 1984, a twin-engine plane touched down briefly on an unopened section of I–95 in Florida, leaving behind 1,200 pounds of high-grade cocaine. Authorities seized the coke and later found the plane, but they could not make any arrests.[8]

The War on Drugs may succeed in weaving a finer mesh for the Customs net, but for every law enforcement move smugglers have a countermove. They respond to intelligence gathered by Customs agents with counterintelligence (gained by bribery) to discover patrol patterns, planned inspections, or the identity of informants. They also use decoy shipments and disinformation (false "tips"). They shift smuggling routes; following the South Florida Task Force's infusion of Customs personnel into Florida, record seizures occurred in areas of the country previously untouched as transit or distribution points: for example, 610 pounds of cocaine at the Brookhaven Airport on June 24, 1982, and 1,254 pounds in Cleveland, Tennessee, on July 11, 1982.[9]

Despite the intensive interdiction efforts of the South Florida Task Force, record amounts of cocaine reached the United States in 1983 and 1984, as much as 90 metric tons. The figure rose to over 100 tons in 1985. The enforcement system cannot regularly achieve a high rate of interdiction because most seizures occur upon random inspection or in response to a specific suspicion. Routine processing of cargo and travelers without prior informant tips accounted for 97 percent of the number of drug seizures and 80 percent of the number of cocaine seizures in 1979.[10] Interdiction is mostly a matter of chance.

Here are some typical scenarios. A local police officer in Everglades City, Florida, notices that a Winnebago rides very low on its suspension. He pulls the driver over, notices "green, leafy matter" on the driver's pants, and searches. The result—a load of nearly one ton of cocaine.[11]

A Piper Seneca shows up on radar over the Bahamas. It enters United States air space and turns off its lights. Its pilot has not filed a flight plan. It carries 1,000 pounds of cocaine.[12]

In August, 1984, Customs inspectors used drug-sniffing dogs to uncover 2,754 pounds of cocaine base concealed in the interiors of 180 large industrial pulleys shipped from Peru to Miami. Three men were indicted.[13]

In yet another variation, a confidential informant "approached Miami police officers on the street" and led them to a boat on the Miami River stuffed with 1,500–2,000 pounds of cocaine in duffelbags.[14]

These basic interdiction techniques—radar, personal observation, cargo checks—show the hit-or-miss nature of enforcement by interdiction. Proactive operations really do not produce very much in the absence of an informant to pinpoint time and place for Customs agents. For this reason concealment of cocaine in ordinary cargo shipments, such as Colombian flowers or fruit from Central America, continues to find favor as a smuggling technique. The magnitude of such smuggling operations showed up in a series of unusually large cargo seizures by Customs: 3,748 pounds at Miami International Airport on March 9, 1982; 233 pounds on an Eastern Airlines flight on April 14, 1982; 236 pounds on an Avianca flight on May 16, 1982; and 1,197 pounds on a chartered jet on May 18, 1982.[15]

Cargo smuggling offers the potential for delivering very large quantities with minimal risk of arrest. No arrests occurred in the seizures just cited. The high markup makes the risk of product loss worth taking, as the out-of-pocket cost to the smuggler, say $7,000-$10,000 per kilo in Colombia, constitutes perhaps only one-quarter to one-third of the wholesale value of cocaine in Miami. Smugglers appear willing and able to absorb such losses as a cost of doing business. Even doubling the smuggler's product losses would not end profitability at present price levels.

Since the out-of-pocket costs of cocaine smuggling (exclusive of the premium for risk taking) are relatively low, rational smuggling decisions will hinge primarily on assessment of the risks of arrest. If the War on Drugs is to succeed, the smugglers must perceive a drastic elevation in the level of risk. But as we have seen, cargo concealment and other smuggling techniques enable smugglers to insulate themselves from the risk of arrest.

This analysis suggests three conclusions about the Government's program of interdiction. First, a permanent increase in the interdiction rate of cocaine above the present 10 percent or so will be extraordinarily difficult and expensive for Customs to achieve. Customs itself claims only that its program "reduces the smugglers' options for choosing the time, method and place for entering contraband."[16] But not by much. It claims only a 1 percent interdiction rate for airborne drug smuggling and only a 6 percent interception rate of smuggling vessels (300 of an estimated 5,400 sorties by smuggling ships on both coasts). The ability of smugglers to get their goods to market is hardly even impaired.

Second, even a permanent doubling of the present interdiction rate would not significantly reduce the total size of the black market in cocaine. All it would do is take out of circulation an additional 10 or 12 tons of a total of about 100 tons, a dubious benefit to be sure. Greater product losses, if sustained over the long run, would mean higher costs and therefore higher prices for the stuff that does make it to market, but it might also mean greater total revenues for the traffickers. Third, an undesirable but predictable (and proven) impact of a sustained interdiction program is to drive out amateur and semiprofessional smugglers, leaving the "hard-core" criminal elements, i.e., those who have the resources, organizational skills, corrupting powers, technology, and ruthlessness necessary to penetrate the Government's defenses on a consistent basis. Are such results worthwhile or desirable?

BUSTING THE TRAFFICKER

Because inter-agency rivalries and administrative reorganizations play a central role in the drug enforcement story, a bit of enforcement history is an appropriate prelude. In 1973, the Nixon Administration created the DEA as the chief drug enforcement agency of the federal government. The historical roots of the DEA reach back to 1915, when 162 IRS collectors and agents were placed in the Miscellaneous Division of the Department of the Treasury to enforce the revenue provisions of the Harrison Narcotics Act of 1914. In 1920, the Prohibition Unit was created within the Department of the Treasury, and it became a separate bureau in 1927.

In 1930, the Federal Bureau of Narcotics (FBN), still under the jurisdiction of the Department of the Treasury, was formed. It remained the FBN until 1968, when President Lyndon Johnson merged it with the Food and Drug Administration's (FDA) Bureau of Drug Abuse Control under the Department of Justice as the Bureau of Narcotics and Dangerous Drugs (BNDD). In 1973, President Nixon sought to consolidate primary drug enforcement authority in one agency controlled by the White House through the Attorney General. Accordingly, the Customs Service's Drug Investigation Unit was merged with BNDD, becoming the DEA, and Customs thereby lost its role as the primary agency for the collection of narcotics-related intelligence. The DEA also absorbed the Office of National Narcotics Intelligence (ONNI) and the Office of Drug Abuse Law Enforcement (ODALE), both from the Department of Justice. This plan was based on a position paper drawn up by White House staffer G. Gordon Liddy, later convicted of participating in the Watergate burglary. Edward Jay Epstein, in *Agency of Fear,* theorizes that Nixon created the DEA out of the same malevolent spirit that produced the White House Plumbers.[17]

Whatever its lineage, the DEA's official mission is to immobilize, by arrest and prosecution, "major drug violators" of the Controlled Substances Act "operating at interstate and international levels."[18] In short, the law makes the DEA the principal case-making agency of the United States in this domain, a national drug police force. In addition to case-making by investigation and arrest, the officially stated functions of the DEA include asset seizure and forfeiture; management of a national narcotics intelligence system; supervision of the prescription of controlled substances; cooperative enforcement efforts with officials of federal, state, and local agencies; coordination of drug enforcement programs with foreign nations; and liaison with the United Nations, Interpol, and other international organizations on matters relating to drug control.

Despite this weighty mission, the DEA is rather a small agency. As of February 28, 1981, the DEA employed a total of 4,003 persons, only 1,946 of whom were special agents.[19] Under the War on Drugs, that figure rose by some 400–500.

To further augment DEA manpower, the Administration made history of a sort in bringing the FBI into drug enforcement in a significant way. Historically, the FBI had played only an incidental role in drug enforcement. In 1981, the Attorney General ordered a "realignment of responsibilities" between the DEA and the FBI, conferring concurrent drug investigative jurisdiction on the two agencies.[20] The DEA continued as the lead drug enforcement agency, but the DEA Director was made subordinate to the Director of the FBI, rather than reporting directly to the Attorney General. Additionally, the FBI committed roughly 10 percent of its agents' hours to drug investigations, particularly those involving "complicated financial" expertise. As of December 31, 1983, the FBI had a total of 1,085 agents "working 1692 drug-related matters," up from 100 in January, 1982. Still, the FBI budgeted only $17.8 million for drug law enforcement in fiscal year 1983, and only 300–500 work years of FBI agents went to drug cases.[21] Nevertheless, FBI work in drug enforcement produced 1,200 defendants indicted and 653 convicted in that year.[22]

Under the terms of the "Implementation Directive for Concurrent Drug Investigative Jurisdiction Between DEA and FBI," the FBI is to "focus its resources on drug investigations involving traditional organized crime (OC) families (La Cosa Nostra), violence prone nontraditional OC groups such as the outlaw motorcycle gangs, and ethnic or racial OC groups such as the Israeli, Mexican and Black Mafias and La Nuestra Familia." The DEA is to continue its focus on "major drug organizations according to established priorities." Intelligence is to be shared and good faith cooperation is "expected from all personnel of both agencies," a dictum issued in apparent recognition of persistent inter-agency rivalry, suspicion, and antagonism.

So much for the statistical profile of the DEA/FBI drug enforcement effort. How are cases made in the field, and what problems do agents confront? In a nutshell, the principal challenge to a case agent comes to this: he must produce sufficient evidence against a suspect to justify an indictment and successful prosecution under the law, usually under provisions of the Controlled Substances Act. The most commonly charged offenses include unlawful distribution, possession with intent to distribute, and attempt or conspiracy to distribute a controlled substance, and related import/export offenses. The law authorizes seizure and forfeiture of drug-related assets without an arrest or indictment. Usually, civil forfeiture and criminal prosecution occur together, arising out of the same investigation. Financial offenses—tax and currency law violations—also offer additional prosecutorial tools.

Title 21 of the United States Code defines a "controlled substance" to mean "a drug or other substance, or immediate precursor, included in schedule I, II, III, IV, or V."[23] The law lists cocaine as a Schedule II drug, i.e., one that has "a high potential for abuse," "a currently accepted medical use [as topical anesthesia] in treatment in the United States," and abuse of which "may lead to severe psychological or physical dependence."[24] The law defines "narcotic drug" to include cocaine, contrary to its pharmacological properties as a stimulant of the central nervous system.

Many courts have acknowledged the discrepancy between law and medicine regarding the classification of cocaine. They nevertheless (unanimously) sustain the "narcotic" classification against constitutional attack on the grounds that science or medicine do not control the law.[25] Drug law is explicitly political in this sense; and the law delegates the power to classify controlled substances to the Attorney General rather than, say, the Surgeon General or the Food and Drug Administration.[26] As a result, judicial review of drug law disregards completely the teachings of science and medicine.

The intentional misclassification elevates the maximum punishment for what otherwise would be a "non-narcotic" drug offense from 5 years in prison (and a fine of $15,000) to 20 years in prison (and a $250,000 fine) for a first distribution offense. The maximum penalty doubles in both cases for a repeat offender.

Two federal statutes target the major drug trafficker or recidivist drug violator with severe criminal penalties and property forfeiture provisions. A Continuing Criminal Enterprise (CCE) case requires proof of a series of controlled substance violations undertaken by the defendant "in concert with five or more other persons with respect to whom such person occupies a position of organizer . . . or any other position of management, and from which such person obtains substantial income or resources."[27] Conviction carries a minimum mandatory term of ten years in prison without probation or suspended sentence. In addition, upon conviction of CCE the jury may order forfeiture of money or property acquired from or traceable to the crime.

The Racketeer Influenced Corrupt Organization (RICO) was enacted as part of the Organized Crime Control Act of 1970 and was originally directed toward more traditional patterns of racketeering activity. Its purpose is "the elimination of the infiltration of organized crime and racketeering into legitimate organizations operating in interstate commerce."[28] RICO is broad enough to encompass any illegitimate enterprise affecting interstate or foreign commerce, including a drug importing or distribution business. RICO defines four offenses: illegal derivation of funds used for investment in or acquisition of an enterprise; illegal acquisition of an interest in an enterprise by racketeering; use of an enterprise to commit illegal acts; and conspiracy to violate any of the foregoing sections. The statute imposes a jurisdictional requirement of interstate or foreign commerce and requires proof of two predicate acts of racketeering. The RICO penalties, a maximum of 20 years in prison and forfeiture provisions (of all interests acquired in violation of the statute), resemble those for a CCE violator. In some cases there may be some overlap in the conduct of a drug violator that would bring him under both statutes. Enforcement of RICO has developed slowly. As of early 1979, the Department of Justice estimated that it had filed about 200 RICO cases since the effective date of the act.[29] Proposed RICO and CCE indictments for fiscal year 1983 grew to 64 and 70, respectively.

Financial aspects of the drug business, such as currency violations (the Bank Secrecy Act) or tax evasion (the Internal Revenue Code) generally fall within the enforcement domain of the Department of the Treasury, rather than the Department of Justice, but the recent emphasis on the task force approach has tended to blur some of the former lines of demarcation of agency function. Task force operations are analyzed in Chapter Six.

To the extent that DEA or FBI agents investigate controlled substances violations (rather than financial crimes), case agents concentrate on assembling evidence of possession or transfer of the drug, or related conspiracies and attempts. The major obstacle confronting them arises because drug deals are consensual: obviously, no participant seeks the intervention of the law. The nature of drug law enforcement therefore differs radically from the investigation of conventional crimes against person or property.

In cases involving robbery, for example, investigators typically work backward from a reported crime to discoverable facts about the perpetrator. In this regard, the police depend almost entirely upon information supplied by the victim(s) or the witness(es) for establishing the identity and whereabouts of the robber. What did he say and do? What did he look like? Where did he go? But even for crimes where police have a cooperative or motivated victim, the clearance rate of reported crimes runs very low, about 30 percent for robbery.[30] That is, the police succeed in arresting a suspect in only 30 cases out of 100 reported robberies. The quick encounter between criminal and victim, under conditions of stress and fear, renders many victims inadequate as sources of information; lacking specific leads to work with, the police will generally fail to find the perpetrator.

The clearance rate for drug crimes, by comparison, can not even be quantified in any meaningful way because of the general absence of complaining witnesses. Voluntary participants have no incentive to report a crime to the police. Of perhaps 200–300 million cocaine transactions per year, arrests for cocaine offenses probably do not exceed .01 percent of the total. This miniscule clearance rate for drug offenses reveals something fundamentally twisted about the process of drug enforcement. Some type of undercover operation or clandestine surveillance is usually required, and agents must "act aggressively to uncover offenses, sometimes to the point of promoting crime."[31] Agents must generally rely on snitches and undercover agents, using deception and other methods that border on entrapment or otherwise "rub against Constitutional restraints on police authority,"[32] especially in the realm of surveillance (body bugs, wiretaps) and searches and seizures. The aggressive promotion of drug crime reaches its zenith in so-called reverse sting operations, where agents or informants pose as drug dealers seeking to unload their wares on uncautious (often amateur or novice) buyers. Let us undertake a brief overview of basic case-making techniques in drug cases.

The most elementary technique of case-making is buy and bust. In this scenario, undercover agents, working through an informant, make a connection for a buy. Typically, the informant arranges a meeting to introduce the parties, the agents use departmental purchase-of-evidence money as a "flash roll," and a later meeting is set to consummate the transaction. Upon delivery of the kilo or two (the most common quantity), the agents arrest the seller and seize the drugs as evidence.

This technique suffers from obvious limitations. A circumspect distributor will rarely put himself in the position of selling directly to strangers (who might be "narcs"). As a result, cocaine is sold at this level by lower-level dealers, or simply delivered by mules; both, in effect, are paid to take the risk of an arrest and to maintain silence should it occur. Thus, the buy-and-bust technique will rarely produce an arrest of a dealer above the kilo level. Major distributors or importers insulate themselves from the risk of arrest through the use of underlings and intermediaries.

For years, buy and bust was the mainstay of DEA operations. DEA agents perceived pressure to "put powder on the table," and buy and bust was a proven technique of generating arrest and seizure statistics. Recent departmental pressures for higher-impact cases have produced a shift to long-term investigations. In a more sophisticated, but still conventional, variation on the buy-and-bust theme, agents seek to climb the pyramid of dealers to the apex by repeat purchases. Over time, the undercover agents (or informants) develop the trust of the sellers; they become regular customers; they buy in increasing quantities; and ultimately they contrive a business reason for demanding to meet with and deal directly with the principal figure in the organization. If they succeed, secretly recorded conversations by body bugs or phone taps provide the basis for a conspiracy indictment.

The problems with this technique are many. First, it is time-consuming. Depending on its size and scope, an investigation of this type can take from 6 to 30 months, with two years being a typical time frame.[33] If it fails, the agency has no caseload statistics to justify its time and expenses. Expenses raise a second reservation. Buying drugs costs a lot. To buy five kilos a month used to cost a quarter million dollars (although the price has fallen considerably since 1983). The DEA spent $880,000 to buy heroin in one 1983 heroin conspiracy investigation. The supervisors of case agents get understandably nervous about doling out cash in such amounts. Apart from the obvious opportunities for corrupt diversion of cash, anyone carrying large amounts of cash for a drug deal presents an attractive target for robbery or murder.

One way to avoid these problems has emerged in the sell-and-bust technique. Here, undercover agents, usually in collaboration with an informant, pose as drug dealers with a product to move. In this "reverse sting," undercover agents look for prospective drug buyers, offer them attractive terms, and arrest them after they pay for the drugs.[34] This technique has the distinct administrative advantage of selling drugs from the agency property room; rather than having to finance drug purchases, agents earn cash for the agency. The cash is ultimately forfeited to the United States (or the state enforcement agency) after its use as evidence. While this source of finance for drug enforcement continues to grow in importance, the long-term impact of the technique is limited: someone who buys cocaine from a stranger is more likely to be an amateur than a major dealer, who would have his own source of supply. Nevertheless, local police departments have seized on this scam with gusto, selling drugs in public parks and beaches, and even operating undercover drug supermarkets out of private homes in order to arrest buyers. Sell and bust has become very popular with them: not only is it a proven money-maker, it often leads to seizures of vehicles and other property useful to the police.

The actual sale of drugs by law enforcement agents raises disturbing moral and legal issues: it is right for officers of the law to resort to sales techniques or other enticements in the sale of drugs? The answer of the courts has generally been positive—no unlawful entrapment occurs by an agent's inducements so long as the buyer has the "predisposition" to commit the offense and the police merely provide the opportunity. DEA and FBI guidelines cautiously permit agents to carry "show drugs" for use in investigations where they pose as suppliers.[35]

In any event, the ethical questions raised by the sale of drugs become moot in more sophisticated variations of the reverse sting, where agents appear in other guises in the drug business, serving as pilots of drug planes or financial backers of drug deals. These roles permit the undercover agents to gather valuable intelligence about particular drug syndicates. One of the most successful formats for a reverse sting involved a phony money-laundering operation. In Operation Bancoshares the FBI set up a currency exchange house which accepted $170 million in cash from traffickers over a 13-month period. The FBI actually "laundered" the money by wiring it abroad to foreign banks. At the conclusion of the investigation, the money was out of the reach of the FBI, but the agency obtained numerous indictments for violations of the Bank Secrecy Act.[36]

This brief account presents only a few of the many variations on the drug investigation theme. Whatever the specific technique used by DEA and FBI agents, they succeed (when they succeed) only in pressuring different facets of the drug business, whether it be the distribution of drugs, the transportation of drugs, or the laundering of drug money. The ultimate reality remains largely unaffected: once the cocaine makes its inevitable penetration into the United States, the secrecy of transactions and their vast number simply overwhelm the capacity of the drug enforcement system. The several thousand low-level arrests made each year, and concomitant seizures of a few tons of cocaine, do not significantly disrupt the system of distribution over the long run.

In order to have any enduring disruptive impact on the networks of distribution, law enforcement must take out the importers and other major traffickers at the top levels of the drug hierarchy. In fact, DEA priorities call for ignoring low-level dealers while selectively targeting "major drug law violators who operate at national and international levels." But successful case-making at the highest levels of distribution remains a relative rarity because of an ironic fact about the drug business. The structure of the cocaine industry and the structure of law enforcement combine so that the littlest fish are the easiest to catch, while the major traffickers enjoy a substantial degree of immunity from the law.

Several factors account for the relatively safe position of major violators. First, many of the principal suppliers are foreign nationals residing abroad, such as the Ochoa family in Colombia or the Suarez family in Bolivia. These figures are protected in their own domains by a combination of weak enforcement and corrupt government officials. Corruption in the judiciary, the police, and elsewhere in government is so commonplace that it hardly deserves mention. But the blatancy of some arrangements requires special note. For example, the Suarez family is reputed to have bought the complicity of Bolivia's Garcia Meza regime for millions of dollars, and at one point trafficking operations were protected by the military forces of Bolivia.[37] Similarly, fugitive financier Robert Vesco allegedly bought the complicity of Bahamian Prime Minister Lyndon O. Pindling to protect his island-based cocaine transshipment operations to the United States.[38]

Until recently Colombia provided a wide-open base of operations for both marijuana and cocaine, including cultivation of coca; processing of leaf, paste, or base; and transportation of marijuana and cocaine from Colombia to the United States and to various Caribbean transshipment points. The Colombian government had refused to spray paraquat on marijuana fields or to agree to extradite its citizens to the United States following indictment by American grand juries. Many sectors of Colombian society prospered, directly or indirectly, from the influx of drug money. And the political climate was very favorable: the Colombian Legislature (Parliament) debated legalization of marijuana, and many members enjoyed generous campaign contributions from those in the drug trade. Carlos Lehder, a major cocaine trafficker reputedly allied to Vesco, even published his own newspaper and started his own political party until he was driven into exile by his indictment in the United States.

The climate of public opinion shifted significantly in 1984 when Minister of Justice Lara Bonilla was executed in retaliation for strong anti-drug enforcement actions, including the largest cocaine seizure in history (almost 14 tons). President Belisario Betancur then announced his willingness to extradite indicted Colombians to the United States if the United States would reciprocate. He also declared a state of siege on drug traffickers, who responded to the pressure with a remarkable offer to cease business, give up major holdings of property, and invest billions in drug wealth in Colombia in exchange for amnesty.

> Although Betancur's assault caused the drug kings to lie low for a while, they were by no means cowed. Within a month of the Lara murder, Entrepreneur Escobar and a few colleagues, claiming to represent a group of *coqueros* controlling 80% of the drug market, meet first with Alfonso Lopez Michelsen, former Colombian

President, and then with Attorney General Carlos Jimenez Gomez in Panama City to offer the Colombian government a deal: in exchange for total amnesty, they said, they would dismantle their illicit empires and repatriate $5 billion into Colombia's troubled economy. The government replied that it would accept nothing short of the traffickers' unconditional surrender.

To make the point, the 1,500 men of Colombia's U.S.-supported antinarcotics squad persevered in their search-and-destroy missions and, for a time, scored one spectacular victory after another. In early December, for example, they intercepted more than 550 kilos of high-grade cocaine, packed and readied for shipment at a rambling ranch known as Villa Julia, and flushed it down a sewer in nearby Medellin. Four days later, in northern La Guajira province, squad members came upon 1,054 kilos of pure coke that had been stashed in lunch boxes, leather pouches and even official-looking CARE packages, and dumped it into the Caribbean. In the following weeks they eliminated 32 cocaine-processing plants in the llanos, the sparsely populated areas along the Brazilian border, accessible only by foot, boat or light aircraft.

. . .

But the key figures in the cocaine business continue to elude the authorities. Washington has stationed 16 antinarcotics agents in Colombia and hopes to budget a record $9.2 million for its Colombian campaign in fiscal 1985. By comparison, Drug King Escobar is said to command a personal army of more than 2,000 retainers and a fortune estimated at more than $2 billion. Escobar, who is suspected of having taken out the contract on Lara's life and [who] is wanted in the U.S. on charges of smuggling ten tons of cocaine into the country, at one time faced just one charge in Colombia: illegally importing 82 of the 1,500 exotic animals in his private zoo.

Even if "Los Grandes Mafiosos" could be caught, moreover, it is unlikely that they would be held for long. When the drug war was declared, ex-smuggler Fabio Ochoa voluntarily gave himself up to the police. "I have nothing to fear," he announced. Sure enough, the authorities could muster no more serious charge against him than illegal possession of firearms. Six weeks later he was released on bail, and the case is now in limbo. "We know who [the cocaine kings] are, and we can't nail them," says Police Captain Guillermo Benavides. "But the worst thing is that even if we could get all the bosses, new ones would immediately take their place. They'd pop up like mushrooms."[39]

The attack on distribution networks within the United States fails for different reasons: the deep-rooted American tradition of limited governmental powers, reflected in respect for individual privacy, constrains the investigative powers of law enforcement officers. Because drug transactions are consensual, private, and secret, case agents encounter obstacles to their effectiveness at almost every stage of the investigative process. Not only are the principal means for piercing the veil of secrecy in such conspiracy cases—informants, infiltration, and surveillance—inherently inefficient and tedious, but constitutional, statutory, and administrative restraints make the operations of drug agents still more cumbersome. Let us examine the investigative process in more detail to see how radically it differs from the enforcement of laws against traditional crimes.

At the risk of oversimplifying, investigations generally fall into one of two major categories—those in which agents have developed suspicions about the culpability of specific individuals or businesses, and those in which agents have observed patterns of movement and property transfers in the drug business and seek to trace those patterns to the actors in charge. In both types of investigation, the foremost need of agents is to gather information—the identity of conspirators or other violators, their customers or suppliers, quantities, times, dates, and places. In short, agents must ultimately develop evidence sufficient to prove a crime beyond a reasonable doubt, although lesser standards will suffice for intermediate investigatory stages, e.g., probable cause for the issuance of a search warrant or wiretap. With or without a specific target of investigation, pursuit of information dominates the investigatory process.[40]

Confidential informants (CIs) are the standard, indeed indispensable, source of information in the drug enforcement business. As a top prosecutor in the United States Attorney's office in Miami puts it, "If you want me to catch a criminal, give me a criminal to start with." Without a CI, agents would not get the introductions, connections, or other investigatory leads they need. Even so, a CI can rarely provide evidence sufficient to convict a target unless he is an insider or co-conspirator who has been "flipped," i.e., immunized or promised leniency in exchange for cooperation. Instead, a CI functions to supply information at a preliminary stage in the case-making process, such as furnishing probable cause for the issuance of a search warrant or a wiretap. Evidence acquired from the contacts, leads, warrants, or taps becomes part of the total case against a target, justifying (if successful) the issuance of an indictment.

A second technique—infiltration by an undercover agent—is sometimes employed in a long-term conspiracy investigation. But working up through the ranks of a drug-distributing organization, or posing as a drug entrepreneur in order to gain a position of intimacy with trafficking targets, presents many risks. The long time frame required makes the technique unsuitable for run-of-the-mill investigations. Lack of credibility also presents a major obstacle. Drawn from the ranks of mainstream America and alien to the values and styles of the underworld subculture, most agents lack the ability to carry off the ruse for very long. For one thing, obvious barriers of language and ethnic origin come between the typical Anglo agent and Colombian "businessmen" in the cocaine industry. Bureaucratic codes also interfere: they forbid agents to ingest drugs, an abstinence that can easily generate suspicion. For these reasons, DEA policy for such investigations is restrictive: "Undercover operations are not regarded as a 'standard' investigative technique. They are dangerous, expensive, and highly speculative ventures."[41]

Nevertheless, the infiltration technique is sometimes used and occasionally produces spectacular results. In one exceptional investigation of this type, DEA agents posed as American *mafiosi* seeking to establish a regular supply line for South American cocaine. They convinced Roberto Suarez, Jr., son of the godfather of the Bolivian cocaine traffic, to sell them 854 pounds of cocaine base, which he allegedly ordered loaded on a cargo jet in Bolivia. Suarez, Jr., was indicted by the United States, extradited from Switzerland, and tried in Miami. Alas for the DEA, a jury acquitted him of all charges and he went free.[42]

A third and more basic technique of drug investigation requires labor-intensive watching and following of suspects, aided by electronic surveillance and research of financial records. Physical surveillance generally provides nuts and bolts information about a subject: residence, family, office, associates, patterns of movement, travel, and other activities. From this information, agents may acquire further investigative leads, such as new persons to interview or to place under surveillance. An agent may also draw inferences about the culpability of the subject and the probable productivity of the investigation. Sometimes higher priorities will dictate aborting an investigation, but where continued investigation is warranted, the agents' labors—interviews of witnesses, (computerized) file information, physical surveillance, in conjunction with information supplied by an informant or derived from documents—may produce evidence sufficient (probable cause) to justify issuance of a warrant for electronic surveillance under controlling federal law, Title III of the Omnibus Crime Control and Safe Streets Act of 1968.[43]

That goal collides with the competing goal of protecting privacy from the peering and prying of police officials. So, once a wiretap is sought, the investigation becomes still more labor-intensive and time-consuming because the law imposes a wide array of procedural obstacles to overcome.[44] It is worthwhile surveying those impediments in order to comprehend the difficulty of the process. In order to obtain an order approving a wiretap, an agent must first submit a written request, approved by the local United States Attorney, for authorization by the Department of Justice (DOJ) to apply to a court for an intercept order.[45] This request must travel up the chain of command from the field agent to the head of the investigating agency to the Assistant United States Attorney General. Authorization from DOJ to apply for the order must be approved by the Attorney General or a specially designated assistant.[46] The process then requires presentation of the application to a court; issuance of an intercept order by a court; installation of the intercept device; recording the intercepted communications; monitoring the intercept and maintaining a contemporaneous log of the intercepted communications; compliance with administrative and judicial oversight requirements; compliance with notice and inventory requirements; transcribing recordings; and protecting their evidentiary value.[47]

Implementation of the wiretap requires still more agent energy. A wiretap, for example, ordinarily requires the ministrations of a crew of six: the technical agent, who sets up a listening post and the intercept equipment; the supervising attorney; a supervising agent, who acts as liaison between the supervising attorney and the monitoring agents who prepare and deliver daily written reports to the supervising attorney; and a minimum of three agents for 24-hour monitoring, which includes monitoring all interceptions and maintaining a contemporaneous log.[48] In addition to the monitoring process, if the prosecutors intend to use the tapes as evidence, they must be transcribed and the transcripts have to be "checked and rechecked for accuracy." (Of course, that presupposes that the tap is productive. It may not be so.) The process, according to federal prosecutors, is highly demanding and inefficient, "an incredibly time-consuming job."[49]

The objects of all this unwanted attention typically make wiretapping even more difficult by taking precautionary steps. A wary suspect can thwart electronic surveillance by technological countermeasures or by simple prudence, including the use of coded messages, speed dialing devices, voice disguises, and warning devices designed to detect a tap. Even where prudence fails to defeat the surveillance, it can slow it down considerably. A typical mid-level conspiracy investigation of this type takes one to three years to complete.

Let us consider the process and results of an investigation that was presented to the House Select Committee on Narcotics and Drug Abuse as a prototype of effective law enforcement against the cocaine trade, appearing as an appendix to a printed hearing of the committee in 1979.[50] The investigation started blind, i.e., without a specific suspect or target; the object was to find major cocaine suppliers in the District of Columbia. Through a cocktail waitress, an undercover agent made a connection, followed by several small buys of cocaine. The seller and associates were then placed under physical surveillance, and with the information thereby derived, agents obtained authority for installation of a pen register device on a suspect's telephone to print out the numbers of all outgoing calls. Agents then subpoenaed telephone company subscriber records and cross-checked the names attached to these numbers with DEA file information. After the fourth buy, the agent's connection introduced him to the principal subject, Michael Tillery. There followed more surveillance, more buys from Tillery, installation of a Title III wiretap, identification of the D.C. group's supplier in New York City, grand jury indictments, and execution of search warrants at four locations. The searches produced six pounds of cocaine and four ounces of heroin, marijuana, hashish, PCP, and other pills. Nine arrests were made and a total of $49,000 in buy money was expended.

The process took about one year from the date of the connection to the date of the defendants' convictions, a relatively quick pace. It required the full-time work of a prosecuting attorney for eight to nine months. The number of agent hours expended was not revealed, but for the 29 days of the wiretap, three agents staffed the listening post around the clock. More than 2,000 telephone calls were intercepted, but only 400 were relevant to the investigation. The taps produced 60 hours of tapes. Preparation of the transcripts took two months.

The case was successful in knocking out a substantial drug distributorship and procuring convictions. But the agents who made the Tillery case observed in their testimony to the House Select Committee that the busting of the Tillery ring did not lead to a general decline in the availability of cocaine in the Washington, D.C., area or to a rise in its price. This same stubborn resistance to law enforcement has persisted nationwide.

In this respect, the black market functions like a white (legal) market in which there is no oligopoly: a multiplicity of buyers and sellers prevents the operations of any one from affecting market price. In a fruit and vegetable market, for example, the disappearance of one vendor leaves market price unaffected so long as competitors remain. The same is true of cocaine. Accordingly, the price/purity index of cocaine compiled by the DEA for the United States shows only minor variations from 1977 through 1982. Had law enforcement succeeded in significantly restricting supplies or elevating the costs of dealing in cocaine, the law of supply and demand would have sent up the price. This did not happen. On the contrary, the nominal price of cocaine remained roughly constant between 1977 and 1982, and the real price declined after correcting for inflation.[51] Furthermore, the worldwide cocaine glut that began in 1983 moved prices sharply down (and sent average purity up), despite a significant increase in the number of seizures, arrests, prosecutions, and convictions. Clearly, the black market in cocaine is too large to be affected directly by knocking out a few tendrils of supply. Organizations and individuals alike are fully replaceable: "Criminal organizations have demonstrated remarkable powers of regeneration for developing new appendages to replace those shorn off by law enforcement."[52]

But what of the impact on the cost of doing business? Arrests factor into cost as risk premium. A systematic campaign of arrests could drive the price up if it elevated risk. But arrests have had little impact on the black market in cocaine. The data show both low quantity and poor quality of arrests for cocaine-related offenses. In gauging the impact of arrests on the importing and distributing hierarchy, the DEA has used a four-tiered classification system called the Geographic Drug Enforcement Program (GDEP). In fiscal year 1981, 29 percent of 4,379 cocaine arrestees fell into Class I (4 kg per month or more), and 17.3 percent into Class II (at least 1 kg). Class III is 1/4 kg per month and Class IV is all others.[53] Both the absolute and relative numbers of Class I violators rose in 1981 over fiscal year 1980, in which only 26.4 percent of 4,021 cocaine arrests were in Class I, and 16 percent were in Class II.[54] The DEA has apparently stopped publishing GDEP data, but the emphasis of the Reagan Administration on "breaking the power of the mob in America" points to a continuation of this trend, as evidenced by a rise in proposed CCE indictments from 29 in fiscal year 1981 to 70 in fiscal year 1983, and a rise in requests for RICO wiretaps from 53 to 108 in the same time period.[55] Although it should be noted that a single indictment frequently charges multiple defendants, these are still very modest numbers.

In evaluating the drug enforcement system, the role of state and local enforcement agencies deserves only brief mention. The majority of arrests at the state and local levels occur for simple possession or for sale of relatively small quantities and have no discernible impact beyond the maintenance of pressure on street-level sale of drugs in parks, bars, and other public places. For example, Florida authorities, with more opportunity for high-level cocaine trafficking cases than in any other state, made more than two-thirds of 3,559 cocaine arrests (in 1981) for simple possession.[56] Generalizing from newspaper reports of cocaine arrests, most of the remainder probably consisted of gram sales, with a noticeable minority proportion of kilo sales. The typical pattern of undercover work by local narcs follows the buy-and-bust model for a kilo of cocaine. More systematic research into state enforcement efforts elsewhere was impossible because no other state maintained official crime reports that separated cocaine cases from other drug cases. While it is therefore impossible to arrive at an aggregate figure for all cocaine-related arrests at the state level, there is little reason to think that enforcement patterns or results would vary in any meaningful way. The fundamental constraints of limited jurisdiction and limited resources in conjunction with the international and interstate structure of the cocaine industry (and its money-laundering operations) dictate that the federal enforcement apparatus play the dominant role.

FINANCIAL CONTROLS

As federal law enforcement officials became more sophisticated about the cocaine business, they learned that the supply of cocaine remains virtually invulnerable to traditional attacks on the drug itself. As a group, smugglers *always* get most of their product to market. Major trafficking organizations take years to break up. Once disrupted, employees often reconstitute under new leadership. Even the permanent crippling of an organization has no perceptible effect on price or availability of drugs in the black market. Even worse, the cocaine industry has blossomed in the intensified enforcement environment of the War on Drugs. "I have never seen more cocaine on the streets than I have in the last year," the Senior Commander of the Metro Dade Organized Crime Bureau told the President's Commission on Organized Crime in 1985.[57] The major mobilization of the War on Drugs has not even succeeded in keeping the price from declining as a result of massive oversupplies of coca leaf and cocaine in South America. Despite the crackdown, business is better than ever.

For this reason, law enforcement officials have shifted their traditional emphasis from border interdiction and case-making under the Controlled Substances Act to financial investigations and "asset removal." "Hit 'em in the pocketbook" is the current theme:

> We recognize that the conviction and incarceration of top-level traffickers does not necessarily disrupt trafficking organizations; the acquisition of vast capital permits regrouping and the incarcerated trafficker can continue to direct operations. Therefore, it is essential to attack the finances that are the backbone of organized drug traffickers.[58]

"Attacking the finances" takes two main forms: (1) seizure and forfeiture of assets, and (2) prosecution for financial crimes under the Bank Secrecy Act and the Internal Revenue Code.

Seizure and Forfeiture of Assets

A variety of federal statutes authorize the initial seizure and ultimate forfeiture of assets to the United States. Older statutes provide for the forfeiture of vehicles, vessels, aircraft, and other conveyances used to transport drugs or to "facilitate" a transaction in contraband.[59] The 1970 Bank Secrecy Act authorizes the Government to forfeit currency as a sanction for some violations of the law.[60] Perhaps the broadest in scope is a 1978 amendment to Title 21, which authorizes the seizure and forfeiture of anything of value used or intended to be used in exchange for illegal drugs, all money used or intended to be used to facilitate any illegal drug transaction, and "all proceeds traceable" to an illegal drug exchange.[61] This last broad provision includes real estate, securities, precious stones, and all other tangible or intangible property. Going even further, the Comprehensive Crime Control Act of 1984 amended the foregoing statute to add to the list of forfeitables "all real property . . . which is used or intended to be used . . . to commit or facilitate the commission" of any felony under the Controlled Substances Act.[62] As a result, homes, offices, or any other real property in which a drug deal is made or planned can be forfeited to the Government.

It deserves emphasis that none of the foregoing forfeitures requires that the owner be convicted of a drug crime, which would itself justify forfeiture. Indeed, forfeiture may proceed without any criminal charge being filed. Moreover, a defendant who has been tried and acquitted of a drug charge still runs the risk of having his property forfeited in a separate civil proceeding. Under legal theory, "guilt" attaches to the property itself. Federal agents may thus get a second bite at the apple by financially hurting a defendant who escapes conviction.

These civil forfeiture laws facilitate the goals of reducing the rewards of drug dealing (and perhaps deterring others) by dispensing with the necessity of criminal convictions and by permitting forfeiture to the Government without proof of crime beyond a reasonable doubt. The civil standard of proof applies because the law deems a forfeiture action to be *in rem*, i.e., an action against the *property* rather than the person. Under this legal fiction, all the Government need prove is that the property was (probably) used unlawfully or derived from unlawful sources, in connection with a drug transaction, actual or intended; the burden then shifts to the property owner to prove by a preponderance of the evidence that the property was not so used or derived.[63] An asset bought with drug money can be traced by the Government to its origin for the purpose of forfeiture.

Whether the proceeding is civil or criminal, however, asset removal by the Government can occur only at the end of a relatively small number of successful investigations or serendipitous seizures. Even then, the Government is likely to find only visible assets to seize and forfeit. Although the law permits tracing of proceeds, the concealment of cash, jewelry, collectibles, foreign bank or securities accounts, and silent-partner interests in business or properties is not difficult and constitutes a common evasion.

The statistical data illustrate the modest achievements of the seizure program to date. In fiscal year 1982, the DEA seized $106.6 million in assets. In the same year it forfeited $39.5 million, a figure that may tend to mislead because it applies mostly to assets already in the pipeline, i.e., those seized at an earlier time. Now, $39.5 million more than triples the $12.9 million forfeited in fiscal year 1981, and the DEA has accelerated its asset removal program (partly in the hopes of becoming self-financing). But even if the Government succeeds in realizing its projected figure of $235 million seized and $214 million forfeited by all federal agencies (excluding the IRS) for fiscal year 1983, how significant is it really?[64]

The impact of this forfeiture program must take its measure from a comparison to total black market revenues (from all drugs) of about $100 *billion* per year. According to an IRS study, at least 50 percent (and up to 90 percent) of drug revenues represents profit.[65] As a result, even an exceptionally ambitious forfeiture program producing, say, $1 billion a year in assets (four times the stated goal), would at best remove not more than 2 percent of the $50 billion in drug profits! Clearly, seizure of assets can "punish" some individuals severely. But it cannot pose a serious threat to the profitability of drugs on an industry-wide basis.

A more realistic framework for asset forfeiture would view it as a source of off-budget finance for law enforcement operations. The Attorney General has the authority to retain forfeited property for use by the Department of Justice or any law enforcement agency, state, federal, or local, or to sell it. Proceeds of assets sold are to be deposited in a Department of Justice Assets Forfeiture Fund, which the Attorney General can use for payment of rewards for information leading to civil or criminal forfeiture.[66] Rewards may run to 25 percent of the amount realized by the United States, up to a cap of $150,000. A similar Customs Forfeiture Fund was created by the 1984 Comprehensive Crime Control Act. Local police departments also rely more and more on drug seizures for cash and equipment to finance their operations. Rather than making a serious dent in the black market in drugs, asset forfeiture makes the Government a "partner" in the drug enterprise.

Financial Crimes

The second main financial strategy against drug importers, distributors, and financiers relies on tracing the money flow. A successful financial investigation will establish a basis for criminal prosecution under the Bank Secrecy Act or the Internal Revenue Code and may also provide a basis for civil forfeiture of dirty money.

Bank Secrecy Act Investigation

In 1970 Congress enacted the Bank Secrecy Act (BSA)[67] in response to the increased use of overseas money-laundering techniques to evade the payment of taxes and to conceal the illegitimate origin of income. Congress declared its purpose "to require certain reports or records where they have a high degree of usefulness in criminal, tax, or regulatory investigations or proceedings."[68] Compliance with the act generates a domestic paper trail to facilitate the detection and documentation of criminally based currency flows.

The Bank Secrecy Act requires financial institutions and depositors to record and report certain cash movements. Three types of activity necessitate a report to the federal government under Title II of the Bank Secrecy Act. First, whenever a bank or other covered financial institution engages in a currency transaction in excess of $10,000, it must file a Currency Transaction Report (CTR) with the Internal Revenue Service, naming the depositor and amount. Second, whenever a person physically transports currency or other monetary instruments in excess of $10,000 into or out of the United States, he must file a Currency and Monetary Instrument Report (CMIR) with the Customs Service. Third, whenever a person subject to the jurisdiction of the United States has a financial interest in, or authority over, a financial account in a foreign country, he must file a Foreign Bank Account Report (FBAR) with the Treasury Department. The act provides criminal penalties for most violations, in addition to civil fines and forfeitures of unreported money.

Enforcement of the act was slow getting started. Congress enacted it in late 1970, but the Treasury Department did not promulgate regulations implementing it until 1972. Then a lawsuit by banks, depositors, and the American Civil Liberties Union (ACLU) challenging the act on grounds of privacy and self-incrimination followed.[69] Then widespread noncompliance in the late 1970s and early 1980s was uncovered by authorities. A study by the Comptroller of Florida disclosed that one state chartered bank had apparently not filed 48 percent of the CTRs in its files, so that the IRS had no record of those cash transactions.[70] Dozens of other financial institutions ignored the CTR requirement in cash transactions running into the billions.

In recent years, enforcement of the BSA has become more systematic. One of the symbols of the new enforcement climate is Operation Greenback, which officials have called "the most significant single law enforcement effort developed to date from the Bank Secrecy Act."[71] Greenback was initiated by a Treasury Department study of currency transactions in the Federal Reserve System that revealed a multibillion dollar excess of cash in the Miami branch. It developed into a cash-flow project designed to trace the assets of major drug-trafficking organizations for seizure and forfeiture and criminal prosecution. About 17 months after it began, 14 indictments against 51 defendants were filed, with 32 other investigations remaining open. The Government seized $20 million in currency.[72]

Treasury officials portrayed Greenback's early phase to Congress as a successful "pilot program," an "innovative approach," and "a learning process for everybody concerned."[73] The Customs Service asserted that "intensified enforcement of the Bank Secrecy Act may be one of this country's most powerful weapons against narcotics traffic."[74] Greenback-type enforcement was in fact intensified: investigative hours spent on currency cases escalated from 111,032 agent hours in fiscal year 1979 to 376,320 agent hours in fiscal year 1981;[75] and post-Greenback indictments have exposed several massive money-laundering schemes by drug financiers and compliant banks. For example, the federal government indicted the Great American Bank of Dade County (Miami) for allegedly laundering $96 million in cocaine money in a 14-month period.[76] A New York banking institution was similarly indicted for illegally processing 400 cash deposits of more than $150 million.[77] Beno Ghitis-Miller, a Colombian convicted of BSA offenses, passed $242.2 million through his account at the Capital Bank of Miami in an eight-month period. A $500,000 fine was levied against the Bank of Boston in 1985 for not reporting $1.22 billion in cash shipments to banks in Switzerland and other European countries. Soon afterward, the Government set a new record in imposing $2.75 million in penalties against Crocker National Bank of San Francisco for failing to report almost $3.88 billion in cash transactions as required by law. The bank committed 7,877 reporting violations in a four-year period. Such banking prosecutions have become a staple item of the War on Drugs.

But the Bank Secrecy Act surely offers no panacea for controlling the drug traffic. Several factors limit its value as an investigative tool. The mere filing of a CTR for cash deposits of $10,000 does not by itself incriminate, as filing requirements apply to all cash deposits. While the law exempts certain retail businesses such as race tracks, sports arenas, bars, restaurants, and hotels from the reporting requirements, the reporting system still produces informational overkill because of the vast volume of both legitimate cash transactions and suspected illegal money laundering. For example, Greenback investigators identified approximately 50 currency exchange houses in the Miami area that moved over $2 billion through their bank accounts in three years. Similarly, of all currency transactions in the United States involving amounts of $10,000 or more which were reported in 1981, 51 percent were made by individuals and companies with addresses in foreign countries. Individuals and companies in Colombia and Peru accounted for $427 million of such transactions.[78] How does one separate the wheat from the chaff without extensive, time-consuming investigation?

The Government's answer relies in part on computerization. Data required by the BSA are assembled and analyzed by the Financial Law Enforcement Center (FLEC), the Treasury Department's clearinghouse for intelligence on cash flow generated by criminal activity. From its data banks, FLEC may develop evidence against a pre-existing suspect. But to identify new targets for investigation requires tedious research of the data banks for patterns of excessive cash deposits represented by CTRs without informant tips. Reconsider Operation Greenback itself. There the prime defendants brought themselves under suspicion by repeated and blatant movements of cash: some carried suitcases and cardboard boxes to the bank to deposit over $2 million, uncounted, in small bills in just a few weeks. The arrest of those defendants served as a warning to other banks. Since Greenback became public knowledge, the number of CTRs filed by Florida banks with the IRS has quadrupled, and their dollar value has gone up 400 percent. Now, what do investigators do with all those data? In Florida alone, in October and November, 1984, the state counterpart of the federal BSA produced reports of cash deposits of $600 million dollars, an annualized rate of $3.5 billion.[79] The State Comptroller believes that most of it is drug money, but proof requires investigation, which in turn often requires an informant's tip. In the interim, the IRS estimates that banks, brokerage firms, and savings and loans launder about $80 billion per year for drug syndicates.

Sophisticated offenders can find ways of finessing the CTR, developing schemes to defeat the law. For example, in one obvious method of evading the BSA, a drug dealer or courier can avoid the CTR filing requirement by making deposits in amounts less than $10,000 at a number of banks. This simple method can generate suspicion if the pattern is detected, and the method is too slow and inefficient for moving large volumes of money. An alternative technique involves making large cash deposits in excess of $10,000 to a fictitious-name personal or corporate account (using false identification if necessary), filling out the CTR, and shortly thereafter wiring the funds to a foreign bank account or offshore corporation. Unless the depositor is at that moment under surveillance or has been informed against, an investigator would not ordinarily discover the falsity of the CTR.

Another variation dispenses with the CTR altogether by taking advantage of the statutory exemption for businesses that do a large cash business. Evidence discovered at a later date might permit prosecution of the depositor but would be too late to prevent the movement of the money out of the country. While the wire transfer is recorded and therefore discoverable, the paper trail would lead nowhere because of foreign bank secrecy. Yet another technique for evasion calls for the complicity of a bank employee to destroy copies of the CTR filled out by the depositor so that the Government gets no record of the transactions involved. This evasion will show up in an audit of the bank's books.

Perhaps the most effective scheme of all uses the purchase of banks by foreign nationals fronting for drug traffickers. When the entire bank has been thus corrupted, its capability for concealing large cash movements by nonreporting or keeping dual sets of books dramatically increases. In 1981, the Bank of Perrine (in Miami) was acquired by Colombian cocaine traffickers in this manner.[80] In 1984, the Government indicted officials of the Sunshine State Bank for various federal offenses, including money laundering for a Colombian drug syndicate over a five-year period.[81] The bank pleaded guilty and paid a corporate fine.

Clearly, then, the BSA cannot promise an end to drug money laundering. Even when banks comply with the law, many transactions escape its net. For example, the BSA does not cover interbank transfers within the United States and wire transfers with foreign banks because it would not be practical to do so: reporting requirements would disrupt the flow of transfers and impose enormous costs. The $587.35 billion in wire transfers handled by the Miami branch of the Federal Reserve Bank of Atlanta in 1980 illustrates the massive volume of transactions by wire transfer, as does the 1.5 to 2 million checks that the Miami branch processes each day.[82]

Nor is the problem of policing wire transfers simply a matter of volume and cost. Identifying suspicious transfers poses the ultimate challenge. Money-laundering operators, relying on highly skilled attorneys, accountants, and money-managers, follow very sophisticated patterns in moving drug profits around. Transactions, involving letters of credit, putative "loans," phony invoices for goods, or even legitimate investments, leave false clues for the investigator, especially when the transactions are "layered," funneling money back and forth from United States corporations or banks to offshore corporations and banks. Some idea of the magnitude of drug money funneled to foreign banks is conveyed by the fact that one bank in Panama returned $1 billion more to the Federal Reserve System than it took out, a sum that must include substantial drug trafficking revenues.[83]

Ultimately, drug financiers can ignore the domestic banking system altogether by the simplest and most direct device of all—smuggling cash to a foreign country. The Customs Service, for lack of sufficient personnel, does not routinely check passengers leaving the United States on commercial flights or sea voyages, although it does perform occasional spot checks for currency violations. In one lucky strike, federal agents caught a woman with two small children attempting to depart Miami International Airport with $400,000 concealed in boxes of Pampers. For really large quantities of cash in $10- and $20-dollar bills, the smugglers' solution lies in packing the money in boxes and flying them by privately chartered small aircraft to the Bahamas, the Caymans, Panama, or elsewhere. Importation of currency to these countries violates no law of theirs, although the export of $10,000 in cash from the United States requires a CMIR under the BSA. However, investigators have no evidence of the CMIR violation in this scenario unless they receive a tip from an informant. For example, in April, 1985, the DEA stopped a Piper Navahoe Panther taxiing onto a runway in Fort Lauderdale for takeoff. Agents found $1.3 million in small bills.[84] An anonymous caller tipped off the police. Without the call, enforcement could not have occurred. For this reason, the Government succeeded in filing only nine prosecutions during the period from 1977 to 1980 based on CMIR violations.[85] The number may well rise, but the order of magnitude speaks for itself.

Once the currency safely reaches a shell bank in a tax haven such as Panama, investigators have no paper trail to follow. Again, the BSA offers no investigative leverage. The failure of an account holder to report the existence of a foreign account in a tax haven on the FBAR form creates no risk of detection: the offshore record of that account is confidential under the law of the tax haven and will not be disclosed officially in response to a United States subpeona or other official inquiry, with some limited exceptions. In the Caymans, for example, there is one theoretical exception to the rule of nondisclosure. After an indictment for a crime which also constitutes an offense in the Caymans, a request by the United States Department of Justice for bank records will be entertained. Note, however, that neither income tax evasion nor drug *conspiracy* offenses violate Caymans law; only the subtantive narcotics offenses are crimes in the Caymans and other tax havens. But even this limited exception permitting disclosure has no investigative value. Investigators must build their case against a suspect based on other evidence, benefitting from the offshore bank records only after they have indicted the suspect and begun preparing the case for trial.

Thus, astute use of tax havens effectively nullifies the ability of United States law enforcement agencies to prosecute drug smugglers and distributors for financial crimes. For this reason, the United States is bringing intense pressure to bear—pursuing "diplomatic initiatives," in the polite phrasing of the State Department—on tax havens. These pressures include the effort to renegotiate tax treaties, and the demand for investigative access to bank records and other financial documents now protected from disclosure by the laws of countries like the Bahamas and the Caymans. Such pressures have been resisted and resented. After all, banking secrecy provides the raison d'etre of tax haven nations. Thus, the chief counsel of the Senate Permanent Subcommittee on Investigations reported in 1981 "absolutely no indication of a willingness to alter banking secrecy laws" by governmental officials of the Cayman Islands, although the Caymans subsequently softened their resistance.[86]

The government of the Bahamas has been especially antagonistic because of what it regards as infringements of its national sovereignty. One of the sore points, Operation Tradewinds, involved a breach of Bahamian bank secrecy by IRS agents working with a Bahamian informant. Prime Minister Lynden Pindling, who is himself accused of complicity in drug smuggling operations, may nevertheless reflect national sentiment in sarcastically describing the prevailing DEA attitude that the Bahamas is just a suburb of Miami.

In the face of foreign resistance to its pressures, the United States continues to seek concessions from tax havens on the secrecy issue with a variety of (dis)incentives. One of the recently devised "carrots" appeared in a 1983 Department of Justice plan proposing to permit Caribbean tax havens to forfeit bank accounts as the *quid pro quo* for supplying information leading to prosecution of drug traffickers for offenses against the United States. But the truth of the matter is that the United States has little leverage on nontreaty tax havens. A variety of measures in retaliation for noncooperation have for this reason been proposed. One Senator suggested that the United States might deny landing rights at United States airports to the airlines of noncooperative nations. Other proposed sanctions focus on denying or reducing United States foreign aid. Actual retaliation occurred in the United States cancellation of a tax treaty with the British Virgin Islands for lack of cooperation on information exchanges. The Government did succeed in achieving one breach of the wall of secrecy with the Bahamian Bank of Nova Scotia. A federal court ordered it to honor a United States grand jury subpoena for bank records because it operated within the United States, despite the contrary mandate of the bank's national laws.[87]

This conflict does not lack irony. Under United States law, the Right to Financial Privacy Act greatly restricts governmental access to customer records of financial institutions. The law requires investigators to issue a summons to the bank for such records and provides the depositor an opportunity to contest the summons in court. Tax returns were even more closely guarded by the Tax Reform Act of 1976, which made disclosure very cumbersome, an obstacle that the 1982 amendments lowered to a considerable degree. Ultimately, United States law now permits investigators to lift the veil of secrecy. Despite our domestic reforms, most tax haven countries have held firm in protecting bank secrecy under their laws. Competitive pressures in the tax haven industry mean loss of business to a country that becomes too compliant with investigative demands. Indeed, new havens spring up all the time to service restless capital, including drug money. The Caribbean is saturated with havens, and the Pacific and Far East offer many others: Hong Kong, Guam, Singapore, Nauru, Vanuatu, and the Marianas. The United States will never tame them all.

For all these reasons, prosecutions for violations of the BSA can do no more than increase the cost of financing the drug business by compelling drug dealers to adopt more sophisticated patterns of finance and money laundering. In this regard, the law's greatest success is that the cheapest and most convenient method of processing cash, bulk deposits of multimillion dollar amounts in local banks, can no longer be used. Also, banks now generally comply with the CTR requirement, because audits expose consistent nonfiling of CTRs. As with most controls, refinements of the recordkeeping regulations may achieve further enforcement gains, but the net effect on market price add supply is marginal. Transaction costs add little to the market price of cocaine, most of which comes from the risk premium. Thus, the analysis set out in Figure 5 (see Chapter Six) applies equally to the Government's attempt to raise the transaction costs of the cocaine industry. On balance, the post-Greenback evidence shows that while the BSA provides the investigators an additional pressure point against the cocaine industry, the profits are too extraordinary for occasional indictments to scare away the dealers and financiers. Indeed, the extra risk probably enhances profitability. In any event, they are willing to assume the risks of getting caught, and business goes on.

Internal Revenue Code Investigations

Criminal tax prosecutions against major organized crime figures are the legacy of the case against Al Capone, whom the United States could not bring to justice for murder, extortion, bootlegging, or the like. Instead, he went to prison for failing to pay his income taxes.[88] While a full consideration of enforcement methods used by the IRS lies beyond the scope of this book, we can survey its investigative procedures sufficiently to see that the threat of criminal prosecutions for tax evasion has not been and cannot become a major impediment to trafficking in cocaine or other drugs.

The IRS vests jurisdiction over criminal offenses in its Criminal Investigation Division (CID), staffed by about 2,600 agents. The IRS divides its CID program into general (GEP) and special enforcement programs (SEP), with SEP directed at income derived from illegal activities, including drug trafficking. SEP assigns about 600 agents to the narcotics program, the single greatest commitment of resources.

Following the post-Watergate disclosures of abuses of power by the IRS, Congress reduced the role of the IRS in criminal law enforcement by enacting the Tax Reform Act of 1976.[89] The act required IRS agents to maintain the confidentiality of tax returns and tax return information, subject to several exceptions, making it more difficult for other agencies to use that information in their investigations. In addition, administrative adoption of a new enforcement priority occurred under the tenure of Commissioner Donald Alexander. He restored the role of the IRS to traditional revenue collection functions and rejected "selective priority-setting" in response to "socio-political phenomena" such as drug dealing. Accordingly, he changed the criteria for IRS involvement in anti-narcotics and strike force activities to those that "satisfy the revenue and professional criteria . . . for channeling our resources."[90]

By 1980, however, a new administration sent the pendulum swinging in the opposite direction, bringing the IRS into a more prominent anti-crime role. As a result, the IRS increased its allocation of personnel to SEP as a whole and to that part of SEP assigned to narcotics investigations. Staff years allocated to narcotics cases rose from 232 in fiscal year 1980 to about 600 in 1982.[91] The expanded commitment by the IRS to prosecute drug traffickers is also reflected in its decision, reported in 1983, to increase its undercover operations, use of paid informants, and deployment of agents assigned to federal task forces.[92]

Nevertheless, resources remain limited, and this expansion of IRS drug enforcement actions starts from a very modest base. Thus, even though the CID's entire inventory of narcotics cases under investigation has more than doubled in recent years, the absolute numbers remain quite small. Thus, in fiscal 1983, the IRS initiated 826 investigations and recommended 421 prosecutions, of which 265 resulted in indictments yielding 167 convictions for the entire United States. In some respects, a tax case carries more bite than a drug charge, as prison sentences have tended to be higher than those for convicted drug violators: three-quarters of those convicted of drug-related tax violations received prison sentences averaging 45 months. But the force and effect of those longer prison terms are offset by their low number; a few hundred indictments per year hardly pose a major threat of punishment.

The main reason for the paucity of drug-related tax cases stems from the IRS's conception of its role: despite its more aggressive posture with respect to drug cases, the prevailing view is still that the IRS "is not primarily a criminal law enforcement agency. Rather, its primary mission is to collect taxes."[93] For this reason, and because of the high value we place on protecting the privacy of individuals, the law imposes a series of limitations on the power of law enforcement officials to obtain the tax and banking records of a suspected violator. For example, the Tax Reform Act of 1976, which law enforcement–minded officials have derisively labeled the "Organized Crime Relief Act of 1976," restricts the disclosure of IRS tax returns and tax information to other law enforcement agencies.[94]

Under the original Tax Reform Act, the IRS was required to keep tax returns confidential, subject to three exceptions. First, disclosure to federal law enforcement agencies was authorized by a judge upon written request of an agency head showing "reasonable cause" and meeting other criteria of relevance and need. Second, disclosure was authorized where the requesting agency was engaged in a judicial proceeding or criminal investigation. Third, the IRS itself could initiate the disclosure to the appropriate federal agency of information not provided by the taxpayer constituting evidence of a crime.[95] In 1982, amendments to the Tax Reform Act broadened the scope of authorized disclosure to permit, for example, any United States Attorney, special prosecutor, or attorney in charge of a strike force to obtain tax returns upon request.

Other legal obstacles slow down the ability of the IRS to pursue financial investigations. The law governing summonses provides, in most circumstances, that the bank or other third party recordkeeper must notify the person whose records are sought by the summons. That person may stay compliance merely by giving written notice to the bank not to comply. The IRS must then go to court to enforce the summons, and that person may intervene in the court proceedings.

Perhaps the most critical limitation on the CID's case-making ability arises from the fact that the cocaine industry operates on a cash basis and with few, if any, written records. Occasionally, a drug dealer falls victim to a net worth investigation prompted by a lavish lifestyle and no apparent source of income. The IRS can sometimes prove unreported income by reconstructing the transactions in question and further proving the illicit sources of the funds. More sophisticated dealers acknowledge the need for discretion in at least two areas. First, a circumspect dealer must hide his income behind a legitimate source of income, or at least one appearing to be so. Businesses dealing in cash—bars and restaurants—find favor with underworld people precisely because of the ability to skim profits or pump in excess cash in order to launder the money as income. Dealers must also be discreet in investment and consumption. Items such as jewelry, precious metals, objects of art, rare stamps, and coins offer non-traceability. Titled assets can be acquired in fictitious or corporate names or through anonymously owned offshore corporations. For large amounts of cash, the astute use of tax havens offers the same kind of protection from tax investigators as from investigations for currency violations. For example, the Commissioner of the IRS testified before the Senate Permanent Subcommittee on Investigations that the refusal of countries with bank secrecy laws to cooperate with the United States in tax evasion cases caused the IRS to abandon 57 potential prosecutions over a five-year period.[96]

Of course, it would be foolish for a drug dealer not to respect the potential for discovery by the IRS. Nor is criminal prosecution the only weapon in the IRS arsenal against drug trafficking. In fiscal year 1982, the IRS's Examination Division assessed about $225 million in taxes against drug traffickers; about $181 million of that amount resulted from the IRS's special jeopardy and termination assessments. But the quarter billion dollars in tax assessments in context constitutes a tiny fraction of the $100 billion in black market drug revenues, of which at least $50 billion represents profit. Thus, the need to take precautions to conceal income and assets in order to avoid investigation and liens by the IRS is simply one more cost of doing business. Even the careless dealer can expect a hassle-free run of some years before feeling the wrath of the IRS. To the extent that the IRS restricts the fluidity of transactions in the drug business, it facilitates the supply reduction strategy. But as long as the profits remain great and the risks of short-run deduction remain insignificant, enforcement of the tax laws poses no insurmountable obstacle to the drug business.

The IRS has apparently conceded that reality by its own somewhat radical contingency planning proposal to compel old-for-new $100 bill exchanges. In a 1982 confidential report called "Closing the Gap," the IRS canvassed a number of options for collecting more taxes on unreported income, especially in the "underground economy."[97] In one option, $100 bills would be recalled and replaced with new ones of a different size or color. In order to make the exchange, people would have to provide identification and run the risk of calling investigative attention to themselves. Apart from its obvious expense and disruption of the economy, the scheme offers only one-time benefits. New accumulations of dirty cash would call for repetitions of the exchange plan. But even repetitions of this plan would leave smaller bills untouched by the exchange. Ultimately, cash itself must be abolished as a medium of exchange in order to make a serious dent in the drug business. Proposals for doing so by substituting a universalized electronic funds transfer (EFT) system exist. Still, one doubts that the criminal mind could not conjure up ways of defeating or evading an EFT system. In any event, the cashless society will be a long time in coming.

In summary, many of the previous restraints on the IRS have been relaxed by changes in law and the administrative policy shift in favor of nontax (i.e., drug) law enforcement. Undoubtedly, the IRS will in the future prosecute more criminal cases against drug dealers for tax evasion. In addition, more Bank Secrecy Act prosecutions may occur as the IRS, which enforces the CTR requirement, assumes a more active role in money-laundering investigations such as Operation Greenback. But it defies experience to assume that the deterrent impact of such activity can ever loom large enough to reduce the volume of cocaine trafficking. Just as with traditional drug enforcement methods, investigative resources for tax cases are limited, violations are endemic, and, as the statistics show, the likelihood of detection by the IRS remains low. Even successful investigation by the IRS ordinarily takes so long that it greatly attenuates its deterrent value. The dominant psychology goes for cash in hand in the face of long odds of detection.

6

Escalating the War on Drugs: No Light at the End of the Tunnel

The central strategy of the War on Drugs relies upon the supposedly synergistic benefits of the multi-agency task force approach to law enforcement. This strategy employs two different kinds of task forces, one focusing on the interdiction of drugs at the border and the other on the investigation and prosecution of major importers and distributors.

THE INTERDICTION NETWORK: FROM MIAMI TASK FORCE TO NATIONAL NARCOTICS BORDER INTERDICTION SYSTEM

The interdiction network grew out of the Miami prototype, the Task Force on Crime in South Florida. In January, 1982, President Reagan, responding to the entreaties of some prominent Miamians, including the publisher of the *Miami Herald* and the president of Eastern Airlines, created the Task Force in order to fulfill the federal government's "special responsibility" to control "[m]assive immigration, rampant crime and epidemic drug smuggling."[1] The President placed the Task Force under the direction of Vice President George Bush, who announced its goals and organization in February, 1982.[2] The Task Force became operational shortly thereafter, starting with the temporary reassignment of existing law enforcement personnel to the Miami offices of their respective agencies. Some 374 federal agents were thus deployed to Miami.

The Task Force began its attack on drugs by forming an inter-agency Task Group of 256 Customs and 81 DEA agents.[3] The primary mission of this Task Group was to spearhead an intensified air and sea interdiction effort designed to constrict the flow of illegal drugs into the South Florida area. In that undertaking, the Task Group drew on the resources of other federal agencies, particularly the Coast Guard, the CIA, and the Department of Defense (DOD).

The Coast Guard assisted the interdiction effort by intensifying its patrolling of known marijuana smuggling routes in the Caribbean, such as the Windward and Yucatan passages. For that purpose, the Guard received 285 additional seamen and other personnel and new equipment—initially, two high-speed surface-effect ships and two new cutters and later, helicopters and new Falcon jet long-distance search aircraft.[4]

The CIA, which traditionally had maintained a low profile (so far as we know) in drug enforcement, also significantly expanded its role. In an Executive Order issued in 1982, the President directed the CIA to gather intelligence concerning "criminal narcotics activities" abroad. The order authorized CIA agents to "participate in law enforcement activities to investigate or prevent . . . international terrorist or narcotics activities" and to render "any other [lawful] assistance and cooperation to law enforcement authorities."[5] Accordingly, the CIA apparently tapped into surveillance satellites of NASA and the Pentagon, which produced aerial photographs of all major coca and marijuana fields in South America.

The DOD also joined the War on Drugs. "One of the most significant accomplishments of the Task Force has been the forging of prototype linkages between the military and civilian law enforcement agencies under the amendments to the Posse Comitatus Act."[6] The Posse Comitatus Act, a statute of post–Civil War vintage passed in reaction to military occupation of the South during Reconstruction, made it a felony for the Army to perform the law enforcement functions of civilian authorities. In 1956, Congress added the Air Force, and the Navy and Marine Corps bound themselves by administrative regulation to adhere to the statutory prohibitions. In practice, a cautious approach to the act evolved in which the military confined itself to the occasional rendering of "indirect" forms of assistance. The Army, Air Force, and Navy rendered assistance to law enforcement agencies by lending equipment, training civilian personnel, and permitting the use of military facilities. Between 1971 and 1981, the DOD received 156 requests for military assistance and approved more than 140. As an example of the latter, the Air Force permitted a Customs patrol officer to fly aboard certain Airborne Warning and Control System (AWACS) border patrol flights.[7] Direct participation in drug investigation or interdiction was abjured by the armed services.

In 1981, as part of the "legislative offensive" in the War on Drugs, Congress enacted amendments to the Posse Comitatus Act,[8] putting its stamp of approval on the DOD's previous practices and authorizing a greater degree of military support services to track and report on the movement of suspect aircraft and ships. Once liberated by the statutory amendments to the Posse Comitatus Act, the DOD, responding to political pressures from the White House (through the office of the Vice President, who headed the

Miami Task Force), began more freely supplying equipment and smuggler-tracking technology. The Army, for example, lent Cobra and Blackhawk helicopters to Customs Service pilots for use in the air interdiction program.

Tracking assistance began as one of the earliest activities of the Task Force, starting with the high-technology capabilities of the Navy Hawkeye E2–C radar plane.[9] Conventional radar installations of the Federal Aviation Administration (FAA) and NORAD scan the skies at high and mid-altitudes and generally miss the low-flying smuggler. Of 1,013 Customs air interdiction missions in 1981, only 26 originated with NORAD detection. The Hawkeye E2-C, by contrast, flies at high altitudes and provides "look-down" radar coverage over a 200-mile radius. Enthusiasm for this high-tech scanner of smugglers led to initial deployment of the E2-Cs in South Florida from March 15 through June 30, 1982, for 435 hours at a cost of $715,000. This high cost, coupled with impairment of military training missions, led to a tapering off of Hawkeye surveillance (down to zero hours for some months). Customs later wrote an evaluation stating that the E2-C "was not all that effective in detecting and tracking small vessels of 30 feet and under."[10] We may infer from this that many of the small speedboats used for transshipment of cocaine from the Bahamas to Miami went largely undetected.

To reduce costs and placate the political pressures for radar coverage, DOD substituted an aerostat radar system consisting of a lighter-than-air balloon beneath which hangs a radar unit.[11] This system stays aloft 24 hours a day on a long cable tethered to the ground. It provides look-down capability over an area 150 miles in radius, at altitudes from 10,000 feet to the surface. The Air Force maintains one Seek Sky Hook balloon in the Florida Keys, one at Patrick Air Force Base, and a third in the Bahamas. In July, 1985, the Coast Guard launched STARS (Small Tethered Aerostat Relocatable System), consisting of radar-equipped helium-filled balloons to detect drug boats in the Caribbean passages. Starting with two STARS in Key West, six others will be placed around the United States. It remains to be seen whether the Sky Hook and STARS system will provide any greater interdiction protection against cocaine smuggling than the E2-Cs. Tracking, after all, is only a first step; suspicious vessels or aircraft still have to be intercepted and searched.

Perhaps the most dramatic change of all has occurred by administrative regulation rather than statute. Stimulated to take a much more aggressive enforcement posture by the political and legal environment of the War on Drugs, the DOD issued administrative regulations which had the effect of releasing the Navy from the administrative prohibitions that had confined its law enforcement role in the same manner that the Posse Comitatus Act had restricted the Army and Air Force. In response to the Coast Guard's certification to the Secretary of Defense of the need for assistance in its drug interdiction mission in order to protect "the national interest of the United

States," the Secretary of the Navy waived the administrative prohibitions that otherwise applied and authorized the Navy to engage directly in drug enforcement operations.[12] The Navy then began providing air and surface surveillance of "suspected drug trafficking vessels." It also began carrying Coast Guard detachments on naval vessels for "law enforcement boardings of United States flag and stateless vessels." To maintain the fiction of an "indirect" law enforcement role, the Secretary's directive stipulated that "[t]actical control of Navy vessels will shift to the Coast Guard prior to any interdiction."[13] In other words, the Navy ship "becomes" a Coast Guard ship during the interdiction.

Thus, in November, 1982, while on maneuvers in the Caribbean, a plane from the United States aircraft carrier *Nimitz* spotted a suspicious tugboat, took reconnaisance photos, and informed the Coast Guard Tactical Law Enforcement Team aboard the *Nimitz*. The Coast Guard unit then helicoptered from the *Nimitz* to the escort cruiser U.S.S. *Mississippi*, which intercepted the tug laden with 30 tons of marijuana.[14] Presumably, a change of command from Navy to Coast Guard occurred during the mission. A defense motion to suppress the marijuana on the grounds that the Navy's "support" activities violated the statute and regulations was denied by the federal district court in Puerto Rico.

In a subsequent incident, in July, 1983, the U.S.S. *Kidd*, a Navy guided-missile destroyer, chased, fired upon, and seized a marijuana cargo ship.[15] Presumably, this historic naval firing upon a civilian vessel did not violate the no-direct-participation rule if one assumes the presence of a Coast Guard contingent aboard the *Kidd* to qualify under the "supporting role" rationalization set forth in the Secretary's instruction. No repetition of so direct an involvement has been reported, and the exclusionary rule, so long as it survives, provides one built-in brake on this process. Direct involvement in interdiction operations will likely prove disruptive to the Navy, as defense lawyers may well subpoena officers and crew members to testify at evidentiary hearings on motions to suppress seized evidence, alleging that their testimony is relevant to issues of the lawfulness of the search or seizure. Naval officials will undoubtedly want to minimize their entanglement in judicial proceedings because of the interference with military assignments.

Compromise of classified information is another risk of court hearings: technical aspects of the detection and surveillance systems leading to the seizure might be revealed. Presently, the Navy's most common form of assistance to the Coast Guard includes the reporting of sighting suspect smuggling vessels and towing or escorting vessels seized by the Coast Guard. This permits Coast Guard cutters to stay at their patrol stations while the Navy transports their prisoners and seized ships to port.

Apart from the unique situation of the Navy under the Posse Comitatus Act, the DOD has restrained the participation of all the armed services out of considerations of military preparedness. The loan of airplanes, the flying of anti-smuggling patrols, the training of customs pilots or DEA agents in the use of military equipment, the maintenance of aircraft and other authorized assistance all have the effect of diverting military equipment and personnel from military missions. Defense Secretary Caspar Weinberger went public with the concern of a "negative impact on readiness" in a letter to the House Armed Services Committee. He also expressed concern about the possible disclosure of national security information. Cost imposes further restraints, as the DOD directive generally requires reimbursement by the civilian agency requesting the assistance, and military operations are very expensive compared to civilian ones. At the same time, frustration over the limited results of the War on Drugs fuels a drive toward more fully involving military forces in direct enforcement operations. Congressman Charles E. Bennet (D., Fla.), who lost a son to a drug overdose in 1977, advocates a full-blown military role in the War on Drugs.

In his October, 1982, speech "nationalizing" the Florida-based War on Drugs, the President pointed to the Task Force as an "unqualified success." The General Accounting Office performed an independent evaluation of the work of the South Florida Task Force and reached more modest conclusions.[16] In assessing the impact of the Task Force on drug supply, the GAO compared federal drug seizures and arrests made in the state of Florida for the period March 15 to December 31, 1982, to the same period in 1981. The data showed that marijuana seizures increased from 1,074,000 pounds to 1,245,000 pounds; cocaine seizures went up from 1,617 pounds to 2,891 pounds; and drug arrests rose from 742 to 945. The GAO estimated the cost of operations for that March–December period at $66 million.[17]

The GAO also found that in response to expanded radar coverage and other Task Force pressures on sea lanes, marijuana smugglers shifted routes to different areas of the United States. Marijuana seizures in the northeastern United States, for example, rose more than 400 percent during the test period, suggesting that smugglers shifted their mothership routes away from the intensified patrols in the Caribbean.[18] In addition, an expanded domestic marijuana crop took up whatever slack (if any) resulted from interdiction of supplies from abroad. With respect to cocaine, supplies were *more* plentiful one year after the inception of the Task Force than before, despite substantial increases in both the number and size of cocaine seizures. Higher-quality cocaine became more readily available in Miami at lower prices (and higher purity) than those prevailing prior to the inception of the Task Force. In addition, the Task Force "succeeded" in partially diverting cocaine smuggling routes to other areas, as evidenced by the sudden outbreak of record-quantity seizures around the country. On a national basis, during 1982 the average price of cocaine declined to a then record low (see Figure 5).[19]

Nor was this a momentary aberration of the market. Task Force pressures continued to intensify throughout 1983. Through September 30, 1983, the Task Force and all federal agencies operating in South Florida made 1,677

Figure 5
Effects of Increased Interdiction Rates on Quantity and Price of Cocaine

An effective increase in the interdiction rate would result in an upward shift in the supply curve: lower quantity and higher price.

But greater interdiction (and other enforcement pressures) cannot reduce quantity very much because the largest component of production costs (perhaps 80%) is the risk premium. Out-of-pocket costs such as product and smuggling costs are a relatively small component of total cost and do not offer much leverage on market price. An increase in such costs will therefore not affect supply significantly. Because demand is relatively inelastic, a strategy directed at further increasing costs will yield only a negligible decline in the quantity of cocaine delivered to market and consumed. Thus:

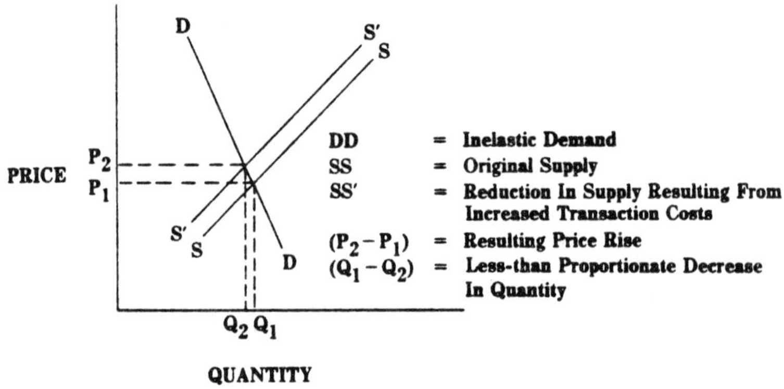

arrests and the drug and asset seizures shown in Table 9. Yet the prices of cocaine fell further, to as low as $15,000-$18,000 per kilo by the summer of 1983, probably the lowest in modern history. In 1984, prices rose slightly and stablilized in the range of $20,000-$30,000 per kilo, about 40–50 percent of what they had been in the 1980–1981 period before the President declared war on drugs. In 1985 the price hovered in the $30,000-$35,000 range.

Noting that federal resources devoted to interdiction of all drugs more than tripled from 1977 to 1982, and that the number of persons arrested by federal agencies for drug offenses in Florida increased 40 percent (from February 15 to June 30, 1982, compared to the same period in 1981), the GAO reached the following conclusions:

- Cocaine, heroin, and dangerous drug seizures for fiscal years 1977 through 1982 comprised less than 10 percent of the estimated supply of these drugs.
- Less than 20 percent of the estimated marijuana supply was seized over this same time frame.

Table 9
Seizures in South Florida by Miami Task Force and Other Federal Agencies (Through September 30, 1983)

Drug	Number of Seizures	Amount Seized
Heroin	2	0.4 Kilograms
Cocaine	412	3,555.6 Kilograms
Cannabis	606	874,083.6 Kilograms
Methaqualone	10	160,470 dosage units
Others drugs	13	39,092 dosage units

Asset	Number of Seizures	Estimated Value
Vehicles	79	$ 679,825
Vessels	194	17,115,550
Aircraft	27	1,765,500
Currency	143	2,590,964
Bond	1	50,000
Weapons	351	135,566
Other	25	241,935

Source: Compiled by author.

- Drug price and purity statistics, measures of availability, indicate little change.
- Most individuals arrested in interdiction cases are low-level violators.
- The bulk of those arrested spend less than a year in jail.[20]

Theoretically, a highly committed program of interdiction, with a level of border security characteristic of closed societies, might become more successful. But such a program would also be very costly:

> [T]he Coast Guard has estimated that it would have to seize 75 percent of the marijuana entering the United States before drug traffickers would be driven out of business . . . [at a cost of] $2.3 billion in additional operating funds. . . . Estimates to seize 75 percent of the cocaine, heroin, and dangerous drugs entering this country are not available, but it would also take billions of dollars.[21]

Even this multibillion dollar estimate might prove inadequate in the face of the resilient demand for cocaine and the ease with which smugglers bring it in with clever ruses or high technology. We saw in Chapter Three that the compactness of cocaine renders it easy to conceal by a variety of relatively undetectable techniques, including cargo shipments, and that in the event of a seizure the cargo has passed through so many hands that the Customs Service ordinarily cannot prove who smuggled it in and perhaps cannot even identify a suspect. Many large cargo seizures have occurred since the advent of the Miami Task Force. Few produced any arrests.

The limitations of interdiction are well known to the federal government. Indeed, the Department of Justice comment on the GAO evaluation concedes the point: "[Y]ears of experience have shown that this band-aid approach to controlling illegal drugs—stopping them midway along the delivery chain—is nothing more than a maintenance effort which, standing alone, will never have any permanent effect on drug traffic."[22] In other words, the drug supply is a bottomless pit.

The Administration, of course, counters that interdiction should be regarded as only one component of an overall drug enforcement program. Nevertheless, it has emphasized the visible results of interdiction: drugs and cash on the table and prisoners in jail to show "progress" in the War on Drugs. Accordingly, in March, 1983, the Administration began to implement the National Narcotics Border Interdiction System (NNBIS), under the direction of the Vice President, for the purpose of refining its interdiction program. Using South Florida anti-smuggling efforts as a model, NNBIS extended the federal interdiction net along borders near New York, Chicago, New Orleans, El Paso, and Long Beach. The six NNBIS centers are staffed by redeployed Customs and Coast Guard personnel. The centers serve as coordinating mechanisms, relying in part on increased tactical intelligence from CIA[23] and drawing upon the resources (equipment and personnel) of the DEA, Customs, the Coast Guard, and the DOD.

NNBIS has two divisions performing two distinct but related functions. The Interdiction Operations Intelligence Center (IOIC) is designed to inventory all law enforcement assets (location of ships, airplanes, and other deployable personnel) and to track suspect vehicles, making real-time "matching" recommendations to the operational agencies regarding "intercept potential." The Intelligence Information Command Center (IICC) is a future or "strategic" planning unit that makes recommendations based upon anticipated smuggling activity to operational units.

Since it is not an operational entity, but a coordinator or facilitator of existing agency personnel, the success of NNBIS hinges on its capacity to enhance organizational effectiveness. If NNBIS succeeds in that mission, it may end up boosting interdiction rates, but for all the reasons discussed above, improved interdiction of the drug supply remains a treadmill to nowhere. It is also worth noting that enterprises like NNBIS, designed to make the existing enforcement agencies more productive, must first transcend traditional inter-agency rivalries and struggles for bureaucratic turf or glory. For example, a memo from DEA Administrator Bud Mullen to Attorney General William French Smith lodged a number of complaints against NNBIS for making "grandiose claims" of drug seizures of a magnitude that could not be documented and taking "false credit" for arrests and seizures that should properly have been attributed to the DEA and other agents in the field. He further claimed that instead of being "a cost-free operation that would not become another bureaucratic entity, NNBIS diverted resources" (including "first class word processing and desk top computers") for its own staff of 125 and duplicated efforts of other federal agencies.[24] It is useful to keep this perspective in mind in assessing the War on Drugs, lest the rhetoric of agency cooperation come to overshadow the real-world limitations on the effectiveness of federal enforcement.

THE ORGANIZED CRIME DRUG ENFORCEMENT TASK FORCE PROGRAM

Without question, the heart of the War on Drugs strategy is the Organized Crime Drug Enforcement Task Force Program, which the President announced in his War on Drugs speech of October, 1982. By the end of 1983, the Administration had fully staffed 12 regional OCDETFs with 1,000 agents and 200 prosecutors, supported by paralegals and clerical personnel. The total Task Force Program appropriation for fiscal year 1983 was $127.5 million. Of this amount, $92,569,000 was allocated for law enforcement activities, $11,731,000 for prosecutorial expenses, $23,000,000 for correctional facilities, and $200,000 for the Policy and Management Division. A reprogramming of $500,000 from the prosecution allocation later provided funds for the establishment of the President's Commission on Organized Crime. Funding for the Task Force initiative provided for a total of 1,630 additional personnel in fiscal year 1983.[25]

In March, 1984, Attorney General Smith transmitted to President Reagan the first annual report on the OCDETF program, reviewing its work for 1983. Because 1983 was the start-up year for OCDETF, the Attorney General claimed, with some justification, that its case load statistics were untypically low. Still, the report provides a basis for some preliminary conclusions about the potency of OCDETF.

Recognizing that the "traditional approach to drug enforcement has had minimal impact" on major trafficking organizations, the Task Force program constituted a nationwide structure combining the resources of enforcement agencies in "concentrated, long-term operations designed to attack and destroy narcotics trafficking organizations."[26] OCDETF created a national structure of 12 regional multi-agency task forces based in "core" cities: Detroit, Houston, Los Angeles, Baltimore, Denver, Boston, New York, Chicago, San Francisco, St. Louis, Atlanta, and San Diego. A thirteenth OCDETF was added in Miami in October, 1984. In each core city, the United States Attorney, who is accountable for Task Force activities to the Associate Attorney General, has under his supervision a Task Force office staffed by Assistant United States Attorneys and agents from the DEA, FBI, Customs, Bureau of Alcohol, Tobacco and Firearms (BATF), IRS, Coast Guard, and U.S. Marshals Service. Each Task Force has its own organizational identity and a central office and administrative staff. Although all investigative agents remain under the direction of their respective agencies, they work together, conducting collective investigations on major cases selected according to OCDETF criteria.

As with NNBIS, the superimposition of an additional layer of enforcement on the existing structure created concerns about coordination. Some of these concerns surfaced during the groundwork for the Miami OCDETF.

Clearly, a major area of concern, particularly in the Southern District, is that a new program added on to the existing crowded environment will cause additional coordination problems. Many officials in South Florida have indicated that there are already too many programs and special investigatory units in South Florida. Even the professionals currently assigned to the area find the situation confusing.

Most participants in the South Florida criminal justice system state that it is currently impossible to keep track of all the activities, let alone identify the relationships among all of the separate programs of the agencies, special groups and task forces.[27]

Despite this organizational complexity and the inevitable problems of coordination and friction, the premise of this design is the synergistic blending of diverse enforcement skills:

Effective and comprehensive attacks on major drug organizations are often beyond the capacity of a single agency. Agencies working together can accomplish things that the same agencies working separately cannot. A multifaceted attack on drug organizations requires many kinds of expertise, combined into a comprehensive and orchestrated investigation. Thus, for example, by uniting the physical and electronic surveillance abilities of the Federal Bureau of Investigation, the undercover skills of the Drug Enforcement Administration, the tax and financial knowledge of the Internal Revenue Service, the resources of the U.S. Customs Service for tracking international movements of people and funds, and intelligence gained from U.S. Coast Guard maritime activities, the full forces of the drug enforcement community are brought to an investigation. The Task Force Program further broadens this base with the local intelligence resources of State and local law enforcement agencies and adds to the impact by utilizing attorneys' skills at an early stage of investigation. Joining such diverse abilities and resources is the underlying thrust of the Task Force Program.[28]

The OCDETF program has four specific objectives designed to further its ultimate goal of destroying the operations of high-level traffickers:

1. To target, investigate, and prosecute individuals who organize, direct, finance or are otherwise engaged in high-level drug trafficking enterprises, including large-scale money laundering organizations;
2. To promote a coordinated drug enforcement effort in each Task Force area and to encourage maximum cooperation among all drug enforcement agencies;
3. To work fully and effectively with State and local drug enforcement agencies; and
4. To make full use of financial investigative techniques, including tax law enforcement and forfeiture actions, in order to identify and convict high-level drug traffickers and enable the government to seize assets and profits derived from high-level drug trafficking.[29]

Starting by adopting 200 pre-existing agency investigations as Task Force cases, the total number grew to 467, with 2,072 principal potential defendants by the end of 1983 (see Figure 6). The report explained the first year's progress as follows:

The original 200 Task Force cases were already at various stages of development when they became Task Force cases. Hence, the 467 first-year cases fall at different points on the case timeline. Though a few cases have run their course, most are still approaching completion. There is a considerable time lag before the program's activities are converted into results. . . . Since the time frame for an average major drug trafficking case is from twenty to forty-two months [a pre-indictment phase of 6–30 months], the achievement of program goals cannot be measured by the first twelve months of the Task Force Program's operation.

The cases that qualify for Task Force selection are invariably those that require long-term dedication of personnel from more than one agency. These cases will not have quick turnover or results. The Task Force Program, by putting aside the numbers game of rapid and numerous prosecutions, is able to dedicate resources for better and higher achievements . . . to reach targets that are untouchable through traditional approaches.[30]

The Task Force resisted the "numbers game" and the short-term pressures to put "powder on the table," so its efficacy must be judged by its impact on the "high level kingpins who make the drug organization[s] function." One measure relied upon by the Attorney General's report is the number or percentage of investigations involving RICO and CCE charges. Fifty-one Task Force investigations resulted in the indictment of 90 persons under RICO and 71 under CCE.[31] Putting aside the quibble that indictment under these statutes does not automatically signify that the defendant is a "high-level kingpin," these numbers have a long way to grow.

The Attorney General's report goes on to celebrate the following examples of high-level targets in successful Task Force cases:[32]

- One principal defendant was a high-level target in his own right, a "Top leader" in a large organization, responsible for the importation of tons of cocaine over

Figure 6
Task Force Cases, Indictments, Convictions, and Estimated Potential Defendants in 1983

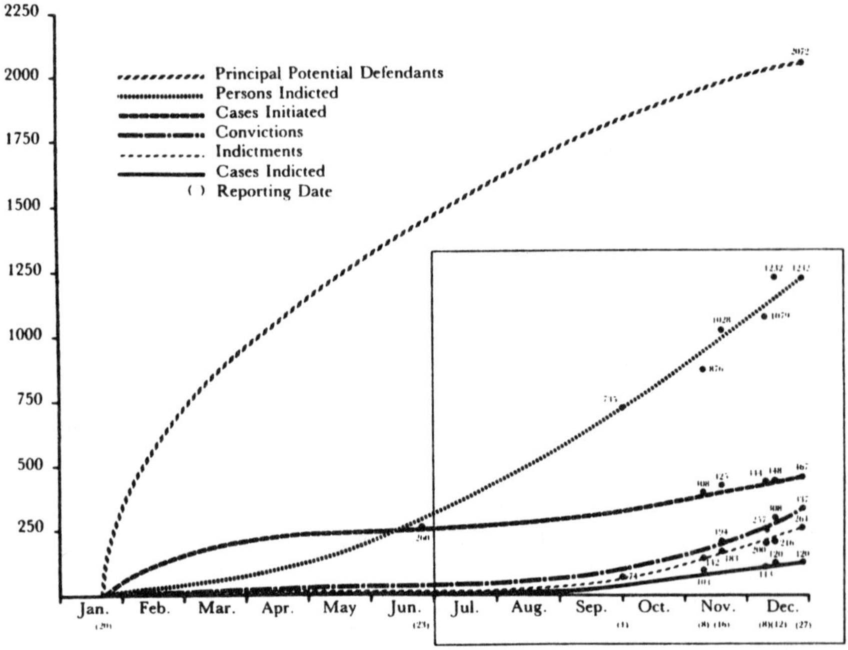

Source: U.S. Attorney General, *Annual Report of the Organized Crime Drug Enforcement Task Force Program* (March, 1984), p. 103.

the past three years. While he could have been indicted in mid–1983, the Task Force continued its investigation until the *organization* was more fully identified, resulting in the simultaneous indictment of fifty key figures, enough to severely cripple the organization.

- Another case focused on the "respectable" people—businessmen, lawyers, etc.—who were making fortunes on marijuana importation. The Task Force financial investigation approach resulted in multiple indictments of over fifty people, of whom six were charged with CCE violations. . . .
- An outlaw motorcycle gang heavily engaged in PCP and methamphetamine sales was another Task Force target. The result was multiple indictments against the bikers, including several of the gang's national officers.
- A drug ring operating out of a Federal prison was rounded up by a Task Force operation, resulting in the indictment of eight inmates and fifteen of their associates in five states. . . .

Table 10

Drugs, Cash, and Property Seized and Fines Levied in OCDE Task Force Cases in 1983

Region	(a) Drugs Seized (by kilos)			(b) Other Seizures	(c)	(d) Forfeitures	(e)	(f)	(b + d + f) Totals	(c + e)
	Heroin	Cocaine	Marijuana	Cash ($)	Property ($)	Cash ($)	Property ($)	Fines ($)	Cash ($)	Property ($)
Great Lakes	2	33	668	1,982,377	4,232,130	741,180	1,395,284	288,000	3,011,557	5,627,414
Gulf Coast	4	30	73,450	1,055,700	1,422,000	5,600	107,100	555,000	1,616,300	1,529,100
Los Angeles/Nevada	0	145	6	416,640	312,500	448,000	2,500,000	0	864,640	2,812,500
Mid-Atlantic	1	15	94,128	964,110	2,966,975	157,500	70,500	397,400	1,519,010	3,037,475
Mountain States	0	9	1,726	1,581,727	164,000	0	0	5,000	1,586,727	164,000
New England	8	39	93,773	1,137,925	3,333,082	40,000	33,000	20,000	1,197,925	3,366,082
New York/New Jersey	27	3,219	12	265,000	30,000	74,950	247,445	85,000	424,950	277,445
North Central	5	413	7,530	1,031,696	1,178,375	85,108	886,000	45,000	1,161,804	2,064,375
Northwest	0	657	11	1,892,100	1,005,994	0	1,211,000	0	1,892,100	2,216,994
South Central	0	756	76	0	0	177,200	933,800	150,000	327,200	933,800
Southeast	0	2,424	20	1,465,600	5,338,500	1,168,037	2,486,370	50,000	2,683,637	7,824,870
Southwest	0	8	10,000	2,834,250	930,305	0	300,000	0	2,834,250	1,230,305
Totals	47	7,748	281,400	14,627,125	20,913,861	2,897,575	10,170,499	1,595,400	19,120,100	31,084,360

Source: U.S. Attorney General, *Annual Report of the Organized Crime Drug Enforcement Task Force Program* (March, 1984), p. 102.

- An entire heroin organization—shippers in Italy and importers, distributors, and dealers in the United States—was the target of a major Task Force case, resulting in indictments of ten key figures in the United States. Some of the organization's other members in Italy have already been arrested and are awaiting trial.
- A West Coast organization that grew from school-yard sales to a multi-million dollar, multi-ton marijuana importation and distribution organization became a target, and Task Force agents and attorneys have identified and prosecuted over a dozen top and middle leaders in the organization.
- Ten years of corruption by a free-wheeling sheriff were brought to an abrupt conclusion by a Task Force investigation that netted eighteen assorted drug dealers, gambling and prostitution operators, including the sheriff and his assistant.

Viewed individually, some of these prosecutions appear very impressive indeed. The first case on the list, for example, appears to be the Harold Rosenthal case, "the biggest drug case in United States history," in which the Government alleged that his organization smuggled over $2 billion worth of cocaine into the United States in a 27-month period. In another spectacular hit announced in April, 1984, the Government concluded a three-year investigation by charging 31 persons directed by the Joe Bonanno Mafia family with importing $1.68 billion worth of heroin into the United States over a five-year period. "It is the most significant case involving heroin trafficking by traditional organized crime that the federal government has ever developed," the Attorney General said. "This is a classic Drug Task Force case—massive resources, widespread coordination, and significant contributions by a variety of law enforcement agencies, [FBI, DEA, Customs], including state and local agencies." Two hundred FBI agents worked on the case full time for nine months.

So, the "biggest drug case in United States history," the "most significant" heroin trafficking case—clearly, the Task Force approach works to produce arrests of "high-level" drug traffickers. But what results does it produce in terms of overall drug supply, the ultimate goal of the War on Drugs? How do these "biggest ever" cases differ from the "biggest ever" cases of a few years ago, when, for example, Nicky Barnes, the "Mr. Big" or "Mr. Untouchable" of New York heroin was sentenced to a life term? Or Operation Grouper, the nation's "biggest and most successful" marijuana investigation, in which $1 billion in drugs was destroyed, 53 persons were convicted, and some 30 vessels, 2 planes, and $1 million in cash were confiscated. Aren't these the same type of cases that the Government has always made against the drug trade?

Perhaps OCDETF will produce more of such giant cases, but record-setting indictments and even convictions have no intrinsic meaning whatever. In the context of the War on Drugs, the practical (as distinct from symbolic) value of such enforcement—if any—lies in its impact on the supply of illegal drugs. The purpose of the War on Drugs, after all, is to squeeze the supply of drugs in order to prevent or minimize drug abuse. And even if we make an appropriate discount for political rhetoric in the President's call in his Proclamation for National Drug Abuse Education and Prevention Week, 1984, to "eliminate" drug abuse, the Government will not be able to claim victory in the War on Drugs without showing an actual reduction in supply and consumption. Even the GAO, in its review of OCDETF, argues that it is "particularly relevant" whether the disruption of organizations reduces the supply of drugs.

This, of course, the Administration cannot show so far and can never show as long as consumer demand holds. All the Administration can do is boast of its bigger numbers, as it did in a September 27, 1984, White House press release titled "Summary of Accomplishments [of] the National Campaign Against Drug Abuse," listing these results:

- Arrests of the top-level organizers and financiers of the drug traffic have increased 18 percent, from 195 per month in 1981 to about 231 per month in 1984. Total arrests averaged about 1,000 per month.
- Convictions for all drug law violations have increased 90 percent, from 485 per month in 1981 to about 921 per month in 1984.
- Convictions for top echelon organizers and financiers have increased 186 percent, from 88 per month in 1981 to about 252 per month in 1984.
- U.S. seizures of cocaine during the first seven months of 1984 are 216 percent greater than cocaine seizures during all of 1981. Heroin seizures are 67 percent greater for the first seven months of 1984 than in all of 1981.
- In the first half of 1984, over 25 metric tons of cocaine were seized in the United States and Latin America, compared to approximately 3.7 metric tons in 1981.

The "bottom line" of burgeoning cocaine supplies renders these numbers meaningless. In order to succeed at supply reduction, what the War on Drugs must do is to knock out and scare off so many actual and potential suppliers as to spread a generalized perception of increased risk. That in turn will translate into a higher cost of doing business (higher risk premium) and reduce the supply of cocaine. This scenario would unfold. The drop in supply would raise consumer prices. To the extent that demand is price-sensitive (elastic), consumption would decline to reflect reduced purchasing power. If consumption declines, overdoses, deaths, and dependency would also decline, although the "hard-core" users most prone to those fates would be the least likely to cut back on consumption. Conversely, the uncommitted dabbler most likely to respond to higher prices is least at risk of addiction, overdose, or death.

At some nominal level, the War on Drugs might succeed in realizing this scenario. But supply reduction on a meaningful scale is a lost cause. It has not succeeded and can never succeed, except temporarily—twice in modern history, the supply of heroin was shut down substantially, World War II causing the first shortage—because of the limits of the criminal sanction. As one anonymous drug enforcement official put it, "We can bust the trafficker, but we never really hurt the traffic." The OCDE Task Force program may well be more efficient in making cases, but at bottom the investigative process remains the same: informants, undercover work, surveillance, body bugs, wiretaps, computerized data banks, grand juries, cash flow forms, tax returns, and so on. Synergistic interaction of multi-agency task force personnel does not eliminate the limits on investigative powers or the need for pavement-pounding and other traditional methods of assembling a provable case under the rules of law. As the Attorney General himself points out, two to three and a half years is the required time frame for that process. In the meantime, dealers find markets to service and vast profits to make.

Thus, despite the Administration's bigger-than-ever statistics in every category—seizures, forfeitures, investigations, indictments, arrests, and convictions—the fact remains that the black market in cocaine has grown to record size, about 74–96 metric tons imported in 1984. In fact, by 1980, Americans had consumed twice as much cocaine per capita as they did in the basically free market that prevailed in the years before enactment of the Harrison Narcotics Act of 1914.[33] Moreover, this rapid market growth occurred in the face of Reagan's doubling of the federal drug enforcement budget from $645 million in fiscal year 1981 to over $1.2 billion in fiscal year 1985. This budgetary expansion seems all the more remarkable when compared to the equivalent budget for fiscal year 1969 of $34.2 million. The social return on the extra billion dollars spent during that decade and a half is a drug trafficking and drug abuse problem of record size.

How is it possible for so much enforcement energy, producing such impressive-sounding statistics on arrests, drug seizures, and property forfeitures, to fail to make a visible dent in the black market? Can it really be that the supply of cocaine and cocaine distributors forms a bottomless pit? The Attorney General's report suggests that it is simply a question of time, since the "United States drug market, approaching $100 billion annually, cannot be expected to yield to first-year assaults." With more time to make the full force of its prosecutorial power felt, runs the implicit argument, OCDETF will succeed in its goal of destroying the operations of drug-trafficking organizations. Certainly, the case load statistics will rise and many such organizations will be knocked out. Just as certainly, such organizations will be replaced by others. The law can imprison a black marketeer, but not the market itself.

This conclusion is vehemently resisted by some law enforcement officials. The former United States Attorney in Miami argued in a guest editorial in the *Miami Herald* that there simply cannot be an endless supply of people willing to risk imprisonment and loss of assets, and that ultimately the drug industry must bow to relentless enforcement pressure:

> It may seem at times that the resources of this criminal import industry are limitless; they are not. There are only so many people willing to go to jail for the industry and one surely would expect that this number would sharply decline with a significant increase in the certainty and severity of punishment. Moreover, there are only a fixed number of ships and planes—only a fixed amount of cash and property—that this industry can afford to lose before it will run in the red. In Florida we have begun a massive effort to press this criminal enterprise to the limits of its solvency. While we most assuredly haven't reached those limits yet, we continue to intensify our efforts on the firm conviction that those limits are not ultimately beyond our reach.[34]

Other government officials do not share this naked belief in the potency of law enforcement: in testimony before Congress, one Deputy Assistant Attorney General conceded the invincibility of the black market.

> [An improved] ability to ferret out and convict the major offenders and to deprive them of their illicit gains . . . will not halt illicit drug traffic and its attendant high profits. As long as there remains a strong demand and a ready market, there will be individuals willing to run the risk to supply them.[35]

Which of these two diametrically opposed assertions captures the truth of the matter? The "firm conviction" of the former United States Attorney depends upon a naive faith in the power of deterrence that cannot find support in either theory or experience. The study of deterrence—the inhibiting effect of sanctions on the criminal activity of people *other than* the sanctioned offender—is a field unto itself, and a barren field it is. The state of knowledge is such that deterrence, rather than economics, may deserve the title of "dismal science."

The National Academy of Sciences in 1976 convened a panel to make "an objective assessment of the scientific validity of the technical evidence . . . of any crime-reducing effects" of criminal sanctions.[36] Its study, *Deterrence and Incapacitation: Estimating the Effects of Criminal Sanctions on Crime Rates*, reached no firm conclusion. On the one hand, "[t]aken as a whole, the reported evidence consistently finds a negative association between crime rates and the risks of apprehension, conviction, or imprisonment."[37] On the other hand, the panel was unable to conclude that high sanction rates *cause* low crime rates (or vice versa):

> Any conclusion that these negative associations reflect a deterrent effect, however, is limited principally by the inability to eliminate other factors that could account for the observed relationship, even in the absence of a deterrent effect.
>
> The most important such factor is the possibility that crime rates influence sanctions as well as vice versa . . . a simultaneous relationship between crimes and sanctions.[38]

Jurisdictions with high crime rates, for example, may typically impose low sanctions for the sake of expedience in processing a massive case load and out of greater tolerance for crime as a fact of life.

Despite weaknesses in the scientific evidence for the deterrent effect of increased sanctions, the idea of deterrence certainly has strong intuitive appeal, derived from the general proposition that human behavior can be influenced by incentives. The idea of deterrence claims a respectable lineage. A rational calculation of pains and benefits formed the heart of Jeremy Bentham's utilitarian argument for the deterrent efficacy of criminal penalties. A more deterministic view of human behavior, however, sees little or no direct relationship between crime and punishment. Acting out of their existential situations, people do what they do, and then suffer the consequences of the law or not, depending largely on the fortuity of getting caught and convicted. In this view, enforcement and punishment can affect only the number of prisoners and the length of their sentences, while the supply of criminals and crimes remains more or less fixed. Committing crimes is what criminals do. Conscious choice plays little or no role in the commission of those crimes. Instead, crimes are committed as the effect of external forces or influences such as poverty or psychological deficiency.

The question of whether law deters crime need not be resolved at so metaphysical a level for purposes of this inquiry, and I have accepted the intuitively compelling proposition that threats deter at least some people from committing some crimes. Having made that assumption, the most meaningful question for drug policy concerns the strength of deterrence: whether more certain or more severe punishment would deter (and to what extent) those who now work in the drug industry or those who might enter it. More specifically, what impact on the supply of cocaine or other drugs might the OCDETF initiative in the War on Drugs produce, assuming that it is able to increase the risk of detection (arrest and conviction) and the risk of higher penalties (fines, forfeitures, and prison terms)?

The extent to which the War on Drugs can achieve supply reduction through increasing the risk factor is probably *very* small. In order for the enhanced risk to work as a deterrent, two things must occur: the increase in risk must be perceived by the risk taker, and it must be unacceptable to him. Technically, the extra law enforcement pressure must shift the perceived risk-reward ratio into the unacceptable range of his indifference curve between money (taking the risk of crime) and freedom (not committing crime). Some dealers may already operate at the margin of acceptable risk, and they will be scared out of the black market by the War on Drugs. Others will remain in business until caught or killed. Still others will enter at the first opportunity.

In assessing the prospects for deterrence, it is important to take account of the target group. Probably drug dealers as a group tend to discount the "objective" threat posed by the law more than other groups in society.

Several factors operate to support a high tolerance for risk among drug dealers. The very willingness to supply (and to take) drugs presupposes a certain defiant attitude toward the law, reinforced by the cockiness born of apparent (statistical) safety. While law enforcement can impose severe sanctions upon the few who are caught and convicted, it can never pose a meaningful risk of detection for any single transaction. There are simply too many buyers and sellers to police, and their deals take place in secrecy. In addition, those who operate by paying bribes for protection often have *de facto* immunity from the reach of the law. (This is especially true for those based in South America.) These safety factors, coupled with extraordinary profits, make the cocaine business look very attractive, a perception exaggerated perhaps by the psychological tendency to value highly the short-term, tangible rewards (the certainty of immediate gratification) and to ignore or to undervalue the longer-term, intangible costs (the potential sanctions of an uncertain future). Crime does pay in the cocaine business, at least in the short run, and it pays extraordinarily well.

Even those who recognize that the law of averages may catch up with them in the longer run believe, usually correctly, that they can succeed in the short run and perhaps retire early with a modest nest egg, if not a small fortune. A distributor, dealer, pilot, courier, or other employee of the drug industry can expect a "run" of several years before an informer turns him in or sets him up, and perhaps several more years, if ever, before his day in court comes up. In the meantime he can reap the rewards of extraordinary opportunities for making money. Under these circumstances, if the risk of getting caught, measured by some objective standard, should actually rise, the day of reckoning remains seemingly so remote that the subjective tendency will be to disregard or discount it.

Additionally, when his luck does run out, the plea bargaining process offers some chance of getting off with a reduced sentence or wiggling off the hook completely. Deal-making lies at the heart of the prosecutorial process. On average, about 90 percent of all cases end in a guilty plea, with the defendant receiving some consideration at sentencing for not putting the Government to its proof. A few defendants really profit from a plea by "cooperating" with the Government in making other cases by giving evidence against co-defendants. A defendant who "rolls over" on an important target may receive a variety of considerations: immunity, money, or enrollment in the Witness Protection Program with a new identity and relocation to a new city. So, all things considered, the prospect of a favorable plea bargain for a crafty or duplicitous few probably misleads others to think they can also strike such deals and thereby attenuates the force of deterrence.

Most defendants will not have the kind of information against important targets required to deal at that level. For them, lawmakers have consistently overestimated the deterrent value of penal sanctions by projecting stereotypical white, Middle American attitudes about freedom and imprisonment, neglecting to consider the ethnic and social class composition of the cocaine industry. A prison term looms much larger for middle-class whites because their opportunity costs are generally much higher than those for American blacks, Hispanics, or illegal aliens from South America. For the underclass, the uncertain risk of even a long prison term some years in the future is an acceptable price to pay for the rewards of wealth, status, and sexual opportunities not available through legitimate channels, even if the success only lasts for a few years. Drug dealing thus provides for the underclasses a rare opportunity for upward social mobility. And life in the fast lane of drug dealing has proven to be a powerful magnet in a country that celebrates material success with few reservations. Making it is both a universal aspiration and an honored goal. Television purveys the vicarious experience of wealth in broadcasts like "Life Styles of the Rich and Famous," and cocaine dealers vibrate to the capitalist chord like everyone else. Successful dealing requires all of the traditional qualities of entrepreneurship and service in delivering goods to market to satisfy consumer demand. Apart from the law, drug dealing remains one of the last bastions of free-wheeling enterprise.

Moreover, the risks posed by the legal system cannot loom very large for the many who accept the risk of torture and violent death as part of the reality of life in the cocaine business. The Colombian mentality may be unique in this regard, but it is important because Colombians control the production and import/export phases of the cocaine industry. Their "inordinate propensity" for violence, in the language of the NIE report, has already been noted. It has shown up repeatedly in cocaine cowboy shootouts in public places and in the execution of whole families, including infants. As one anonymous cocaine importer put the matter, "The Colombian attitude toward making money is very similar to the American attitude. But the Colombian attitude toward life is very different. Under their Code, one who betrays his friends should be killed, as should his family." Against the risk of execution, the threat posed by the legal system pales in comparison.

Finally, the attractiveness of risk as an end in itself should not be ignored. Certain undertakings command respect in our society precisely because they are risky. Professional auto racing and boxing, for example, reflect glory on the participants and pay them so highly because they require great skill and courage, including the willingness to face death. The public rewards that bravery with adulation and sometimes considerable wealth. Dealing drugs stands on the same footing—a high-risk, high-reward, macho endeavor. True, public admiration is contaminated by the condemnation of law. Even so, an ambivalent, grudging respect for the ambition, talent, and daring of many smugglers remains. Portrayals on "Miami Vice" sometimes capture those qualities. Other dealers come across as sleazy, vicious, and repulsive, motivated solely by greed.

The last point raises another consideration. For some, smuggling and dealing are strictly business. Others deal for more than money, responding to the challenge of confronting danger and beating the system. As the slogan puts it, "Smuggling: not a job, but an adventure." Those for whom dealing (and taking) drugs constitutes a way of life do not yield readily to heightened legal pressures. Thus, when the system ups the ante, those who savor risk taking may actually welcome the extra challenge, along with the extra rewards, like skiing the black-diamond trails. In their naiveté, the squareheads who make drug enforcement policy do not understand the seductiveness of the adrenalin rush that comes from walking the edge. Real players like the game.

For all these reasons, smuggling or dealing cocaine remains remarkably resistant to the threats posed by the law. Of course, resistance to legal sanctions does not mean total immunity to deterrence. The question remains to what degree the cocaine trade is vulnerable to legal pressure. The cocaine industry/law enforcement interface is characterized by three parameters: a very low (short-run) risk of being caught, which risk varies at different strata of the business; a high probability, if caught, of being convicted and fined, and deprived of assets through forfeiture; and extremely high profits or benefits of committing the crime if not caught.

The War on Drugs, through its OCDETF program and its "legislative offensive" in the area of criminal law and procedure, has attempted to raise the risks and reduce the benefits. Although the Government offers no empirical evidence, we may assume for the purpose of this analysis that the War on Drugs has succeeded in raising the statistical risk of getting caught. Once caught, changes in the law regarding bail, search and seizure, and other aspects of pretrial procedure probably have raised the likelihood of conviction. Conviction now carries higher fines and penalties, including forfeiture of assets and fairly long prison terms. In short, once apprehended, defendants in federal drug-related cases have very little chance of beating the system. On the contrary, they must pay a substantial price.

The Achilles heel of the War on Drugs, so far as deterrence is concerned, is the system's limited ability to catch a significant percentage of drug offenders. This greatly weakens its deterrent impact. Optimists in the Government might argue that the rapidly rising number of prosecutions and convictions holds out an eventual promise of deterrence. As one official put the matter, "If we are to ever make a meaningful dent in our national drug abuse problem we must reduce the incentive to participate in the narcotics business by significantly increasing the risk of conviction and certainty of long prison sentences."[39] But this "commonsense" thinking suffers from a major flaw.

In addressing this issue, we can learn much from the analysis of Professor Stuart S. Nagel in "Tradeoffs in Crime Reduction Among Certainty, Severity and Crime Benefits."[40] Nagel's tradeoff analysis posits interrelationships among these variables:

1. the probability of being convicted;
2. the fine or penalty imposed upon conviction;
3. the benefits of committing a crime.

Assuming a utilitarian model of criminal behavior, in which the would-be criminal intuitively judges the potential costs and benefits of his proposed crime, Nagel asserts that it is "common knowledge" that crime varies inversely with the first two factors and directly with the last factor. These variables also interact, i.e., changes in one or more produce nonlinear changes in the other(s), that is to say, a change in one of the decisionmaking variables may produce a disproportionate change in the others. His conclusions regarding these interrelationships suggest very limited prospects for deterrence by turning the War on Drugs (through the OCDE Task Force) into a more efficient arrest and conviction machine:

> First, the amount of crime reduction which an increase in certainty is capable of achieving depends on how much certainty initially existed. If the probability of being arrested, convicted, and imprisoned is quite low, then small increases in the probability are likely to produce a substantial reduction in crime.[41]

Because the low-certainty characterization applies to the War on Drugs, it appears at first that higher arrest rates produced by the Task Force would produce a deterrent effect. But other considerations, principally the effect of high crime benefits, alter the equation.

> Even if certainty is low and would normally have a high marginal rate of return when other relevant variables are held constant, and even if severity is high, an increase in certainty will still not have much impact on crime reduction when the crime benefits are high. Similarly, even if severity is low and would normally have a high marginal rate of return, and even if certainty is high, an increase in severity will still not have much impact on crime reduction when the crime benefits are high.[42]

Indeed, "[i]n the extreme case, when the benefits become extremely great, the actual perceived probability of being caught would have to be close to unity [100 percent] to deter the would-be criminal."[43] In other words, the two principal stratagems of the OCDE Task Force war machine, increasing the probability of being caught and the fine or penalty upon conviction, offer little leverage on the drug crime rate because the benefits of committing the crime remain so high in the cocaine industry. The risk factor needs to climb near 100 percent in order to convert an otherwise profitable deal into an unacceptably risky undertaking.

For all these reasons, an elevated risk factor has very limited potential for "reduc[ing] the incentive to participate in the narcotics business." Even former Attorney General Smith conceded that "unless you can eliminate the demand for drugs, the amount of money is so large that the dealers will continue to take whatever risk is necessary."

So, the former United States Attorney's "firm conviction" that deterrence can press the drug industry to its limits is wrong in every conceivable way—wrong in theory, wrong in human psychology, and wrong in experience. The case for deterrence rests entirely on hope or ideology, not on fact or reason. And there is an ultimate trump card played by the drug industry on deterrence: even if it did work to reduce drug supply, the heightened risk/penalty factor would almost certainly be socially counterproductive. Here's why. Higher risk would raise the cost of doing business in two ways: (1) by increasing costs of security and evasion strategies in order to avoid arrest, and (2) by causing the seller to demand a higher price in order to monetize the extra risk of getting caught. Perception of a higher risk would then raise the cost of cocaine, and this increased crime tariff would reduce the supply. A reduced supply of cocaine at higher prices will not necessarily make the cocaine business less *profitable*, however. Supply reduction might even increase total gross revenues, depending upon the elasticity of demand.

There are three possibilities: unitary, inelastic, and elastic demand. Elasticity defines the tendency of total revenue (P x Q) to rise when price drops and the increase in quantity sold more than compensates for the price cut. With unitary elasticity, price decreases bring an exactly compensating increase in quantity sold so that total revenue remains unchanged. Only if demand is relatively elastic will the other important goal of the War on Drugs—reducing black market profits—also be achieved by raising the crime tariff.

It is impossible to do much more than speculate about the elasticity of market demand for cocaine. In addition to the impossibility of maintaining *ceteris paribus* conditions in real markets, no one has sufficient information about the price-quantity relationship in the black market to permit the necessary measurements of the interactions. Moreover, the cocaine market probably consists of fairly distinct submarkets with varying degrees of inelasticity along lines suggested by Siegel's adaptation of the National Commission typology. Clearly compulsive users would generate more inelastic demand than social-recreational users. Based on NIE's assumption that 63 percent of market demand comes from heavy users (four or more times per month),[44] it seems very likely that the overall demand for cocaine is moderately to highly inelastic.

If the price of cocaine were to rise, consumers would experience a decrease in real purchasing power if they continued the same level of consumption. The "income effect" would therefore tend to promote a reduction of consumption, but the strength of that tendency is limited by inelasticity. Those who regard cocaine as a staple item, or those who have high incomes, may not care very much if the price were to rise from $70 or $80 back to $100.

Moreover, drug dealers at retail tend to disguise price increases by holding the dollar price constant and cutting purity instead. This effective price increase goes unnoticed by the consumer, who has no convenient way to measure the purity of his product. (Of course, the hidden price increase would mean that consumers would be using the same amount of powder but less cocaine.) So, if the demand for cocaine is on balance relatively inelastic, then the higher prices brought about through intensified risk will serve the goal of the War on Drugs of lowering consumption. At the same time, higher prices will raise the total revenues of the cocaine industry. In other words, the risk factor will be higher, the costs of production will be "taxed" higher, supply will be lower, but the price will rise more than the decline in sales, so that industry-wide revenues will be even greater (see Figure 7).

And what will be the societal gain? In their wildest fantasies, do law enforcement officials dream of cutting the black market by as much as one-

Figure 7
Effects of the War on Drugs on Cocaine Production Costs

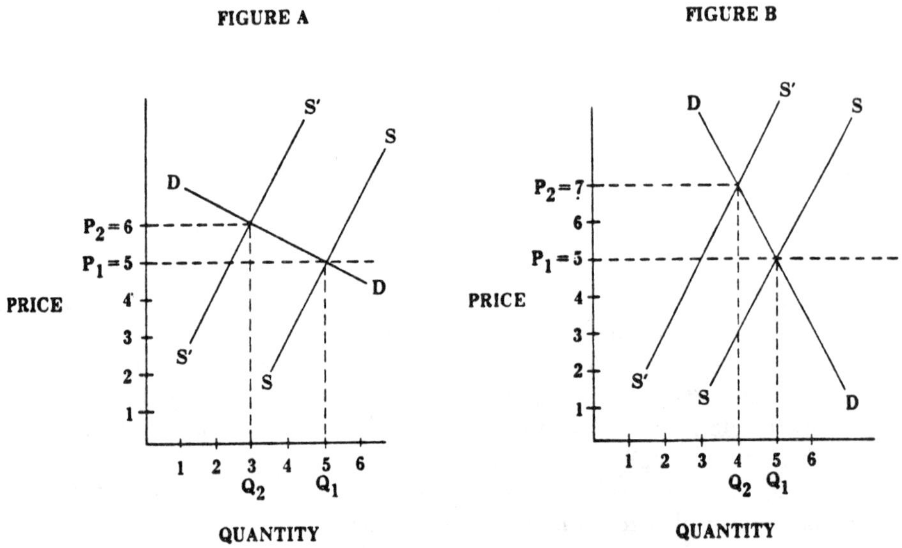

In both Figures A and B, the shift from SS to SS' represents increased production costs caused by the war on drugs. In Figure A, representing elastic demand, this shift causes total revenue to decline from 25 (P1 to Q1) to 18 (P2 x Q2). In Figure B, representing inelastic demand, total revenue rises from 25 (P1 x Q1) to 28 (P2 x Q2). Thus, when demand is inelastic, the war on drugs causes sellers of cocaine to earn more revenue as a result of higher price, despite a restriction in quantity sold.

half? While that would be a heroic achievement, given the limited powers of law enforcement, its impact on public health would be minimal. It would, after all, only roll back the black market to its 1980–1981 level, which triggered the War on Drugs hysteria in the first place. It would save perhaps a hundred lives and a few thousand emergency room visits, far less than would be accomplished by comparable expenditures, on, say, highway safety. And as the *quid pro quo* of that accomplishment, law enforcement will have raised black market revenues, further enriching drug dealers as a class and exacerbating the grievous secondary costs that the black market imposes on society.

7

The Pathology of the War on Drugs: The Assault on Justice and Civil Liberties

Society pays dearly for the war on cocaine. The aggressive effort to "ration" drugs by maintaining hyper-inflated prices institutionalizes the black market and pumps vast sums of money into it. The flow of these illegal billions through a subterranean network generates a set of pathologies harmful to important societal interests and values. The interests and values jeopardized by black market pathologies fall into three categories: (1) the social interest in avoiding or minimizing the aggrandizement of governmental enforcement powers at the expense of individual rights; (2) the social interest in avoiding the secondary crimes committed as a necessary adjunct of cocaine trafficking and money laundering; and (3) the social interest in avoiding subversion of basic social, political, and economic institutions. Within each category, black market effects manifest themselves in many forms, enough to occupy an army of political scientists, economists, and sociologists for years to come. This chapter and the next concentrate on several of the most destructive manifestations of black market pathology.

The first category, the growth of governmental power and the correlative squelching of personal liberty, forms the subject of this chapter. It focuses on two related phenomena: (1) the Government's sustained attack, motivated by the imperatives of drug enforcement, on traditional protections afforded to criminal defendants under the Bill of Rights; and (2) the gradual but perceptible rise of Big Brotherism against the public at large in the form of eavesdropping, surveillance, monitoring, informing, and other intrusive enforcement methods.

Chapter Eight considers elements of the other two categories of pathologies. In the second category fall what might be called derivative black market crimes, i.e., those committed in order to protect or facilitate the illegal transactions of the drug business. Tax evasion, bribery, kidnapping, and murder all seem standard adjuncts to drug trafficking. In the third category belongs the social and institutional impact of the War on Drugs: the corrosion of the work ethic, the subversion of the integrity of government, and the general decline of the moral authority of the law. These impacts extend beyond the borders of the United States to other nations; the War on Drugs finances the spread of corruption and narco-terrorism, inflicting grave damage on the foreign policy interests of the United States in promoting stability in the Caribbean and the Americas. Chapter Nine considers these black market pathologies overseas.

In its narrow focus on attacking the supply of drugs, the Government has mindlessly sacrificed things of great value, without ever acknowledging the real cost of the war or asking whether the "casualties" are worth it. The thought process—if it can be called that—animating the War on Drugs is so obsessively fixated on drugs that it pays no heed whatever to the consequences for the overall well-being of American society.

THE ASSAULT ON JUSTICE

When the President initiated the War on Drugs, he harnessed the power of a pre-existing momentum in the Congress. Both the Senate Drug Enforcement Caucus and the House Select Committee on Narcotics Abuse and Control had spurred the President on, urging him to declare war on drugs. After he did so, the judiciary, the "least dangerous branch" in James Madison's phrase, played a vital role in the war effort, validating the legality of the Government's many incursions into the Bill of Rights whenever they were challenged by criminal defendants. War fever brought a rare measure of unity to the three branches of government.

In his original declaration of war, the President announced a "legislative offensive designed to win approval of reforms" with respect to bail, sentencing, criminal forfeiture, and the exclusionary rule.[1] He succeeded in almost every respect. The Administration's march toward a tougher set of investigative and prosecutorial powers drew much of its energy from the widespread belief that the criminal justice system was treating drug traffickers with excessive leniency. In 1981, the United States Attorney for the Southern Distrct of Florida (Miami), a Democratic appointee (whose job was presumably on the line after Reagan's election), articulated that perception in a statement to Congress and a guest editorial in the *Miami Herald*:

> Currently, a first time offender associated with multiton quantities of marihuana, kilogram quantities of cocaine or tens of thousands of methaqualone tablets expects: not to be arrested; if arrested, to be immediately set free on bail pending trial; if tried to have representation by the best lawyers money can buy; if convicted, to remain free on bail pending appeals, all the way to the Supreme Court; if eventually sentenced, to receive a sentence of two to three years and to serve less than 10

months in "a clean well-lighted place" (perhaps even receive probation); and when released after a few months in prison, to have millions of dollars in narcotics profits waiting.[2]

In short, the system was too soft all the way down the line. What was needed, according to this view, was a general toughening of all phases of the criminal justice system, from investigation through pretrial procedure, sentencing, and the appellate stages of a prosecution. The goal of the crackdown was to make the system more effective in catching drug violators, to facilitate their conviction once indicted, and to punish them more severely upon conviction. News of the heightened severity would deter others from trafficking in drugs, and drug abuse would therefore decline. In other words, extend, expand, and intensify the pre-existing system of enforcement. Doing more of the same and doing it better would correct the failures of the past and the drug control system would begin to work.

However simpleminded the analysis, it prevailed. In the late 1970s and early 1980s, representatives of the DEA, Customs, and other enforcement agencies came before Congressional committees and repeated that theme. Drug traffickers had a free hand because enforcement was underfunded, understaffed, and underequipped. Not only that, agencies were hampered by excessively restrictive laws that tied their hands in the fight against drug violators. Legal obstacles to efficient investigative action needed to be removed. One Congressman agreed that the laws were a nuisance to enforcement, observing, without apparent irony, that "in the war on narcotics, we have met the enemy, and he is the U.S. Code. I have never seen such a maze of laws and hangups."[3] The entire Congress apparently shared that perception, responding with alacrity to the call for a crackdown. Indeed, Congress became a prolific source of anti-drug initiatives. In just the first year of the 97th Congress, for example, over 100 bills proposing to "reform" some aspect of the criminal justice system were filed; more than three-quarters specifically proposed harsher treatment for drug offenses or drug offenders.[4] Most of the bills concentrated on restricting bail for accused drug offenders, followed in frequency by proposals for more severe (or mandatory) sentences for convicted drug traffickers.

To facilitate conviction of those arrested, two bills proposed to amend the Constitution to eliminate the exclusionary rule that bars the Government from using at trial evidence obtained by means of an illegal search or seizure. Two others proposed to dilute the exclusionary rule by adopting a "good faith exception," a step soon taken by the Fifth Circuit Court of Appeals in a drug case and later validated as the law of the land by the United States Supreme Court. A variety of other proposals sought to toughen the criminal justice system, including changes to the laws on asset forfeiture (more), the Bank Secrecy Act (more), sanctions against foreign drug producers (more), the Posse Comitatus Act (more), the Tax Reform Act of 1976 (less), and the Freedom of Information Act (less).

Apart from the sheer number of proposed laws, this legislative activity was noteworthy for its manifestation of a get-tough, do-whatever-is-necessary attitude. In its most reasonable form, legislators voiced the matter as one of creating disincentives, of raising the ante, i.e., making the drug business riskier (and therefore less attractive) "by significantly increasing the risk of conviction and certainty of long prison sentences."[5] It showed its most pugnacious mentality in the proposed Arctic Penitentiary Act, creating "an American Gulag" of remote prison camps for drug (and some other) offenders. So great was the legislative activity that one could fairly say that drug enforcement became both the top priority and the organizing or focal point for the entire federal criminal justice system. And, in its zeal to shore up the sagging system, the Congress did not hesitate to attack the "enemy." If the Bill of Rights or statutory protections stood in the way of the war effort, then they had to go.

Probably the most aggressive and effective assault on justice emerged from passage of the Comprehensive Crime Control (CCC) Act of 1984,[6] a major rollback of the rights of the criminally accused. The first impact of the act is felt soon after the arrest of a defendant on drug charges, when he applies for pretrial release on bail. The courts had previously "upped the ante" in this area by restricting the use of cash bonds through what lawyers call a *Nebbia* hearing.[7] Devised in response to cases in which defendants had posted large cash bonds and then absconded, *Nebbia* permitted the court to interrogate a defendant about the source of his bail money and to reject drug money (or any cash bond) where it did not provide adequate assurance that a defendant would appear for trial. Nevertheless, the traditional legal test for release on bond remained whether a released defendant would appear for trial.

The CCC Act of 1984 broke new legal ground in authorizing pretrial detention upon a judge's "finding" that a defendant's release would pose a "danger to the community." The law dispenses with pretrial bail altogether for most charges under the Controlled Substances Act if the court decides, upon "clear and convincing" evidence, that detention is necessary to insure the appearance of the defendant *or* to protect the safety of the community, even from nonviolent crimes like drug trafficking. Furthermore, the law creates a rebuttable *presumption* of a defendant's dangerousness upon a judicial finding of "probable cause to believe that the person committed an offense . . . [under] the Controlled Substances Act" punishable by ten years or more in prison. In other words, a (serious) drug charge *alone* can justify pretrial detention, which all authorities agree severely handicaps the preparation of an effective defense.

The potency of the preventive detention provision in the act shows up in its early track record: between October 12, 1984, and May 10, 1985, the

Department of Justice won 704 motions for pretrial detention and lost only 185.[8] At this writing, the law has yet to face and survive a challenge to its constitutionality under the Eighth Amendment, which forbids "excessive bail." Pretrial detention is surely "excessive," although an analogy to the capital crimes exception to the Eighth Amendment can be made and the Supreme Court almost always sides with the Government on drug issues. However the courts finally rule on that issue, the act's authorization of pretrial detention marks a historic shift in legislative attitude toward criminal procedure in attempting to destroy a large part of the constitutional right of pretrial liberty.

Greater restrictions now apply under the act to post-conviction bail as well. Formerly, courts granted bail pending appeal liberally unless the Government could show that a defendant was likely to flee or pose a danger to others. The act shifts that burden to the defendant and mandates that a convicted defendant be detained unless his appeal "raises a substantial question of law or fact likely to result in reversal or an order for a new trial."

The CCC Act of 1984 also makes several important changes in sentencing. First, it raises the maximum term of imprisonment for many drug offenses, including one kilo or more of cocaine, to 20 years, and increases the maximum fine tenfold to $250,000. Second, it provides a powerful stick for the collection of fines through devices such as imprisonment for willful failure to pay the fine. Third, it provides for an alternative fine of twice the gross gain of the drug deal or other crime. Fourth, its adds forfeiture, formerly limited to CCE and RICO offenses, as a penalty for all felony violations of the Controlled Substances Act. Upon conviction (in addition to fines), the Government gets title to any "property used or intended to be used" to facilitate commission of a drug violation and any money or property, including land, that was obtained directly or indirectly through such violation. Money or property realized by forfeitures goes to a law enforcement fund for use in paying informers, rewarding state and local enforcement agencies, and a variety of other purposes.

One of the most serious incursions into the rights of criminal defendants arises from the Department of Justice tactic of using the criminal forfeiture provisions of the act against fees paid to defense counsel. When so used, prosecutors claim that the fee received by counsel represents the proceeds of a controlled substances violation, and upon conviction of the client, the Government asks the court to order the fee forfeited to the United States. Since very few cases result in complete acquittal of defendants charged in multicount indictments, defense counsel confronts a thorny problem. Preparation and trial of a major drug conspiracy case, typically involving multiple defendants and multiple counts, takes months of concentrated work. Even if one agrees that defense lawyers have come to expect excessive fees in drug cases, the prospect of no fee at all is an extreme curative. The potential for forfeiture in effect converts the fee arrangement to a contingent fee, which ironically, the Code of Professional Responsibility prohibits in criminal cases.

Forfeiture of fees seriously cranks the balance wheel of justice in the Government's favor. It hurts defendants by discouraging experienced attorneys from wanting to work on such cases, and by diverting energy of counsel from defense of the charge to defense of the fee. While it would be easy to overdramatize the impact of the assault on defense counsel, it has succeeded already in driving out one of Miami's most highly regarded drug defense lawyers, "Diamond" Joel Hirschhorn. In announcing his retirement from drug cases, Hirschhorn cited both the stigma of drug defense and the threat to fees: "It's just not worth the aggravation to represent major drug dealers. The government comes after your fees. It's not worth it. . . . I'm doing tax fraud. And I like to do one murder case a year. It's OK to represent a murderer. Everyone approves of that."[9]

While the DOJ has issued guidelines to constrain prosecutorial discretion on this issue, its constitutional validity under the Sixth Amendment remains unresolved. Whatever the final resolution of the issue, the attempt to apply forfeiture to attorneys' fees is most noteworthy for what it reveals about the attitude of the forces of justice in the War on Drugs. In an article in the *American Criminal Law Review*, two Department of Justice prosecutors displayed a rather cavalier attitude toward the Sixth Amendment's guarantee of the right of assistance of counsel:

> If all of the defendant's ill-gotten gains are subject to forfeiture, then any fees paid from illegal sources are appropriately included. Under the Constitution, defendants are entitled to legal advice, not to high priced advice. Moreover, such advice cannot be paid for by ill-gotten gains.[10]

The superficial logic of the argument ignores more fundamental questions. How can the law justify isolating drug offenders for this special treatment? Does not the "ill-gotten gains" logic apply with equal force to tax evasion, bank robbery, or almost any other offense? If taken at face value, the Government's rationale would mean that no criminal defendant could retain private counsel without first proving that he has an untainted source of money for the fee. What, after all, is the point of such a rule except to weaken an accused's ability to defend himself? Forfeiture of defense fees is a simple stacking of the deck against the defense, effectively requiring that drug defendants be defended by young, inexperienced public defenders with excessive case loads. Even if such a law can claim technical justification, it debases the processes of justice, tipping the scales in favor of the Government. This ruthless mentality characterizes the entire federal criminal justice system vis-à-vis drug offenders.

The hostility reflected in the attempt to forfeit attorneys' fees in drug cases shows up in other assaults on the attorney-client relationship: the

Government's frequent use of subpoenas against defendants' lawyers to get information and records harmful to their clients. This scenario occurs in a variety of ways, all involving the Government's efforts to convert defense lawyers into witnesses against their own clients. The process frequently starts with a grand jury subpoena compelling defense counsel to disclose the amount, source, and method of payment of the fee received, information that the courts deem not protected by the confidentiality of the attorney-client relationship. Thus, attorneys must testify or turn over the subpoenaed records. A defendant's knowledge that his lawyer is giving potentially incriminating testimony to a grand jury certainly casts a pall over the attorney-client relationship and often requires the lawyer to disqualify himself as defense counsel. If new counsel is retained, however, the grand jury may begin the process all over again *ad infinitum*.

In some cases the Government has exercised its power to pit the defense lawyer even more directly against his client. For example, in a CCE case, the Government must prove that the defendant derived "substantial income" from a series of drug violations. By subpoenaing defense counsel to testify as to the amount of his retainer, the Government may attempt to prove the element of income. The lawyer becomes a witness against his own (former) client. One of the nation's leading criminal defense lawyers calls this "reprehensible" and "disastrous."

> When the lawyer is a witness called by the prosecution, there is actual prejudice to the client. Even a mere production of the attorney's records is counter to the defendant's interest. The records showing payment on account of the specific case might be circumstantial evidence tending to prove the substantial income; however, these records are not a full and fair description of the genesis of the financial relationship. In either circumstance, whether the attorney is called as a witness or whether the records are subpoenaed, the attorney becomes a witness for the prosecution or a witness for the defense. Because the attorney's testimony is directed to a material element of the offense, it seems that withdrawal is mandated. The next step is painfully obvious. There appears to be an unlimited discretion within the government to select the defendant's counsel.[11]

The Government drove yet another wedge between lawyer and client by passing the Deficit Reduction Act of 1984.[12] It applies cash reporting requirements similar to those of the Bank Secrecy Act to lawyers. Now attorneys' fees of more than $10,000 in cash must be reported to the IRS on Form 8300. It requires the lawyer to report the amount of the fee and the name, address, and tax number of the person who paid it. The very filing of the form puts the client, who may not (yet) have been charged with any crime, at risk of (further) investigation. For these reasons, the 1984 legislation is generally perceived by defense laywers as "one of the most threatening steps yet taken by Court or Congress against traditional attorney-client relationships."[13]

One last thing should be said about these various offensives in drug cases. When viewed in isolation, each measure may appear to be reasonable. But their cumulative impact is another matter. They appear calculated to render the defendant as helpless as possible to mount a successful defense. The prevailing attitude seems to be that drug defendants deserve the worst, and that indictment should be tantamount to a conviction, with trial a mere formality or foregone conclusion. This approach is a historic reversal of "the bedrock, axiomatic assumption" of our system that presumes an accused innocent until the Government proves him guilty beyond a reasonable doubt. The new, almost vindictive attitude pays little regard to tradition or principle in its single-minded dedication to "getting" drug violators. That the end has come to justify the means is a fair inference from the forfeiture of fees, the subpoenaing of defense lawyers to give evidence, Form 8300, and so on. Indeed, since the overall effect on drug supply is nonexistent, the *only* point of these mean-spirited methods is their symbolic value—we (the Government) reserve our nastiest procedures, our most potent legal weapons, for drug cases. Is this not a form of scapegoating?

In the past, those whose rights were savaged by legislative or prosecutorial excesses could turn to the federal courts for protection. But the War on Drugs steamroller has flattened judicial barriers as well. In case after case, the courts have whittled away or discarded vital procedural rights of the accused. This process has reached its apogee in drug cases. There the individual's right to be free from unlawful searches and seizures conflicts directly with the inherent invasiveness of drug enforcement techniques. Historically, drug enforcement has precipitated a tug-of-war between the search and seizure powers of the drug agents and the privacy rights of individuals, shaping the contours of contemporary Fourth Amendment jurisprudence in a decisive way.

In recent years, the courts have ruled overwhelmingly for the Government. For example, the 1982–1983 term of the Supreme Court was marked by "the overwhelming importance of the Fourth Amendment in drug cases."[14] In almost every one of these test cases, the Supreme Court puts its imprimatur on the enforcement techniques of the drug agencies, upholding use of the airport drug courier profile to stop, detain, and question citizens without probable cause; submitting a passenger's luggage for sniffing by drug detector dogs without probable cause; permitting warrantless searches of automobiles and packages inside them; authorizing surveillance of vehicles by attaching radiotracking devices or "beepers"; and conferring unrestricted powers of search of most ships on the high seas and inland waterways. That term, the Court also abandoned the relatively restrictive *Aguilar-Spinelli* test for obtaining a search warrant based on an undisclosed informant's tip for a more loosely structured "totality of the circumstances" test.[15]

In later terms, the Supreme Court adopted a "good-faith exception" to the exclusionary rule and authorized warrantless searches of "open fields" adjacent to a residence. The Court significantly enlarged the powers of the police to stop, question, detain, investigate, and search vehicles on the highways. In the realm of search and seizure and other areas of criminal procedure, the Government won almost every test case in the Supreme Court.

The question whether the Government deserved in law to win these cases misses the point: such issues are always debatable. But the relentless drive to pursue the drug supply generates the pressure to exercise these enforcement powers and sets up these test cases. Moreover, when the Supreme Court "balances" the collective interest in "effective" law enforcement against the individual's interest in being left alone, the right of privacy must almost always lose. The net result of the War on Drugs is gradually, but inexorably, to expand enforcement powers at the expense of personal freedom.

Several years ago, defense lawyers began to joke darkly of the "drug exception to the Fourth Amendment." Apparently, their perception had some basis in reality, for the Supreme Court was moved to say in the 1984 case of *United States* v. *Karo*, one of its few rulings in recent years against the Government, that "[t]hose suspected of drug offenses are no less entitled to that protection than those suspected of non-drug offenses."[16] Even so, Professor Silas Wasserstrom captured the essence of the defense perception in the title of his article, "The Incredible Shrinking Fourth Amendment."[17] Moreover, the Government's assault on justice goes beyond the Fourth Amendment cases; and changes wrought by Congress in the CCC Act of 1984, along with court rulings in other areas of criminal procedure, suggest an even bleaker quip: "the drug exception to the criminal law."

Congress certainly has manifested some sympathy for the idea of a drug exception to the law. Its legislative offensive exhibits uniquely punitive attitudes toward drug violators, and it has shown an eagerness to change or repeal almost any law that "interferes" with drug enforcement. In a strictly positivist sense, of course, the new laws create the legitimacy for the enforcement enterprise. But when law becomes purely instrumental, when it loses its mooring in precepts of fairness and fundamental rights, then the notion of the rule of law degenerates into whatever majoritarian oppression commands a consensus at a given time in history. Were not the Nuremberg Codes a parliamentary product? Does not South Africa obey its own laws in matters of race? The American constitutional tradition, by contrast, draws heavily upon the "self-evident" truth that citizens are endowed with "inalienable rights." The War on Drugs disrespects that natural law tradition. In doing so, it has set in motion forces or attitudes that society may someday regret. Already, anecdotal evidence suggests that the disrespectful attitude of the War on Drugs toward individual rights—the idea of a drug exception to the law—has seeped into the public consciousness:

3 FAKE POLICE OFFICERS RANSACK HOME

. . . At about 8 a.m. Friday, a 27-year old woman thought she noticed a car following her as she drove home on Bird Road after dropping her two children off at a junior high school on Coral Way.

"She decided to pull off the road to see if the car would pass her," [Detective] McDermott said.

The car pulled up behind her and three casually dressed men got out. They brandished handguns and identified themselves as police.

"They got into her car with her," McDermott said. "She said they flashed some kind of badge. It looked like a silver badge. She didn't get a good look at it."

The men drove the woman to her house, where they handcuffed her and her husband.

"They just said they were police and they were there to search the place and they proceeded to handcuff the couple and ransack the place," McDermott said. "Her husband asked them if they had a search warrant and they said, 'We don't need one, we work in the drug department.' "[18]

THE GROWTH OF BIG BROTHERISM

Perhaps the public at large has no interest in the malignant effects of drug enforcement on justice or the attack on the rights of criminal defendants. After all, drug enforcement ordinarily affects only an alien "them," those who inhabit the drug underworld, not "us," the mainstream of society. Its procedures seem to have no impact on daily life. But in fact the tentacles of drug enforcement have begun to reach into the lives of ordinary people, not just those involved in the drug business. Civilian casualties in the War on Drugs continue to mount as a result of increasing resort at all levels of government to an impressive array of Big-Brother-is-watching enforcement techniques.

Wiretapping

Because of the War on Drugs, the United States has become an increasingly monitored country. Wiretaps open all conversations on the line in question to scrutiny, although monitors are supposed to minimize interception of calls unrelated to the purpose of the investigation (after listening long enough to make that decision). In 1983, court-authorized wiretaps rose 60 percent, primarily in cases of suspected drug trafficking.[19] The Government sought and obtained 648 wiretaps. Not one of its applications was denied. In a nation of 230 million the number 648 seems small, and the Department of Justice has no doubt exercised restraint in selecting wiretap targets. On the other hand, the number undoubtedly would be much greater if the DEA and the FBI had the personnel necessary to staff the listening posts and otherwise administer the taps. The number also would be larger if Congress lowered the substantial statutory barriers under Title III of the

1968 Omnibus Crime Control Act to obtaining an intercept order from a court. The pressures of the War on Drugs will sooner or later crystallize that issue, as expanded wiretap powers are one of the most potent investigative tools in existence. With or without that legislative "reform," the widening of the War on Drugs will almost certainly produce more wiretaps next year and the year after that. In any event, the precise number of wiretaps should not be allowed to obscure the significance of the rapid growth in this form of invasion of privacy. Wiretaps implicate a fundamental principle, and the War on Drugs continues to erode it by encouraging the proliferation of electronic surveillance.

Stopping Cars on Public Highways

TROOPERS AIMING AT DRUG FLOW ON TURNPIKE

. . . For years, cars and trucks laden with marijuana, cocaine and pills have been travelling north on Florida's Turnpike taking the cargo to northern buyers, lawmen say.

. . .

Last month, troopers routinely patrolling the turnpike from Palm Beach to St. Lucie counties arrested 64 people on drug-related charges. A month earlier, troopers had arrested only 14 persons.

The seizures and the arrests are the result of a heightened awareness among the troopers who are now making a serious effort to arrest suspected smugglers.

"We want them to stop using the turnpike," said Sgt. Phil Moan of Troop K, which is responsible for patrolling the entire length of the turnpike.

. . .

Troopers, he said, became more suspicious of cars riding low in the back. They also started looking closely at cars with out-of-state tags if there w[as] no luggage or clothing visible. Frequently, Moan said, smugglers will use air fresheners and perfumes to mask the odor of the narcotics.

"They look harder and harder at every vehicle," Moan said.

DEA's Lloyd said that police agencies in other states are also making an effort to stop the ground transportation of narcotics.

In New Mexico, he said, a state police program has been operating for several months. One of the indicators officials in New Mexico watch for is Florida tags, he said.[20]

According to the article, the Florida Highway Patrol relied upon a drug courier profile that cautioned troopers to be suspicious of rental cars, "scrupulous obedience to traffic laws," and drivers wearing "lots of gold," or who do not "fit vehicle," and "ethnic groups associated with the drug trade."[21] The Florida Highway Patrol's reliance on the drug courier profile was interrupted by a court ruling in Palm Beach County that articulated the civil liberties impact of the challenged practice:

Circuit Judge Carl Harper blasted the profile as "so broad and indistinct as to ensnare the innocent as well as the guilty."

Harper ruled that the hypothetical description of drug smugglers used by troopers to combat drug trafficking violates constitutional protections against unreasonable searches and seizures.

"While we have a horrendous drug smuggling problem here in South Florida, the ends simply do not justify the unlawful means occasionally employed to combat the problem," Harper said.

The Judge said the profile gives troopers too much leeway in pulling over cars to check out hunches that the vehicles may be carrying drugs.

. . .

[Defense lawyer] Natale, hailing the ruling as a blow for the rights of the public, said "Judge Harper was confronted with the question of, do we let the Florida Highway Patrol decide who can proceed up and down our highways free of unreasonable searches and seizures, or do you decide to use the Constitution and follow the laws?"

Natale said patrol records showed a majority of the motorists arrested through the drug profile were black, suggesting the profile merely gave troopers an excuse to pull drivers over and search their vehicles.[22]

Another tactic that police sometimes use is the roadblock. Police set up a barrier, stop every vehicle at a given location, and check the driver's license and registration. While one officer checks the paperwork, another walks around the car with a trained drug detector dog:

Under the watchful eyes of government attorneys, nearly 1,500 vehicles stopped last month by the Florida Highway Patrol for safety inspections were also checked for hidden contraband by drug-sniffing police dogs.

One drug arrest was made. Lady Luck and Citizen Band radios were suggested as possible causes for the lack of more arrests.

Still, authorities said they were sufficiently pleased with the operation, staged at four roadblocks in North Florida, to expand it to other areas of the state as part of an intensified crackdown on drug trafficking.

"I don't know how, where or when [they will resume], but we want to send the message out that we will be aggressive in the War on Drugs and will use every available tool," said Lee Gilreath, a special agent who coordinated the Florida Department of Law Enforcement's role in the multi-agency operation.[23]

The law does not regard the dog's sniffing as the equivalent of a search on the theory that the odor of contraband is an exterior olfactory clue in the public domain. As a result of this theory, no right of privacy is invaded by the sniff, so the police do not need a search warrant or even probable cause to use the dog on a citizen. If the dog alerts, moreover, that fulfills the probable cause requirement, and the police may then search the driver or vehicle for drugs.

Monitoring of Students and School Personnel

The political climate supporting the War on Drugs has generated increasingly invasive monitoring of personal behavior. In one manifestation of the anti-drug pressure, drug detector dogs have been brought into the public schools to sniff out student lockers, followed by searches when the dog alerts. The procedure is no doubt motivated by the doctrine that the school official stands *in loco parentis* to the students, but the question arises whether students can claim the benefit of the Fourth Amendment's protection from unreasonable search and seizure. In one case involving the search of a New Jersey high school student's purse, the Supreme Court held that students do have privacy rights under the Fourth Amendment, and that searches may occur on reasonable grounds to believe that the student is violating the law or school rules.[24] In a case starting with a canine sniff, the Seventh Circuit Court of Appeals held that a nude body search of a school girl violated her constitutional rights. The Fifth Circuit upheld canine sniffs of student lockers and cars, however. And in any event, the real meaning of it all arises not from the court decisions but from the pressure felt by the schools to "do something."

The anti-drug drive shows up in yet more intrusive ways. A school system in Bergen County, New Jersey, voted to implement a more comprehensive method of detecting drug violations by compelling students to submit samples of their urine for testing in a drug laboratory. The ACLU filed suit challenging the program, and the court enjoined it as too broad. The Dade County (Miami) school system in 1985 considered, but did not adopt, a "voluntary" urine testing plan for teachers, counselors, and other school officials.

Once again, outcomes matter less than the efforts and the attitudes they reveal. The pressures underlying these plans, abortive or not, continue to mount and take other forms. "Tipster" programs are another manifestation of the felt necessity to respond to "the drug problem."

DRUGS, PAYOFFS AND THE AMERICAN HIGH SCHOOL

[W]ell-meaning civic leaders have asked local citizens to turn in their peers . . . town elders in Lewisville, Texas, (population 24,000) are offering a $100 reward to students who provide information about drug users or sellers at the local high school.

Though various American high schools have encouraged students to make anonymous tips on local drug pushers, only Lewisville's has been desperate enough to post "wanted" signs and offer bounty.

Last September, Lewisville High School's principal, C. Douglas Killough, solicited community leaders for commitments to pay for the drug-reward program.

. . .

Lewisville's business community responded enthusiastically to the proposed program. So many commitments were received, in fact, that the local PTSA ceased its solicitations. "It only took us a few days," recalled John Zepka, an executive committee member of the Lewisville group.

To date, the program's practical success has turned out to be less certain. An assistant principal at Lewisville High, Malcolm Dennis, told the Dallas Morning News last week that "you'd be astonished at how well the students are cooperating. Some have even turned in their best friends."

But of the 30 students turned in to school authorities, principal Killough himself told us, only half have actually been found in possession.[25]

Abusive Enforcement

Abusive enforcement, like beauty, is often in the eye of the beholder. One's view of the importance of an enforcement goal tends to color one's judgment about the legitimacy of the enforcement tool. But when the *Miami Herald*, one of the principal advocates of the War on Drugs, editorializes against "Drug War Overkill," the transgression must be gross.

Judge Jose Gonzalez admonished U.S. marshals for seizing a $3.5-million Martin County resort without first seeking a Federal-court hearing. Prosecutors asserted that the Manatee Resort had been purchased with drug profits, but the owner had not—and still hasn't—been charged with any crime. In voiding the seizure, Judge Gonzalez noted that "neither Congress nor the people intended that the Bill of Rights be a fatality in the War on Drugs."[26]

In a more sinister vein, the pressure to "get" the drug kingpins and their lawyers occasionally tempts drug agents to cross the boundaries of ethical law enforcement practices into the domain of entrapment or worse.

JUDGE CALLS AGENTS' TACTICS 'OUTRAGEOUS'

Citing "outrageous" misconduct by government agents, a U.S. magistrate Wednesday sternly recommended dismissal of a 13-count federal indictment against accused cocaine kingpin Harold Rosenthal.

U.S. Magistrate Peter Nimkoff accused undercover Drug Enforcement Administration agents from Atlanta of trying last October to trick defense attorney Alan Ross of Miami into making incriminating statements about an alleged jailbreak attempt by Rosenthal.

When Ross refused to take the DEA's bait, Nimkoff ruled, Atlanta prosecutors then used a deceptive affidavit to get a search warrant to read privileged attorney-client letters between Rosenthal and Ross.

DEA agents later told the court that a cellmate of Rosenthal's had told them that attorney Ross would furnish the money and cocaine for the escape. And so DEA agent Donald Carter, posing as a friend of Rosenthal's, went to Ross' office in Miami Oct. 25 to talk about the plot.

But every time Carter mentioned drugs and escape, Ross kept replying that he didn't want to know anything about it. Ross repeatedly told Carter that all he did for Rosenthal was represent him in court. And at his next meeting with Rosenthal, Ross blasted his client for sending Carter to him.

Though rebuffed by Ross, Carter and federal prosecutors in Atlanta didn't give up. According to the file, they swore out an artfully drafted affidavit, suggesting that Ross was involved in the escape plan and avoiding mention of Ross' refusals, in order to get the search warrant to intercept Rosenthal's mail.

It is as clear a misrepresentation of facts as ever there w[as]," Ross argued to Nimkoff in June. "Their zeal has blinded them to the parameters of decency."

Nimkoff ultimately agreed.

The prosecutors and agents "consistently and surreptitiously sought to breach the attorney-client privilege," he ruled Wednesday, calling the action "so outrageous" as to require dismissal.[27]

Perhaps the attempt to ensnare Ross should be disregarded as an aberrational case. On the other hand, some form of enticement of defendants is more or less built into the system of drug enforcement, varying only in its subtlety or blatancy. The institutionalization of "entrapment" (in lay terms) stems from the Government's dependence on informants to make cases. Informants are paid, in effect, to encourage or to "create" crime. In the most blatant cases, the incentive system includes payment contingent upon the making of an arrest, or worse, payment in proportion to the number of pounds or kilos or the value of property seized.

An example of this type of behavior involves a woman who "set up" at least 40 men in South Florida. Her tactics included seducing an intended defendant and establishing a sexual relationship. After a few weeks of gentle pressure, she would arrange a drug deal between her reluctant "boyfriend" and drug enforcement agents. The "boyfriend" would be busted, and the woman would get paid. Magistrate Peter Nimkoff recorded his disapproval of this technique by recommending dismissal of cocaine charges against a defendant victimized[28] by this technique.

Even without the temptations of greed, the Government's reliance on unpaid informants seeking leniency or dismissal of charges introduces a systematic incentive for distortion of truth. An amateur informant in this situation clearly has an axe to grind in implicating others, and it easily leads to shaded if not false testimony. The same pressure often results in targeting as a defendant someone who genuinely has no background in drug trafficking. Automaker John Z. DeLorean, acquitted of trafficking in cocaine, claimed that he was enticed into a drug deal by an informant who needed to make a big case in order to get himself off the hook. The jury believed him.

Getting oneself out of trouble by implicating others forms the very foundation of the system in some states. Florida plays a leading role in this regard. Under the state's trafficking law, which mandates long prison terms—15 years for 400 grams (less than one pound) of cocaine without probation or parole—the law provides only one escape valve. A defendant who provides "substantial assistance" to the state may receive the benefit of a prosecutor's recommendation for leniency, including probation.[29] In practice, this means making a controlled buy (or delivery) to one's associates or otherwise providing the state with evidence sufficient to make a case against them. In some districts in the state, prosecutors have adopted creative plans for "implementing" the statute, such as requiring a 3:1 ratio, i.e., a person arrested on a one-kilo charge must produce a three-kilo arrest in order to qualify for substantial assistance. Three one-kilo arrests might also qualify.

Whatever the details of the particular deal, the Florida system has put into the field a band of "informers" or amateur police agents who are more or less desperate to set up their friends or acquaintances in new drug deals in order to escape the wrath of the excessively punitive mandatory minimum sentence. While their activities do not (necessarily) constitute illegal entrapment, this system does exact a heavy price. First, many defendants simply do not have the contacts to avail themselves of the "mercy" offered by the law, typically because they played only a minor role as courier, go-between, or provider of a stash pad. Ironically, the higher-ups with good contacts or sources of supply can deal much more effectively, while their underlings must suffer sentences disproportionately severe to their level of culpability. Fifteen years for transporting a pound or kilo of cocaine robs the criminal justice system of balance and fairness when one considers that it exceeds the typical sentence for second degree murder.

Beyond the unfairness to the defendant with no one to set up, one can only speculate about the trickle-down effect of all the mistrust and deception generated by this small army of amateur informers. The informer system can certainly enhance the effectiveness of law enforcement; it also has overtones of the police state. Do we as a society want to create a climate of fear and betrayal, where people need to be wary of friends and business associates, to suspect the motives of others, to be on guard against the set-up, the body bug, and the wiretap? That's what the informer system promotes in its zeal to catch the "bad guys."

Keeping Tabs on the Citizenry by Computer

DRUG AGENTS KEEPING TABS ON LEADERS, STARS, CLERGY

The federal Drug Enforcement Administration is keeping computer files on more than 1.5 million persons, including U.S. congressmen, entertainers, clergymen, industry leaders and foreign dignitaries, according to DEA Administrator Francis M. Mullen Jr.

Many of the famous persons named in the computerized index system, known as NADDIS (Narcotics and Dangerous Drug Information System), are the subject of "unsubstantiated allegations of illegal activity," Mullen said.

. . .

Mullen's letter stated that "less than 5 percent [of the total 1.5 million persons whose names were added to the computer since 1974] . . . are under investigation as suspected narcotics traffickers by DEA."

The NADDIS computer system contains data from informants, suspects, surveillance and intelligence reports compiled by DEA and other agencies, Mullen said.[30]

The information in NADDIS is available to federal drug enforcement officals in other agencies (FBI, Customs, IRS). Probably state law enforcement officials can also gain access on request. Obviously, this method of oversight has troubling implications for one's personal interest in privacy and good reputation, especially for the 95 percent named who are not under investigation. A data bank of this kind becomes objectionable for other reasons: the quality of the data, controls on access and disclosure, and the consequences of being included. Does one become a target or suspect as a result of such a listing? And what about the sheer number of listings—at what point does the number grow too large for comfort? Again, the data bank by itself may not pose much of a threat, but the cumulative weight of the various programs and methods should give cause for concern.

Stigmatizing

"Public embarrassment" is the federal government's goal in publishing a list of names of people caught bringing small amounts of drugs into the United States—beginning tomorrow—says Dennis Murphy, a U.S. Customs spokesman in Washington.

But critics of the plan, including Charles Sims, staff counsel for the American Civil Liberties Union in New York, says the list amounts to "slander" of people who have not been found guilty of any crime.

The punish-by-publishing list, to be supplied to news organizations each Wednesday, will include only small-scale smugglers who were neither arrested nor prosecuted for their alleged crimes, said Harry Carnes, Miami customs district director.

The "drug blotter" will include the name of each alleged smuggler, address, occupation, age, type and quantity of drugs being smuggled, method of travel and point of origin, customs said in a prepared statement.

Carnes said persons whose cases are dropped from prosecution will automatically be put on the press list—with no option to request arrest as an alternative.

"One principal reason for trials in this country is to decide who is innocent and who is guilty," Sims said.

"When the police undertake to announce that people are guilty without a trial, then they are slandering people. . . . They will be damaging people's reputations."

Miami attorney Richard Sharpstein labeled the plan "disgusting." According to Sharpstein, people who are arrested on drug charges would have more legal rights than those who aren't arrested, but find themselves on the customs list.[31]

Extraditing United States Citizens for Trial Abroad

After years of American pressure on the government of Colombia to extradite its citizens to the United States to stand trial in drug cases, Colombia acceded. It also made a demand for reciprocity, which the United States honored in the case of John Tamboer:

> Tamboer, a compact, mustachioed man, said he was being sacrificed for political reasons. Tamboer, recently transferred to another Massachusetts jail, which officials asked not to be named, after his cell in the Plymouth House of Correction was set on fire, said in an interview that he is innocent. He said that a Colombian hit man was responsible for the prison fire and that he will be murdered if he is extradited.
>
> He cited death threats from drug mobsters that led the State Department to order some diplomats' families to leave Bogota in January, and he noted that a State Department report calls Colombian jail conditions "deplorable."
>
> "Here the U.S. government said Colombia is so dangerous that Americans must leave the country, but they are willing to have me, an American citizen, flushed down the toilet so they can follow through on this treaty." Tamboer said, "I have become a pawn in an international chess game."
>
> Because Tamboer faces Colombian charges, he has few of the usual constitutional rights in his extradition fight. For instance, prosecutors are allowed to submit hearsay evidence.
>
> Once in Colombia, he would be subject to that country's justice system, which essentially said he is guilty until proven innocent, says Tamboer's attorney, Richard Emerson.[32]

Obstructing Medical Practice

The overkill mentality characteristic of the War on Drugs extends even to the regulation of medical practice, preventing doctors from making authorized use of many controlled substances having valuable therapeutic applications. Because of a hostile attitude and fears of illicit diversion to the black market, a clear pattern of governmental denial of legitimate medicines to doctors has emerged over the years. Several recent examples illustrate the point. In 1984, the House considered H.R. 5290, a bill that would have made injectable heroin available under procedural safeguards to dying cancer patients suffering "severe, intense and intractable pain" as a "drug of last resort." The AMA, citing "security problems of hospitals" and other reasons, opposed the bill, as did the International Narcotics Enforcement Officers Association.[33] The House killed the bill.

A second example comes from an experiment in California where patients with extremely debilitating cases of rheumatoid arthritis smoked freebase cocaine. Many of the test subjects responded to the cocaine by exhibiting remarkable, pain-free agility. Press disclosure of the experiment resulted in embarrassment to the researchers, and it appears from the press report that the Government (DEA) swiftly brought pressure to kill off what apparently was an unauthorized experiment. The fact that cocaine may effectively alleviate the pain of rheumatoid arthritis is clearly less important to the law enforcement mind than that cocaine should be condemned as a dangerous drug and exiled for practical purposes (except surgery) from the United States pharmacopeia. Even its use as an anesthetic was attacked by the National Commission on Marihuana and Drug Abuse. Doctors since Freud have known that cocaine has a variety of potential applications, including use as an antidepressant. Its short course of action may well limit that usefulness. But the critical fact is that the law will not permit doctors to make that judgment case by case with their patients. Even worse, obstructionist legal regulations make clinical research designed to find therapeutic applications of the drug nearly impossible. The Government simply does not want to encourage *any* positive information about cocaine.

Addiction treatment is the third and perhaps paradigmatic example of the way the United States has displaced medical authority with legal force. In the years following passage of the Harrison Narcotics Act, the enforcement agencies succeeded in breaking the power of the medical profession over drug control by redefining drug abuse and addiction as predominantly the concern of law enforcement rather than medicine. As a result, federal agents succeeded in closing virtually every addiction maintenance clinic in the United States during the 1920s. They arrested approximately 25,000 doctors (3,000 of whom were imprisoned) for "unlawfully" prescribing morphine, cocaine, or other "narcotic" drugs to patients.[34] The Supreme Court put its imprimatur on this campaign by interpreting the Harrison Act's *permission* for a doctor to prescribe narcotics "in the course of his professional practice" to *prohibit* the maintenance of an addict.[35] Only an attempt to "cure" (wean) the addict was deemed medically legitimate. Accordingly, the Supreme Court rejected the doctor's best medical judgment and denounced a prescription for cocaine as an unlawful "gratification of a diseased appetite."[36] The Court thus appeased the enforcement agencies at the expense of doctors and their patients.

As a result of this transfer of power, the law enforcement bureaucracy succeeded in establishing supremacy over all drug control issues. Today, the power to classify or reclassify controlled subtances rests in the hands of law enforcement authorities—the Attorney General (not the Surgeon General). The Attorney General, in turn, has delegated that power to the Administrator of the DEA. In 1985, for example, reacting to a sudden, though small, spate of drug overdoses from MDMA ("ecstasy"), the Attorney General used his newly enlarged emergency powers to place MDMA on Schedule I ("no currently accepted medical use").[37] Many in the medical community thought the decision precipitous, as it completely blocked therapeutic applications of the drug, which they regarded as having a low or moderate potential for abuse. Of course, within a legalistic regulatory framework and a paramilitary political environment, medical views on the needs of patients carry little weight. Law enforcement concerns always trump medical concerns.

Militarizing Law Enforcement

By amending the Posse Comitatus Act in 1981 and authorizing the Navy to interdict smuggling vessels at sea, Congress inflicted the first major breach in the century-old wall of separation between civilian and military law enforcement roles. Of course, even that sacrifice of principle to expedience proved insufficient to fulfill the illusory quest to bring the illegal drug supply under "control." Accordingly, several members of Congress soon began seeking a wider military role. Some sought full and direct military participation in drug enforcement, while others sought merely to expand the military's back-up role. In 1985, Congress reached a "compromise" position:

> Congressional negotiators have agreed on a plan that allows the military to stop more drug traffickers headed for South Florida but does not give them the power to make civilian arrests.
>
> Rep. Charles Bennett of Florida had pressed for a stronger plan that would have given the military the authority to search, seize and arrest drug traffickers at sea.
>
> The Jacksonville Democrat settled for a compromise after his plan became a sticking point in negotiations.
>
> "The compromise isn't bad at all," Bennett said. "It strengthens our hand against drug smugglers, and that's what we were after."
>
> . . .
>
> The conferees agreed to spend $15 million for 500 new Coast Guard officers who will be stationed on naval ships in the prime drug trafficking routes in the Caribbean and off the Gulf Coast.
>
> The Navy ships will be available to stop vessels suspected of carrying drugs and the Coast Guard officers will be able to board and search the vessels and make arrests.
>
> The compromise allows the Navy to become more involved in drug interdiction while avoiding the legal ramifications of having the military make civilian arrests.
>
> Opponents of more naval involvement fear that military arrests would infringe civil liberties and end up in lengthy court cases.[38]

But what will happen next? Surely this latest enlargement of military "assistance" will not win the War on Drugs; and therefore it cannot placate the demands for still more intervention. On the contrary, the 1985 compromise represents only a transitional phase; its real significance lies in the momentum generated for further enlargements of the military's enforcement role. And the dynamics of the War on Drugs will support that escalation to the next level, and the next.

The historic dynamics of the American drug control movement always has been expansionary. As observed by the Supreme Court, "[T]he history of the narcotics legislation in this country 'reveals the determination of Congress to turn the screw of the criminal machinery—detection, prosecution and punishment—tighter and tighter.' "[39] Pretrial detention, longer or mandatory prison sentences, enhanced fines and property forfeitures, good faith exception to the exclusionary rule, roadblocks, drug detector dogs, compulsory urine samples, wiretaps, informants, undercover agents, extradition treaties, tax investigations, computers, currency controls—the list grows and grows. And still it is not enough. Always the Government needs more.

That, ultimately, is the truly insidious quality of the War on Drugs: the drug enforcement system can never have enough power, never enough resources, to win the war. In the futile quest to control the uncontrollable, the Government follows an imperative to expand. Legislative reforms, doubling of "troops," administrative directives, task forces, executive coordination—all of these have proven ineffective in controlling the drug supply and, short of a police state, always will. Yet the reflexive response of the system is always to do more, always to expand. "In one sense," said former Attorney General William French Smith, "to deal with this problem, we have to blanket the world."[40]

Blanketing the world, of course, begins at home. When one initiative and then the next fails to produce any discernible or lasting impact on the black market in drugs, the frustrated impetus for control carries the system to its next "logical" extension. And the internal logic of the War on Drugs, coupled with its insatiable appetite for resources and power in its futile pursuit, leads inevitably to repressive measures. The authoritarian logic of drug control was noted, although not endorsed, by the National Commission on Marihuana and Drug Abuse:

> Under certain conditions, perhaps, law enforcement alone might eliminate the illicit market in drugs. To achieve this, though, would require, at the least, multifold increases in manpower, a suspension of Fourth Amendment restraints on police searches, seizures and wire-taps, wide-scale pretrial detention, abolition of the exclusionary rule and border controls so extreme that they would substantially hinder foreign commerce.[41]

In a nutshell, the commission suggested, a successful drug enforcement program requires a police state.

In the United States, warnings about a police state sound a bit excessive, if not jejune, if one has in mind the nations of the Soviet bloc. Our contemporary reality is quite different. The gradual accretion of enforcement powers moves so slowly as to be invisible to the untrained eye. The rights of citizens recede by gradual erosion, by relentless nibbling rather than gobbling. Yet the danger to civil liberties is no less real, especially in the realm of criminal justice. Magistrate Peter Nimkoff dramatized that reality in his resignation from the court in protest of the continued erosion of the rights of those accused of crime. In an exit interview with the press, Nimkoff focused on the War on Drugs as the source of governmental abuses of power.

According to Nimkoff, many people have decided "that because drugs are such a horrible thing, we will bend the Constitution in drug cases," or "that there are two constitutions—one for criminal cases generally, and another for drug cases. . . . I think that's wrong. . . . It invites police officers to behave like criminals. And they do."

Among his specific areas of concern are

- Government sting operations in which it is considered "sound police practice to get people to do bad things in order that they can then be accused," Nimkoff said.
- Use of informants who pretend to be criminals during ongoing investigations and then testify about what they did. Nimkoff said that the use of civilian informants and assignments of police as undercover agents are "very, very dangerous" practices.

"Justice Brandeis said about 60 years ago that government is the omnipresent teacher, especially in a democracy," he said. "And that the police practices of our government teach moral lessons to our society. And I think it is wrong and dangerous for the police to make a norm of deception. . . . "

"It's a very dangerous practice for the police to begin to behave like criminals in order to catch criminals, and to encourage the commission of the offense instead of preventing its occurrence."

Nimkoff said he's also troubled by the Comprehensive Crime Control Act of 1984, which he said undercut the presumption of innocence and removed the traditional presumption that a defendant is entitled to bond before trial.

Although most criminal defendants are eventually found guilty, Nimkoff said, "I'm very reluctant to discard the presumption of human freedom or the presumption of innocence. . . . To discard them is to engage in classically authoritarian behaviors."[42]

Judge Nimkoff's resignation, however unusual, reflects a traditional concern. Even Justice Hugo Black, an advocate of aggressive enforcement against the drug trade, warned of its ready capacity for excess: "[T]he narcotics traffic can too easily cause threats to our basic liberties by making attractive the adoption of constitutionally forbidden short-cuts that might suppress and blot out more quickly the unpopular and dangerous conduct."[43] As the War on Drugs converts paramilitary rhetoric into social reality, the nation's tolerance for extremist ideas rises. Thus, the politics of the War on Drugs generates proposals that only a few years ago would have been rejected as unacceptably repressive or unconstitutional. Witness what happened with pretrial detention.

In this climate of repression, politicians advocate capital punishment for drug dealers, or isolation of them in Arctic gulags, or simply shooting drug planes out of the sky without charges or trial.[44] What will tomorrow's political agenda find tolerable? A bill in the Florida Senate proposed prohibiting the sale of "any magazine or other printed matter the dominant theme and purpose of which, taken as a whole, is to advocate, advise, encourage, or glorify the unlawful consumption, purchase, or usage of any controlled substance."[45] Despite the bill's analogy to valid anti-obscenity statutes, it almost certainly violates free speech and related rules on vagueness and overbreadth, under existing case law. (Even advocacy of the violent overthrow of the Government finds protection under the First Amendment, absent a "clear and present danger" of [intended] imminent violence.) But case law also demonstrates that wartime emergencies can justify curtailment of constitutional rights, and the analogy to the War on Drugs beckons. After a few more years of frustration with the War on Drugs, proposals of dubious legality may not seem so far fetched. Repeated expansions of governmental powers have already gained acceptance as reasonable measures to fight the War on Drugs. Given the nature of the beast, we can expect the demands to spiral upward toward infinity. There is no light at the end of the law enforcement tunnel.

Already, some of the authoritarian methods mentioned by the President's Commission in 1973 have become law. Why not go further and abolish the exclusionary rule altogether, authorizing drug agents to search for drugs, tap telephones, or seize financial records without warrant or probable cause? Why not adopt a bounty hunter system for suspected drug dealers and teach school children to report their parents for drug possession? Why not, in fact, bypass entirely the cumbersome criminal justice system, with its tedious set of impediments to investigation, prosecution, and conviction, and substitute a control system consisting of civil sanctions: fines, asset seizures, and forfeitures. Control over the offender's future conduct would come, as one professor has already suggested,[46] through a civil injunction forbidding the defendant from violating the drug laws in the future. Violation of the injunction would be proved in a civil contempt proceeding by a mere preponderance of the evidence, rather than by proof beyond a reasonable doubt. What a masterstroke: no need for grand jury indictment, right to counsel, or even trial by jury. After all, if the U.S. Code is the "enemy," it must be overcome. In the drug enforcement field, we clearly face the danger of losing the ability, in Madison's timeless warning, to "oblige [the Government] to control itself."

8

The Pathology of the War on Drugs: Corruption and Violence in the Black Market

While the drug enforcement system mutates to more virulent forms, it continues to prop up a gigantic black market whose illicit billions inflict terrible harms upon our society's domestic and foreign policy interests. Indeed, the destructiveness of the black market is so great that rational policy makers would find it essential to balance off the very different set of harms caused by the drugs themselves. The qualitative differences between the problems of drug abuse and the social pathologies of the black market would make such a "cost-benefit" analysis difficult. But it is impossible simply to ignore the cost side of the social ledger. Yet proponents of the War on Drugs have never acknowledged that enforcement itself causes serious problems. In seeking to confine sales of cocaine and other illicit drugs to the black market, enforcement necessarily promotes other forms of crime. Because the cocaine industry functions entirely outside the law, its operations require the commission of subsidiary crimes, such as murder and the bribery of public officials and bank officers. In its creation of a vast underground pool of income and wealth, it subverts many institutions and values in ways that could never be done openly and directly. And while there is much public hand wringing over these lamentable side effects of drug policy, public officials never accept responsibility for producing these effects. Since the War on Drugs has, by agreement, such an unquestionably legitimate mission, social and political conventions support denial of the obvious damage caused by drug enforcement.

TAX EVASION

Perhaps the most obvious mark of the black market comes from the money—vast, unknowable, and uncontrollable sums of money, the conspicuous and the hidden fruits of crime, that circulate in the underground economy. As early as 1978, Federal Reserve Banks in Florida had received a surplus of $3.5 billion in currency from financial institutions in Florida. This contrasted starkly with the need of Federal Reserve Banks everywhere else in the nation to supply currency to member banks, about $3.4 billion worth. By 1984, the Miami branch alone had accumulated a cash surplus of $7 billion, nearly all of it suspected to be untaxed drug money.

Although the scope of drug-related tax evasion can never be known, prevailing assumptions about the volume of black market sales generate proportionate estimates about the amount of untaxed income. Using DEA figures on the gross tonnage of cocaine imported into and consumed in the United States, the IRS estimated in 1976 that approximately 50 to 90 percent of the value of gross sales of cocaine constituted net income; that about 10 percent of that net income was actually reported to the IRS as income; and that unreported income from the cocaine traffic was $4.4 to $9.1 billion. The figure for 1980 computed in the same manner ranges from $13 to $23.4 billion.[1] The 1984 number would run about double that figure, again considering only the cocaine market. With total black market revenues running a guesstimated $100 billion a year, total unreported drug income may be $70 to $80 billion. This underground economy has created a world unto itself.

Tax evasion, an inevitable by-product of any black market, does not by itself constitute serious crime. Moreover, it would be a mistake to assume that the Government could ever capture the revenues now lost to the black market; under a regime of legalization, the crime tariff would disappear or fall sharply and prices would plummet to pharmaceutical levels, about 1/200 of current black market prices. This would obviously shrink the revenues subject to taxation. No, the real significance of the underground economy lies in its cumulative social and political impact. Billions of untaxed dollars take their toll in many ways—the inflationary effect (especially on South Florida real estate and the economies of Colombia, Peru, and Bolivia), the negative impact on the United States balance of payments ($3.5 billion to Colombia alone in 1979), the competitive disadvantage to the legitimate businessman who operates with taxed dollars, and the various seductions of easy money.

CORROSION OF THE WORK ETHIC

One of the hidden costs of the black market is its strong tendency to convert drug users into either thieves or drug dealers. Thievery tends to be a problem among chronic or compulsive users. The high price of cocaine puts it beyond the reach of the average budget, and "addiction" drives people to do things they ordinarily would not do. A cocaine hot line survey in 1984 revealed that about one-quarter of addicted cocaine users had stolen or embezzled on occasion in order to buy cocaine. Whatever the number of such persons, their existence clearly represents the law's self-inflicted wound. Legal cocaine, by doctor's prescription, at a few dollars a gram, costs too little to drive anyone into theft. No doctor can write such a prescription, however, in the ordinary course of medical practice.

Dealing provides another avenue of access to cocaine. In fact, low-level retail dealing often begins in this way. People who simply want to use cocaine on occasion find that its high price steers them into selling it in order to be able to pay for personal consumption. Other customs lead in the same direction—buy wholesale, sell at retail. Almost anyone using illegal drugs may at some time make a sale, if not for profit, then as a favor to a friend or family member. In addition, consumers often pool their resources in order to get a discount for volume; one person makes the buy and divides it with friends. Thus, the entry-level cocaine dealer often begins as a user who wants to sell enough cocaine to cover or defray the cost of his personal consumption.

> "I began by using half a gram a week," he said. "Soon it was one gram. Then I realized I could buy one-eighth of an ounce, which is three and a half grams. I would sell three grams and keep a half. Before long I went from one-eighth of an ounce to one-eighth of a kilo—that's 125 grams. It took 11 and a half months for this to happen." Eventually he quit his job to deal full time, said the suburban dealer, who is 33 years old.[2]

From there, many graduate to even higher levels of entrepreneurship, seduced by the fast-lane lifestyle of easy cash, late hours, material well-being, and independence: no nine-to-five, no clock punching, no union, no boss, no regimentation. Little or no start-up capital is necessary to climb the ladder of the distribution pyramid, as shown by the suburban dealer. In fact, it is easy, at least in Miami, to start at the kilo level, with supplies "fronted" by kilo distributors to promising sales personnel on credit.

While drugs are condemned by prevailing mores, dealers command quite a bit of social status in some circles, often attracting a large retinue of sycophants, hangers-on, and willing sexual partners (coke groupies). For young people in their twenties or thirties, dealing offers exceptional material rewards and a relatively low level of short-term risk, especially at the retail level, where one sells only to friends, or perhaps to friends of friends. It's a life of drugs, sex, and rock and roll. "Miami Vice" captures the sleek and chic of the disco/dealer culture, populated by slim, young, attractive, and well-dressed (if vacuous and sometimes treacherous) people who stay up late and party all night at glitzy pleasure palaces. It's quite a lure. As put by one young woman after her arrest, selling cocaine offered a "beautiful life." In fact, the attractions of selling cocaine have pulled in many middle-class entrepreneurs.

The cocaine trade in the [New York City] area has become so lucrative and widespread that many in the middle class with comfortable careers have been drawn into its illegal operations, according to law enforcement officials and people involved in the drug trade.

. . .

A small group of professional people—including lawyers, doctors, nurses, police officers and teachers, as well as construction workers, plumbers and electronics and telephone experts—have now become a part of the cocaine trade, the officials say. These professionals are drawn both by financial rewards and the need to support expensive drug use of their own.[3]

This easy-money climate subverts traditional notions of hard work and deferred gratification. As the Government puts it, "The work ethic of those citizens who are struggling to make an honest living can only be undermined by the general awareness of an ostentatious display of ill-gotten gains."[4] The psychological impact is speculative, but consider this story:

In Miami last year, a teenager named Randy Randall found $800,000 in cash. He gave away shopping bags full of money to friends and bought a few dream items—a Jaguar, an Eldorado—but almost $700,000 was still unspent when the police caught up with him. Randy told them he had come across this lode in the trunk of a car he'd stolen. Although charges of car theft were filed, the prosecution went nowhere; the owner of the car, a man who professed to be a grocer, said the money wasn't his and then skipped town. Randy's lawyer is now testing whether the theory of finders-keepers can be applied to unclaimed drug money. It is assumed that Randy's good luck was made possible by the business of illegal drugs, most likely the business of cocaine, which per ounce is worth more than thousand dollar bills.[5]

Randy's pot of gold is certainly exceptional. It nonetheless conveys a potent symbol of the power of drug trafficking. Signs of nouveau riche drug wealth abound in every community. They are especially visible in remote towns that find favor with drug traffickers as smuggling routes. Outposts of civilization as diverse as Everglades City, Florida, and Tocache, Peru, suddenly become boom towns in which formerly marginally employed laborers begin buying cars and trucks and generally displaying the accoutrements of success. Making it in the drug business, moreover, is not a remote fantasy like winning the lottery but a plausible, accessible option for the masses. Opportunity abounds because drug deals are everywhere. Despite the stigma that surrounds the drug business, its flash and panache have captured the imagination of the American public, at least at some subliminal level, as a cultural ideal. So the following satire suggests.

GOLD CHAIN FAD GIVES FLORIDA A TOUCH OF SLEAZE

Gold-chain fever owes its roots to South Florida drug smugglers, who were looking for a flamboyant way to distinguish themselves from honest, hard-working citizens. Believe me, the world was a simpler place when only coke dealers wore gold.

By the late 1970s, the fashion had spread to young lawyers, who thought that sporting gold was a sure way to impress doper clients.

The next to succumb were undercover cops, who had to drape themselves in chains in order to blend in with all the smugglers and lawyers.

Pretty soon, every geek, hustler and two-bit scam artist in South Florida was wearing gold. It became the definite badge of sleaze, the pinky ring of the 1980s.[6]

In short, the work ethic is getting serious competition from the get rich quick promises of the drug trade. For the economically deprived underclasses confronting minimal opportunities for upward social mobility through traditional channels, jobs in the drug business must seem especially desirable. Thus, one of the trade-offs for the prohibition of cocaine is the creation of disincentives to adhere to the traditional ethic of work and school. The black market sings a siren song of opportunities for riches in the drug underworld, producing a society where tens of thousands of its citizens can prosper while thumbing their noses at schooling and honest work. Prohibition thus exacts its hidden toll on the social welfare.

CORRUPTION OF PUBLIC OFFICIALS

Just as the easy money climate of the black market lures many consumers into sales, so the successful functioning of the black market requires the corrupt services of law enforcement officers of all types: local police; DEA, FBI, and Customs agents; Coast Guard officers; judges; prosecutors, and so on. After all, in economic theory, these officials possess "a highly marketable service—the sale of nonenforcement of the law."[7] Nonenforcement occurs in many ways. The activities of a pair of Customs agents illustrate a common pattern of "overlooking" enforcement. In exchange for money and Caribbean trips, two customs officers at Miami International Airport were allowing drug couriers to carry cocaine through their posts. The average fee was $3,500 a kilo.

More proactive forms of agent-dealer relationship center on the supply of information relating to wiretaps, search warrant applications, planned arrests, names of informants, surveillance operations, and related sensitive information. Such information helps smugglers or distributors protect their operations and themselves from arrest. For example, a DEA agent gave information to a Miami attorney that his client was going to be indicted. The client then "disappeared" (although she was later captured).[8] In another case, the identity of an informant was apparently supplied to a dealer; the informant's body was later found, along with three others, in a burning car. Trussed hand and foot, the victims had been beaten with baseball bats and stabbed. One had been shot. In the home of the chief murder suspect were found confidential DEA surveillance reports.[9]

The destruction of evidence or damaging information might also be the object of a corrupt agreement. Twelve thousand dollars was offered to a Customs agent for each person he would erase from Customs' computerized suspect list.[10]

Bribery often consists of taking money at the time of or after the arrest. The easiest and most risk-free method of opportunistic bribery is achieved by the on-the-scene release, where the suspect offers the officer money or drugs to let him go without arrest. This type of bribe is very difficult to detect since there is no relationship or regular interaction between the parties involved. As a result, the bribe easily escapes detection unless the officer offered the bribe reports it (in which case it is no longer corruption).

Another form of more regularized bribery occurs when a drug agent protects a dealer from arrest by conferring *de facto* immunity, i.e., by claiming that person as his confidential informant. Some officers charge for providing this "protection" by taking periodic payments or a percentage of sales and revenues. At the level of street sales, dealers commonly make payoffs to police to be free to operate. One author reported that New York City street dealers in heroin paid up to 40 percent of gross sales in bribes to avoid arrest.[11]

Yet another type of payoff from dealers to cops or drug agents buys favorable testimony at a hearing or trial. The Knapp Commission found that it "was not uncommon for defense attorneys in narcotics cases to pay policemen for such favors as lying under oath."[12] Less blatantly, a police report or affidavit about an arrest can be written with sufficient ambiguity to leave the door open for the officer to shade his testimony so that a motion to suppress "illegally" seized evidence will succeed.

Conversely, dealers who do not pay for protection or who fall out of favor may be ensnared by the so-called dropsy gambit. A policeman covering up an illegal search of a dealer's body or car will claim that the defendant threw away some drugs as he was approached. This pattern of perjured testimony became so commonplace that the District Attorney of New York County joined with defense counsel in arguing for a shift in the burden of proof to the prosecution on motions to suppress evidence because "it is very difficult in many cases to distinguish between fact and fiction."[13]

In the late 1960s, the Knapp Commission exposed pervasive corruption in the narcotics section of the New York City Police Department that went beyond the nonenforcement of the law. The commission demonstrated that narcotics agents frequently extorted money from dealers, illegally retained seized drugs or money, accepted bribes from dealers, and gave false testimony, especially on pretrial motions to suppress unlawfully seized evidence. A high level of corruption also prevailed in the New York office of the Federal Bureau of Narcotics and Dangerous Drugs, where in the late 1960s "almost every agent . . . was fired, forced to resign, or transferred."[14] "Collusion between BNDD agents and drug traffickers was "deeply ingrained."[15] Most of the heroin seized in the notorious "French Connection" case "disappeared" from the N.Y.P.D. property room. These corrupt phenomena became the subjects of popular entertainment in books and films *Serpico* and *Prince of the City*.

Such pervasive corruption does not present an aberration of the enforcement system; it is not something that better management can guard against. Rather, it is inherent in the drug enforcement system. Within that system, an unholy alliance between drug dealers and drug agents becomes extremely valuable to both parties. For all these reasons, past exposés have not resulted in a "clean-up." On the contrary, media accounts of drug-related corruption of law enforcement officers have become even more commonplace than in the past. While the full extent of corruption necessarily remains hidden from view, the known corruption runs wide and deep. Some examples quoted without comment should suffice to make the point.

Almost the entire homicide squad (nine detectives) of the Metro Dade Police Department was indicted on federal charges:

> [T]he suspected police are accused of selling out to a dope pusher. The 39-page indictment accuses them of racketeering, bribery, extortion and dealing in narcotics and dangerous drugs. It says they used their official positions to solicit money, gifts and cocaine from known criminals which influenced them to assist in the commission of crimes, prevent arrest of the criminals and get charges against them dropped. They are accused of robbing the dead—murder victims among whose belongings cash, marijuana and cocaine were found—and of arresting and robbing five rivals of [cocaine dealer] Escandar. They are accused, too, of bribing other police to help them steal money and drugs officially seized as evidence from suspects under investigation and to sell the stolen contraband.[16]

Four detectives were convicted at trial.

> U.S. AGENT PLEADS GUILTY TO HELPING DRUG SMUGGLERS
>
> A veteran federal drug agent has pleaded guilty to obstruction of justice and receiving unlawful compensation from a smuggler who was importing planeloads of cocaine, marijuana and methaqualone from the Bahamas to Palm Beach County. Jeffrey I. Scharlatt, a former group supervisor in the Miami office of the U.S. Drug Enforcement Administration, quietly made the plea this week before U.S. District Judge Norman Roettger. The plea, made public Friday, ended an unprecedented corruption case in which as much as $385,000 may have changed hands. It is the

story of a partnership of greed between one of the DEA's brightest agents and one of its most productive confidential informants.[17]

30-YEAR CUSTOMS AGENT CONVICTED IN DRUG CASE[18]

. . .

EX-GUARDSMAN: I STOLE, SOLD DRUG-FIGHT PLANS

Derrick Warren James bowed his head Wednesday and told a Miami federal judge he was ashamed of stealing and selling secret U.S. drug-fighting plans. Then the former Coast Guard reserve lieutenant pleaded guilty to nine felonies.[19]

EX-PROSECUTOR IS INDICTED FOR BRIBERY IN DRUG PROBE

A federal grand jury indicted a former federal prosecutor Tuesday on charges that he tried to sell for $200,000 sensitive information about a U.S. drug investigation to the subjects of the probe.[20]

METRO POLICE 'LOST' DRUGS STORED IN PROPERTY ROOM

[An] incident in the spring of 1981 helped trigger an investigation that revealed the estimated loss of nearly $1 million worth of Quaaludes, cocaine, marijuana and jewelry from Metro's property and evidence bureau.

Handled quietly for months, a series of internal investigations into separate disappearances have culminated in early retirements, suspensions or transfers of property room employees.[21]

SUPREME COURT REMOVES JUDGE LEON FROM BENCH

Thirteenth Judicial Circuit Judge Richard E. Leon was removed from the bench by the Supreme Court of Florida October 20 following review of Judicial Qualifications Commission findings that found him unfit to hold the office.

In the much publicized case, the commission found Leon guilty of improper ex parte conversations with Circuit Judge Arden Mays Merckle in which Leon sought to improperly secure an alteration of a sentence in a [cocaine] case, State v. Alisa Dean Avery.[22]

3 KEY WEST POLICEMEN, FORMER COUNTY ATTORNEY NABBED ON DRUG CHARGES

Seventy-six FBI agents spread throughout this island city shortly after dawn Friday and arrested three top-ranking city policemen, a prominent attorney and others at their homes on racketeering and drug charges.

The surprise arrests of 22 suspects came on the heels of two lengthy indictments handed up by a federal grand jury in Miami that charged the Key West Police Department was "used as a racketeering enterprise" between June 1978 and June 1984.[23]

CORRUPTION RUNNETH OVER
Tough prosecutors, drug trade and informants
mean record number of cases

From the pudgy, balding Northeast Florida sheriff indicted a week ago on charges of stealing marijuana to the Key West public defender accused days before of grand theft, Florida's elected officials are facing corruption charges in record numbers. More aggressive prosecution, the insidious influence of the drug trade and the public's willingness to tell on them have produced a wave of cases that has forced the suspension of 18 county commissioners, sheriffs, judges and other elected officials since the start of 1983.[24]

DRUG MONEY LURES GEORGIA POLICE

Arrests of lawmen for drug smuggling in rural Georgia have become so numerous that investigators are beginning to compare conditions here to Prohibition, when police more often than not were on the payroll of the bootleggers. "It's shades of the 1920s all over again," one federal investigator said as he recounted arrests within the past two weeks of a sheriff, a police chief, a judge, a former Georgia Bureau of Investigation agent, two former sheriffs and two former deputies. The charges involve present and former officials in rural Henry County, about 20 miles south of Atlanta, and in heavily wooded Appling County, once a major hangout for South Georgia moonshiners. Most are charged with trying to smuggle or provide protection for planeloads of marijuana[,] methaqualone and cocaine from South America and the Bahamas. Besides shaking residents of these rural counties to their roots, the arrests have fanned long-held fears that the vast amounts of money to be made from marijuana and cocaine are becoming too tempting for the generally low-paid lawmen who once watched airstrips in the Georgia backwoods in hopes of breaking a big dope ring.

"When you talk about the vast amounts of money involved in drug smuggling, that's something you always have to be concerned about," said Roger Boles, director of the Criminal Investigations Division of the Georgia Bureau of Investigation. Indeed, in the past two years, a Georgia public official has been arrested every 19 days, on the average, for drug-related activities.[25]

Corruption, of course, arises from many sources other than drugs, but the black market in drugs provides a uniquely fertile field for corruption. The special danger of corruption from drug trafficking arises from three facts. First, drug trafficking generates more money than any other type of crime. For this reason, since the 1970s "narcotics trafficking has replaced gambling as the major illegal activity associated with official corruption."[26] Similarly, the FBI reports that "about one-quarter of current traditional organized crime investigations of public corruption involve drug trafficking."[27] Within that category of drug-based corruption, cocaine trafficking probably comprises the principal source because of its dominant share of black market revenues. Historically, it was Prohibition (of alcohol) that did "more than anything else in American history to corrupt the police and to destroy respect for the law."[28] The contemporary equivalent is the prohibition of cocaine and other drugs.

A second and closely related reason why the black market in drugs poses special dangers of corruption arises from the sheer number of opportunities presented by one of the nation's largest industries. There is so much importing, distributing, and sales activity, and so much law enforcement activity, that opportunities for corruption abound. Finally, the temptation to succumb to bribery exerts extra pull because of the moral ambiguity of drug crime. Many people regard drug crimes as victimless crimes, or matters of individual taste, judgment, and freedom. Others see illegal drugs as relatively harmless, or "no worse" than legal drugs. Clearly, the prohibitions against marijuana and cocaine cannot command the moral force of traditional crimes against the person or property—murder, rape, robbery, arson, burglary, and so on. The shakiness of the social consensus for drug enforcement makes it particularly easy for cops and other officials to rationalize a corrupt arrangement with drug entrepreneurs. After all, drugs are what the people want.

This triple-threat combination of moral ambiguity, frequent opportunity, and extraordinary payoffs strongly suggests that the corruption so far exposed constitutes only the tip of a very large iceberg. No one knows for sure, of course, but the illegal drug industry, propped up by the enforcement apparatus, presents very strong cause for concern about the integrity of Government. Concern, moreover, extends to levels of authority much higher than street cops or agents in the field, as exemplified by the federal prosecutor who pleaded guilty in 1985 to theft of a kilo of cocaine, a kilo of heroin, and $41,800 in cash from the evidence safe of the United States Attorney's office in Manhattan. As put by an anonymous State Attorney in Dade County:

> We're drawing the battle line at trying to maintain the integrity of our institutions. If we can maintain integrity in politics and police and other institutions—some of our large financial institutions—we'll be ahead of the game. I would be ecstatic if we could do that, because there is so much money.[29]

But former U.S. Attorney General Smith saw no cause for optimism: "The dollar amounts are so great that bribery threatens the very foundation of the law and law enforcement."[30] Of course, he did not ask whether the benefits of drug enforcement could justify such a weighty risk.

VIOLENCE

Violent crime is yet another way in which the drug enforcement system harms society. We have seen how legal prohibition has the purpose and effect of maintaining high prices. By "taxing" the cocaine industry and funding the black market, drug enforcement creates extraordinary incentives for the systematic commission of violent crimes. Lacking recourse to the law, the drug industry must protect or "police" itself by private self-help methods, in accordance with its own code of ethics.

The Colombian "Code" regards kidnapping and murder as legitimate enforcement tools for punishing those who commit betrayals—ripping off cash or drugs entrusted to them or providing information to rival gangs or to the authorities. When intramurally contained within the cocaine industry, such retaliations only occasionally (and accidentally) spill over into the civilian sector. But the drug killers have shown a ready willingness to go outside the business, to go after judges, prosecutors, witnesses, and even their relatives. For example, the press reported that the FBI received informant tips of a plot to kidnap and ransom a federal judge in exchange for the freedom of Roberto Suarez, Jr. (before his acquittal on cocaine smuggling charges).[31] In April, 1984, three men armed with a submachine gun executed the 48-year-old mother of a witness on the eve of his scheduled appearance to testify in federal court against two major cocaine importers.[32] If the readiness to kill as a warning to others were not scary enough, Colombians display an especially cold-blooded attitude toward the extermination of groups of victims. The Code embraces a notion of blood feud and permits the families of traitors to be put to death. Thus, the wives or female companions of those marked for execution have several times been killed in groups of two or three. In at least one instance, an entire family was wiped out—man, woman, housekeeper, and a one-year-old infant.

Execution-style homicide of those who transgress against an importing or distributing organization has become commonplace.

> You can just about rule out all other motives when you arrive at a homicide scene in a remote area of Dade County such as an open field or canal. The victim is a Latin male, well dressed, a large sum of money in his pocket, still wearing expensive jewelry, hands and feet bound[,] and shot in the back of the head execution style.[33]

This scenario recurs with great frequency. In 1980, the Metropolitan (Miami) Dade County Public Safety Department investigated 303 homicides and attributed 24 percent of those cases (72) in which the motive could be attributed to drugs.[34] Similarly, the City of Miami Police Department investigated 244 homicides and determined 15 percent (36) of the cases to be drug-related.[35] In total, about 108 people were killed in Dade County as a by-product of the black market in drugs; almost all the killings involved cocaine, where the monetary stakes are so much higher than for other drugs. (In 1980, a pound of commercial grade marijuana cost about $400, while a pound of cocaine cost about $30,000. Moreover, the near doubling of the Dade County homicide rate in the 1978 to 1980 period coincided with an approximate doubling of the volume of the cocaine traffic to the United States, while marijuana imports were approximately level.)

Drug homicide should not be regarded simply as a Miami phenomenon. A study of homicides by the New York City Police Department produced comparable results: about one-fourth (393 of 1,632) of homicides stemmed from the drug business. Like the Miami killings, the label "drug-related" encompassed a variety of scenarios, from executions as punishment to more conventional motives of robbery of a dealer's drugs or cash. " 'The use of drugs has become more extensive and pervasive, and when you have people selling drugs, you have guns, rivalries, rip-offs and, inevitably, violence,' said James T. Sullivan, the chief of detectives."[36]

The Colombian-style killings instill by far the greatest public fear because of their audaciousness and viciousness. First, the killings are cold-blooded, gun-to-the-head executions, sometimes committed while the victim is sleeping, sometimes after prolonged infliction of torture. Second, because the killings frequently occur within a closed society of foreign nationals, some of whom are illegal aliens, they almost defy solution. Often the victim cannot even be identified by investigators. Police call these murders who-done-it/who-is-it? As a result, the clearance rate for murder, traditionally the most solvable of all crimes, has fallen precipitously wherever drug killings form a noticeable portion of the total.

Third, the shootings often occur in public places, thereby endangering innocent persons. The term "cocaine cowboys" was coined by the press to capture the wild character of some of their public shoot-outs, such as one in a suburban shopping mall. In another daytime episode, two drivers raced along the Florida Turnpike, exchanging semi-automatic weapons fire at each other. In April, 1983, three or four cars pursued Thomas Adams on I–95 in Miami. Seven shots hit his truck, one striking his head and killing him.[37] Sometimes an innocent bystander becomes a casualty, as when a 25-year-old woman was accidentally shot to death "in the gunfire of a drug deal gone bad."[38] Whether or not the public actually gets hurt, a daylight execution on a public road understandably undermines one's sense of security.

Killings such as these are frequently invoked to justify ever more repressive measures against the cocaine trade. But that is very bad advice, based on the illusion that the law enforcement pressure adds to public control of the black market. The more sensible question asks whether stricter enforcement might *promote* such violence. Of course, this question does not get asked by Government officials precisely because the War on Drugs would not be viable without denial that drug enforcement in some meaningful sense "causes" these crimes. In reality, they constitute a necessary by-product of or adjunct to the black market in cocaine.

In much the same way that the traditional Mafia uses professional contract killers to settle its disputes, cocaine traffickers also require private methods of security, discipline, and punishment. Recourse to the courts or other agencies for the settlement of disputes in the cocaine trade is obviously out of the question. Killing is thus predictable, almost routine. The brutality and heinousness of the killings might be regarded as exceptional, but not the killings themselves. For these reasons, even though the number of drug-related killings in Miami declined significantly in 1982 and 1983 from the peak reached in 1980 and 1981, violence remains intrinsic to the black market. Indeed, in 1984 Dade County regained its former title as murder capital of the United States. Police again attributed many of the killings to the drug business.

While the Chamber of Commerce and other civic groups fret about the bad public image and the impact on tourism, they remain blind to the contribution to the high murder rate made by the War on Drugs. Men would not torture and kill to protect their operations if cocaine sold at its legal price of less than $2 per unadulterated gram. The crime tariff is what makes cocaine so inordinately profitable. Because it is so valuable, people are willing to kill and risk being killed for it. Murder is simply part of the business. Not all the enforcement in the world can change that reality.

DISRESPECT FOR THE LAW

The obvious failure of the War on Drugs to control the cocaine industry tends to bring the criminal justice system into disrepute. It is not simply that the black market in cocaine is large and growing but that it has expanded so dramatically in the face of a doubled budget, stricter laws, and a greatly intensified enforcement effort in which the United States has literally sent in the Marines.

The burgeoning black market in cocaine proves the ability of traffickers to maneuver through the Customs and NNBIS nets and around the rest of the enforcement system. One year after the inception of the Task Force on Crime in South Florida, record drug seizures and concomitant arrests coincided with greater availability of cocaine at lower prices and higher purity. Cocaine seizures nearly tripled, from 4,353 pounds in 1981 to 12,535 pounds in 1982; yet the average price of cocaine declined and average street purity rose. Eighteen months after the Task Force began its work, a glut of cocaine supplies in South America caused wholesale prices of kilos in Miami to plummet to less than half of what they were in 1981. Thirty months afterward, prices had risen somewhat, but supplies still set new records. In fact, in fiscal year 1985, federal authorities in the Florida region alone confiscated 50,360 pounds of cocaine, double what had been seized in the whole United States the previous year. Still, market prices held stable. The black market mocks the War on Drugs.

The gap between the rhetoric and the reality of the war on cocaine justifiably erodes confidence in the criminal justice system. The system has been made to look very foolish indeed—more drugs than ever accompanied by rampant corruption, shoot-outs on the public streets, and murders with victims the police cannot even identify. At the same time, ordinary street crime as measured by the FBI index—murder, rape, robbery, burglary, assault, larceny, auto theft—reached historic levels during the 1980s. The massive mobilization in the War on Drugs has not produced an iota of gain in terms of public safety and well-being. Fear of violent crime has soared, along with the rate of victimization. To the extent that the public inevitably becomes aware of the incompetence and waste of the War on Drugs (and in state enforcement, with one-half million marijuana arrests per year), the system must lose credibility. The fatuous pretense that "we've begun to win the War on Drugs,"[39] according to Associate Attorney General Dr. Lowell Jensen, cannot long survive.

9

The International Pathology of the War on Drugs: Corruption, Instability, and Narco-Terrorism

The violence, corruption, and other black market pathologies spawned by the cocaine industry within the United States take a particularly dangerous and intractable form overseas. In country after country throughout the Caribbean and the Americas, the drug trade has gone beyond corrupting individual governmental officials to enlisting entire governments in the drug enterprise, as in Bolivia and the Bahamas. In other countries, such as Peru and Colombia, the War on Drugs has seriously undermined the power and stability of the central governments, delivering effective operational control of large regions of the country to drug traffickers or "narco-terrorist" alliances of drug traffickers and guerrilla armies.

In a related development, the War on Drugs has provided a rich source of finance for hostile governments in Nicaragua and Cuba to fund the export of violent revolution to other nations in the hemisphere through a drugs-for-arms cycle of trade. In perhaps the keenest irony of the War on Drugs, the staunchly anti-Communist Reagan Administration has unwittingly strengthened the forces of revolution and terrorism throughout the Western Hemisphere; by exporting the deleterious side effects of the War on Drugs to countries that service our black market, it has increased their vulnerability to subversion or violent overthrow.

Just as the War on Drugs has pressed severely on our values, laws, and traditions, so has it weakened even more the fragile institutions of friendly Third World nations—increasing hyper-inflation, the opportunities for corruption, the leverage of the terrorists, and the weakness of the central governments. In short, American drug enforcement has been profoundly destabilizing to our allies.

CORRUPTION AND NARCO-DESTABILIZATION

In outlining the futile and destructive efforts to police the drug supply at its source, Chapter Four has already presented much of the drug enforcement story in Bolivia and Peru. That story has three closely related themes: pervasive drug-based opportunities for corruption overlaid on previously corrupt police, judicial, and military institutions; economic crisis accompanied by growing dependence on the drug trade; and worsening political instability. Indeed, Bolivia has only the most tenuous grip on governance of the nation, and Peru has lost *de facto* control over large regions of the country, at least temporarily. But there is more. In 1980, Bolivia established a new paradigm of corruption: an entire nation captured by black marketeers.

On July 17, 1980, a democratically elected civilian government was deposed by a coup d'etat that later came to be called the "cocaine coup." After the coup, the military government of General Garcia Meza formed a syndicate with producers of cocaine in order to share in the profits of the business. It was the first known instance in which an entire government became a trafficking organization. Lieutenant Colonel Arce Gomez became, in Mike Wallace's descriptive phrase on a "Sixty Minutes" broadcast, the "Minister of Cocaine."

In the months before the coup, Gomez had used his position as head of Army Intelligence to set up paramilitary squads that used bombings and killings to destabilize the democratically elected regime of Lidia Gueiler. After the coup, Arce Gomez received a reward for his work—appointment as Minister of Interior. From that post, he organized his 1,000 *paramilitares* into the Special Security Services (SES), which he used to shake down cocaine traffickers for millions of dollars in protection payments. Further details come from this journalistic account:

> U.S. Drug Enforcement Agency officials in La Paz have said Arce Gomez charged Bolivia's top five traffickers $75,000 every two weeks in return for freedom to export cocaine.
>
> Colombians and small-time traffickers who didn't pay ran the risk of losing their cocaine and cash to Arce Gomez's heavily armed enforcers.
>
> In October 1980, Customs Maj. Jose Abraham Baptista seized $6 million from a Colombian plane that landed in Santa Cruz on a cocaine run. Baptista made the mistake of going directly to President Garcia Meza, who pocketed $4 million and ordered that Arce Gomez receive $2 million.
>
> Shortly thereafter, reportedly on the orders of Arce Gomez, Baptista was machine-gunned to death as he walked out of a pizzeria in Santa Cruz.
>
> U.S. court documents charge that, independent of the drug shakedowns, Arce Gomez built up his own cocaine trafficking empire. In a matter of months, Bolivia's interior minister became a millionaire in a country where the annual per capita income is $497.

He had a fleet of 11 airplanes, a mansion in Santa Cruz, a hacienda with a private lighted airstrip in the Beni and another mansion in La Paz. He kept his mistresses in La Paz's best hotel, the Plaza.

One of Arce Gomez's planes crashed in 1980, and, according to a Bolivian air force official who investigated, the plane was loaded with cocaine, Israeli submachine guns and large amounts of U.S. currency.[1]

In 1981, Garcia Meza himself was ostensibly deposed in a palace coup. Both he and Arce Gomez fled to Argentina, where they received asylum. Bolivian authorities later indicted Gomez for nine murders. A request for Gomez's extradition to the United States for trial on cocaine trafficking charges was pending at the end of 1985. Despite the ouster of Garcia Meza and Gomez, real power remained concentrated in a group of cocaine-trafficking, right-wing military allies of Garcia Meza, known as the Black Eagles. The Black Eagles maintained their power through the Gomez-recruited private army of paramilitary squads led or trained by German and Austrian neo-Nazis, many of them recruited by former Nazi Gestapo chief Klaus Altmann, the "Butcher of Lyon." Italian terrorist Luigi Pagliai had also worked for Gomez.

When the popularly elected civilian government of Hernan Siles Zuazo acceded to power in 1982, he bowed to United States diplomatic pressures and pledged to crack down on the cocaine trade with a "war to the death." Starting by purging the corrupt Narcotics Control Board and firing about 250 customs officials, he later committed his government to crop substitution and the destruction of illegal coca plants. Very little enforcement of consequence actually took place, however, although a number of semi-abortive raids occurred.

The critical factor enfeebling Bolivia's enforcement campaign is the rival power of the cocaine trafficking empire in Bolivia. The government simply does not control the countryside beyond La Paz, where powerful cocaine traffickers deploy their own security forces. Interior Minister Mario Roncal estimated that some 6,000 *paramilitares* protect cocaine traffickers from the reach of the law. The government's lack of power also arises from the combined effects of geographical remoteness and popular support, typified by the case of Roberto Suarez. Suarez, who allegedly financed the 1980 cocaine coup, has in effect created his own "state" in the Beni region:

BOLIVIA'S COCAINE "GODFATHER" UNTOUCHED BY CRACKDOWN

LA PAZ, Bolivia—Roberto Suarez Gomez is the flamboyant godfather of this country's booming cocaine traffic.

The 52-year-old Suarez likes to surround himself with lovely women, enjoy the good life and spend his free time financing goodwill projects in his hometown of Santa Ana de Yacuma, where he is referred to affectionately as Papito—"Daddy."

Last week, he defied authorities by taking out advertisements in all major Bolivian dailies, accusing the government of complicity in the cocaine trade. He rules with total impunity over an area in the Beni department that makes up one-tenth of the country.

Suarez is wanted in Bolivia on cocaine-trafficking charges, and in Miami for conspiracy to import cocaine, charges that could earn him a total of 300 years in jail upon conviction.

. . .

Drug-enforcement sources describe Suarez Gomez as head of one of the largest cocaine operations in Bolivia, although Suarez denies this.

On June 18, the Bolivian government sent 150 policemen to search for Suarez in San Borja, a small cattle-raising village in the Beni, 350 miles northeast of La Paz. The operation headed by Interior Minister Mario Roncal has, not surprisingly, resulted in no arrests.[2]

The United States bears a large measure of responsibility for the parlous political and economic position of Bolivia. Of course, the pattern of poverty, corruption, feeble government, and ineffectual enforcement certainly existed in Bolivia long before the emergence of the mass market for cocaine and the War on Drugs. But the destabilizing effects of the cocaine enforcement policies of the United States can hardly be denied. They created the necessary conditions for a cocaine coup, an Arce Gomez, and a Roberto Suarez by providing a system of "price supports" to foreign producers. Just as the black market distorts the economy of the United States and fuels corruption, kidnapping, murder, and the assault on justice, so also it wreaks its havoc on the much weaker institutions of Third World nations such as Bolivia.

The Bahamas presents a second case of a government captured by the cocaine trade, although the "takeover" there was less complete than in Bolivia and lacked the ruthlessness of the Black Eagles. Rather than an overt coup d'etat by cocaine traffickers, it appears that traffickers quietly bought the complicity of a broad range of governmental officials, including those at the highest levels—the Prime Minister and several of his Cabinet members. Although these allegations have not been proven in a criminal prosecution, the circumstantial evidence seems compelling.

The importance of the Bahamas to drug trafficking operations stems from the geography of this nation of 700 islands spread out over thousands of square miles off the Florida coast. They are at once remote—many uninhabited and unpatrolled islands—and yet accessible to Florida Atlantic and Gulf coast staging areas. Bimini, for example, lies less than one hour's run from Miami in a speedboat. For small aircraft, too, the Bahamas provide an ideal transshipment point for cocaine and marijuana brought in from Colombia or Central America.

The details of the Bahamian connection reflect a bit more sophistication than the Bolivian cocaine coup. It started in 1983 when NBC News broadcast allegations that Prime Minister Lynden O. Pindling and several Cabinet ministers were receiving $100,000 per month in drug-money bribes. The network also reported that fugitive American financier Robert Vesco had teamed up with Colombian smuggler Carlos Lehder to ship cocaine out of a tiny Bahamian island owned by Lehder. Pindling denounced the charges, sued NBC, and empaneled a commission of inquiry to investigate the charges.

While the commission was hearing testimony, *Miami Herald* investigative reporters Jim McGee and Carl Hiassen produced their own five-part study, "A Nation for Sale." The first article summarized their conclusions:

> Some of Pindling's closest political allies allegedly offered protection to smugglers in exchange for large cash payoffs. Smugglers say they were promised unrestricted travel, immigration favors and a guarantee that drug shipments could pass unmolested through the Bahamas.
>
> - One confidant of the prime minister, Cabinet Minister Kendal Nottage, has been implicated in a scheme to launder millions of dollars for an accused smuggler and New England Mafia figure. Nottage denies any wrongdoing.
> - Records show that the prime minister, or companies in which he held a secret interest, accepted nearly $17 million in gifts and loans from foreigners during the last 12 years. The money came from investors and businessmen who owned or sought government-sanctioned enterprises in the Bahamas.
> - The prime minister has been accused of accepting a $100,000 payoff from a Boston marijuana trafficker, a charge Pindling vigorously denies.
> - As the Commission of Inquiry pressed its investigation the prime minister summoned three witnesses crucial to his defense and questioned them about their testimony. One of those men, Nassau real estate agent Lester Brown, later allegedly bragged that he was asked "to lie for" the prime minister. Brown denies saying it. Pindling says there was nothing improper about questioning the witnesses.
> - The Bahamas government has been slow to crack down on the most notorious smuggling hotspots in the 750-mile archipelago, despite repeated warnings by senior police officers. Most notable is Bimini, which is riddled with corruption and remains a thriving drug center despite years of embarrassing publicity.
> - Smugglers in the Bahamas rely on a nucleus of Nassau lawyers who allegedly have fixed cases, laundered money, tampered with evidence, compromised judges or passed on secret police intelligence. One attorney, F. Nigel Bowe, was accused of raking 10 percent of a cocaine smuggler's profits. Bowe says it's a lie.
> - The Bahamas remain a sunny magnet for U.S. fugitives who use bribery to ensure themselves safe haven. One robber-turned-smuggler told The Herald he paid $25,000 for Bahamian citizenship papers that enabled him to start a new life in Nassau and evade U.S. authorities.[3]

Summarizing the major smuggling operations that had been based in the Bahamas with a map of their respective turfs, the reporters concluded that corruption was all-pervasive.

You can buy an airstrip, or an island. You can buy citizenship. You can buy protection. You can buy justice.

And should your drug cargo get seized by police, you can even buy it back.

. . .

Bahamian courts have adopted a demonstrable no-jail policy for foreign drug suspects.

Since 1980, more than 978 Americans have been arrested on drug charges in the Bahamas; only four are serving prison terms.

The common punishment for smugglers is a fine, sometimes large, sometimes small. For example, a Colombian boat captain caught with 760 bales of marijuana was fined $50,000 and set free. For an American caught with seven bales, the price of freedom was $10,000. Another caught with a boatload of grass was released after paying only $3,000.

In recent months, with the drug crisis in Nassau's headlines, some magistrates have cracked down—at least by Bahamian standards. A few weeks ago two men caught with $12 million worth of cocaine were fined $70,000 each and released. Still, the smugglers were allowed to buy their airplane back for $75,000.

. . .

"I felt that the government of the Bahamas was a payable situation," says convicted pot smuggler Robert L. Frappier. "If you paid enough money, you were protected in the Bahamas."

Corruption, spawned and fueled by American drug millionaires, has stained every strata of Bahamian officialdom, from constables to Cabinet ministers. The scandal has enfolded some of those nearest to Prime Minister Lynden O. Pindling—and Pindling himself.[4]

Of the $17 million received by Pindling, $14 million came from Vesco's bank. The bank that Vesco controlled financed companies in which Pindling had an undisclosed one-third interest. Several of Pindling's Cabinet ministers and closest associates were also implicated.

The moral of the Bahamian tale parallels that of Bolivia: the leadership of an impoverished nation with shaky political institutions and a natural (geographic) affinity for drug smuggling operations betrays the public trust, either seeking out or succumbing to the lucre of the black market. In one world view, both countries were simply sold out by selfish and unscrupulous politicians acting out of ancient motives of greed, with the law enforcement policies of the United States playing no causal role in that corruption. But that atomistic view of human behavior ignores the structural function of the War on Drugs in channeling human behavior by creating lucrative black markets. It is of course true that government officials should obey the law; it is much less compelling to assert that while surrounding them with the opportunity for almost instantly acquiring the riches of Midas for tolerating drug traffic, a crime of moral ambiguity. Without excusing their betrayals, especially the outrages of the quasi-fascist Bolivian regime, is it not true at some level that both nations became combat zones in the War on Drugs? Can the United States really expect the fragile governments of the Third World to withstand pressures that have damaged our own institutions?

Destabilization in Colombia comes less from the "sale of a nation," although there is certainly plenty of corruption, than from the violent resistance put up by Colombian traffickers to the enforcement efforts undertaken by the Colombian government at the instigation of the United States. The conflict has created a climate of fear, violence, and instability, although some of the violence is directed at officials of the United States Government in retaliation for increasing enforcement pressures. For example, a bomb exploded under a car parked outside the U.S. embassy in Bogota, killing a woman. Related telephone death threats caused 17 U.S. officials and their families to leave the country. Intelligence agents in Bolivia discovered that Colombian and Bolivian cocaine traffickers had paid a gunman $500,000 to murder U.S. Ambassador Edwin Corr. The traffickers especially hate President Betancur's capitulation to United States requests for extradition; they have sworn to kill five Americans for every compatriot extradited to the United States. They have even placed a $300,000 bounty on the heads of U.S. drug agents, dead or alive.[5] Of course, the traffickers also attacked Colombian law enforcement officials and succeeded in executing the Minister of Justice, Lara Bonilla.

Corruption, too, has become entrenched, as drug traffickers have attained great influence in Colombian society. Several dozen Congressmen are thought to be traffickers, while many others have received campaign contributions from them. One hundred Air Force personnel and 200 national policemen were discharged because of drug connections. Attorney General Jimenez ordered investigations of 400 judges suspected of complicity in the drug trade. Even the personal press secretary of President Betancur was arrested on suspicion of helping to smuggle 2.7 kilos of cocaine into Spain in two diplomatic pouches.[6]

By South American standards, Colombia is a rich and powerful nation, enjoying the relative political stability that goes with those conditions. Nevertheless, the corruption and violence of the black market have taken their toll on Colombian society, which even before the rise of the mass drug trade suffered an extraordinary rate of homicide (more than ten times that of Western Europe) and street crime. The changes brought by the cocaine boom have greatly exacerbated those problems. A secret diplomatic cable analyzed the impact of the black market on Colombian society:

> Illegal drugs have become one of Colombia's most serious and complex problems. Enormous profits from marijuana and cocaine corrupt all levels of Colombian society and aggravate an endemic crime problem. Over time, this pervasive corruption could fatally erode Colombian institutions.
>
> . . .
>
> The drug industry also exerts significant influence on Colombia's economy. Illegal

earnings complicate economic policymaking by substantially increasing the money supply, a major cause of the government's meager results in fighting inflation. . . .

The drug industry also contributes to many social ills. The increase in drug-related crime, for example, has been dramatic in the marijuana-growing regions. Murders, kidnappings, and common assaults occur almost daily. The military's presence has not only failed to reduce crime but causes resentment among the rural population.

Finally, the drug industry appears to be creating a newly affluent stratum of society with impressive economic power and the potential to influence—or even control—political power. Illegal profits are channeled into legitimate business ventures, creating a new, corrupt elite that may eventually challenge the domination of the Liberal-Conservative oligarchy and strain the fabric of democracy.[7]

Because of Colombia's relative strength, the economic dislocations, the corruption, the violence, and the threat to existing institutions might all present manageable, if very serious, problems. But on top of this array of drug-based social ills comes a new and profoundly threatening one—narco-terrorism. Narco-terrorism has the potential to force struggling democracies over the edge into civil war.

NARCO-TERRORISM

The black market in drugs has for many years provided common ground for apolitical, entrepreneurial smugglers and ideologically motivated revolutionaries. Henrik Kruger's *The Great Heroin Coup* furnishes an interesting, if fairly speculative, account of the many unions of coup-makers (of both left and right) with drug smugglers around the world. In the United States Congress, committee hearings have unearthed "hard" evidence of "narco-guerrilla" connections in the Far East and elsewhere. In fact, that connection has long been known to the CIA: alliances among political intriguers, tribal chiefs, would-be coup-makers, guerilla commandos, and so on in the opium traffic in Burma and Thailand, the hashish traffic in Lebanon, and the marijuana trade of the Mexican highlands are an old story.

Now it has spread through Central and South America. Although the motivations for and details of these alliances vary from place to place, they all have one fundamental thing in common—a mutuality of interest in the money generated by the black market in drugs. In this sense, the marriage of convenience between smugglers and guerrillas pairs natural allies rather than strange bedfellows. Their community of interest derives from drug money and the arms or political power that it can buy. Their unholy alliance poses obvious dangers to the survival of elected governments.

In the nature of the case, knowledge about this phenomenon is difficult to come by, lying primarily in the domain of classified information obtained by intelligence operatives in the field. Some of the information has been selectively "leaked" or intentionally disclosed for the purpose of embarrassing adversarial governments in Cuba and Nicaragua. The full story remains to be told some time in the future by an enterprising investigative reporter. Nevertheless, having made these necessary caveats about the quality of data disclosed to the public by journalistic sources and selectively declassified diplomatic and national security information, it seems clear that a "narco-terrorist" connection exists in the Americas; and it grows more significant with the continuing growth in black market drugs.

Perhaps more is known about the situation in Colombia than anywhere else.

> Evidence and rumor have been mounting for several years about the ways in which guerrillas and drug traffickers cross paths in Colombia's underworld.
>
> The relationship today lies at the heart of the two most potent and divisive issues facing Colombia: a crackdown on the drug trade prompted by the April 30 contract murder of justice minister and anti-narcotics crusader Rodrigo Lara Bonilla; and the Betancur-inspired cease-fire scheduled to go into effect May 29 between the government and guerrillas of the Colombian Revolutionary Armed Forces.
>
> In March, Colombian narcotics police confiscated 13.8 metric tons of cocaine and dismantled a gigantic jungle processing complex. It was the most lucrative drug bust in recorded history.
>
> During the raid, the cops also found what they believed to be a base camp belonging to the Colombian Revolutionary Armed Forces, known by their Spanish initials as FARC.
>
> The camp, complete with a communications center, barracks, tailor shop and firing range, and littered with FARC documents, propaganda, logbooks, insignia and an assortment of automatic weapons, was linked by a dirt path to an abandoned cocaine lab a half-mile away.
>
> . . .
>
> The conclusion, voiced for months by the U.S. Embassy in Bogota and echoed and amplified upon by the Colombian army and police, is that the FARC provides cocaine industrialists with base security and perhaps intelligence. In turn, the guerrillas receive protection money and perhaps weapons.[8]

FARC, a Moscow line Marxist-Leninist organization, is not the only insurgent group on the Colombian scene. The newer M–19 organization competes for adherents with FARC, drawing support from left-intellectuals and student leaders. But the nature of the connection between M–19 and drug smugglers is more obscure: the major allegations point to a "Cuban connection" funneling arms to M–19, arms paid for with drugs (or drug money) run through Cuba with the complicity of officials of the Cuban government. Secretary of State George Shultz articulated the official position of the United States Government on Cuban complicity as follows:

> Over the years, the case against Cuba mounted until, finally, in November 1982, four high level Cuban officials were indicted by a Miami grand jury for helping a

major Colombian narcotics trafficker. That case provided startling evidence of Cuban complicity in Latin American narcotics trafficking.

According to evidence revealed in the course of that investigation, a Colombian drug smuggler, Guillot Lara, was recruited by Cuba's Ambassador to Colombia. The Ambassador offered Cuban Government help in smuggling drugs to the United States. Cuban waters were provided as a safe haven for the transfer of narcotics to boats bound for Miami. Certain Cuban authorities were instructed to leave Guillot and his men alone while they went about their business. In return, the Cuban Government received payments, in hard cash, of hundreds of thousands of dollars.

But there was another element in this elaborate deal. In return for help with his drug smuggling racket, Guillot participated in a plan to provide weapons to the M–19, a terrorist group that operates in Colombia.

The pattern, long suspected, was finally and clearly established. Cuba was using drug smugglers to funnel arms to terrorists and Communist insurgents.[9]

The situation in Peru also suggests an even closer alliance between the Sendero Luminoso (Shining Path) and the coca growers for mutual political advantage. With a base of operations in the remote, mountainous coca-growing region, Shining Path has carved out a niche for itself as protector of the peasant coca farmers from oppression by a hostile government in Lima, servilely carrying out the imperialist coca eradication policies of the United States. Shining Path has succeeded in exploiting the unpopularity of coca eradication for political advantage, using it as a focal point for episodic bouts of guerrilla warfare against the government.

The Peruvian government and some police say the Maoist guerrilla group Shining Path (Sendero Luminoso) has joined forces with Colombian and national cocaine traffickers in the central jungle highland where a U.S. coca eradication project is centered.

There, armed bands have staged bloody raids on banks, police stations and U.S. rural development officers, killing at least 25 policeman, 21 farmers and a mayor in the last five months.

Death threats have forced most government authorities throughout the area, including 24 mayors, to resign.

The latest intelligence information suggests units of Shining Path are moving 280 miles north of the group's Andean base, Ayacucho, to the 200,000-square-mile swath of coca-covered jungle that starts with the city of Tingo Maria, 190 miles east of Lima, and continues northeast toward Colombia along the Huallaga River.

The Upper Huallaga valley is also headquarters for a $27.2 million program to wipe out coca, sponsored by the State Department, the Agency for International Development, and the Drug Enforcement Administration.

"The terrorists and traffickers have struck a mutually advantageous deal," Col. Juan Zarate of the Peruvian Narcotics Police said in an interview.

He said the guerrillas, in exchange for weapons, attack to divert police from a hundred or more clandestine airstrips the traffickers use to ship out the drug. Shining Path may also receive money from the drug traders.[10]

In apparent response to the threat of a full-fledged partnership among growers, traffickers, and guerrillas, President Garcia Perez in August, 1985, ordered a "frontal attack" on the traffic in the jungle area of the northeast, bordering on Colombia. Aggressive enforcement is a rather perverse policy for the government to pursue. In light of the alienation of the populace, more pressure can only strengthen the hand of the guerrillas as legitimate competitors to the power of the central government. This, in turn, bodes ill for the foreign policy interests of the United States in supporting friendly, democratic governments in South America.

Given the rapid spread of the narco-terrorist phenomenon throughout the Americas, the United States reacted predictably. Rather than questioning the soundness of its underlying policy attacking coca, it reflexively intensified the war effort.

U.S. HELPING MOUNT COUNTERATTACK ON VIOLENT LATIN DRUG TERRORISTS

WASHINGTON—New evidence linking drug traffickers to political terrorists is prompting the United States to put firepower behind its anti-narcotics efforts in Latin America.

The Reagan administration and Congress are each mapping plans to help embattled Latin American governments fight a guerrilla war against drugs that has been marked by mass killings, assassinations and car-bomb attacks.

Key proposals call for a firm counterattack against what drug enforcement officials are calling "narco-terrorism."

The House Foreign Affairs Committee has approved a measure that would arm more than 70 U.S. aircraft on loan to Latin governments with .50-caliber machine guns.

The proposal stems from State Department reports that aircraft used to pinpoint and spray illegal crops with herbicides have themselves been sprayed with machine-gun fire from guerrillas protecting the fields.

. . .

"Some of these [aircraft] have been shot and downed. This would at least give them the capability to shoot back," said Rep. Larry Smith, D-Fla., chairman of the Foreign Affairs task force on international narcotics control.

. . .

The House Foreign Affairs panel is also supporting a State Department plan to help outfit and train Latin American SWAT teams to counter violence from both narcotics producers and political insurgents.

Robert Oakley, U.S. ambassador to Somalia and director for counter-terrorism and emergency planning for State, said Colombia already has signed on and other Latin nations are being encouraged to follow suit.[11]

Given the (incorrect and unexamined) premises of the War on Drugs, the "logic" of the crackdown on narco-terrorism is impeccable. It is sad, nonetheless, for its lack of awareness in missing the inevitable obviousness of "mutual assistance" pacts between growers or traffickers and guerrillas, both united in their opposition to governing authority and both in quest of money. But United States policy depends upon denial. It is essential to block recognition of the truth that narco-terrorism, like corruption and the rest of the black market pathologies, flows inevitably from the War on Drugs. The War on Drugs must fail in attempting to suppress narco-terrorism because it promotes it, just as the war must fail to suppress production of cocaine because it promotes it. Narco-terrorist alliances will prosper and spread to other countries.

One press account speculates on the existence of a "Salvadoran Connection" between drug traffickers and Roberto d'Aubisson's Arena Party:

> The detention of a leading Salvadoran ultrarightist and three fellow travelers at a Texas airport last February has raised suspicions of a Salvadoran connection. The group was nabbed with $5.9 million in unexplained cash by Customs officials who spotted their names on a computer list of suspected drug traffickers, according to a Customs search warrant application.[12]

Firmer suspicions of a planned Guatemalan coup surfaced in the press:

> WERE DRUGS SOLD TO FUND LATIN COUP?
>
> Three men arrested during a cocaine bust in Miami may have been planning to finance a coup in Guatemala with their drug profits, according to information released Friday by the Metro-Dade Organized Crime Bureau (OCB).
>
> The suspects—a Venezuelan National Guardsman and two well-known Guatemalan citizens—were arrested at the Westland Mall last month in what was initially considered a routine drug case.
>
> However, The Herald has learned that within days of the arrest, OCB detectives notified the Guatemalan Consulate in Miami that the three men may have schemed to use millions in cocaine profits to bankroll a coup against the government of Oscar Humberto Mejia Victores, military chief of state of Guatemala.
>
> . . .
>
> Police and Guatemalan authorities are exploring the possibility that some of the cocaine profits were to be used to purchase a large shipment of arms from an unidentified Venezuelan supplier. The weapons ostensibly were to be sold to anti-government guerrillas in Guatemala, according to sources familiar with the investigation.[13]

Whether or not these particular speculative accounts prove true is almost beside the point—weak Latin American governments remain especially susceptible to corruption, subversion, and violent overthrow. The failed Honduran and Guatemalan coups represent an intrinsic part of the pathology of the War on Drugs, not an aberration. Other would-be kings will no doubt seize upon the extraordinary opportunities for profits in the black market, profits for "the cause," even if the cause can muster no greater nobility than the age-old lust for power. In 1985, the United States Government filed an indictment alleging that a cocaine smuggling conspiracy had as its purpose the assassination of the President of Honduras. Prospects for these black market pathologies to develop further can only increase as the War on Drugs intensifies.

Narco-terrorism has yet another dimension. Governments motivated by ideological or competitive hostility to the United States may well be harboring or protecting drug trafficking operations within their borders. Secretary Shultz's accusations against Cuba were set out earlier in this chapter, including the indictment by the Department of Justice of four officials of the Cuban military on drug conspiracy charges. Secretary Shultz made similar claims about the government of Nicaragua, stating that Frederico Vaughan, an aide to Nicaraguan Minister of Interior Tomas Borge, conspired with drug traffickers to put 1,500 kilos of cocaine aboard a plane parked on the military side of Managua airport. Furthermore, he said that photographs show Sandinista troops helping to load the cocaine on the plane. The press account is a bit spicier:

U.S. PROSECUTORS: NICARAGUA LINKED TO COKE CARTEL

One of the world's biggest cocaine cartels transported its merchandise in a monster cargo plane called The Fat Lady and relied on support from Nicaragua's Sandinista government, federal prosecutors said Tuesday as they began presenting evidence in one of the most significant drug-smuggling cases ever tried in Miami.

In a series of allegations that have heightened tensions between the United States and Nicaraguan governments, the prosecutors have said the Sandinistas participated in an enormous smuggling business. They said the operation funneled thousands of pounds of cocaine through several Central American countries to sophisticated distribution networks on both coasts of the United States.

. . .

The Sandinista government denies the prosecutors' assertions and says that [defendant] Vaughan once held a minor position in the Interior Ministry, but left nearly two years before he was charged in this case.[14]

Of course, given the ideological and military tensions between the United States and Nicaragua, allegations of Nicaraguan complicity in the drug traffic would yield political benefits to the Reagan Administration. Nevertheless, additional circumstantial evidence supports those claims:

U.S. INDICTS 11 IN DRUG OPERATION

Four of Colombia's most notorious cocaine suppliers, worried by their government's crackdown on drug trafficking, have found safe haven in Nicaragua for their operations, Miami's chief drug agent said Friday.

Peter Gruden, agent in charge of the Drug Enforcement Administration's local office, pointed to new drug laboratories, an improved airstrip and the volume of cocaine traffic to illustrate his point.

"It is part of a growing trend," Gruden said in announcing the indictment of the four Colombian suppliers, an accused Nicaraguan accomplice and six other suspects in a 1,452-pound cocaine delivery. "This is certainly not the first shipment ever to come out of Nicaragua."

Gruden said he believes that Nicaragua's friendly reception of the cocaine czars was approved by high-ranking Sandinista officials who profited handsomely. But he reported that the DEA has no proof that cabinet ministers took part.

"The extent of trafficking, the establishment of cocaine processing laboratories and the ability to secure the release of other individuals after their arrest would indicate to me that there had to be knowledge," Gruden said.

Asked why prosecutors did not seek indictments against ranking Nicaraguan officials, Gruden replied: "The evidence didn't exist."[15]

If the DEA's charges are true, it still remains an open question whether the complicity in Nicaragua and Cuba constitutes an expression of government policy, as opposed to renegade action by individual officials. The State Department claims that it does, Secretary Shultz asserting that it serves the Cuban and Nicaraguan need for dollars to buy foreign goods, as well as advancing the ideological "goal of attempting to weaken the fabric of Western democratic society" by "smuggling massive amounts of drugs into Western nations."[16] Again, it should not be surprising if Shultz is proved correct that it is governmental policy, for it represents a natural exploitation of black market opportunities created by the War on Drugs. If left-wing guerrillas can exploit the drug trade for revolutionary purposes, why should not left-wing governments also do so as a matter of policy? The only surprising element is the naiveté of the United States in seeking to foreclose those opportunities by pursuing the very policies that create them, i.e., by aggressive law enforcement. Just as it promotes or nurtures other black market pathologies, the War on Drugs inevitably creates market conditions for someone—governments, guerrillas, or men who would be king—to capitalize on the drug trade. Cuba, Nicaragua, and others yet to come thus finance and pursue their own foreign policy objectives.

Short of invasion or coups d'etat, it is impossible to see how the United States can shut down those opportunities. But logic plays little part in the War on Drugs. The Administration just gets mad at the natural consequences of the very market forces that it so systematically, if unwittingly, generates. Because of those forces, all its actions and all its threats remain absolutely powerless to do anything other than perpetuate the existing system. Indeed, neither drug smugglers, narco-terrorists, nor hostile governments could design a system better suited for the advancement of their interests. Viewed from the perspective of the Administration, of course, the situation is rapidly getting worse. Events in the drug trade move faster than United States bureaucracies can possibly react, and the tide clearly runs against us. The crisis management style of the Administration cannot begin to respond to the proliferating worldwide drug industry. Soon the United States will run out of fingers to plug the leaking dike.

The latest evidence adumbrates the future.

VENEZUELA BECOMES BRIDGE FOR COCAINE ON U.S. DRUG ROUTE

Over the past six months, Venezuelan law enforcement agents have seized more than 3,500 pounds of cocaine, up from virtually nothing in previous years.

. . .

The recent cocaine seizures have raised suspicions that drug smugglers could have good connections within the Venezuelan armed forces.[17]

"Scandals hint at Panama role in drug trade," says a *Miami Herald* front-page story on the arrest of the fourth-ranking officer in the Panama Defense Forces. In 1984, in Panama's Darien rain forest, authorities came upon an elaborate cocaine laboratory and arrested 22 Colombians who claimed that they had earned the right to process cocaine by paying off a leading Panamanian official. Panamanian agents later found 17,000 55-gallon barrels of ether, worth about $1 million and enough to process around 200,000 kilos of cocaine. Shortly afterward, Julian Melo, the General Secretary of the Panamanian National Defense Forces High Command, was arrested and accused of allowing the Colombians to transport the ether through the country in exchange for a $2 million bribe.[18]

On and on it goes—Brazil and Ecuador growing new crops of coca; the Chief Minister and the Commerce Minister of the Turks and Caicos convicted on marijuana and cocaine-related charges; massive drug-based corruption and racketeering in the Mexican police and judiciary; new tax havens sprouting in the Caribbean—hardly a single nation in all the hemisphere not caught up in some significant way in the drug traffic. The ironic result of the War on Drugs promises to be a major affliction on the well-being of our allies through the violence, corruption, and subversion spawned by drug trafficking. A scenario in which the United States confronts a hemisphere rimmed by governments held in a semi-captive state by a deeply entrenched drug trade and their narco-terrorist allies is beginning to appear more likely as time passes. Even relatively stable Colombia finds itself in an incipient civil war. "Kidnappings, terror bombings and bloody guerrilla army clashes have taken an increasing toll since the M–19 tore up its truce in June [1985]"[19] More than 1,000 soldiers, guerrillas, and civilians died subsequent to the signing of a truce in 1984, and kidnappings rose 40 percent. Colombia's ability to maintain its own intensified anti-drug initiatives in the face of such pressing concerns is in doubt. In any event, while feeding its narco-terrorist threat, neither the Colombian nor United States War on Drugs seems to make much difference: still the drugs continue to pour into the United States. The Administration's solution to both problems? Why, stricter enforcement, of course.

PART TWO

Breaking the Impasse in the War on Drugs

Cocaine is really our Public Enemy Number One.
—Roberto Fabricio, *Miami Herald* columnist

Time for a new paradigm.
—Anonymous

10

Sources of the Impasse

The War on Drugs is clearly stuck, mired in paramilitary rhetoric that obscures understanding while worsening the problem. Enforcement does not work to control supply. Therefore we must intensify enforcement. That creates terrible black market pathologies at home and abroad. Therefore we must intensify enforcement even more, further worsening the consequences. This vicious circle represents a complete failure of courage and intelligence, perversely working against our own self-interests.

A government committed to intelligent, workable policy would at least probe for other alternatives, perhaps convening a commission of the best and brightest minds to consider and recommend. Of course, the National Commission on Marihuana and Drug Abuse failed to achieve any enduring reform, but at least it represented a step on a path toward enlightenment. By contrast, the current Administration has given us the President's Commission on Organized Crime, which in the guise of fact-finding hearings routinely conducts "dog-and-pony" shows with hooded witnesses from the drug underground confessing their dark deeds. Clearly, no one in the Government has any stake or interest in critical study of the issue. Worse, no one in Government bears any responsibility for the real-world results of the War on Drugs. The only imperative is to keep it going (and growing).

It is difficult to find in modern American History an obviously defective and destructive policy so rigidly locked in place. A partial explanation for this unique rigidity lies in the fact that the ordinary corrective mechanisms that operate for some other failed governmental policies do not function here. First, the lack of even a minimal standard of performance by which to measure results precludes responsible political dialog within the Government. Without real goals, there can be no accountability. Not once in the history of the War on Drugs, Nixon's or Reagan's, has the Government ever stated a realistic objective. Vague and ridiculous aspirations of "ending" drug abuse are all the public ever hears. This lack of goals guarantees that the system will continue to generate its infinite spiral of unworkable policies to "crack down" on the drug supply. Second, the Government has effectively immunized itself from outside criticism, managing to preempt any serious public debate calling into question the premises of drug enforcement policy. The sole exception—the convening of the National Commission on Marihuana and Drug Abuse in the early 1970s—turned out to be an illusory promise, as Nixon's Attorney General John Mitchell anticipatorily repudiated any movement toward decriminalization of marijuana even before the commission issued its report. Drugs are bad, enforcement is good, and let's not waste time questioning the matter.

Public criticism does not occur very often because seven decades of Government propaganda about the evils of drugs have deprived the public of the power of critical thought respecting drugs and cowed it into silence. Fear of arrest and prosecution silences consumers of illegal drugs (unless they get into trouble, in which case public confession and denunciation of drugs become obligatory). This "chilling effect" deprives the public of a critically important perspective—the positive experience of successful, long-term, controlled drug users. People who do not use drugs but who object to the status quo on grounds of principle or cost also rarely speak out; most back off from the controversial nature of the issue, silenced by the powerful social stigma attached to those who "favor" drugs. In this respect the Government's misleading and useless formulation of "the drug problem" as one arising from the substances themselves rather than human action renders intelligent discussion impossible. For the same reason, institutional advocacy of freedom of choice to use cocaine or other drugs has not fared well. No organizational counterpart of the National Organization for the Reform of Marijuana Laws (NORML) exists for LSD, cocaine, or heroin, and NORML itself has fallen on hard times as a political force. As a result of these governmental and social pressures, criticism of drug prohibition is confined almost entirely to a small coterie of academicians, whose influence is diminished by lack of political clout or access to channels of communication necessary to precipitate a rethinking of the issue.

Additionally, the weak budgetary constraints that might reign in a failed governmental policy have even less force as applied to drug control. Because drug enforcement proceeds almost as a categorical imperative, arguments about excessive cost lack persuasive power. As Professor David Richards points out, when the public perceives a strong moral reason for criminalizing certain conduct, whether it be drugs, gambling, or prostitution, then it quite willingly pays extraordinary enforcement costs,[1] although with the War on Drugs, the public cannot possibly know just how extraordinary are the non-monetary costs. Even the limited tendency to question the cost-effectiveness of the War on Drugs that occasionally surfaces in Congress will weaken and disappear when drug law enforcement becomes a self-financing, or even money-making, operation, a process that is now far advanced. The Department of Justice has already declared its intention to make drug law enforcement "pay its own way." In fact, in the 1985 *Annual Report on the Organized Crime Drug Enforcement Task Force Program*, the Attorney General was "proud to report that the value of forfeitures, fines and seizures . . . surpassed the [$90 million] expense of operating the program."[2] It should not be too long before the billion dollar budget of the entire War on Drugs comes entirely from seizures and forfeitures. In the three-year period from 1979 to 1982, for example, the DEA alone confiscated over a quarter-billion dollars in assets from drug dealers in civil and criminal seizures, although not all of these assets were successfully forfeited to the United States. Moreover, the United States Customs Service already claims to be a money-making agency for the Government by virtue of its seizure of thousands of cars, boats, and planes.

Local governments also find drug enforcement a very profitable operation. Metro Dade police seize an average of eight cars, six boats, and more than $100,000 in cash a month.[3] In one six-month period, the city of Fort Lauderdale, Florida, "earned" about $2.57 million in reverse stings, an amount double its annual budget for the organized crime section.[4] The city also built a $1 million mini-jail with drug money. For the state and local police, seizure and forfeiture of cash and conveyances (cars, boats, and planes) has proved to be a bonanza.

Governmental dependence upon the revenues realized from this "partnership" in crime poses a real danger to the ability of society to break the impasse. Drug enforcement could easily become a perpetual motion machine, with drug dealers and drug agents operating in a state of symbiosis: black market profits can finance both the police and the policed in mutual prosperity forever after.

Not even the war in Vietnam, fired by the fear of global Communism, proved so intractable. One of the critical factors in breaking the impasse in Vietnam was the role of the media. Television reporting in particular, with its vivid images of death, destruction, and apparent futility, galvanized mainstream public opposition to the war. Rightly or wrongly, large and influential segments of the public became convinced that Vietnam was a no-win situation (short of some objectionable, catastrophic act like nuking Hanoi). While many factors distinguish the real war in Vietnam from the paramilitary War on Drugs, especially the absence of maimed young veterans returning to their hometowns, the analogy to the destabilizing effect of negative media coverage remains valid. As the realization of the futility and destructiveness of the War on Drugs becomes part of the vocabulary of news coverage, public skepticism about the Government's claims and promises will grow.

Actually, in November, 1981, the *Miami Herald* had already published

"The Billion Dollar Bust,"[5] an incisive exposé of drug enforcement during the Nixon-Ford-Carter years. But after President Reagan declared his war the following year, overwhelming national and community support (not to mention the unequivocal enthusiasm of the *Miami Herald* Editorial Board) discouraged critical reporting. As a minimum response, it was time to wait and see. By 1984, however, the doubts began to emerge quite sharply in the *Herald*: "Local Drug Agents Pan South Florida Task Force,"[6] "U.S. Losing Key Drug-War Battles,"[7] "Congress Questions Success of Bush Anti-Drug Program."[8] *Herald* reporters were not alone. The *New York Times* asked, "Is Drug War Merely a Holding Action—Dramatic Seizures Appear to Leave Supplies Unaffected."[9] The *Wall Street Journal* joined the doubters: "War Against Narcotics by U.S. Government Isn't Slowing Influx."[10] The thrust of *Time*'s cover on the "Cocaine Wars"[11] and *Newsweek*'s on the "Evil Empire,"[12] both in 1985, was the same. Local television news began to run similar stories. Even conservative columnist William F. Buckley, Jr., who had previously advocated capital punishment for heroin dealers (by lethal injection of heroin), radically reversed course and proposed legalization as the only solution to the impasse in an article entitled "After We Admit Drug War's a Failure."[13] Ironically, the media that for years uncritically accepted Government propaganda claims about the War on Drugs and did so much to distort and sensationalize the "drug problem" may now contribute to its demise.

The dawning realization of the failure of the War on Drugs brings us to a historic point of transition. As media revelations feed public awareness that we are losing the war because it is unwinnable, the next evolutionary stage should bring a questioning of the validity of the drug enforcement enterprise. Once that occurs a search for alternatives inevitably will follow. Some may dismiss this assertion as mere speculation, but in fact the social consensus supporting the War on Drugs is crumbling, if not crashing. Perhaps the most compelling evidence of that shift comes from the sheer number of drug users and their distribution throughout all educational and occupational segments of society. The power of the Government to stigmatize drug users as deviants cannot withstand the onslaught of empirical reality. One amusing example occurred in Broward County (Ft. Lauderdale) when the sheriff's office was forced to reject, for illegal drug use, 80 percent of 446 applicants who applied to work as corrections officers at a new jail.[14] Illegal drug use is now commonplace in all social strata and rapidly gaining acceptance. The media, once again, prove that phenomenon:

Cocaine's Appeal Sifts into the Mainstream[15]

Use of Cocaine Grows Among Top Traders in Financial Centers[16]

Drug Use in Silicon Valley Is Running Rampant[17]

Pervasive Use of Cocaine Is Reported in Hollywood[18]

Baseball Stars Linked to Drugs[19]

Drugs: Crisis for the Bar?—Users and Dealers Abound in the Legal Profession[20]

Cocaine Crossing Middle-Class Line[21]

Cocaine Usage Rising Among Women, Minorities[22]

12% of Teen-agers Admit They Combine Drugs, Alcohol—Poll[23]

Cocaine Use Among Young Latins Becoming Major Crisis[24]

Psychedelic Scene, Sounds Are in Again[25]

The last article, describing LSD's comeback in the 1980s, shows that the cocaine explosion represents part of a much larger phenomenon of widely spread and deeply rooted drug taking of all kinds. Even heroin, for decades stigmatized as a ghetto drug or a loser's drug, has (re)gained a middle-class constituency. In 1983, *Rolling Stone* reported that "[t]he social acceptability of smack has been ballooning in Europe. It is now spreading to the United States."[26] The mainstream press followed with its own reports. The *Herald*'s "objective" coverage included an article called "Smart Set Stupidly Adopts Heroin,"[27] portraying the burgeoning of recreational heroin by the Palm Beach crowd and other affluent types. Notorious deaths of the rich and famous, including David Kennedy and comedian John Belushi, confirmed the polydrug trend of mixing cocaine use with opiates. Belushi's death also increased awareness of the popularity of the formerly obscure "speedball," a push/pull combination of cocaine and heroin in a single injection.

While fear and loathing are understandable emotional reactions, none of these trends should prove surprising in a nation with a voracious appetite for *legal* drugs. It has been remarked to the point of cliché—for which it is no less true—that the United States is a drug-taking nation. More than 25 million prescriptions for hypnotics (sleeping pills) are written annually, with Valium representing the most commonly used single drug. In such an environment, does it really shock when the *New York Times* reports that "U.S. Social Tolerance of [Illegal] Drugs Found on Rise"?[28] The two phenomena cannot realistically be separated. In legal theory, the physician's "supervision" over pill-taking legitimates and differentiates it from "drug abuse." In practice, however, that "supervision" translates into self-medication at the time and place of the patient's choosing (including, generally, the right to several refills). Thus, the buzz derived from legal drug use, though restricted, is a commonplace experience in contemporary society. A person receptive to the psychoactive action of tranquilizers need take only a small step to enter the realm of experimentation with illegal drugs.

That in fact has happened on a very large scale. The 1982 NIDA Survey found that a full one-third of Americans age 12 and older had used marijuana, hallucinogens, cocaine, heroin, or other psychoactive drugs for "nonmedical" purposes.[29] Of course, as the survey itself recognizes, many others probably denied such illegal use. Even more important is the generation gap—the percentage would come out much higher if the drug-naive population over age 50 (56 million) were removed from the calculation. Whatever the precise ratio, the fact remains that a significant plurality of Americans has experience with illegal drugs.

Nor does this represent only an American phenomenon. The drug revolt has spread throughout the world, from the nations of Western Europe to those of Latin America. It has spread, in fact, even to the closed societies of Eastern Europe. Bulgaria, Yugoslavia, and Hungary have begun cooperating with the DEA in response to trafficking in heroin, hashish, and marijuana. Czechoslovakia had a major customs drug smuggling scandal. In Poland, government statements and state-controlled media estimate the number of drug abusers in six figures. Yugoslavia estimates as many as 60,000 heroin users. Even in the Soviet Union, hashish, heroin, and opium circulate, much of it brought back by Soviet soldiers from Afghanistan. The "drug problem"—meaning illegal drug use—exists worldwide.

While some countries make war on drugs, others have tried more flexible approaches. The Dutch decriminalized marijuana in 1978 when the government concluded that the substance was "relatively innocuous" and dropped criminal penalties for possession. Spain, of all places, not long emancipated from Franco's rule, followed a few years later. Whether the governments have or have not changed their laws, however, the underlying reality in nearly all countries is the same: proliferating drug use. Clearly, prohibition does not harmonize with social reality in the United States or elsewhere.

Against this background of pervasive public disregard for the drug laws, especially among the generations under age 50, the War on Drugs can be seen clearly for what it is—an attack on shifting cultural norms repugnant to the narrow "majority" (one-half of the one-half of eligible voters who voted) who control the Government. The War on Drugs thus represents a rear-guard action supported by men and women who fear drugs, or what they symbolize, and who do not understand the world they live in. Drug taking has become a normal rite of passage rather than an aberrational descent into deviance or degradation.

Perhaps the Government realizes that and makes war on drugs to fend off the threat to the cultural hegemony of its values. That would explain the desperate defense of the status quo, the tenacious clinging to an unworkable and destructive policy. In fact, its redoubling of efforts—budgets, troops, rhetoric—completely coincides with the syndrome captured so incisively by Hazel Henderson's phrase, "Politics of the Last Hurrah." Just as the war in Vietnam pursued a path of constant escalation up to a half-million troops until final collapse of public support, so too the War on Drugs spirals upward toward oblivion. South Africa presents another parallel: can there be any serious doubt that apartheid in South Africa must inevitably fall? Nevertheless, the Botha regime there redoubles its defense of a doomed policy, undoubtedly sharing the fear of Louis XVI, "*Après nous, le déluge.*" But the Politics of the Last Hurrah always fails to comprehend that forceful resistance to powerful forces causes destructive impact. Oriental philosophy—embodied in martial arts such as aikido—recognizes the superior leverage offered by gracefully harnessing the energy of one's opponent. As the aphorism puts it, "It's easier to ride the horse in the direction he's going."

The social forces now at work make change in the drug laws or their enforcement inevitable. But the process has only begun. It will take some time before the continued erosion of public support finally discredits the War on Drugs sufficiently to set the stage for serious inquiry. When that time comes, it will be important in the search for a sensible framework of drug control to understand the origins of the present impasse. Otherwise, as George Santayana observed, those who are ignorant of history are condemned to repeat it. What explains the complete absence of critical thinking at all levels of government on the drug issue? For this question, we require some historical perspective.

Like many other policy disasters, the War on Drugs began as a well-intentioned reform of a perceived social problem. Its roots go back to the Progressive Era of American history. At the turn of the century, according to Richard Hofstadter's *Age of Reform*, a broadly based coalition of middle-class reformers and workers, often led by an activist Protestant clergy, sought to meliorate the worst excesses of capitalist production—the use of child labor, contaminated food and drugs, sweatshop working conditions (no wage and hour laws), and a range of environmental problems.[30] In addition to these material concerns, the Progressives also focused on matters of morality and vice, and out of this era came a great variety of federal laws regulating public morality: the Mann Act (forbidding interstate travel for prostitution); the Anti-Lottery Act; the Harrison Narcotics Act (1914); and the Volstead Act (1919), creating National Prohibition.

In *The American Disease*, David Musto presents the history of the American narcotics control movement leading to passage of the Harrison Act. He describes it as a relatively minor issue—"not a question of primary national interest"—having "none of the controversy associated with the prohibition of liquor."[31] Whether or not the two movements were politically tied, they emerged from the same milieu and shared a common reformist impulse in addressing social problems.

Musto argues that reformers on the narcotics issue fell into two groups:

> One group thought in moral abstractions while another was interested in a practical solution. The Right Reverend Charles Brent, who played an important role in the movement for narcotics control, was an abstract reformer who saw the narcotics problem, like any other social problem, to be a question which required first of all a moral approach to the decision. Did narcotics have a value other than as a medicine?

No: unlike alcohol they had not beverage or caloric value. Should such substances be permitted for casual use? No: there was no justification, since there was the possibility only of danger in narcotics for nonmedicinal uses. Therefore recreational use of narcotics should be prohibited, their traffic curtailed on a world scale, and a scourge eliminated from the earth.

. . .

Other reformers sought a practical and partial solution which edged toward total narcotic restriction but was modified to allow for the cravings of addicts. These compromises often came from political divisions smaller than the federal government. In contrast to Bishop Brent's proposals, the compromise programs were based on the assumption that the supply of and the desire for narcotics could not be eliminated, and therefore any attempt at total prohibition would be a failure.[32]

Whether pragmatic or moralistic, however, both groups agreed on the necessity of control. "The only question publicly debated with reference to narcotics was *how* to control, not (as in the case of liquor) *whether* to control."[33] In short, the predominant attitude justified the need to protect the drug user from himself and society from the user.

In this latter respect, racial fears and ethnic hostilities played a large role:

By 1900, America had developed a comparatively large addict population, perhaps 250,000, along with a fear of addiction and addicting drugs. This fear had certain elements which have been powerful enough to permit the most profoundly punitive methods to be employed in the fight against addicts and suppliers. . . .

In the nineteenth century addicts were identified with foreign groups and internal minorities who were already actively feared and the objects of elaborate and massive social and legal restraints. Two repressed groups which were associated with the use of certain drugs were the Chinese and the Negroes. The Chinese and their custom of opium smoking were closely watched after their entry into the United States about 1870. At first, the Chinese represented only one more group brought in to help build railroads, but, particularly after economic depression made them a labor surplus and a threat to American citizens, many forms of antagonism arose to drive them out or at least to isolate them. Along with this prejudice came a fear of opium smoking as one of the ways in which the Chinese were supposed to undermine American society.

Cocaine was especially feared in the South by 1900 because of its euphoric and stimulating properties. The South feared that Negro cocaine users might become oblivious of their prescribed bounds and attack white society.

. . .

One of the most terrifying beliefs about cocaine was that it actually improved pistol marksmanship. Another myth, that cocaine made blacks almost unaffected by mere .32 caliber bullets, is said to have caused southern police departments to switch to .38 caliber revolvers. These fantasies characterized white fear, not the reality of cocaine's effects, and gave one more reason for the repression of blacks.[34]

These, then, are the impulses that animated the drive for control of narcotics—motives of sincere paternalism and self-protection, mixed with pharmacological ignorance and racial fear and hostility. Nevertheless, control began in a moderate way—with regulations designed to confine cocaine and the opiates to medical uses for patients upon a doctor's prescription.

In the years following passage of the Harrison Act, the Government hardened its regulations far beyond the law's initial taxing and record-keeping requirements into a flat prohibition. The aggressive campaign, described in Chapter Seven, conducted by Treasury agents against doctors who treated addicts by prescribing maintenance doses of drugs set the tone of moral fervor that now animates the War on Drugs. For example, in upholding the legitimacy of prosecuting a doctor for so treating an addict, the Supreme Court condemned the practice as unlawful "gratification of a diseased appetite for these pernicious drugs."[35] Other cases of the era contain similar emotionally charged and denunciatory language. Even during the comparatively drug-free decades of the Great Depression through the 1950s, public officials continued to champion the cause of drug control in shrill language grossly disproportionate to the actual supply of, or dangers posed by, black market drugs. Much of the present attitudinal rigidity stems from that relentless propaganda campaign of the Government.

In a selective review of the systematic distortions generated by drug officials and politicians, we should begin with Harry J. Anslinger, Director of the Federal Bureau of Narcotics from 1930 to 1962, who initially opposed federal law enforcement against marijuana as unnecessary. Several years later, he reversed course. In asking Congress for funds to expand the Bureau, he published an article entitled "Marijuana: Assassin of Youth," in which he warned of an epidemic of violent crimes committed by young people under the influence of marijuana. Unlike opium, which, he told Congress, could be good or bad, marijuana was "entirely the monster [Mr.] Hyde."[36] The film *Reefer Madness*, now regarded as a camp classic of the scare-tactic genre, came out of this milieu. Congress responded to such fears, and over the opposition of the American Medical Association enacted the Marijuana Tax Act of 1937, empowering the federal government to police the marijuana supply.

During World War II, Anslinger waged a press campaign to convince the American public of the baseless charge that Japan was systematically attempting to addict its enemies, including the American people, to opium, in order to destroy their civilization.[37] In 1950, he used the same ploy, updated to meet the propaganda needs of the Cold War. Thus, during the Korean War, Anslinger leaked a report to the press claiming that "subversion through drug addiction is an established aim of communist China," and that the Communist Chinese were smuggling massive amounts of heroin into the United States to "weaken American resistance." Change the details of time and place, and we find politicians such as Senator Paula Hawkins (R., Fla.) making essentially the same claims about Cuba in 1984, i.e., that the Government of Cuba, as a matter of policy, is flooding the

United States with cocaine in order to subvert our society by ruining our youth.

Similar rumors of subversion through distribution of cocaine circulated during World War I. Reports in the press alleged that German agents were attempting to enslave America by selling or giving cocaine to school children in an attempt to convert them into addicts. But there is a critical difference between popular fears or rumors and the falsehoods propagated by public officials. The first usually represent honest if misguided alarm about a situation not understood. The second represent a disreputable form of pandering to popular fears by leaders in a position to know better. So powerful is the demonology of drug abuse that appointed and elected public officials find it convenient, a half-century after Anslinger's absurdities, to manipulate the issue for political reasons. Politicians on the campaign trail mine the vein of public fear surrounding the drug issue, causing irreparable harm to the cause of rational policy making.

In New York, for example, Nelson Rockefeller began exploiting the drug issue in his 1966 gubernatorial reelection campaign, warning that an epidemic of heroin addiction was spreading like the plague to the sons and daughters of the middle class. He demanded "an all out war on drugs and addiction" and successfully pressed the New York legislature to adopt a statute providing for involuntary "treatment" of addicts without regard to the commission of a crime. A few years after his reelection, the Governor wrote an article describing with hysterical excess the threat of drug addiction as "akin to war in its capacity to kill, enslave and imperil the nation's future."[38] Rockefeller's crusade against drugs reached its climax when he convinced the New York legislature to adopt "the nation's toughest drug law," which provided mandatory life sentences for many drug violations. A successor in office, Governor Hugh Carey, continued the tradition of exploiting public ignorance and fear of drugs. He reached new peaks of excess in explaining the "cause" of a 1980 wave of jewelry snatching on subways and commuter trains: "The epidemic of gold-snatching in the city is the result of a Russian design to wreck America by flooding the nation with deadly heroin."[39] He presented no evidence in support of this claim.

Exploitation of the drug issue has also been a prominent feature of Presidential politics. In *Agency of Fear*, Edward Epstein makes the persuasive point that Richard Nixon built his 1968 "law and order" campaign on public fear of street crime after realizing that "the menace of communism on which he built his early reputation no longer was an effective focus for organizing the fears of the American public."[40] Epstein's interpretation derives support from the shift in domestic policy concerns: as the politics of Communist subversion from within waned in the 1960s, the politics of drugs as the enemy within waxed. Both "dangers" served the role of scapegoat. Whatever his actual motivation, Nixon developed his law and order theme while in office by taking a hard line against drugs, claiming that drug addicts were responsible for most crime in the streets. This stratagem also permitted his Administration to produce superficially impressive anti-crime statistics in the form of rising drug seizures and arrests of drug dealers. Additionally, it provided the justification for his doubling of the manpower of the BNDD to 1,500 agents during his first term.

Perhaps the most cynical of all of his Administration's manipulations of the drug issue occurred in the precipitous "manufacture" of an eightfold jump in the estimated number of heroin addicts—from 69,000 in 1969 to 560,000 in 1971—by applying a different formula to the *same raw data*. Relying in large part on these figures, the President went public with the "news" of a drug abuse crisis. In a message to Congress on June 17, 1971, he declared that the drug abuse problem had "assumed the dimensions of a national emergency."[41] The next day, in an address to media executives, he stated that "[d]rug traffic is public enemy number one domestically in the United States today and we must wage a total offensive."[42]

Acting on that offensive, and circumventing bureaucratic opposition in the Bureau of Customs and the BNDD, he issued an executive order creating an anti-drug agency operating directly under the Executive Office of the President. The new agency, the Office of Drug Abuse Law Enforcement (ODALE), had been proposed in a Presidential option paper drafted by G. Gordon Liddy. Formation of ODALE was the first critical step in the ultimate consolidation of all drug investigation power in the White House, through the Attorney General in 1973, when all drug agencies were merged in the DEA under the authority of the Department of Justice. Epstein argues darkly that Nixon used the powers of the Presidency to implement, by executive order, a hidden plan to create new "investigative agencies [including the DEA] having the potential... to assume the functions of the [Watergate] Plumbers on a far greater scale."[43] With or without that sinister intention, Nixon's actions showed a great deal of exploitation of the drug abuse issue.

Acknowledgment of the long tradition of political manipulation of the drug issue is a very important step in breaking the present impasse in drug policy for at least two reasons. First, it will serve to call into question future politicians' claims about the severity of the drug problem and the "need" to wage war against it, tempering the crowd psychology now lending support to the War on Drugs. Second, it shows that much of the conventional folk wisdom about the dangers of drugs can trace its roots to politics rather than medicine. Certainly, irresponsible rhetoric has played a decisive role in shaping contemporary public consciousness about drugs: "assassin of youth," "subversion," "Communist China," "kill, enslave and imperil," "Russian design," "national emergency," "public enemy number one." This powerful imagery cannot fail to make an impact and to find its way into the unconscious.

Sophisticates, of course, may roll their eyes at the evident nonsense. But the naiveté of the public at large is more easily exploited. Hitler's Big Lie technique proved that reinforcement through official endorsement and repetition, especially in the absence of a competing reality, can convert falsehood into truth. Reality, after all, is a function of social agreement. How else did "witches" get burned at Salem? Indeed, even the mythmakers themselves probably believe in the truth of the imagery of darkness, death, and destruction, since they have grown up in and been acculturated by the demonology of illicit drugs. That social environment makes impossible critical thinking about drugs, drug abuse, and the role of the law in their regulation. As shown later in this chapter, even our leading jurists, who learned in law school to "think like lawyers," fall into this same unconscious mindset of reflexively stigmatizing drugs in the guise of adducing facts about them.

Self-conscious awareness of this historical source of contempoary attitudes would go a long way toward breaking the impasse. But attitudes toward drugs often seem not to be attitudes at all. The consensus prevails that we have made certain drugs illegal because of a solid foundation of scientific evidence of dangerousness or harmfulness—the proven capacity of illegal drugs to produce impaired functioning, death by overdose, or dependency through repeated use. In contempoary society, majority opinion accepts as fact that all drugs are potentially harmful and supports the legal standard that only a doctor's prescription can justify the taking of a drug. Otherwise, as the President says, "drugs are bad."

In his inimitable style, Thomas Szasz captures the universality of the negative consensus about drugs:

> There is probably one thing, and one thing only, on which the leaders of all modern states agree; on which Catholics, Protestants, Jews, Mohammedans and atheists agree; on which Democrats, Republicans, Socialists, Communists, Liberals, and Conservatives agree; on which medical and scientific authorities throughout the world agree; and on which the views, as expressed through opinion polls and voting records, of the large majority of individuals in all civilized countries agree. That thing is the "scientific fact" that certain substances which people like to ingest or inject are "dangerous" both to those who use them and to others; and that their use of such substances constitutes "drug abuse" or "drug addiction"—a disease whose control and eradication are the duty of the combined forces of the medical profession and the state.[44]

Ironically, of course, the groups named by Szasz do not agree on what needs to be banned. For Muslims, it was alcohol but not opium. In the West, danger was defined the other way around. Because of such obvious discord, Szasz argues persuasively that drug prohibitions are culturally rather than medically based, reflecting deep-seated, quasi-religious attitudes toward drug taking. In the West these attitudes claim objective justification through the authority of modern medicine, falsely relying on "scientific fact" to prove the "dangerousness" of selected culturally repudiated drugs.

Szasz does not stand alone in arguing that what we regard as "fact" about drugs and abuse is wholly a matter of convention and culture. Indeed, the very phrase "drug abuse" denotes *not* physical or mental harm to the user, which might constitute a medical "fact," but the unauthorized use of controlled substances. In short, "drug abuse" refers not to a medical condition, as the concrete phraseology implies, but to a type of legal or social deviance. Thus, the DEA calls the 24 million who smoke marijuana marijuana "abusers" regardless of their health. The law punishes the deviance, without regard to any actual physical or mental harm. Manifestly, the control of drug abuse does not concern itself with "scientific facts" or results manifested in the real world. Rather, it proceeds from culture-specific *a priori* "truths." Empirical research plays a role only in finding post hoc justifications for decisions made on cultural and political grounds. As Szasz puts the matter, opium is not illegal because it is dangerous, rather it is called dangerous in order to make it illegal.

Recognition of this point is critical in breaking the present impasse, yet it is also very difficult to communicate. Nearly everyone starts with the presumption that our present framework for controlled substances claims scientific rationalization, i.e., that illegal drugs carry that status because they are more dangerous than legal ones, both the regulated and the unregulated kind. Of course, nothing could be further from the truth. Both marijuana and cocaine, for example, fell into the prohibitionist net without any serious legislative inquiry or medical research, based largely on racial or ethnic prejudices and irrational fears of a nonexistent crime wave. In essence, the drugs we have outlawed represent the habits of alien cultures. By the same token, if we did not give cultural approval to alcohol and tobacco and instead applied the controlled substances framework to them, we would have to place them on Schedule I as dangerous drugs with "no accepted medical use" and "a high potential for abuse" leading to "severe physical or psychological dependence." In *Cocaine: A Drug and Its Social Evolution*, the authors conceive the issue in terms of

> the shared prejudices of a whole society or culture. Our own common sense, for example, makes it necessary for authorities to debate gravely whether possession of marihuana should be decriminalized, even though countless obviously more harmful and dangerous commodities are sold freely. . . . An extraterrestrial being who believed our declarations that drugs were a major problem and then contrasted our attitudes towards cannabis with our attitudes toward alcohol and tobacco would have to conclude that we were insane.[45]

Dr. Andrew Weil makes the point even more succinctly. In *The Natural Mind* he concludes that "the commonly used illegal drugs—narcotics, hallucinogens, marihuana, amphetamines, and cocaine—are much less dangerous medically than alcohol. . . . I would also rate them much less dangerous medically than many used widely in clinical practice (including many antibiotics and hypertensives)."[46]

What is the basis for these startling assertions? The health and mortality data speak for themselves. The evidence of serious organic damage, dependency, and death from the use of alcohol and cigarettes, the institutionalized (ceremonially accepted) psychoactive drugs of Western societies, is overwhelming.

Although the Surgeon General regards cigarette smoking as "the largest preventable cause of death in America," about 54 million Americans regularly smoke cigarettes. The number of annual deaths from diseases caused by cigarette smoking is about 346,000: 80,000 deaths from lung cancer, 22,000 deaths from other cancers, up to 225,000 deaths from cardiovascular disease, and more than 19,000 deaths from chronic pulmonary disease.[47] Cases of nonfatal diseases brought on by smoking number in the hundreds of thousands. In addition, the "passive smoker's syndrome" shows that the effects of cigarette smoking are in a real sense contagious: nonsmokers, (particularly children) who live or work in confined spaces with smokers involuntarily inhale their smoke and show a higher rate of pathology than nonsmokers living in quarters without smokers. In many semi-public places, it is impossible to avoid having to inhale such noxious, toxic "side-stream" smoke.

Finally, cigarette smoking is highly addictive, "the most widespread example of drug dependence in the United States."[48] (The meaningfulness of the concept of addiction is questioned in Chapter 11.) Smoke in the lungs delivers nicotine to the blood, where it travels almost immediately to the brain. The cessation of smoking deprives the chronic smoker's brain of his habitual intake of nicotine and results in tobacco withdrawal syndrome: anxiety, restlessness, craving. For this reason, "intermittent or occasional use is a rarity—about 2 percent of smokers."[49] On the contrary, the "typical pattern of nicotine use is not only daily but *hourly*. . . . No other substance known to man is used with such remarkable frequency."[50] Indeed, most smokers find the craving for tobacco so powerful that, if contronted with the choice, they often prefer to forego food. For this reason, cigarettes play an important role as "money"—a medium of exchange—in many prisons, buying goods and services, including sexual favors.

The high failure rate of stop-smoking clinics, which start with a self-selected population motivated to quit, also reflects the extraordinary strength of the addiction. In fact, some addiction treatment specialists claim that cigarette addiction is sometimes more difficult to break than heroin addiction. Apologists for the status quo might argue that these facts were not fully known until decades after cigarette smoking became popular, so that our drug laws reflect cultural lag. But even today, two decades after the first Surgeon General's report on cigarettes, smoking benefits from the Government's legal protection and financial support. Despite required health warnings on cigarette packs and the episodic antismoking media campaigns of the Public Health Service, the encouragement of smoking proceeds vigorously in several ways.

Cigarette producers advertise pervasively and expensively, spending roughly two billion dollars per year. Even on television, where such advertising is theoretically banned, cigarette manufacturers achieve a high visual profile by sponsoring major sports events or tournaments named for their products. In the print media, brazen promotion of cigarettes panders to new and potential "addicts" by offering free samples through coupons placed in newsweeklies and other mass circulation magazines. The "Free Pack of Sterling" cigarettes coupon campaign would be denounced as a despicable form of drug "pushing" if the drug were, say, marijuana. Once again, attitudes concealed in value-laden language ("drug pusher") perpetuate cultural norms.

Government itself protects and even promotes cigarette smoking in at least two ways. First, the Department of Agriculture has historically supported the tobacco industry with a system of low-cost loans and price supports. Although tax-financed subsidies were replaced in 1982 with a system of self-financing by growers, the Government's concern for the well-being of the industry is reflected by the fact that the Department continues to administer the programs. These policies have nurtured the industry to its position as a major force in the economy. A decade ago, more than 100,000 employees received $500 million in wages annually from tobacco companies.[51] Today, governments at all levels receive important financial support from the multibillion dollar tobacco industry in the form of $6.8 billion in annual tax revenues, 98.8 percent of that from cigarettes.[52] This symbiotic relationship between the Government and the tobacco industry precludes a Government policy toward cigarettes commensurate with their actual impact on human health. Thus, the Reagan Administration in 1982 first endorsed and then retreated from a more explicit health warning on cigarette packs.

Little need be said about alcohol as a "dangerous drug." It is high in toxicity, "addictive" to millions, and a prolific source of traumatic injuries and death in the home, workplace, and everywhere else. Part of the problem arises from the sheer volume and pervasiveness of drinking—about one-third of 145 million adults drink at least once a week, and another third on special occasions. The casualties "caused" by alcohol are well known—13.3 million alcoholics and problem drinkers and 50,000 to 200,000 annual deaths from disease and accident, including one-half of the 46,000 highway fatalities.[53] While the War on Drugs propagates the myth that marijuana poses an equal menace to highway safety, *Car and Driver* magazine tested and disproved that proposition with actual time trials and other techniques that measured driver performance. Drunk drivers showed radical impairment of motor skills. Stoned drivers showed little or none, and several actually improved performance on challenging slalom courses.[54]

As with cigarettes, widespread advertising by industry and governmental dependence upon tax revenue promote the consumption of alcohol. The hustling of alcohol in the air as well as on the ground illustrates the blindness of American drug control laws. Drinking is not merely tolerated but shamelessly promoted through a variety of customary schemes—free drinks in the first class, ladies' night, happy hour, two-for-one, drink-'n-sink, free buffet, and an endless variety of other promotions designed to sell as much liquor as possible to anyone of minimum age. Even in the face of a nationwide campaign against drunk driving, many states, like Florida, continue to permit drinking *while* driving, there being no "open container" prohibition.

If medicine or science really were important in our drug laws, the promiscuous promotion of these drugs through advertising would not be permitted. Nor would prices be so cheap. Ten-dollar-a-pack cigarettes and $30 vodka would more accurately reflect health concerns by rationing consumption. Total prohibition, which is bad on principle and impossible to enforce, would not be demanded, but a serious public health approach would not permit the free-wheeling enterprise that now prevails in these "dangerous" drugs. Clearly, science and medicine play little or no role in these decisions. As Dr. Robert Byck puts the matter, "There is no such thing as a 'bad' drug. People can abuse almost any chemical substance ever invented. . . . We choose our poisons on the basis of tradition, not pharmacology. Societal attitudes determine which drugs are accepted and the extent to which moral qualities are ascribed to chemicals."[55]

Once again, Szasz captures the essence of the matter somewhat provocatively in distinguishing the legal from the illegal on purely ritualistic or ceremonial grounds:

> Organic chemistry, biological chemistry, and pharmacology are all concerned with the chemical properties and biological effects of *drugs*. Ceremonial chemistry, on the other hand, is concerned with the personal and cultural circumstances of *drug use* and *drug avoidance*. The subject matter of ceremonial chemistry is thus the magical as opposed to the medical, the ritual as opposed to the technical dimensions of drug use; more specifically, it is the approval and disapproval, promotion and prohibition, use and avoidance of symbolically significant substances.[56]

In short, our attitudes about legal and illegal drugs cannot claim an objective basis in medical fact but emanate entirely from the realm of culture and convention.

Cocaine presents a classic example. The legislative process by which the law classified it as a "narcotic" was quite casual, as was passage of the

Harrison Act itself. It was not preceded by systematic scientific study or legislative inquiry. In fact, the federal government never commissioned any scientific or medical studies of cocaine until 1974, 60 years after firmly planting the drug in a concrete bedding of illegality. The body of "knowledge" about cocaine before 1914 came almost entirely from the realm of anecdote, usually presented sensationally by a yellow press. Its illegality owes a lot to the southern racist perception of it as a "nigger vice" 70–80 years ago.[57] Certainly, empirical research did not underly the claim of a doctor writing in the *New York Times* in 1907 that cocaine not only improved the marksmanship of blacks but conferred upon them a temporary resistance to the knockdown effects of fatal wounds.[58] In other words, shoot a black on coke through a vital organ and he'll keep coming at you. Similarly, it was not a "fact," though uttered solemnly by another doctor, that "[m]ost attacks upon white women of the South . . . are the direct result of a coke-crazed negro brain."[59] Nor this: "There is nothing that we can do for the confirmed user of the drug. The best thing for the cocaine fiend is to let him die."[60]

We can smile now in our sophistication at these almost charmingly antiquated beliefs. After all, today we know the "real" reasons why cocaine is a "dangerous" drug. We can read about them in today's seemingly informed press. Thus, the *Miami Herald* and other papers publish lurid articles about cocaine focusing exclusively on the worst cases of excess, overdose, addiction, and death. The headlines alone tell the story: "The Dark Side of Snow,"[61] "Cocaine and the Quest for Death,"[62] "Cocaine Kills in Many Ways,"[63] "When You're on Coke, Nothing Else Matters, Not Even the Fact That It May Kill You,"[64] "Cocaine Is Ruining Our Nation and Nobody Seems to Care,"[65] "Cocaine Causes Panic, Paranoia, Many Users Say,"[66] "Habitual Use Can Put Hole in Your Nose,"[67] "Given the Choice, Laboratory Test Animals Get High So Often They Kill Themselves."[68]

Now, no one could deny the dark side of cocaine abuse. Some of it is reviewed in Chapter 1. But the press, following the Government's lead, has been relentlessly irresponsible in portraying the taking of cocaine as the equivalent of playing Russian roulette. Balance and perspective are completely lacking—no comparison to other drugs regarding toxicity or lethality; not even a citation of the Government's own data for some measure of context. Those data undermine the media's presentation of grave danger. In 1981, for example, the DEA estimated that 6.75 million people had used cocaine within the last 30 days and that 15 million had used it during the past year. They consumed more than 34 metric tons at an average gram purity of 25 percent, for a total of five billion lines (at 25 mg. each). The health toll that year was 4,777 overdoses reported to DAWN emergency rooms; 14,354 admissions to federally funded treatment centers; and 326 overdose deaths involving cocaine.[69] Cause for concern? Surely. A plague of deadly consequences? Hardly.

In fact, media presentations of extreme cocaine abuse have become almost completely stylized. A favorite scenario starts with a successful professional or businessperson who tries cocaine, likes it, progresses to chronic, compulsive, and obsessive use, loses interest in job and family, spends exorbitant amounts to feed a passion for freebase, defaults on his mortgage, sells off his belongings to pay for his habit, plunges into the abyss of addiction and near-death, and is saved only at the eleventh hour by the decision to go into treatment.

The story of Dr. ———, a Miami Beach physician, is one such case. He enjoyed a lucrative practice, a waterfront home on a private island in Biscayne Bay, and a prized art collection. In his forties he began taking cocaine:

> "It made my conversation seem sparkling, music sound better, made me feel good," he recalls. It seemed a fountain of youth. He could beat his 19-year-old son in a three-mile run, and his sex life sizzled. "I could be the macho man I always dreamed about." Soon he was spending $1,000 a week, snorting two grams a day with only minutes between "toots." "Even when you drive, you can pour a little sniff on your hand," he says.
>
> After a year of cocaine use, [he] discovered free-basing, and the social highs turned insidiously antisocial. "In the beginning, I felt I was communicating with God," he says with a wry smile. "In the end, I thought I was God." With the help of an unsuspecting nurse, he maintained his medical practice. But his life at home was unraveling. He was unperturbed by the constant small fires he started with his free-basing equipment. He was now smoking $2,000 worth of coke a day. He wanted to be alone, away from his disapproving wife and children. Even sex seemed boring. "You could line up the Latin Quarter. All I wanted was the pipe."
>
> [He] moved out of his house and into a dilapidated apartment. "I was chasing the memory of the high," he says. "The highs got lower, and the lows got deeper." His skin was covered with sores from malnutrition. The free-basing also caused rashes and made his tongue so swollen that he could barely talk. In one of the fits of rage that accompanied the "down" periods, he snapped off two teeth. Shards of broken glass pipes formed a thigh-high pile. The apartment was rancid, filled with unwashed clothes and dishes. The doctor did not notice. He spent most of his time in the shower, even smoking his coke there, to relieve the constant sweating. "I went as low as you can go without dying."[70]

Without in any way denigrating the pain and poignancy of that experience, its exploitation by the media is objectionable. Reading or viewing a steady stream of such accounts conveys the impression that they represent the typical, rather than the aberrational, experience. Clearly, many others, the majority, have no such problem of loss of self-control and balance in life. Never, however, does the press print even an anonymous account of a successful long-term user, i.e., one who uses the drug moderately, occasionally, and responsibly. Why is that? Successful cases have no incentive to come forward, given the law and prospects for stigmatizing publicity. Only those who have problems, who may in fact be under court orders,

speak out. Still, an enterprising reporter could present anonymously what is after all the normal pattern. The explanation must be in the cultural agreement that makes cocaine a wholly negative force and therefore renders such reportage by mainstream institutions impossible.

Because television stations require licensing by the Federal Communications Commission (FCC), television reality is even worse: fewer facts and greater adherence to the Government's position. An hour-long 1985 television program, "Cocaine Blues: Myth and Reality," broadcast on NBC's Miami affiliate, exemplified this type of irresponsible journalism. In fact, the station may not have viewed the show as journalism, but as an important public service, since it was part of "Cocaine Awareness Week." Most of the program consisted of interviews with convicts and former convicts (drug dealers), patients or former patients (cocaine addicts), and their therapists. Researchers and pathologists were also interviewed. Given this cast of characters, the impression conveyed was relentlessly negative. Consider the imagery—crime, sickness, and death. No upbeat stories about using cocaine were presented at all. The nearest thing to a positive statement came from the host of the program, who, in talking about cocaine and mortality, solemnly conceded that "most cocaine users do not end up in the morgue." The program concluded with information about where to call for medical help and where to call to turn in a dealer. The message: cocaine is very bad; law enforcement is the (only) right response.

The criticism here is not that cocaine is "good" or "not so bad," but that the reality varies tremendously with set and setting, frequency and dosage. Most of all, it varies with the character of the individual who takes it, as shown by Aleister Crowley's quote in Chapter 1. Conventional reportage irresponsibly buries these not-so-subtle distinctions. Beyond recognizing the range of cocaine realities, good journalism could raise important questions about the propriety and efficacy of the law enforcement response. Certainly, an exposé of black market pathologies lies within its domain. Even if one starts with a totally negative view of the "effects" of cocaine, does it automatically follow that the War on Drugs offers a useful social remedy or a humane response? Neither the Government nor the media find occasion to consider these important questions in any depth.

Just as it was not necessary to study cocaine in 1914 because of common knowledge about it, so today the tyranny of prevailing opinion, in J. S. Mill's phrase, forms a cultural lens that screens out every fact or option that might destabilize the cultural norm. The possibility of improved physical or mental functioning, of anti-arthritic or antidepressant therapy, or of controlled, long-term, non-addictive recreational use are simply denied by the mental iron curtain. Prevailing social attitudes toward cocaine, built on a tiny nucleus of anecdotal evidence and surrounded by a much larger cell of hostile presupposition, make such inquiry impossible. Don't disturb me with facts, goes the joke, my mind is made up.

Breaking out of this mindset, breaking away from the ubiquitous palette of dark imagery, will not be easy. The demonology of illicit drugs unconsciously reflects the dominant social reality, built on overwhelmingly negative attitudes and false or distorted information about drugs. Even intelligence does not seem sufficient to break the stigma reflex to drugs. Consider statements by two of the most prominent and respected Supreme Court justices in modern history, Hugo Black and William O. Douglas. In each case we find attitudes masquerading as facts, and no evidence of the justice's awareness of that conflation.

Hard-headed, independent-minded Justice Hugo Black, who during his long career repeatedly rebuffed the attempted incursions of law enforcement authorities into the Bill of Rights with the position that the Constitution by design makes it difficult to convict a citizen of crime, fell into the trap of conventional wisdom about drugs:

> Commercial traffic in deadly mind,-soul,-and body-destroying drugs is beyond a doubt one of the greatest evils of our time. It cripples intellects, dwarfs bodies, paralyzes the progress of a substantial segment of our society, and frequently makes hopeless and sometimes violent and murderous criminals of persons of all ages who become its victims.[71]

Justice Black may have intended "mind,-soul,-and body destroying drugs" as a rhetorical flourish, not meant to be taken literally but designed as a clarion call to action, for "the most vigorous laws to suppress the traffic." His second sentence, however, in its use of active verbs—"cripples," "dwarfs," "paralyzes," "makes"—strongly smacks of factuality. Those are the actual effects of the drugs, his presentation argues. Of course, he does not trouble to cite any authority to provide a factual basis for those claims. Rather, he relies on his sense of the common knowledge about drugs, not realizing that he, too, has fallen victim to the tyranny of what everyone "knows" about drugs.

The great civil libertarian, Justice William O. Douglas, also approached the drug issue from a similar perspective—one of victimization. His approach was more subtle, however, apparently empirical in its citation of authority and its lengthy recitation of the "medical" details of heroin addiction:

> To be a confirmed drug addict is to be one of the walking dead. . . . The teeth have rotted out; the appetite is lost and the stomach and intestines don't function properly. The gall bladder becomes inflamed; eyes and skin turn a bilious yellow. In some cases membranes of the nose turn a flaming red; the partition separating the nostrils is eaten away—breathing is difficult. Oxygen in the blood decreases; bronchitis and tuberculosis develop. Good traits of character disappear and bad ones emerge. Sex organs become affected. Veins collapse and livid purplish scars remain. Boils and abscesses plague the skin; gnawing pain racks the body. Nerves snap; vicious twitching develops. Imaginary and fantastic fears blight the mind and sometimes complete insanity results. Often times, too, death comes—much too early in life. . . . Such is the torment of being a drug addict; such is the plague of being one of the walking dead.[72]

It should be noted that Douglas was writing with benign intention here, by way of ruling in *Robinson* v. *California* that imposing a prison sentence for the "crime" of being addicted to heroin violated the Eighth Amendment's ban on cruel and unusual punishment. Nevertheless, good intentions cannot excuse the absurdly livid and wildly inaccurate account of heroin addiction he cites. Quite to the contrary, the physiological effects of heroin are quite benign, and often associated with longevity in the addict. Dr. Arnold Trebach informs us in *The Heroin Solution* that "putting aside the problem of addiction, the chemical heroin seems almost a neutral or benign substance. Taken in stable, moderate doses, it does not seem to cause organic injury, as does alcoholism over time."[73] Furthermore, Norman Zinberg's research in *Drug, Set and Setting* demonstrates that a great many heroin users have developed stable, non-addictive patterns of occasional use ("chipping") over long periods of time.[74]

Perhaps the state of knowledge about heroin was not as advanced when Justice Douglas wrote as it is today. On the other hand, from the nature of the nonmedical source he cited, a law journal, it seems likely that he searched for the most grotesque and damning account he could find. He was able to succeed in his gross distortion of medical reality precisely because the surrounding social reality encouraged it. Everyone "knew" that heroin was bad, dangerous, and destructive, and that "knowledge" made irrelevant to the justice's purposes a bona fide statement of contrary medical fact. After all, it was an "established fact" that "narcotic drugs are dangerous. Not that they are poisons within themselves, but are worse than poisons. Their excessive use destroys will power, ambition, self-respect, and in the end, mentality. They make men and women moral perverts."[75]

Yet refuting the common mistakes and/or misunderstandings about heroin or any other drug can hardly lead to reform, given the tyranny of what everyone knows. We deal in the realm of drugs, with deeply held metaphysical notions that transcend mere "facts." Rational argument can contribute no more to breaking society's present impasse on drugs than Galileo's astronomy contributed to the Church's acceptance of the heliocentric structure of the solar system during his lifetime.

The impotence of rational thinking in a confrontation with the tyranny of social agreement was demonstrated quite clearly by the failure of the movement to "decriminalize" marijuana. An impressive number of respectable, mainstream organizations—AMA, ABA, National Educational Association, Consumers' Union, American Public Health Association, National Council of Churches—considered the evidence on marijuana and concluded that its harms were small enough that possession of marijuana for personal use should not be a crime. Even the National Commission on Marihuana and Drug Abuse agreed that *private* possession for personal use should be allowed. Despite this extraordinary consensus, however, the movement gained virtually no headway at all. About 10 or 11 states reduced penalties to the level of a misdemeanor or traffic-type offense, but only in Alaska did a restricted form of possession (in the privacy of the home) become fully legal. Even that limited breakthrough took a constitutional ruling by the state supreme court to circumvent the political process. Ultimately, the "liberalization" of the 1970s proved abortive. In 1982, President Reagan asserted as "truth" that marijuana was "dangerous." Now the War on Drugs disdains any distinction between "hard" and "soft" drugs and has mounted a major enforcement effort against both domestic and foreign production of marijuana. Forget the "scientific" evidence. Forget cost-benefit balancing. Forget black market pathologies. Forget individual rights. As the President says, "[Illegal] drugs are bad and we're going after them."[76]

The tyranny of what everyone knows about illegal drugs keeps our present impasse in place, just as it has retarded every major breakthrough in human thought and social organization, from Galileo's struggle against the geocentric orthodoxy of the Catholic Church to the emancipation of the American slaves. In all such cases, deeply held belief systems masquerading as objective truth erect mighty bulwarks against the penetration of a competing truth or world view. As Thomas Kuhn argues in *The Structure of Scientific Revolutions*, real progress proceeds not from the discovery of new facts but from the creation of a new paradigm to make such facts possible, to give them meaning, to permit scientists to "see new and different things when looking with familiar instruments in places they have looked before."[77] Modern astronomy is not possible if the social reality requires that the earth be the center of the universe. Similarly, progress on the drug issue has been rendered impossible by the social reality of deviance, danger, and destructiveness that makes it impossible to see the truth, or at least a different truth. A shift in this context is a necessary precondition to constructive action on the drug issue.

If unconscious attitudes about drugs, not facts, keep the impasse locked in place, how is it possible to break their grip? It may prove illuminating to consider how past social realities that once seemed very solid later gave way to competing realities. The transformation of attitudes about race and gender—attitudes underlying critical aspects of social structure—illustrates the kind of contextual shift needed for a breakthrough in thinking about drugs and drug abuse. For both race and gender, we may take a landmark decision of the United States Supreme Court as fairly embodying the prevailing social reality of the age in question.

In the case of *Dred Scott* v. *Sanford* (1855), Scott had been taken as a slave by his owner into Illinois, a free state. Upon returning to Missouri, Scott sued his owner in federal court to gain his freedom, claiming that his physical presence in Illinois had emancipated him. Rather than simply relying on a narrow ground of decision, such as the slaveowner's property rights under Missouri law, Chief Justice Roger Taney wrote a wide-ranging opinion denying Scott the right to bring suit because he lacked citizenship. Slaves were not intended by the Constitution to become citizens, wrote Taney, because they were "a subordinate and inferior class of beings, who had been subjugated by the dominant race."[78] Moreover, as inferior beings, they comprised a class of untouchables in the social order, "altogether unfit to associate with the white race, either in social or political relations; and so far inferior, that they had no rights which the white man was bound to respect."[79] Slavery, in short, found justification in the "fact" of white racial superiority, a "fact" that required no proof because it was part of the *volksgeist.*

A similarly narrow world view disguised as universal truth determined the outcome of a Supreme Court opinion considering the rights of women. In *Bradwell* v. *State* (1872), the Supreme Court of Illinois refused to grant Myra Bradwell a license to practice law on the sole ground of her sex. The fact that she possessed the requisite qualifications to practice law did not matter because "God designed the sexes to occupy different spheres of action" and it was "an almost axiomatic truth" that "it belonged to men to make, apply and execute the laws."[80] A concurring opinion went even further in rejecting any role for women in professional or business life:

> The civil law, as well as nature's law, has always recognized a wide difference in the respective spheres and destinies of man and woman. Man is, or should be, woman's protector and defender. The natural and proper timidity and delicacy which belongs to the female sex evidently unfits it for many of the occupations of civil life. The interests and views which belong, or should belong, to the family institution

[are] repugnant to the idea of a woman adopting a distinct and independent career from that of her husband.[81]

Given the high moral ground of late twentieth-century ideas about sexual and racial equality, we may sigh gently about the court's wrongheadedness and take comfort in the comparative enlightenment of contemporary thinking. That would miss the point. In the twentieth century, as in the nineteenth, the role of women in society or the status of blacks turns on a belief system—a world view based on equality replacing a world view based on hierarchy—not on matters of fact. Equality is preferred not because it is more factual or more "scientific," but because it more closely embodies our ideals. One paradigm for organizing reality simply gave way to another. Can we apply these lessons of history to produce a contextual shift for the drug problem? That kind of sophistication about our own way of thinking is the beginning of wisdom about drug abuse control. Short of that, public discussion of policies for drug abuse control will remain dominated by attitudes as enslaving as those manifested toward blacks in *Dred Scott* and women in the *Bradwell* case.

Attitudes—irrational, unexamined, and destructive—not facts, control our drug policies. Yet in focusing obsessively on the chemical properties of illegal drugs (while ignoring those of legal drugs), we obscure our own conceptual apparatus regarding drugs and drug abuse, and disable ourselves from dealing effectively with those phenomena. Given the tyranny of what everyone knows about drug abuse, mere rationality can hardly liberate us from the death grip of the War on Drugs. Looking for the solution to the drug problem in the control of drugs seems sensible only if the prevailing reality regards drugs as "worse than poisons." But if the reality has regard to issues of choice and responsibility, it is as foolish as looking for the solution to the obesity problem in food control. If ever we are to make any progress, we must emancipate ourselves from the "axiomatic truths," the crippling attitudes, that keep us locked in the present impasse. We must create a new context.

11

Beyond the War on Drugs: Creating a New Context

Where lies the path out of the drug enforcement wilderness? The reader who accepts the validity of the argument in Chapter Ten that unconscious attitudes about drugs and the drug problem—the ideology of victimization—not medical facts, keep the impasse in place is nevertheless entitled to issue a challenge consisting of two main questions. First, given that we are prisoners of our own unexamined concepts and reflexive "thought" processes about drugs and drug abuse, what is the "correct" model of thinking to replace them? Second, assuming the new model is discovered, what type of social or cultural engineering could possibly succeed in implementing the needed change? In short, how can society create a new paradigm for understanding and regulating what is now conceived to be the "drug problem"? These questions form the core of this chapter and the next.

The starting point for creating a new context is as simple as it is profound. It begins by acknowledging the social reality that drug taking of some kind forms the statistical rule rather than the exception. In the United States, illicit drug taking has become the cultural norm rather than an aberration, and the rest of the world—even the Communist world—is following our lead. Second, it recognizes that drug taking responds to universal human needs, comparable to the sex drive, and that it therefore cannot be outlawed, only channeled. As a result, a war on drugs has no legitimate or effective role to play. In a democratic society, regulation cannot succeed unless it appropriately defers to social custom and individual autonomy. The new context thus holds the individual legally and morally accountable for specific acts of wrongdoing, but not for drug taking itself, just as the criminal law generally holds a drinking defendant responsible for offenses but not for the drinking. Like drinking, moreover, drug taking must be socialized by informal, customary restraints that seek to domesticate drug taking and prevent or minimize the excesses of drug abuse.

In order to reach "critical mass," the new context must produce (or reflect?) a movement away from the present preoccupation with the "effects" of drugs to focus on ethical questions of freedom, informed choice, and social responsibility. The government's extraordinary, expanding commitment to law enforcement against drugs—eradication, crop substitution, interdiction—blocks awareness of a critical fact: as inanimate objects, drugs cannot harm anyone or make an addict of anyone. Even if drugs be regarded as poisons, as the political rhetoric often puts it, the obsessive fixation on their physiological effects and supposed dangers obscures the fundamental role of individual choice in voluntarily exposing oneself to the risks. People take drugs because they like or need the experience they produce.

In *The Natural Mind* Dr. Andrew Weil argues that drug taking is a universal phenomenon, practiced by nearly every known culture, and may be driven by innate yearnings, arising from the structure of the brain, to transcend the limits of human experience imposed by ordinary ego-centered consciousness. The drugs themselves do not produce the persistence and force of that drive to get high. They merely constitute the object of desire or the vehicle for its expression. Therefore, a war on drugs hopelessly confuses cause and effect, means and ends. Logically and legally, as Szasz retorts, the War on Drugs makes as much sense as a war on sexual organs as a means of controlling rape or prostitution. Viewed in this light, the War on Drugs actually is a war on the American people—their values, needs, and choices, freely expresssed in the marketplace of consumer goods.

If it is possible to break out of the present impasse, I think the process of transforming the context surrounding the drug issue must start with this most fundamental realization. The transformative power of that perspective springs from shifting the conception of drug taker as slave or victim of drugs to responsible agent pursuing the expression of psychic drives. That fundamental shift, in turn, would make possible a new paradigm of individual responsibility and accountability for drug taking to replace the War on Drugs, which is predicated upon the helplessness and consequent irresponsibility of the individual.

Reconsider Chapter 10's review of the dominance of negative and erroneous conceptions about drugs and drug abuse. Although the details vary with time, place, and drug, they all reflect one overriding meta-conception—the drug taker as victim. It was not always so. We may assume that the tolerant attitude toward unregulated drug taking in the late nineteenth century reflected the *zeitgeist* of laissez-faire capitalism—freewheeling entrepreneurship, self-reliance, and a near absence of governmental regulation. At the turn of the century, the Progressive movement produced, or perhaps reflected, a profound shift in this paradigm, from an individualistic ethic to a collectivist ethic. Acting largely on materialist assumptions—the detrimental effects on people of poor environmental conditions, physical and social (including drugs and liquor)—reformers succeeded in justifying the "need" for governmental regulation to displace individualistic or market approaches. With the advent of the Great Depression and the New Deal, the societal transformation to a collectivist paradigm operating through a modern bureaucratic state was more or less complete. Solving social problems became the job of government rather than individuals or organizations in the private sector. Through this process, drug control was wrested from individuals and doctors by a police-medical bureaucracy that dominates to this day.

> The alliance of the organized medical and pharmaceutical professions with government and police established during the Progressive era produced a rationalized system of control over psychoactive drugs that has endured until the present.... In spite of its intellectual and moral inadequacies, it serves a protective and conservative function required by the organizations that support it.[1]

Under this new institutional arrangement, all drug taking not authorized by doctors was literally out of control. The doctors themselves, subservient to the enforcement agencies, had limited powers and could prescribe only certain approved drugs for certain, approved purposes. With patients now deprived of the earlier right of self-medication, even with their doctors' consent, it became a short, and politically logical, step to portray "freelance" drug taking as sickness or helplessness. A benign, paternal authority found it more congenial to its deterministic assumptions about human behavior to understand it as victimization rather than volition. The general tendency of the modern welfare state to attribute causation to environmental factors in shaping or controlling human behavior encouraged the perception of drug taker as helpless or sick victim.

The conventional imagery of addiction more particularly promotes the concept of drug taker as victim. At least since Freud's time, much of the hysteria surrounding drug abuse has emanated from the fear of potent drugs overpowering and dominating weak-willed humans. Political rhetoric reflects that perception. New York's Governor Nelson Rockefeller put the matter as one of conquest:

> Drug addiction represents a threat akin to war in its capacity to kill, enslave and imperil the nation's future.... Are the sons and daughters of a generation that survived a great depression and rebuilt a prosperous nation, that defeated Nazism and Facism and preserved the free world, to be vanquished by a powder, needles and pills?[2]

The rhetoric is striking, a classic example of the Cartesian reductionism. Consider its structure. An external force—drug addiction—threatens to vanquish our sons and daughters. Not, our sons and daughters are taking risks—

even life-threatening risks—with drugs by (foolish?) choice. That would concede their own choice and responsibility in the matter and would tend to color it as a problem for individual or family resolution. A powerful threat from the outside, however, more readily justifies a collectivist or governmental solution. In short, drug addiction is done to people—passive voice—not something they do or choose—active voice. In its most extreme form, *it* kills *them*. Hence, according to Senator Paula Hawkins (R., Fla.), "Drug traffickers are mass murderers."[3] Given that "understanding" of the drug problem, government must act to protect people against drugs, against their will if necessary. The individual's ethics cease to matter; "protecton" requires that he or she become an object to be regulated, conditioned, threatened, and institutionalized if necessary. Human choice and responsibility vanish, replaced by a *Clockwork Orange* conception of the sanitized and properly conditioned (drug-free) human being. The irony could not be greater: if drugs are in fact a moral evil, prohibition destroys the opportunity for the spiritual growth that comes from confronting evil and making the righteous choice.

In this regard, the disease metaphor plays a useful role in obscuring the morality of choice. By stigmatizing drug taking as sickness, it suggests a condition of body or mind needing cure by medical or other experts. It reinforces the idea of victimization and further serves to frighten the public. For example, former DEA Administrator Peter Bensinger wrote a guest column for *USA Today* titled "We Can Win the War Against This Cancer."[4] Does he refer to the lung cancer that smokers (including, probably, marijuana smokers) often develop? No. He refers metaphorically to farming: "Domestic growth of marijuana is a cancer that must be fought."[5] By this imagery of disease, he conveys the idea that the body politic is being attacked or invaded by a foreign substance—a deadly one—that must be repelled by the analog of chemotherapy, paraquat. The true state of affairs—that Americans grow marijuana to sell to other Americans who want to buy it because they like it—violates the convention of victimization in which volition plays no role in drug taking. The law disrespects the preferences of marijuana smokers, who are, after all, "drug abusers." The quotes from the opinions of justices Black and Douglas in Chapter Ten rest on similar premises of disease and victimization, Douglas invoking the specter of the helpless, debased, and physically degenerated heroin addict done in by the drug, and Black the drug takers who are "crippled," "dwarfed," or "paralyzed" (passive voice again) by the drugs. Both victims seem weak and pitiful, not even, as in the *Robinson* case, deserving legal blame for their condition. This reductionist denial of the human capacity for choice and the reversal of causation—drugs control the user rather than vice versa—play a critical role in maintaining the status quo. The law must protect society from drugs. Society is presumed to be composed of people helpless and powerless to choose safe and ethical conduct.

The impasse in the War on Drugs thus finds its anchor in this unexamined, unconscious denigration of the human capacity for responsible choice and self-control in the matter of drugs and consciousness. Ironically, that meta-conception violates the fundamental moral premise of our political, economic, and legal systems: that the individual is competent to order his life, to vote, to manage his own affairs and be responsible for whatever results he produces in life. In the economic sphere, despite numerous market interventions and a tradition of limited paternalism, consumer protection legislation centers primarily on disclosure, labeling, truthful advertising, and design safety. Within those broad contours, consumers can buy all manner of dangerous products from poisons to guns to dynamite, often without a permit or license of any kind.

In law, the heritage of our criminal justice system from the common law honors the principle of free will in human conduct. Unlike deterministic notions of modern psychiatry, in the common law all serious crimes require *mens rea*, or criminal intent. No one deserves punishment for serious crime without that guilty mind or intent because the predicate of just punishment is moral blameworthiness. That in turn emanates from the capacity to choose wrongful conduct. Critically, the law presumes that everyone has the capacity so to choose, save only for children under fourteen or the insane. Insanity negates criminality precisely because it precludes the kind of free choice necessary for moral blameworthiness. So does infancy. In both cases, the law recognizes a lack of capacity for meaningful choice because the individual does not appreciate the wrongfulness of his act. But for drunkenness, the condition closest to the drug state, the common law has made hardly any concession at all. An intoxicated defendant remains guilty for his crime despite his drunkenness, except perhaps for "specific intent" crimes if the jury can be persuaded that the defendant was too drunk to form an intent to steal, for example. Or premeditated murder might be mitigated to murder in the second degree. Despite this slight bending of the principle, the law generally holds the drunken criminal accountable for his crime because of the premise that his intoxication was itself an exercise of volition.

By contrast, the War on Drugs violates the fundamental common law principle of responsibility in its reliance on coercive, preventive laws—prohibition—passed in *anticipation* of misconduct, whether or not it actually occurs. It thus proceeds from a platform of disrespect for the idea of individual rights and responsibilities; its premises do not harmonize with those of the legal and political systems, and that dissonance may explain much of its futility and destructiveness.

The conception of drug taker as victim also defies historical experience and psychological knowledge about human motivation. Rather than casting about for weary existential explanations—drug taking as an escape from reality or the pain of existence—it generally makes more sense to look to drug taking as an affirmation of the joy of life. Most societies use drugs for celebratory purposes—alcohol at parties, weddings, bar mitzvahs, state dinners. The use of illegal drugs follows the same social and psychological mechanisms. Indeed, the use of drugs in social rituals is such a universal phenomenon, part of almost every culture, that Dr. Weil theorizes that the

> desire to alter consciousness is an *innate* psychological drive arising out of the neurological structure of the human brain. Strong evidence for this idea comes from observations of very young children, who regularly use techniques of consciousness alteration on themselves and each other when they think no adults are watching them. These methods include whirling until vertigo and collapse ensue, hyperventilating and . . . fainting. Such practices appear to be universal, irrespective of culture, and present at ages when social conditioning is unlikely to be an important influence (in two and three year olds, for example).[6]

Of course, drug taking also has a destructive potential. But only a propagandist or an alarmist would want to place exclusive emphasis on the one dimension and ignore the obvious realm of positive experience and the persistence of the drive to attain it. The use of drugs for medicinal purposes (healing and relief of pain), and various expressions of heightened awareness—celebration, euphoria, sensuality, and sexuality—explains a lot more of drug-taking behavior than does pathology, which is the exclusive perception of the War on Drugs mentality. Furthermore, the taking of drugs can claim as alumni some of the world's most famous people, including President John F. Kennedy (marijuana, cocaine, amphetamines), Sigmund Freud, William Halstead (founder of the Johns Hopkins Medical School), Robert Louis Stevenson, Aldous Huxley, William Burroughs, Allen Ginsberg, and dozens of writers, indeed, tens of thousands of highly accomplished people in all fields of endeavor. Some of the most brilliant jazz improvisation ever played was created under the influence of heroin, marijuana, or other drugs. The rubbish that passes for drug education in the public schools or the media denies all of this, which is not intended to be an endorsement of drugs (especially for on-duty neurosurgeons or air traffic controllers), but a simple recognition of the dualistic character of drugs.

> As soon as we begin to understand that drugs have a positive side that can be developed, we no longer need try to make drugs go away, which, as we have seen, makes them more of a problem. For drugs are perfect examples of the ambivalence of external things. They are potential keys to better ways of using the mind; they are also potential traps that can keep us from using our minds in better ways. As long as we continue to ridicule the possibility that drugs can help us, we have no chance of making them less harmful to us.[7]

The refusal to accept the positive potential of drugs stems largely from the wilful ignorance mandated by the negative consensus on illegal drugs.

Drug users, who already know the truth, cannot share their experience with the straight world for fear of legal action or damage to social or professional standing. The law thus keeps successful, knowledgeable drug users "in the closet," and that silence contributes to maintenance of the present impasse based on the false paradigm of drug taker as victim. For this reason, a moratorium on enforcement of possessory offenses constitutes an important step toward breaking the impasse. It would permit those with accurate information based on actual experience to come out of the closet and educate others. The emergence of an overwhelming number of "successful" drug users would powerfully challenge and ultimately undermine the social agreement that drugs are unidimensional, destructive substances.

People take drugs, as they have throughout history and across cultures, because they need and like the experience. Unlike the politicians and drug enforcers, they do not see themselves as victims of the drugs they take. Yet, a balanced view of the matter must also respect the legitimate concerns arising from drug use. What about those who become addicted? Are they not victimized, and doesn't the law find its greatest justification in trying to prevent that disaster, what Professor David Richards has called "the alienation of moral personality"?

Richards traces the moral condemnation of drug use, and especially drug addiction, to "the perfectionist ideal of the person," which "identifies virtue with personal imitation of Christ, and this in a commitment to extraordinary self-sacrifice in the service of others, requiring the exercise of independent conscientiousness and self control."[8] Drug addiction clearly represents a failure to achieve these Christian ideals. The rejoinder can proceed on at least two levels: first, does addiction in fact mean loss of self-control; and second, if it does, can it provide an adequate justification for the War on Drugs?

The first-level challenge comes from critics like Thomas Szasz, who repudiate the circularity of the concept of addiction: "We call certain drugs 'addictive' because people like to use them—just as we call ether and gasoline 'flammable' because they are easily ignited."[9] This is no mere wordplay; in reality many daily drug takers who might be called "addicts" simply stop taking drugs when sufficiently motivated. This phenomenon occurs commonly with all drugs. The heroin user upon return from Vietnam, for example, decides, or is "compelled" by lack of supply, to quit cold turkey. He goes through "withdrawal sickness," a very uncomfortable detoxification process of a week or more. A cigarette smoker with a track record of failed attempts to quit the habit, after receiving a diagnosis of lung cancer, immediately stops smoking forever. He, too, experiences physical symptoms and psychological cravings. But if these "addicts" can quit, is it meaningful to call them addicted? And if they "can't" quit, is it because of the chemical properties of the drugs or because *they* lack motivation or self-discipline, preferring the immediate, experiential gratification of the drug to the mere abstract thought of being drug-free tomorrow?

In fact, the psychological reality of what we call drug addiction replicates entirely that of the person with a "weight problem" who repeatedly tries but fails to stay on a diet or lose weight. We do not call food addicting (just as we do not call alcohol addicting despite 10 or 12 million alcoholics). Instead, we sensibly regard the cause of obesity as overeating. The ideology of victimization intrudes slightly to the extent that doctors or patients may seek to ascribe obesity to a metabolic disorder, genetic predisposition, or other condition beyond the individual's control. Nevertheless, no prisoner remained fat at Auschwitz, and the centrality of caloric intake in causing obesity must be close to universal. This shifts the focus from object—food and its chemical properties—to the individual's compulsive behavior and his responsibility for it.

Logically, we should frame the issue in the same way regarding drug abuse. But "drug addiction" looks to the outsider so much more powerful than "food addiction" primarily because it often involves extremist behavior as a result of the fact that it is illegal and therefore very costly. There is no need to mortgage a house or embezzle funds from an employer to satisfy the craving for junk food. Similarly, conventional terminology does not describe cigarette smokers as "addicts," because their drug is cheap, legal, and readily available. Is not addiction, then, a function of law and custom rather than medicine or physiology? Is not "addiction" a value judgment applied selectively to stigmatize those who make the socially defiant choice to habituate to an illegal drug?

Even researchers who intend to describe a value-neutral technical dependency by the word have no agreement as to the origins of "addiction." Physical, psychological, biological, sociological, and other theories compete for explanatory hegemony. The literature on the etiology of alcoholism exhibits the same ambiguity, with some researchers emphasizing environmental conditions (family background) and others looking to genetic causes (Jellinek's disease). Some clinicians in the addiction treatment field see addiction itself as a disease, regardless of the drug in question, e.g., "dependency disorder of the cocaine type." This approach has the advantage of unifying various types of drug and alcohol addiction under one conceptual umbrella. It shares the character of other theories in *assuming* that the addict is doing other than what he wants to do. In other words, the possibility of choice is rejected.

The confusion surrounding the idea of "addiction" reflects the poverty of the concept—it is a construct that assumes the very thing in dispute. The truth of the matter is that addiction specialists have no valid means of distinguishing drug addiction from compulsive overeating. Perhaps "drug addiction" offers something useful to people voluntarily seeking treatment. As a political premise, however, it distorts reality by falsely representing drug addiction as a physical dependency. By the same token, the hedged position—addiction as psychological dependency—cannot validly be distinguished from an undisciplined succumbing to temptation or even an emphatic predilection for the pleasures of the drug. Szasz again:

> How, then, shall we view the situation of the so-called drug abuser or drug addict? As a stupid, sick, and helpless child, who, tempted by pushers, peers, and the pleasures of drugs, succumbs to the lure and loses control of himself? Or as a person in control of himself, who, like Adam, chooses the forbidden fruit as the elemental and elementary way of pitting himself against authority?
>
> There is no empirical or scientific way of choosing between these two answers, of deciding which is right and which is wrong. The questions frame two different moral perspectives, and the answers define two different moral strategies: if we side with authority and wish to repress the individual, we shall treat him *as if* he were helpless, the innocent victim of overwhelming temptation; and we shall then "protect" him from further temptation by treating him as a child, slave, or madman. If we side with the individual and wish to refute the legitimacy and reject the power of authority to infantilize him, we shall treat him *as if* he were in command of himself, the executor of responsible decisions; and we shall then demand that he respect others as he respects himself by treating him as an adult, a free individual, or a "rational" person.[10]

Many, especially those in the addiction treatment field, will find Szasz's "radical" critique of the idea of addict as master rather than victim completely unrealistic. Having counseled patients who go through painful withdrawals followed by repeated relapses, who claim with apparent sincerity that they really want to quit but just cannot, and who pay a very high social and economic price for continued dependency, insistence upon individual responsibility for addiction, either as a norm or as a description of reality, must seem harsh and impractical to boot. They accept as fact that drugs "are" addictive because addicts say they cannot control their drug taking. But again, they cannot distinguish an addict's dependency from lack of control or motivation. Moreover, their world view gets twisted by their limited exposure: they treat only people who have come forward with self-described problems. The tens of thousands or millions who have no difficulty living with their "addiction" form no part of the clinician's experience. If it did, the perception of drugs as addicting would not seem so compelling.

Ultimately, it is not necessary to decide whether the addict is or is not a person in control of himself, but whether to treat him *as if* he were. The strongest argument for prohibition presents it as a prophylaxis against addiction because the addict cannot be deemed responsible for his conduct. But the law itself makes no excuses for the addict in terms of criminal responsibility.

In a leading case in point, *United States* v. *Moore*,[11] the Court of Appeals for the District of Columbia affirmed the conviction of a heroin addict of "long standing" for possession of the drug. Moore argued that he had an "overpowering need" to use heroin and therefore lacked the necessary criminal intent to commit the crime of possession. In other words, lacking real choice in the matter, the law could not justly hold him responsible. The court disagreed because of its insistence on the premise of free will, i.e., that the physical craving might be controlled by the addict's "character or his moral standards." The court also correctly observed that exculpating Moore for possession would require exculpating, say, a bank robber motivated by the need to finance a fix. As a matter of principle, held the court, the addict must remain responsible. So the law does not accommodate a case of volition impaired or "overcome" by drugs.

It is important to note that the law comes up with the same answer for the alcoholic. In *Powell* v. *Texas*[12] the defendant challenged his conviction for public intoxication on grounds similar to those advanced by Moore. As an alcoholic, he argued, his public drunkenness was merely a symptom of a disease or condition over which he had no control and therefore no intent—no criminal responsibility. In a five to four decision, the Supreme Court rejected that contention. Although the dissenters accepted Powell's view that he was "powerless to choose," the majority held that his act of going into a public place while drunk was not rendered involuntary by his alcoholism. Therefore, Powell bore criminal responsibility for his act.

Powell, like the *Moore* case, represents a coherent application of common law principles of criminal responsibility. Thus, the law answers Szasz's metaphysical query with the second answer—the law punishes him *as if* he were "a person in control of himself." Szasz's critique turns out not to be radical at all. The inconsistency and confusion for the criminal justice system could not be greater. For the purpose of punishing the addict, the law deems him fully responsible for his crime in taking the drug; for the purpose of "treating" his addiction, with methadone (or even compulsory civil commitment for detoxification), the law regards him as victim of his habit; and, for the purpose of preventing addiction in the first place, *everyone* is regarded as helpless. Thus, the War on Drugs attempts to prevent addiction of legally responsible individuals by denying the entire population access to a drug supply, treating people as though they were not morally responsible.

Accepting drug addiction as a form of free agency encounters so much resistance because of the extraordinary lengths to which many addicts will go in pursuit of and payment for the drug. The choices they sometimes make—to live in the streets, to give up family and friends, to forsake career and professional success—seem irrational to people of a more conventional turn of mind. Surely, the thought process goes, no one in control of himself would choose drug taking over the generally accepted goals of a middle-class life. Such assumptions enshrine bourgeois values and condemn non-conformity. The credo "Live fast, die young and leave a good looking corpse" has its adherents. Perhaps such nihilism should be condemned as a matter of social criticism or the moral education of the young. But the Government should not make it a crime. Certainly, the attempt to engage the issue of the value of life in such an attenuated fashion as a prohibition on the supply of drugs, objects with a dual character, makes little sense. Law, in fact, produces much of the alienation it condemns, converting what would otherwise be relatively innocuous behavior into crime and degeneracy committed in the sleazy environs of a drug underworld—drug markets, freebase houses, shooting galleries, crime syndicates, guns, robberies, cops, paranoia, and so on. These black market pathologies, produced by drug enforcement, but conventionally attributed to the drugs themselves, help reinforce the negative stereotypes surrounding illegal drugs.

Even if one cannot accept the model of the drug user as a person in control of himself, a second approach avoids the conceptual quagmire surrounding addiction and victimization. Practically speaking, the idea of victimization cannot find meaningful statistical support. Historically, drug taking (excepting perhaps cigarettes) does not result in what most people would call "addiction," i.e., some compulsive pattern of use. On the contrary, experience shows that no more than about 10–20 percent of a drug-using population becomes dependent on it or compulsive in consumption.[13] The distinction between social drinking and alcoholism (about 10 percent of the total drinking population) or "problem drinking" that everyone understands and accepts proves equally true for cocaine and heroin. The dominant pattern consists of controlled recreational or social use, not chronic, compulsive, or obsessive use.

I believe that this fact powerfully demonstrates the meaninglessness of the concept of addiction and the meaninglessness of the artificial experiments conducted with caged monkeys. If only 10 or 20 percent of a population exposed to a drug supply becomes "addicted," the condition of that minority cannot reasonably be described as "caused" by the drug unless we accept food as the cause of obesity. Most people will not *permit* themselves to become addicted, just as most people will not consistently overeat to the point of obesity.

In short, people have natural defenses to drug abuse—a sort of internal gyroscope—that brings them back to a "normal" ego-centered consciousness. After all, the importance of the ego as a source of identity and survival and a frame of reference for knowing the world "out there" presents a powerful case for it as a built-in "antidote" to drugs, preventing overdoses in the short run and dependency in the long run. The law of diminishing marginal utility—the powerful tendency to get less and less incremental pleasure out of more and more of a thing—is another way of explaining the same thing. People get bored or tired of endless repetitions. No one wants to stay high all day long, every day, forever. The only thing that keeps it interesting is the *change* from one state to the other and back again.

Like the cocktail hour, the use of illegal drugs most typically occurs with reasonable spaces of abstinence in between, where normal life goes on. If this is correct, Andy Weil's natural drive to get high carries with it a natural balance wheel—the drive to get straight. Of course, some people seem to have a weak gyroscope and succumb to what looks to an outside observer like addiction, but not most and even then not forever. Worst-case scenarios cannot intelligently govern the whole. The best argument the Government can make is that repeated use of drugs has a *potential* to produce addiction, assuming for the sake of discussion the validity of the concept, in the 10 percent or 20 percent who lack natural balance. This provides little justification for the Government's gross overkill in totally prohibiting the taking of that risk, especially in a society that generally relegates to the individual decisions about what risks are worth taking.

Cocaine—like all drugs—is "dangerous" only in the sense that life itself is dangerous. Perhaps it falls on the higher end of the risk scale. Dr. Byck points out that almost any substance can be abused, but that some substances are more frequently abused. People seem to prefer their effects. Still, the prevailing paradigm for life risks in general leaves dangerous activity alone, regarding the matter as one of individual choice. Large and growing segments of the population regularly take to the seas, skies, and slopes for sport and adventure: sky diving, hang gliding, ultralight aircraft, scuba diving, mountaineering, and the like. These are dangerous activities, in the practical sense that people frequently hurt themselves or die.

Mountaineering provides a vivid illustration. On Father's Day, 1981, 16 climbers died in two separate incidents on Mt. Rainier and Mt. Hood. During October-November, 1984, three climbing fatalities in five days occurred at El Capitan in Yosemite National Park. In recording those deaths, the American Alpine Club noted that 799 mountaineering and rock climbing deaths occurred in the period from 1951 to 1983.[14] Certainly, climbers also sustained thousands of nonfatal injuries. Why do people do such dangerous things? Sir Edmund Hilary said he climbed Mt. Everest "because it was there." Others offer a familiar rationale:

> "Climbing is an addiction," said Jerry Moffatt, 21, a British citizen who is one of the world's top rock climbers and who has lost two friends in climbing accidents. "It's such a great buzz, so much better than any other sport. And once you've felt the buzz, you can't stop."[15]

In our society, we let people choose their non-drug "addictions" with no interference at all, usually not even regulation. The flying of ultralight aircraft, skiing, climbing, etc., do not even require a license or other demonstration of competence. Society simply defers to the freedom of the individual. It takes individual rights seriously insofar as it is willing to accept a high risk of injury or death as the natural or inevitable price of such freedom. Guns provide the classic example, with 12,000 homicides by handgun each year. Yet, the political reality accepts that "guns don't kill people, people kill people." The triteness of the formulation should not obscure its expression of a fundamental moral premise. To reverse the flow of causation with drugs violates the political and social premise of individual responsibility. In that sense, the very idea of a "drug problem" has no meaning. To attribute the very real problems that a minority of drug users experience to the properties of drugs as dangerous substances makes as much sense as attributing obesity to the addictive property of food. Like food, drugs "cause" no harm.

This conceptual confusion of cause and effect governing popular thinking about drugs should at least be tempered by some realistic appreciation of the risk factor arising from the consumption of drugs. As discussed in Chapter One, variables of dosage, frequency, route of administration, set and setting all play important roles. No purely objective measurement is possible. Moreover, different drugs pose different risks: with alcohol, the main risk is traumatic injury while intoxicated; with marijuana, long-term respiratory diseases associated with smoking; with cocaine, overdose is possible but dependency is the more usual problem. If some measure of injury or death per time unit of exposure could be devised, it might show a lower level of short-term injury from snorting billions of lines of cocaine than from pursuing the physically risky endeavors mentioned above. Grinspoon and Bakalar argue that such comparisons lie beyond the realm of serious public debate "because what a society regards as rational is inseparable from its traditions and self image . . . [which] are incompatible with any way of classifying social problems that would make a debate like that possible."[16] But breaking the impasse is precisely the goal of this book, and I think the authors overstate the case in comparing the "right" to take drugs to the freedom to climb mountains. That formulation trivializes the real nature of what the drug law seeks (futilely) to suppress.

We deal here with a drive as powerful as the sexual and aggressive drives which Freud conceived as the two main instincts of the human species. Indeed, some Freudians have labeled the consciousness-altering behavior of children "sexual equivalents." The analogy is insightful. As Weil observes, "Like the cyclic urge to relieve sexual tension, . . . the urge to suspend ordinary awareness arises spontaneously from within, builds to a peak, finds relief, and dissipates. . . . In other words, episodes of sexual release and episodes of suspension of ordinary consciousness feel good; they satisfy an inner need."[17] Weil traces the evolution of childhood experience with altered consciousness and concludes that "use of illegal drugs is nothing more than a continuation of a developmental sequence going back to early childhood."[18] Understood in this way, drug taking claims a much higher status than a license to do whatever feels good. It is not mere indulgence, but a response to a primal force. Indeed, it resembles other states that command the highest degree of social approval, including romantic love, religious experience, and scientific discovery or invention. The common thread that ties these states together is the sense of transcendence.

In *Civilization and Its Discontents*, Freud observed that "the ego ordinarily maintains clear and sharp lines of demarcation" toward the outside world, except when in love. "At the height of being in love the boundary between ego and object threatens to melt away."[19] Freud saw the psychological experience of love as a possible explanation or model for religious energy, the "feeling of an indissoluble bond, of being one with the external world as a whole."[20] A similar process of union and transcendence may also lie at the core of "intellectual" discovery or insight; Albert Einstein asserted that he did not arrive at his understanding of the structure of the universe through his rational intellect. Intuition, dreams, and trances similarly embody the process of transcending ordinary ego-awareness and "merging" into the external world, or at least blurring "the sharp lines of demarcation" between the sense of self and the separateness of the material world.

An understanding of the relationship of drug taking to these other accepted (if not revered) states of altered consciousness could play a major role in shifting the prevailing perception of the meaning of drug taking. In fact, these insights should help to confer some level of "respectability" on it because the underlying reality of drug taking replicates those of socially valued experiences. The altered states share an essential similarity in breaking down the ordinary limits of human awareness.

Weil cautions, however, that "drugs are merely means to achieve states of non-ordinary awareness and must not be confused with the experiences themselves. They have the capacity to trigger highs; they do not contain highs. Moreover, the experiences they trigger are essentially no different from experiences triggered by more natural means."[21] This knowledge provides the key to creating a new context of drug management, one that realistically deals with the true nature of the drug-taking experience while insisting on a standard of personal responsibility for the consequences of that conduct. Weil proposes two specific goals: "(1) encouragement of people who want to use drugs to use them intelligently for their own good and thereby for the good of society; (2) encouragement of people to progress beyond drugs to better methods of altering consciousness."[22] This policy poses formidable challenges.

Most societies, like our own, are uncomfortable about having people go off into trances, mystic raptures, and hallucinatory intoxications. Indeed, the reason we have laws against possession of drugs in the first place is to discourage people from getting high. But innate, neuropsychological drives cannot be banned by legislation. They will be satisfied at any cost. And the cost in our country is very great: by trying to deny young people these important experiences, we maximize the probability that they will obtain them in negative ways—that is, in ways harmful to themselves and to society.[23]

Weil's interpretation of drug-taking behavior and his tolerance for it radically diverge from the present paradigm of drug control as necessary to prevent victimization and therefore will encounter fierce resistance. Yet the power and persistence of drug taking to reach altered states of consciousness remain facts of life. To deal intelligently with that reality requires a workable framework. We can continue to approach it from a condition of personal irresponsibility—as the unruly impulses of animals, like the caged monkeys used in experiments with cocaine, requiring maximum restraint by force and conditioning (legal threats and prohibition)—and continue reproducing the mistakes and failures of the past. Or we can approach it from a condition of personal responsibility, in which people are raised and schooled in self-awareness and self-regulation of their drives and held accountable for their conduct. To the extent that people learn what is necessary to know, drug abuse will diminish. By contrast, legal "management" of drugs offers as much leverage on behavior as legal management of sexual drives—not much. Acculturation and socialization offer the only real possibilities for "control," just as they play the critical role in restraining sexuality and aggressiveness.

In *Civilization and Its Discontents*, Freud sought to explain modern culture as a system for the sublimation of the human instincts for sexuality and aggression. About the law, he had almost nothing to say. For in that taming of the human beast, the law plays almost no role at all. Cultural standards historically precede legal ones; Freud asserted that the first laws came from taboos. Of course, in its declarations of the good and the bad, the law symbolically reinforces the culturally generated limits. Operationally, however, the moral code and social customs arising from that morality provide the real force in restraining behavior. As Montaigne put the matter, "custom is the greatest magistrate."

In general, people do not abstain from incest, rape, or murder because of the law; rather, those crimes became crimes because they embody anterior fundamental beliefs about right and wrong. The law alone could not possibly serve as an effective deterrent to the commission of incest; the social taboo reinforced by a sense of guilt (the superego) carries almost the entire behavioral burden. Legal enforcement is rare and has little potential, if any, for operational impact. As Sutherland put the matter, "when the mores are adequate, laws are unnecessary; when the mores are inadequate, the laws are ineffective."

The effective regulation of drug taking does not depart from these principles. The law alone cannot suppress the primal force of the drug-taking, consciousness-altering drive, especially where the social consensus and cultural restraints that formerly supported compliance with the law have broken down. To channel that drive in socially constructive ways requires building a set of cultural norms and customary restraints transmitted from one generation to the next starting in early childhood. Clearly, this requires long-term socializing and educational efforts to inculcate the desired standards and values. Nor does it address the conditions of current adults.

Yet for future generations, the task is quite feasible because it proceeds from truthfulness, respect for individuality, and realistic appraisal of the capacities of social institutions like the family and the school. The various awareness techniques for experiencing non-drug highs are learnable skills, not exercises in mysticism. The schools can teach yoga, Zen, meditation, massage, biofeedback, autohypnosis, mind control, and the martial arts effectively, just as they can and should teach preventive health care and wellness—diet, nutrition, exercise, and the like. They can discourage drug taking as artificial manipulation of the mind and body. They can demystify drug "highs" by teaching the natural techniques of attaining them. They can inculcate body awareness and the intimate relationship of mind and body in producing health and a sense of well-being.

Conventional anti-drug "education" suffers from the false premises and ideological negativism described in Chapter Ten. Factually, presentations are distorted and incomplete. Moreover, sophisticated students know from personal experience the falsity of the propaganda about the effects of drugs. Most of all, since the standard approach denies the legitimacy—the inevitability—of the drive to get high, it does not meet the demand to satisfy that need in constructive ways. Real drug education must honestly confront that issue. Otherwise, it forfeits credibility and effectiveness. As an example, consider the "Chemical People" production hosted by Nancy Reagan and broadcast in 1983 on PBS. Despite substantial advance publicity in South Florida, the event drew a "disappointing" attendance of parents and youth at participating schools.[24] Suppose they gave a war and nobody came?

A well-rounded program of formal and informal schooling in the techniques of staying well and achieving drug-free highs will go a long way toward ameliorating the worst excesses of drug abuse that now seem so common. The mystique attached to drug experiences will tend to diminish once understood as simply an alternative (although quicker) means of altering consciousness. An emphasis on fitness and health, especially vigorous aerobic exercise, will produce the experience of endogenous-drug highs through the release of "nature's opiates," the endorphins. This, in turn, will tend to discourage the taking of drugs or moderate the frequency of use, because in the long run drug highs are inferior to natural ones. Finally, an insistence on personal responsibility for things done under the influence of drugs will discourage harmful or risky behavior, like driving under the influence.

Schooling and training at home provide only the starting points; an effective system of management of drug taking must build a spider's web of customary restraints to discourage irresponsible alteration of consciousness. These restraints must find support in social agreement. For example, the current social consensus will not tolerate prohibition, but it will support restrictions on drugs in the workplace, drugs and driving, drugs for minors, and drugs in public places. The work ethic, the need for education, fitness, and exercise and other types of discipline all support functionally oriented restrictions on the time, place, manner, and social occasion of drug taking.

If our society ever becomes interested in actually managing "the drug problem" instead of throwing an ideological temper tantrum, it will concentrate its efforts on the long-term process of designing community-based regulatory mechanisms, in the public and private sectors, to influence and moderate drug-taking behavior. It will fund research into these alternatives. And once drug taking comes out of the closet, where it is now confined by law and social stigma, it will benefit from a variety of informal, customary controls. These include cultural recipes (such as one or two drinks before dinner), role model influences, peer group influences, media influences, packaging (amounts or doses), social-class customs, peer group sanctions, and many others.[25] Indeed, the simple process of growing up, living, and working within a system of interlocking responsibilities provides the most obvious set of channeling influences.

I have not attempted to map out the specific features of a post–War on Drugs terrain because it seems premature, clearly secondary in importance to the contextual shift itself. As the National Commission on Marihuana and Drug Abuse pointed out, during seven decades of the same drug policy not once "have the underlying assumptions been systematically evaluated and a broad coherent foundation for policy making established." That's what I have attempted to accomplish in this book. Redefining "the drug problem," reorganizing it around a different set of principles, will automatically begin a process in which many of the obvious questions will answer themselves. Just as the historic shift in attitudes from racial and sexual hierarchy to equality set in motion social and legal forces that totally reorganized those relationships, so too will a new paradigm of volitional and responsible (drug and non-drug) consciousness control eventually work itself out. For example, whether public and private employers will have the legal authority to require random urine samples as a means of enforcing discipline in the workplace, or whether they will first need legal cause to administer the test, is a detail that will get answered in time by living within a framework of individual responsibility and accountability to see what that means in concrete settings. Already, many employers are beginning to require urine tests, and the practice raises a substantial privacy issue. Nevertheless, it would offer great promise as an *alternative* to law enforcement, rather than an additional element of force in the present coercive environment.

Substantial benefits in public safety and reduced black market pathologies will be realized as a result of such a contextual shift. First, it will have a calming effect. The hysteria surrounding the image of one-third of a nation doping itself while Washington remains powerless to take any effective action would be fragmented into more manageable individual problems. A national or macro-problem of massive and alarming proportions would break down into a set of micro-problems to be addressed by the individual, the family, and community organizations. Paramilitary panic about losing the war would cease to be relevant because the nation would not be at war. Reportage would reflect the reduced level of conflict. Drug abuse would become like any other health problem, managed by research, prevention, education, and treatment. (By contrast, the Reagan Administration sliced the prevention and treatment budget in half in order to funnel the money into law enforcement.) People will begin to feel safer and more secure, where now they tell pollsters that the drug problem is extremely serious, equal in importance to violent crime.

Once society shifts from a world view of drug taking as victimization, helplessness, and aberration to one of conscious regulation of a natural drive, the drug enforcement enterprise will cease to have validity (except for children). Its very premise will have been crushed. The need for the Government's "protection" from an external enemy will vanish. The War on Drugs will emerge in its true character—a war on one-third of the American people, or more accurately, a stupid and futile attack on their satisfaction of a fundamental human drive. This is not to deny the fact that people will continue to hurt themselves or others with drugs, although precautionary practices should improve as people grow more sophisticated about non-drug alternatives and more careful about the circumstances of drug use. But the appropriate response to any harms that occur will flow from the premise that the individual bears responsibility for his conduct and may deserve social censure, dismissal from employment, or even criminal punishment for misconduct, but not for the drug taking itself.

Many will regard this as "unrealistic." People *do* need protection and restraint, they will argue. And, after all, individual responsibility for consciousness control does seem an impossibly lofty aspiration in a society that deems it necessary to remind people not to spit on the sidewalk or to wash their hands after using the toilet. Human beings clearly cannot be relied upon to do the right thing for their own good, not to mention the public welfare. This line of argument confuses normative and descriptive realities. In crafting a drug policy for the next generation, it would be foolish to be locked into the current level of ignorance and misunderstanding. Moreover, the proper role of the law is to set standards of criminality that reflect fundamental values and that lend themselves to effective enforcement without destructive side effects. Drug laws fail on both counts. In my judgment, the War on Drugs is so wrong, so ineffective, and so destructive that almost any alternative should be preferred by thinking people. It would be hard to do worse than the status quo.

What about the feared trade-off in increased drug abuse? The main argument against relaxing law enforcement pressure has always been fear of opening the floodgates. Dr. William Pollin, former director of NIDA, raises the classic objection: he asserts that the War on Drugs is actually a success because in its absence 60–100 million people would use cocaine.[26] Dr. Pollin's fears embody the fragmented, anti-holistic belief about human behavior that drugs trump people, disregarding the capacity for choice and responsible conduct. He fails to understand the gyroscopic power of the ego to ensure its own survival by returning to normal states of consciousness.

Nevertheless, experience tends to support the view that the level of drug use in a society bears only a slight relationship to the length of the prohibitionist leash. For example, the National Commission on Marihuana and Drug Abuse survey found that only 3 percent of adults and 8 percent of youth would try marijuana if it were legalized.[27] Experience in Oregon, California, and Maine following decriminalization of marijuana in the 1970s showed no significant percentage of new users or an increase in frequency of use.[28] All the surveys suffered methodological faults, but the results correlate with common sense.

The demand for any product at a given price has a natural market size. People do not want unlimited supplies of anything. With marijuana, something approaching full market penetration had already occurred before the law changed in the 1970s. Cocaine has not yet reached that saturation level yet, although an educated guess might put the United States about halfway there, a market of 40 million first-timers and 20 million monthly users. Whatever the exact number, the market for cocaine or any drug must inevitably top out. This is especially true for a stimulant; most people, especially as they age, want to relax and therefore prefer mellowing or depressant drugs. The large market for decaffeinated coffee also reminds us of such limits. People will not demand cocaine *ad infinitum* like the caged monkeys. The ordinary process of aging also provides a natural ceiling on cocaine consumption. Consumers over 35 or 40 generally will drop out of the market entirely or reduce significantly the frequency of consumption. This will contribute to the market's inevitable plateau, as new consumers simply replace the dropouts.

Even if we indulge Dr. Pollin's worst fears, millions of people using cocaine (at present levels of frequency) would present a far rosier health profile than that of an equal number of cigarette smokers. Using 1981 as a base, DEA's 6.75 million monthly users of cocaine would have to be multiplied by a factor of 8 to replicate the population of 54 million cigarette smokers. Assuming a crudely simplistic straight-line extrapolation of problems, the yearly health toll from cocaine would then be roughly 2,500 deaths, 110,000 problem users enrolled in federally funded clinics, and 40,000 nonfatal overdose cases treated in DAWN system hospital emergency rooms. The health toll then comes in a distant second to cigarettes in disease and death, although the effects of the two "addictions" on daily life have very different qualities.

These numbers are not meant to be taken casually; the human costs are real. But they do provide a useful perspective to moderate the hysteria voiced by such as Dr. Pollin. Furthermore, the casualties may well turn out to be far fewer once people moderate their behavior to take account of accumulated experience about cocaine and learn abstinence, restraint, or alternatives to drug highs. Worst-case scenarios assume that people do not learn anything and blindly repeat the mistakes of their predecessors. Dr. Pollin's fears thus reflect assumptions about human behavior that follow the caged-monkey model of mechanical reaction (press the lever) rather than a more complex creature with an integrated personality having plural values and goals.

There is neither freedom nor dignity in such a behavioral model, where people are objects to be controlled or conditioned, rather than responsible actors who can be entrusted with freedom and held accountable for both experiences and actions. Operating under this assumption, the Government must act to suppress the individual's attempt to govern his own consciousness out of fear for what the individual may do or experience. I wonder whether there is any difference in principle between governmental authority to prohibit drug use and the power to compel it?

While the Government's assertion of extraordinary power over human consciousness goes unchecked, the War on Drugs has never been able to conquer the human drive for transcendence. The need to assert independence, to pursue self-expression, to defy authority and alter consciousness seems instinctual and irrepressible, hence the booming black market and its burgeoning pathologies. The premises of the War on Drugs, in addition to being objectionable in principle, fail to offer any practical solution to the problem of drug abuse, which grows worse every year. The War on Drugs has no creative or constructive power whatever. You can't get there from here. Fortunately, the War on Drugs is beginning to collapse of its own weight.

12

Drugs in the Future

The reader who has accepted the argument thus far—that the War on Drugs inevitably is a losing and destructive policy; that it reflects a set of unconscious, prejudicial attitudes portraying the drug taker as victim rather than one exercising personal liberty in the pursuit of fundamental psychic needs; that these attitudes imprison us, disabling us from taking meaningful and principled action; and that breaking the impasse requires a new paradigm of individual responsibility for drug control—should now ask the critical question: How do we create a new paradigm? How can a whole society accept what it cannot even see?

In the abstract, no one can answer this question authoritatively. It poses the equivalent of asking how to produce an idea whose time has come. One suggestion of a break-out comes from the realm of scientific innovation. T. S. Kuhn argues that "the process by which a new candidate for paradigm replaces its predecessor" occurs "only after persistent failure to solve a noteworthy puzzle has given rise to crisis."[1] The War on Drugs certainly meets the test of persistent failure and may soon satisfy the element of crisis. The particular historical circumstances of the War on Drugs suggest that the process of transition to a new paradigm has already begun. The social consensus supporting the War on Drugs continues to erode at a rapid pace. Like slavery and the subjugation of women, the reign of the War on Drugs seems destined to pass into history.

The most striking evidence of the decline of the War on Drugs as a contextual force comes from the pervasiveness of illegal drug use over the last twenty years and its growing social acceptance. The numbers alone suggest a collapse of the consensus for prohibition—one-third of all Americans over age 12 with illegal drug experience. Actually, the presentation of this datum understates its true significance, since few people born before

1935 or 1940 grew up with any choice in the matter—they had few opportunities for exposure to illegal drugs. So if we focus on the age groups relevant to the making of policy for the future—say adults less than 45 or 50 years old—the percentage with some experience of and sophistication about drugs climbs much higher, probably constituting a majority. For example, the eleventh nationwide survey of 16,000 high school seniors reported that 61 percent of the class of 1985 had tried some kind of illegal drug.

But let us not quibble over percentages. The operative fact is that as the hegemonic, senior generation over age 45 or 50 dies off, it will be replaced by one for whom the War on Drugs makes no cultural sense, quite apart from its operational failures and black market pathologies. Occasionally one hears talk about reversing the trend, as though it were a mere fashion or passing fad like the Nehru jacket. But drug use has penetrated even the United States Congress, where the House Ethics Committee investigated allegations of illegal drug use (marijuana and cocaine) by eight former or current representatives.[2] Two were "cleared," two others admitted drug use, and there was "substantial evidence" against others. No, drug use is not only here to stay, but it will continue to grow until the markets reach their natural plateaus.

The shift from furtive underground activity to common social experience in "recreational" drug use could hardly be clearer. But this alone does not necessarily augur a new set of attitudes. Thomas Szasz has argued that a high level of drug use alone does not necessarily reflect acceptance of its legitimacy. He suggests that the drug user may share the stereotypical stigmas of the dominant culture toward his nonconformity, just as homosexuals may feel guilty about their deviance and suffer low self-esteem. Perhaps drug addicts continue to feel guilty about their addiction, since loss of self-control carries some stigma, but non-addicted users, the overwhelming majority, do not encounter such negative attitudes. On the contrary, the high and growing level of drug use finds increasing social acceptance. Peer group attitudes, as distinguished from those of distant authorities—parents or public officials—accept drugs as part of life and to some extent approve them as a positive force. The War on Drugs cannot survive very long in such an attitudinal environment.

The erosion of cultural agreement for the War on Drugs does not proceed in isolation. Rather, it reflects a complex of forces transforming the very structure of society. The full story of that transformation will have to be told in retrospect by a historian. But some of the forces at work in producing social change are already apparent. One useful source of these changes is John Naisbitt's *Megatrends*,[3] a book that is valuable for present purposes precisely because it does not address the drug issue at all. Using content analysis as his methodology, the author identifies social forces that should prove hostile to the very idea of a war on drugs and undermine its viability.

His first megatrend, the transformation from an industrial society to an information society, focuses on the economic importance of the technologies of communication.[4] That shift has a distinctly negative implication for the War on Drugs, which depends in part upon the unquestioning support of an ignorant populace lacking the information necessary to reach independent judgments. Many studies report that the more (accurate) information a person has about drugs, the less likely he is to regard them as dangerous. A better informed society with access to independent sources of information beyond Government propaganda is likely to use more rather than fewer drugs and use them in more careful, knowledgeable ways. That society is also likely to be more aware of and more critical of the ineffectiveness and destructiveness of present policy, again harking back to the media's role in reversing policy on Vietnam.

If this seems a bit speculative, consider Naisbitt's second megatrend. He calls it "high touch," a counterpoise to the "high tech" revolution. "The principle symbolizes the need for balance between our physical and spiritual reality."[5] Here Naisbitt introduces the human response to high technology, the need to compensate for the potentially dehumanizing effects of a sterile or tension-producing work environment. "That is why the human potential movement that advocates both discipline and responsibility is such a critical part of the high tech/high touch equation."[6]

Naisbitt's somewhat hackneyed statement about the human potential movement, which recognizes the need for conditions of life and practices conducive to a full integration of human personality in work and play, also has an important implication for drugs and consciousness control. It is no accident that Silicon Valley, California, the center of the computer industry, also is a center of consumption of cocaine and other drugs. Nor is it coincidence that Silicon Valley lies within the psychic umbrella of San Francisco, center of the human potential movement, Zen practice, Eastern philosophy, martial arts, flower power, and other explorations of human consciousness. On the contrary, Silicon Valley represents a natural marriage of the two phenomena. If high tech represents our material future and high touch the spiritual future, expanded awareness and practice of consciousness-altering techniques, including drugs, will almost certainly follow.

Closely related to the spiritual drives is the movement toward fitness and wellness, in the megatrend from institutional help to self-help.

> For decades, institutions such as the government, the medical establishment, the corporation, and the school system were America's buffers against life's hard realities—the needs for food, housing, health care, education—as well as its mysteries—birth, illness, death. Slowly we began to wean ourselves off our collective institutional dependence, learning to trust and rely only on ourselves.
>
> During the 1970s, Americans began to disengage from the institutions that had disillusioned them and to relearn the ability to take action on their own.[7]

The shift back to traditional self-reliance manifests itself in a variety of ways. Of greatest relevance to a new paradigm of drug control is the growing awareness and practice of health and fitness. Stimulated in part by growing suspicion of hospitals, doctors, and traditional medical care, the pursuit of wellness is gradually replacing the treatment of illness. In particular, Naisbitt cites the pervasiveness of new habits of diet and exercise designed to promote health, such as jogging, vitamins, health food, and a dramatic decline in cigarette smoking, as evidence for the "triumph of a new paradigm of wellness, preventive medicine and wholistic care."[8] Closer attention to nutritional principles has transformed the American diet and the marketing of food.[9]

These developments in individual responsibility for nutrition, health, fitness, and body awareness offer the single most promising counterpoise to the spreading use of drugs. People committed to wellness will tend to avoid or moderate their intake of drugs and alcohol, thereby averting the dangers of long-term, chronic drug use (the most damaging kind). The practices of wellness should also encourage greater awareness of the role of the mind/body interface in producing wellness or illness, and stimulate recognition of Dr. Weil's premise that drugs and non-drug techniques for altered consciousness form part of a single reality. Indeed, many health and fitness centers already offer classes in yoga and meditation as a logical extension of "staying in shape." Anyone who has practiced yoga or tai chi long enough to raise "shakti" or "chi" (energy) knows that it produces an experience of wellness more potent than any drug high. Even something as prosaic as long-distance running, with its release of endorphins into the bloodsteam to produce "runner's high," offers a vivid experience of the potency of natural highs.

Wellness does not, of course, preclude experimentation with drugs or occasional social use. Indeed, the independence of mind and self-sufficiency required to pursue regular physical and mental fitness will more likely lead to experimentation with (and without) drugs than conformity to the law's rigid code. But that type of experimentation poses little danger of destabilizing the balanced, centered, and integrated personality we're speaking of.

The megatrend embracing multiple options tends in the same direction—the development of more drugs and more non-drug techniques of consciousness manipulation as a result of the demands for diversity and new experience. *Megatrends* describes a growing heterogeneity.

> The social upheavals of the late 1960s, and the quieter changes of the 1970s, which spread 1960s values throughout much of traditional society, paved the way for the 1980s—a decade of unprecedented diversity. In a relatively short time, the unified mass society has fractionalized into many diverse groups of people with a wide

array of differing tastes and values, what advertisers call a market-segmented, market-decentralized society.[10]

Naisbitt cites cable television and specialty food as two examples of the public demand for greater choice in the marketplace. That same demand for variety expresses itself in the market for drugs. Alcohol and tobacco, even prescription drugs, do not satisfy. Consumers want a greater variety of products than what the law permits the market to deliver. As Dr. Weil puts it, people use illegal drugs because they produce better highs than legal ones. Even within the black market, consumer demand in the market for marijuana, for example, has produced market segmentation and product proliferation—"57 varieties" of high-potency marijuana, Colombian Gold, Gainesville Green, Panama Red, Maui Zowie, California sensemilla, and so forth. Many cocaine consumers have moved on, or expanded their repertoire, to include heroin, and the "speedball" mixture of the two is becoming very popular.

In 1985, the press minted the term "designer drugs" to cover the manufacture of "China White," a synthetic heroin, and other molecular variations on the chemical formulas of illegal drugs. Underground labs, mostly in California, began slightly altering the molecular composition of drugs to escape the restrictions of the law, which prohibits particular chemical formulas. In their new legal products, clever chemists have foreshadowed a potentially infinite array of mind-altering chemicals to meet the demands of the marketplace in its ceaseless quest for new frontiers of consciousness. These cottage industries operate at a safe remove from the reaches of law enforcement, indeed they operate *within* the letter of the law in introducing new compounds, not prohibited by the law. Naturally, Congress will not tolerate such open defiance of its power over drugs, and on October 3, 1985, the Senate Judiciary Committee approved S. 1437, which outlaws substances having a substantial similarity in chemical structure or effect to a Schedule I or II controlled substance. Closing the loophole (assuming the bill passes the House) may satisfy the sense of outrage that motivates the War on Drugs, but it offers no more real regulatory control than the existing laws muster over cocaine and other controlled substances.

Designer drugs represent just one more aspect of the leading role played by California—a bellwether state and fountainhead of social invention—in the evolution of American life patterns. The emerging pattern is one that endorses the validity of experimentation in drugs and controlled use of drugs. Clearly, the trend calls forth a cornucopia of drugs—new drugs, more drugs, old drugs (LSD is making a comeback). Proliferation of drugs represents the vanguard of the future.

The War on Drugs, by contrast, represents a rear-guard action fought by fearful men and women who do not understand contemporary culture, the needs of the human psyche, or the limits of the criminal sanction to control human behavior. As a result, it scrambles around, tragicomically ineffectual, trying to roll back the rising tide of drugs. Fear and ignorance render constructive action impossible. It is only a matter of time before the gap between the political/legal and cultural realities widens to unbridgeable dimensions, when the cognitive dissonance between the two becomes an unbearable cacophony. When that occurs, the War on Drugs will become an idea whose time has finally gone, and a new paradigm will emerge in the vacuum of authority that it leaves behind.

Notes

Introduction

1. Leslie Maitland, "President Gives Plan to Combat Drug Networks," *New York Times*, 15 October 1982, sec. A.
2. Edward J. Epstein, *Agency of Fear* (New York: G. P. Putnam's Sons, 1977), p. 178.
3. National Institute on Drug Abuse, *National Survey on Drug Abuse: Main Findings, 1982*, pp. 4, 33, 49.
4. President Ronald Reagan, Presidential Statement of 2 October 1982.
5. President Ronald Reagan, Presidential Statement of 14 October 1982.
6. Office of the Attorney General, *Attorney General's Task Force on Violent Crime, Final Report, 1981*, p. 28.
7. Congress, *Charter of Senate Drug Enforcement Caucus, 1982.*
8. House Select Committee on Narcotics Abuse and Control, H. Rep. No. 418, pts. 1–2, 97th Cong., 2d Sess., 1982, p. 50.
9. U.S., Strategy Council on Drug Abuse, *Federal Strategy for Prevention of Drug Abuse and Drug Trafficking, 1982*, p. 74.
10. Ronald Caffrey, "The Strategy of Enforcement," *Drug Enforcement*, Fall 1982, p. 2.
11. Ena Naunton, "Smart Set Stupidly Adopts Heroin," *Miami Herald*, 28 April 1984, sec. C.
12. "Marijuana Third Largest Crop," *The Leaflet*, vol. 11, no. 3, December 1982.

Chapter 1

1. Robert Byck, ed., *Cocaine Papers: Sigmund Freud* (New York: New American Library, 1974), p. xvii. The book contains the five articles that Freud published on cocaine: "Uber Coca" (1884), "Contribution to the Knowledge of the Effect of Cocaine" (1885), "Addenda to Uber Coca" (1885), "On the General Effect of Cocaine" (1885), and "Craving for and Fear of Cocaine" (1887).

2. Ibid., p. 7.

3. Ibid., p. 32. Shortly before Koller's discovery, the famous American surgeon Dr. William Halsted had reported the achievement of nerve block anesthesia by injecting cocaine into nerve trunks. But Koller made the more important discovery that cocaine was an effective topical anesthetic.

4. Ibid., p. 15.

5. David F. Musto, *The American Disease: Origins of Narcotic Control* (New Haven: Yale University Press, 1973), p. 7.

6. Byck, *Cocaine Papers*, pp. 172–73.

7. Joel L. Phillips and Ronald D. Wynne, *Cocaine: The Mystique and the Reality* (New York: Avon Books, 1980), pp. 73–74.

8. Ibid., pp. 49–50.

9. Ibid., p. 56.

10. Act of June 30, 1906, Ch. 3915, 34 Stat. 768; Act of June 25, 1938, Ch. 675, 8902(a), 52 Stat. 1059.

11. Gerald T. McLaughlin, "Cocaine: The History and Regulation of a Dangerous Drug," *Cornell Law Review*, vol. 58, 1973, pp. 560–66.

12. Richard Ashley, *Cocaine: Its History, Uses and Effects* (New York: Warner Books, 1975), p. 120.

13. Edward M. Brecher and the Editors of Consumer Reports, *Licit and Illicit Drugs: The Consumers Union Report on Narcotics, Stimulants, Depressants, Inhalants, Hallucinogens and Marijuana—Including Caffeine, Nicotine and Alcohol* (Mount Vernon, N.Y.: Consumers Union, 1972), pp. 304–5.

14. *Hearings Before the Subcommittee of the Senate Committee on the Judiciary to Investigate the Administration of the Internal Security Act and Other Internal Security Laws, World Drug Traffic and Its Impact on U.S. Security*, 92d Congress, 2d Sess., 1972, p. 295.

15. National Narcotics Intelligence Consumers Committee, *The Flow of Illicit Drugs into the United States and Its Economic Significance, 1978*, p. 13; ibid., *The Flow 1982*, p. 25; and ibid., *The Flow 1984*, p. 25.

16. National Narcotics Intelligence Consumers Committee, *The Flow 1984*. The 1984 report retroactively revises consumption estimates for 1981 through 1983 "to be consistent with the 1984 methodology," described as follows:

Drug prevalence data from the NIDA National Surveys on Drug Abuse for 1979 and 1982 were used to determine the cocaine using population within the various frequency of use categories in 1979 and 1982, and were combined with available information from other sources as an indication of population trends from 1981 to 1984. Since this produces a conservative estimate, a second estimate, which is believed to be exaggerated, was computed for each year based on consumption rates of treatment clients. The two estimates were used to determine a range which was then narrowed based on supply estimates. Actual consumption is believed to be near the midpoints.

17. National Institute on Drug Abuse, *National Survey on Drug Abuse: Main Findings 1979*, 1980.

18. National Institute on Drug Abuse, *National Household Survey on Drug Abuse 1982: Summary of Selected Findings*, April 1983.

19. Ibid. The meaningfulness of this datum is obscured by the crudity of the measurement: any "mention" of cocaine counts as an overdose.

20. National Narcotics Intelligence Consumers Committee, *The Supply of Drugs to the U.S. Illicit Market from Foreign and Domestic Sources in 1981*, p. 44.

21. Michael Demarest, "Cocaine: Middle Class High," *Time*, 6 July 1981, pp. 56–57.

22. House of Representatives, Select Committee on Narcotics Abuse and Control, "International Study Missions" (Summary Report), 97th Cong., 1st Sess., 1984, p. 18.

23. Ashley, *Cocaine*, pp. 182–83.

24. Byck, *Cocaine Papers*, p. xxxiv.

25. Jerome H. Jaffe, "Foreword," in National Institute on Drug Abuse, *Cocaine Use in America: Epidemiologic and Clinical Perspectives* (Washington, D.C.: U.S. Government Printing Office, 1985), p. v.

26. *Cocaine: A Major Drug Issue of the Seventies: Hearings Before the House Select Committee on Narcotics Abuse and Control*, 96th Cong., 1st Sess., 1979, p. 41.

27. Byck, *Cocaine Papers*, p. 60.

28. Ibid., pp. 97–98.

29. In one controlled experiment, 83% of 85 subjects given one gram of cocaine per month for one year reported absolutely no problems. The others reported mostly minor concerns. Gerald Uelmen and Victor Haddox, *Drug Abuse and the Law* (New York: Clark Boardman Co., 1983), pp. 2–71, citing Overend, "Cocaine: The Controversial Drug," *Los Angeles Times*, 4 October 1976, p. 6.

30. Ronald K. Siegel, "Longterm Effects of Recreational Cocaine Use," in F. R. Jeri, ed., *Cocaine 1980* (Lima, Peru: Pacific Press, 1980), p. 16.

31. Ronald K. Siegel, "New Patterns of Cocaine Use: Changing Doses and Routes," in National Institute on Drug Abuse, *Cocaine Use in America*, p. 210.

32. Ibid., pp. 208–9.

33. Ibid., p. 211.

34. Carlos Carbajol, "Psychosis Produced by Nasal Aspiration of Cocaine Hydrochloride," in Jeri, *Cocaine 1980*, pp. 128–32.

35. Charles R. Schuster and Chris E. Johanson, "The Evolution of Cocaine Using an Animal Model of Drug Abuse," in Jeri, *Cocaine 1980*, p. 37.

36. Ibid., p. 34.

37. Mark S. Gold et al., "Cocaine Abuse: Neurochemistry, Phenomenology and Treatment," in National Institute on Drug Abuse, *Cocaine Use in America*, p. 130.

38. Associated Press, "Survey: Cocaine Users Become Addicted," *Ft. Lauderdale News & Sun-Sentinel*, 19 September 1983, sec. A.

39. Ibid.

40. Craig Van Dyke and Robert Byck, *Drugs in American Society* (New York: H. W. Wilson Co., forthcoming).

41. Craig Van Dyke and Robert Byck, "Cocaine," *Scientific American*, March 1982, p. 141.

42. Byck, *Cocaine Papers*, pp. 98, 103.

43. Ibid., p. 99.

44. *Cocaine: A Major Drug Issue*, p. 51.

45. Ibid., p. 91.

46. Ibid., p. 92.

47. Ibid.
48. National Narcotics Intelligence Consumers Committee, *Supply of Drugs*, p. 107.
49. Ibid., p. 39.
50. Ibid.
51. National Institute on Drug Abuse, *Statistical Series: Annual Data 1981*, Series I, No. 1, 1982, p. 53.
52. Byck, *Cocaine Papers*, p. 92.

Chapter 2

1. Herbert Packer, *The Limits of the Criminal Sanction* (Stanford: Stanford University Press, 1968).
2. Mark Moore, "Limiting Supplies of Drugs to Illicit Markets," *Journal of Drug Issues*, vol. 8, 1979, p. 291.
3. *Cocaine: A Major Drug Issue of the Seventies: Hearings Before the House Select Committee on Narcotics Abuse and Control*, 96th Cong., 1st Sess., 1979, p. 54.
4. Paul Samuelson, *Economics*, 11th ed. (New York: McGraw-Hill, 1980), chap. 4.
5. David F. Musto, *The American Disease: Origins of Narcotic Control* (New Haven: Yale University Press, 1973), p. 6.
6. DEA, Offender Based Transaction System, *Case Level Arrests by Drug* (1982).
7. Florida Department of Law Enforcement, *Uniform Crime Report for 1982* (1983).
8. *United States Code*, vol. 21, sec. 844(a), 1982.
9. Thomas S. Szasz, *Ceremonial Chemistry: The Ritual Persecution of Drugs, Addicts, and Pushers* (Garden City, N.Y.: Anchor Books, 1974), p. 155.
10. *United States Code*, vol. 21, sec. 841(b)(1)(A), 1982.
11. Continuing Criminal Enterprise Act, *United States Code*, vol. 21, sec. 848, 1970.
12. United States v. Miranda, 442 F. Supp. 786 (S.D. Fla. 1977).
13. Ronald Caffrey, "The Strategy of Enforcement," *Drug Enforcement*, Fall 1982, p. 2.
14. Gary Becker, "Crime and Punishment: An Economic Approach," *Journal of Political Economy*, vol. 76, 1968, pp. 167, 176.
15. Packer, *Limits of the Criminal Sanction*, p. 266.
16. "The Economics of Heroin: Key to Optimizing the Legal Response," *Georgia Law Review*, vol. 10, 1976, pp. 565, 574.
17. Samuelson, *Economics*, pp. 365–66.
18. Joel Phillips and Ronald Wynne, *Cocaine: The Mystique and the Reality* (New York: Avon Books, 1980), p. 197.
19. Merck & Co. Price List (December 1, 1981).
20. George Gay, *Clinical Management of Acute and Chronic Poisoning*, September 1981 (paper presented at annual American College of Emergency Physicians (ACEP) Scientific Assembly in New Orleans, La.).

Chapter 3

1. Lester Grinspoon and James Bakalar, *Cocaine: A Drug and Its Social Evolution* (New York: Basic Books, 1976).

2. David Lee, *Cocaine Handbook: An Essential Reference* (Berkeley, Calif.: And/Or Press, 1980), p. 30.

3. Ibid., pp. 25–31.

4. National Narcotics Intelligence Consumers Committee (NNICC), *The Supply of Drugs to the U.S. Illicit Market from Foreign and Domestic Sources in 1980*, pp. 44–46.

5. Ibid.

6. Lee, *Cocaine Handbook*, p. 35.

7. Ibid.

8. NNICC, *Supply of Drugs*, p. 48.

9. DEA Office of Intelligence, "Colombia: South America's Cornucopia," *Drug Enforcement*, Fall 1982, p. 23.

10. Johnson, "Coke Glut," *City Paper* (Washington, D.C.), 17 December 1982, p. 7.

11. James Brooke, "Bolivian President Vows to Dethrone New Cocaine Kings," *Miami Herald*, 27 December 1982, sec. A.

12. George Stein, "Another Cocaine 'Cargo Case' Leaves Cops Holding the Bag," *Miami Herald*, 6 June 1982, sec. A.

13. NNICC, *Supply of Drugs*, p. 48.

14. Ibid.

15. George Stein, "Son of Reputed Drug-Smuggling Czar Extradited, Held on $5-Million Bond," *Miami Herald*, 18 August 1982, sec. B.

16. *Cocaine: A Major Drug Issue of the Seventies: Hearings Before the House Select Committee on Narcotics Abuse and Control*, 96th Cong., 1st Sess., 1979, p. 37.

17. Author's interview with Ron Caffrey, Chief of the Cocaine Investigations Section of the DEA (May 11, 1983).

18. Itabari Njeri, "Cocaine Customs Vary Among Ethnic Groups," *Miami Herald*, 24 August 1982, sec. C.

19. Joel L. Phillips and Ronald D. Wynne, *Cocaine: The Mystique and the Reality* (New York: Avon Books, 1980), pp. 242–51.

20. Florida Department of Law Enforcement, *1981 Annual Report: Crime in Florida* (1982).

21. DEA, Offender Based Transaction System, *Case Level Arrests by Drug*, 1982 (report provided by the DEA Office of Public Information; available at Nova Law Center, Fort Lauderdale, Florida).

22. *Illicit Traffic in Weapons and Drugs Across the United States–Mexican Border: Hearings Before the Permanent Subcommittee on Government Operations*, 95th Cong., 1st Sess., 1977, p. 14 (testimony of Peter B. Bensinger, Administrator of DEA).

23. *Financial Investigation of Drug Trafficking: Hearing Before the House Select Committee on Narcotics Abuse and Control*, 97th Cong., 1st Sess., 1981, p. 65 (prepared statement of William P. Rosenblatt, Regional Director of Investigations, Miami, Florida, Customs Service).

24. Mary Voboril, "Drug Money Is Touchy Topic Among Bankers," *Miami Herald*, 19 October 1981, sec. B.

25. Richard H. Blum, *Offshore Haven Banks, Trusts and Companies* (New York: Praeger Publishers, 1984).

Chapter 4

1. Ronald J. Caffrey, "The Strategy of Enforcement," *Drug Enforcement*, Fall 1982, p. 4.

2. *International Narcotics Control: Hearings Before the House Committee on Foreign Affairs*, 97th Cong., 2d Sess., 1982, p. 156.

3. *Single Convention on Narcotic Drugs: Preamble*, 30 March 1961, 18 U.S.T. 1407, T.I.A.S. No. 6298.

4. Ibid., art. 26(2).

5. *Amendment to the Single Convention on Narcotic Drugs of 1961*, 25 March 1972, 26 U.S.T. 1439, T.I.A.S. No. 8118.

6. *United States Code*, vol. 22, sec. 2291, 1982.

7. Public Law No. 92–247, *Statutes at Large*, vol. 86, p. 60 (amending *United States Code*, vol. 22, sec. 284k, 1982). See also Staff of Subcommittee on International Development of the House Committee on Banking, Finance and Urban Affairs, *Oversight on Illegal Drug Trafficking from Bolivia and U.S. Application of the Rangel Amendment*, 97th Cong., 1st Sess., 1981.

8. U.S. Department of Justice, *Drug Enforcement Statistical Report*, 1980, pp. 13, 19.

9. *International Security Assistance and Arms Export Control Act of 1976*, Public Law No. 94–329, sec. 504(b), codified at *United States Code*, vol. 22, sec. 2291(c)(1), 1982.

10. U.S. Congress, H. Rep. No. 1144, 94th Cong., 2d Sess., 1976, p. 55. Reprinted in *United States Code Congressional and Administrative News*, 1976, pp. 1378, 1431; S. Rep. No. 876, 94th Cong., 2d Sess., 1976, p. 61.

11. GAO, Report by the Comptroller General, *Drug Control in South America Having Limited Success—Some Progress but Problems Are Formidable*, 1978, p. 35. The DEA and Customs have trained and equipped large numbers of South American drug agents. The report shows that for fiscal years 1972 through 1977, the DEA and Customs trained a total of 454 agents in Bolivia, 524 in Peru, and 714 in Colombia. For fiscal year 1972 through fiscal year 1977, the Bureau of International Narcotics Matters (INM) provided equipment worth $1 million to Bolivia, $502,000 to Peru, and $3.438 million to Colombia.

12. *International Narcotics Control*, p. 165.

13. Pico Iyer, "Fighting the Cocaine Wars," *Time*, 25 February 1985, p. 26.

14. *Foreign Assistance Legislation for Fiscal Year 1982 (Part 7): Hearings and Mark-up Before the Subcommittee on Inter-American Affairs of the House Committee on Foreign Affairs*, 97th Cong., 1st Sess., 1981, p. 230.

15. *International Narcotics Trafficking: Hearings Before the Permanent Subcommittee on Investigations of the Senate Committee on Governmental Affairs*, 97th Cong., 1st Sess., 1981, p. 345.

16. Dominick L. DiCarlo, "International Initiatives to Control Coca Production and Cocaine Trafficking," *Drug Enforcement*, Fall 1982, pp. 6, 9.

17. *International Narcotics Trafficking*, p. 201.

18. Author's interview with American embassy officials Rob Gehring and Daniel Strasser in La Paz, Bolivia, 22 December 1982.

19. GAO, *Drug Control in South America*, p. 19.

20. Lester Grinspoon and James Bakalar, *Cocaine: A Drug and Its Social Evolution* (New York: Basic Books, 1976), pp. 9–11.

21. U.S. Department of State, Bureau of Public Affairs, *Background Notes: Peru, March 1980; Bolivia, August 1981.*

22. Grinspoon and Bakalar, *Cocaine*, p. 13.

23. Ibid., p. 14.

24. Joel L. Phillips and Ronald D. Wynne, *Cocaine: The Mystique and the Reality* (New York: Avon Books, 1980), p. 15.

25. George Stein, "Concentrated Coke on Sale 'Like Sugar,' " *Miami Herald*, 14 November 1982, sec. A.

26. *The Yearbook of World Rankings*, ed. George Kurian (New York: Fadson File, Inc., 1979), pp. 18, 82, 283, 284.

27. Ibid.

28. Jackson Diehl, "Economy Booms in Clandestine Nation of Cocaine," *Washington Post*, 11 November 1982, sec. A.

29. Mimi Whitefield, "In Bolivia, Traffic Slows Along 'Cocaine Highway,' " *Miami Herald*, 8 October 1984, sec. A.

30. Iyer, "Fighting the Cocaine Wars," p. 31.

31. National Narcotics Intelligence Consumers Committee, *The Supply of Drugs to the U.S. Illicit Market from Foreign and Domestic Sources in 1981*, 1983, p. 40.

32. State Department, Bureau of International Narcotics Matters, Satellite Survey of Bolivian Coca Fields Done by Earth Satellite Corporation, 15 April 1981, slide no. 69.

33. George Stein, "In Rural Bolivia Drug Agents Fear for Their Lives," *Miami Herald*, 10 October 1982, sec. A.

34. Authors's interview with American Embassy officials in La Paz, Bolivia, 22 December 1982.

35. "Church Blasts U.S. Anti-Drug Campaigns," *Fort Lauderdale News & Sun-Sentinel*, 6 May 1982, sec. A. The Church's statement especially denounced the use of herbicides for coca eradication as an environmental danger.

36. Associated Press Wire Service, "Cochabamba Bolivia," 10 May 1983 (available at Nova Law Center).

37. "Bolivia Arrests Two Who Led Drug Agency," *Miami Herald*, 24 October 1982, sec. A.

38. Iyer, "Cocaine Wars," p. 31.

39. *International Narcotics Trafficking*, p. 521.

40. Iyer, "Cocaine Wars," p. 31.

41. Peter McFarren, "Bolivian Pols Speak No Coke Evil: Won't Bite Hand Feeding Rural Voters in Drug Area," *Miami Herald*, 13 July 1985, sec. A.

42. State Department, Bureau of International Narcotics Matters, Satellite Survey, slides 71, 72, 74.

43. "Betancur Orders Amnesty for Illegal Drug Income," *Miami Herald*, 26 December 1982, sec. A.

44. "17 in U.S. Anti-Drug War Slain in Peru," *Miami Herald*, 19 November 1984, sec. A.

45. House of Representatives, Select Comm. on Narcotics Abuse and Control, "International Study Missions (Summary Report)," 98th Cong., 2d Sess., 2 August 1984 (Washington, D.C.: U.S. Government Printing Office, 1984).

46. Ibid., p. 10.
47. Ibid., p. 13.
48. Diehl, "Economy Booms."
49. *International Narcotics Control*, p. 304.
50. *Foreign Assistance Legislation for Fiscal Year 1982 (Part 7)*, p. 61.
51. *Cocaine: A Major Drug Issue of the Seventies: Hearings Before the House Select Committee on Narcotics Abuse and Control*, 96th Cong., 1st Sess., 1979, p. 65.
52. David Lee, *Cocaine Handbook: An Essential Reference* (Berkeley, Calif.: And/Or Press, 1981), p. 31.
53. John Marion, "The Economics of Cocaine" (seminar paper on file at Nova Law Center, Fort Lauderdale, Florida, 1981).

Chapter 5

1. Drug Abuse Policy Office, *1984 National Strategy for Prevention of Drug Abuse and Drug Trafficking* (Washington, D.C.: U.S. Government Printing Office, 1984), p. 122.
2. U.S. Customs Service, *Customs U.S.A.*, 1981, pp. 28–32.
3. U.S. Customs Service, *Customs U.S.A.: A Special Report on the Activities of the U.S. Customs Service During Fiscal 1979*, pp. 19–20.
4. U.S. Customs Service, *Customs U.S.A.: A Special Report on the Activities of the U.S. Customs Service During Fiscal 1980*, p. 33.
5. Ibid.
6. GAO, Report by the Comptroller General, *Federal Drug Interdiction Efforts Need Strong Central Oversight*, 13 June 1983, p. 15.
7. *Cocaine: A Major Drug Issue of the Seventies: Hearings Before the House Select Committee on Narcotics Abuse and Control*, 96th Cong., 1st Sess., 1979, p. 49.
8. Candace Turtle, "Plane Dumps Cocaine Cargo on I–95," *Miami Herald*, 14 August 1984, sec. A.
9. "Notable Cases," *Drug Enforcement*, Fall 1982, p. 17.
10. U.S. Congress, *Oversight Hearings on Federal Drug Strategy 1979: House Select Committee on Narcotics Abuse and Control*, 96th Cong., 1st Sess., 1979, p. 238. Similarly, in fiscal 1983 Customs seized 2,312 lbs. of cocaine by inspection, 14,934 lbs. by patrol, but only 4,489 lbs. by special enforcement operations.
11. State of Florida v. Del Sol, Police case #2140-M, MDPD Records & Id. #353164, Complaint/Arrest Affidavit, 8 May 1985.
12. Mark Potok, "Pilot Arrested; Big Drug Haul Seized," *Miami Herald*, 2 December 1984, sec. B.
13. United Press International, "Second Largest Cocaine Bust Made at Miami," *Fort Lauderdale News & Sun-Sentinel*, 23 August 1984, sec. A.
14. Joel Achenbach, "Police Seize Nearly a Ton of Cocaine," *Miami Herald*, 1 June 1983, sec. B.
15. George Stein, "Another Cocaine 'Cargo Case' Leaves Cops Holding the Bag," *Miami Herald*, 6 June 1982, sec. A.
16. U.S. Customs Service, *Customs U.S.A.*, 1981, p. 14.
17. Edward J. Epstein, *Agency of Fear* (New York: G. P. Putnam's Sons, 1977), p. 8.

18. U.S. Department of Justice, *Drug Enforcement Administration: A Profile*, July 1981, p. 4.

19. Ibid., p. 32.

20. U.S. Department of Justice, *Implementation Directive for Concurrent Drug Investigative Jurisdiction Between DEA and FBI*, 12 March 1982 (undated departmental memorandum available at Nova Law Center).

21. Strategy Council on Drug Abuse, *Federal Drug Strategy*, 1982, p. 73.

22. *State, Justice, Commerce, the Judiciary, and Related Agencies Appropriations, Fiscal Year 1983: Hearings Before a Subcommittee of the Senate Committee on Appropriations*, 97th Cong., 2d Sess. 1982, pp. 292, 302.

23. *United States Code*, vol. 21, sec. 802(6), 1982.

24. Ibid., sec. 812(b)(2).

25. United States v. Alexander, 673 F.2d 287 (9th Cir. 1982); United States v. Harper, 530 F.2d 828 (9th cir. 1976).

26. *United States Code*, vol. 21, sec. 811(a), 1982. See Executive Order No. 11, 727, 3 C.F.R. 785, 1973; reprinted in *United States Code*, vol. 21, sec. 801 app. at 877, 1982.

27. *United States Code*, vol. 21, sec. 848, 1982.

28. Ibid., sec. 1961–8, 1982.

29. *Illegal Narcotics Profits: Hearings Before the Permanent Subcommittee on Investigations of the Senate Committee on Governmental Affairs*, 96th Cong., 1st Sess., 1979, p. 11.

30. U.S. Department of Justice, FBI, *Crime in the United States*, 1982, p. 152.

31. J. Dean Heller, "The Attempt to Prevent Illicit Drug Supply," in *Drug Use in America: Problem in Perspective*, vol. 3, 1973, pp. 383, 395.

32. Ibid.

33. Office of the Attorney General, *Organized Crime Drug Enforcement Task Force Program Annual Report, 1984*, p. 18.

34. Charles Bass, "Cops Selling Dope," *Miami Herald*, 14 August 1982, sec. A.

35. U.S. Department of Justice, *Implementation Directive*.

36. Jay Williams, Lawrence Redlinger, and Peter Manning, *Police Narcotics Control: Patterns and Strategies, 1979* (Washington: D.C.: U.S. Government Printing Office, 1979), p. 17.

37. George Stein, "Son of Reputed Drug-Smuggling Czar Extradited, Held on $5-Million Bond," *Miami Herald*, 18 August 1982, sec. B.

38. Carl Hiassen and Jim McGee, "Vesco Allegedly Passed Bribe," *Miami Herald*, 21 June 1984, sec. A.

39. Pico Iyer, "Fighting the Cocaine Wars," *Time*, 25 February 1985, pp. 29–30.

40. Investigations may also be initiated by grand juries. As a general proposition, the formalities of presenting evidence to a grand jury tend to make this method of investigation most suitable for crimes which are documented, or which have occurred in a patterned way, e.g., tax evasion or money laundering. Such investigations generally look backward to past offenses. Proactive investigations of current drug operations favor pursuit by case agents. In the federal system, of course, the results of the field investigation must always be presented to a grand jury for indictment of a felony.

41. *United States Attorney's Manual*, 11 September 1979, sec. 9–7.160, p. 14.

42. Peter Slevin, "Reputed Drug Czar's Son Freed of Charges," *Miami Herald*, 20 November 1982, sec. B.

43. *United States Code*, vol. 21, sec. 2510–20, 1982.

44. *United States Attorney's Manual*, 11 September 1979, sec. 9–7.270, p. 21.

45. *United States Attorney's Manual*, 8 October 1981, sec. 9–7.110, pp. 9, 11.

46. *United States Code*, vol. 21, sec. 2516(1), 1982.

47. Ibid., sec. 2518, 1982. *United States Attorney's Manual*, sec. 9–7.

48. *United States Attorney's Manual*, sec. 9–7.312.

49. *Cocaine: A Major Drug Issue of the Seventies*, p. 140.

50. Ibid., pp. 136–42.

51. U.S. Department of Commerce, Bureau of Census, Consumer Price Index, *Statistical Abstract of the United States*, 101st ed., 1980, p. 478.

52. *Briefing Paper for the Working Group Organized Crime Drug Enforcement Task Force*, 21 August 1984, p. 160.

53. DEA, Offender Based Transaction System, *Case Level Arrests by Drug*, 1982 (report provided by the DEA Office of Public Information; available at Nova Law Center).

54. Ibid.

55. Office of the Attorney General, *Annual Report of Organized Crime Drug Enforcement Task Force Program*, 14 March 1984, p. 2.

56. Florida Department of Law Enforcement, 1981 Annual Report, *Crime in Florida*, 1982.

57. Ellen Hampton, "Nehrbass Says South Florida Coke Traffic Worst Ever," *Miami Herald*, 12 February 1985, sec. A.

58. *Stopping "Mother Ships"—A Loophole in Law Enforcement: Hearing on S. 3437 Before the Subcommittee to Investigate Juvenile Delinquency of the Senate Committee on the Judiciary*, 95th Cong., 2d Sess., 1978, p. 63.

59. *United States Code*, vol. 49, sec. 781–2, 1976.

60. Ibid., vol. 31, sec. 5317(b), 5321(a)(2), 1983.

61. Ibid., vol. 21, sec. 881(a)(6), 1982.

62. *Comprehensive Crime Control Act of 1984*, Public Law No. 98–473, *Statutes at Large*, vol. 98, sec. 1976, 1984.

63. *United States Code*, vol. 19, sec. 1615, 1982.

64. *State, Justice, Commerce, the Judiciary, and Related Agencies Appropriations*, p. 307.

65. Department of Treasury, IRS, *Estimate of Income Unreported on Individual Income Tax Returns*, September, 1979, p. 139.

66. GAO, Report by the Comptroller General, *Asset Forfeiture—A Seldom Used Tool in Combatting Drug Trafficking*, 10 April 1981.

67. *United States Code*, vol. 31, sec. 5311–22, 1983. See also ibid., vol. 12, sec. 1730d, 1951–9, 1982; ibid., vol. 15, sec. 78g, 1982.

68. Ibid., vol. 31, sec. 5311, 1983.

69. California Bankers Assoc. v. Shultz, 416 U.S. 21 (1974).

70. *Financial Investigation of Drug Trafficking: Hearing Before the House Select Committee on Narcotics Abuse and Control*, 97th Cong., 1st Sess., 1981, p. 92.

71. Ibid., p. 48.

72. Ibid., p. 82.

73. Ibid., p. 81.

74. Strategy Council on Drug Abuse, *Federal Drug Strategy: Prospects for the 1980's*, 1982, p. 75.

75. Ibid., p. 64.

76. Peter Slevin, "Dade Bank Accused in Drug Probe," *Miami Herald*, 14 December 1982, sec. A.

77. Arnold Lubasch, "Court Told of 'Laundry' for Millions in Drug Funds," *New York Times*, 17 April 1983, sec. A.

78. *Crime and Secrecy: The Use of Offshore Banks and Companies, Hearings Before the Permanent Subcommittee on Investigation, Senate Committee on Governmental Affairs*, 98th Cong., 1st Sess., 1983, pp. 59–60.

79. Terence McElroy, "State Says Banks Getting Millions Daily in Drug Cash," *Miami News*, 19 December 1984, sec. A.

80. Warren Hoge, "Colombia's Banking Scandals," *New York Times*, 27 December 1982, sec. D.

81. United States v. Corona, Case No. 84–853-Cr.-Kehoe (S.D. Fla. 1984).

82. Mimi Whitefield, "Cash and a Flood of Customers Mark Miami Federal Reserve Unit," *Miami Herald*, 19 October 1981, sec. B.

83. U.S. Congress, *Oversight Hearings*, p. 9.

84. Anthony Lednovich, "Drug Agents Seize Cash, Plane," *Ft. Lauderdale News & Sun-Sentinel*, 30 April 1985, sec. A.

85. *Financial Investigation*, p. 48.

86. *International Narcotics Trafficking: Hearings Before the Permanent Subcommittee on Investigations of the Senate Committee on Governmental Affairs*, 97th Cong., 1st Sess., 1981, p. 628. Subsequently, the United States signed a treaty with Great Britain that requires Cayman officials to produce information within 14 days upon certification by the United States Attorney General that there is "reason to believe" that a Caymanian bank account is relevant to a United States drug-related investigation.

87. In re Grand Jury Proceedings, Bank of Nova Scotia, 740 F.2d 817 (11th cir. 1984).

88. William Gibson, "U.S. Wages Quiet War on Tax Evaders," *Ft. Lauderdale News & Sun-Sentinel*, 16 April 1983, sec. A.

89. *United States Code*, vol. 26, sec. 6103, 1976, and 5 Supp., 1981.

90. *Illegal Narcotics Profits*, p. 500.

91. *Financial Investigation*, p. 47. The CID opened a total of 6,498 criminal investigations in FY 1982. About one-third of those cases involved illegal activities, and about one-third of those were proxies for drug violations.

92. Michael Isikoff, "I.R.S. Expanding Undercover Operations," *Miami Herald*, 10 March 1983, sec. C.

93. GAO, Report by the Comptroller General, *Disclosure and Summons Provisions of 1976 Tax Reform Act—An Analysis of Proposed Legislative Changes*, 1980, p. 1.

94. *Financial Investigation*, p. 95.

95. *United States Code*, vol. 26, sec. 6103(i), 1983.

96. Robert Jackson, "U.S. May Let Drug Funds Go for Data," *Miami Herald*, 16 March 1983, sec. A.

97. Timothy Robinson and Ruth Simon, "Report Urges Unorthodox Crackdown on Tax Evaders," *National Law Journal*, 30 August 1982, sec. A.

Chapter 6

1. Robert Shaw and Fredric Tasker, "U.S. Tackles South Florida Crime," *Miami Herald*, 29 January 1982, sec. A.

2. Robert Shaw and Fredric Tasker, "Bush Outlines War on Crime," *Miami Herald*, 17 February 1982, sec. A.

3. GAO, Report by the Comptroller General, *Federal Drug Interdiction Efforts Need Strong Central Oversight*, 13 June 1983, p. 24.

4. George Stein, "586 Federal Crime Fighters to Stay," *Miami Herald*, 26 August 1982, sec. D.

5. Executive Order No. 12, 333, 3 C.F.R. 200, 213 (1982), reprinted in *United States Code*, vol. 50, sec. 401, app. at 65 (West Supp. 1983).

6. Cabinet Council on Legal Policy, *Law Enforcement Report*, 1983, p. 16.

7. John Arnold and Liz Balmeseda, "Missile Cruiser Intercepts Pot-Laden Tug," *Miami Herald*, 24 November 1982, sec. A.

8. *United States Code*, vol. 18, sec. 1385 (1982).

9. John Starita, "Radar Planes to Hunt Drugs in South Florida," *Miami Herald*, 13 March 1982, sec. B.

10. Ibid.

11. Robert Shaw, "2nd Blimp Enlisted in Drug War," *Miami Herald*, 20 May 1982, sec. D.

12. 32 C.F.R. 213.10(c) (1982).

13. Secretary of Navy, Memorandum for Secretary of Defense, 29 July 1982.

14. Arnold and Balmeseda, "Missile Cruiser."

15. Liz Balmeseda, "Navy Bullets Riddle Pot-Smuggling Ship," *Miami Herald*, 17 July 1983, sec. A.

16. GAO, *Federal Drug Interdiction*, p. 25.

17. Ibid.

18. Ibid.

19. Ibid., pp. 16–17.

20. GAO, *Federal Drug Interdiction*, p. 10.

21. Ibid., p. 26.

22. Ibid., p. 28.

23. William Gibson, "Anti-Smuggling System Would Have C.I.A. Links," *Ft. Lauderdale News & Sun-Sentinel*, 18 June 1983, sec. A.

24. Bud Mullen, NNBIS—Major Changes Needed (Memorandum), 31 January 1984.

25. Attorney General of the United States, *Annual Report of the Organized Crime Drug Enforcement Task Force Program*, 1984, p. 120.

26. Ibid., p. 16.

27. *Briefing Paper for the Working Group Organized Crime Drug Enforcement Task Force*, 21 August 1984, p. 6.

28. Attorney General, *Annual Report*, p. 16.

29. Ibid., p. 18.

30. Ibid.

31. Ibid., p. 41.

32. Ibid., p. 43.

33. Joel L. Phillips and Ronald D. Wynne, *Cocaine: The Mystique and the Reality* (New York: Avon Books, 1980), p. 56. In 1906, the peak pre–Harrison Act year for cocaine consumption, 21,000 pounds were consumed by a population of about 90 million, an average of .0002 pounds per capita. In 1980, a population of 230 million consumed 96,800 pounds, or .0004 pounds per capita.
34. Stanley Marcus, "How Drug Money Can Corrupt Us," *Miami Herald*, 20 May 1984, sec. E.
35. *Illegal Narcotics Profits: Hearings Before the Permanent Subcommittee on Investigations of the Senate Committee on Governmental Affairs*, 96th Cong., 1st Sess., p. 56.
36. National Academy of Sciences, *Deterrence and Incapacitation: Estimating the Effects of Criminal Sanctions on Crime Rates* (Washington, D.C.: National Academy Press), 1978, p. vii.
37. Ibid., p. 4.
38. Ibid., p. 6.
39. *Sentencing Practices and Alternatives in Narcotics Cases: Hearings Before the House Select Committee on Narcotics Abuse and Control*, 97th Cong., 1st Sess., 1981, p. 3.
40. Stuart Nagel, "Tradeoffs in Crime Reduction Among Certainty, Severity, and Crime Benefits," *Rutgers Law Review*, vol. 35, 1982, p. 100.
41. Ibid., p. 127.
42. Ibid., p. 128.
43. Ibid., p. 129.
44. Joel Brinkley, "The War on Narcotics: Can it Be Won?" *New York Times*, 14 September 1984, p. 1.

Chapter 7

1. President Ronald Reagan, Presidential Statement of 2 October 1982.
2. *Illegal Narcotics Profits: Hearings Before the Permanent Subcommittee on Investigations of the Senate Committee on Governmental Affairs*, 96th Cong., 1st Sess., p. 389 (testimony of United States Attorney for the Southern District of Florida, Atlee Wampler, Jr.).
3. *Financial Investigation of Drug Trafficking: Hearing Before the House Select Committee on Narcotics Abuse and Control*, 97th Cong., 1st Sess., 1981, p. 58.
4. Information based on a computer printout of pending bills provided by the office of Senator Paula Hawkins (R., Fla.). A survey of the contents of these bills, along with particular Senate or House numbers, appears in Steven Wisotsky, "Exposing the War on Cocaine," *University of Wisconsin Law Review*, vol. 1983, 1983, pp. 1386–88.
5. *Sentencing Practices and Alternatives in Narcotics Cases: Hearings Before the House Select Committee on Narcotics Abuse and Control*, 97th Cong., 1st Sess., 1981, p. 3.
6. Comprehensive Crime Control Act of 1984, Public Law No. 98–473, *Statutes at Large*, vol. 98, 1976, 1984.
7. Nebbia v. United States, 357 F.2d 303 (2d Cir. 1966).
8. Senator Edward M. Kennedy, "Foreword," *American Criminal Law Review*, vol. 22, no. 4, Spring 1985, p. viii.
9. Fredric Tasker, *Miami Herald*, 23 August 1985, sec. B.
10. Joseph E. diGenova and Constance L. Belfure, "An Overview of the Com-

prehensive Crime Control Act 1984—The Prosecutor's Perspective," *American Criminal Law Review*, vol. 22, no. 4, Spring 1985, p. 717.

11. Albert J. Krieger and Susan W. Van Dusen, "The Lawyer, the Client and the New Law," *American Criminal Law Review*, vol. 22, no. 4, Spring 1985, p. 742.

12. Deficit Reduction Act of 1984, Public Law No. 98–369, 98th Cong., 2d Sess., 1984.

13. Krieger and Van Dusen, "The Lawyer, the Client," p. 737.

14. Bureau of National Affairs, Review of the Supreme Court's Term (Criminal Law), 52 U.S.L.W. 3151 (13 September 1983).

15. Illinois v. Gates, 103 S.Ct. 2317 (1983).

16. United States v. Karo, 104 S.Ct. 3296 (1984).

17. Silas Wasserstrom, "The Incredible Shrinking Fourth Amendment," *American Criminal Law Review*, vol. 21, no. 3, 1985, p. 257.

18. Jeff Leen, "3 Fake Police Officers Ransack Home," *Miami Herald*, 28 July 1985, sec. B.

19. Pete Early, "Wiretaps up 60 Percent, Reports Say," *Miami Herald*, 16 June 1984, sec. A.

20. Rich Pollack, "Troopers Aiming at Drug Flow on Turnpike," *Ft. Lauderdale News & Sun-Sentinel*, 6 August 1984, sec. B.

21. *Common Characteristics of Drug Couriers*, issued by Florida Department of Highway Safety and Motor Vehicles, Office of General Counsel, 8 May 1985, sec. I.A.4.

22. Jon Peck, "Lawyers: Ruling Will Alter F.H.P. Anti-Drug Effort," *Ft. Lauderdale News & Sun-Sentinel*, 28 June 1985, sec. B.

23. Mark Prendergast, "Highway Drug Searches Raise Questions," *Ft. Lauderdale News & Sun-Sentinel*, 26 February 1984, sec. A.

24. New Jersey v. T.L.O., 105 S.Ct. 733 (1985).

25. Maxwell Glen and Cody Sherer, "Drugs, Payoffs, and the American High School," *Ft. Lauderdale News & Sun-Sentinel*, 26 March 1983, sec. A.

26. "Drug War Overkill," *Miami Herald*, 17 July 1985, sec. A.

27. Steven Doig, "Judge Calls Agents' Tactics 'Outrageous,' " *Miami Herald*, 20 September 1984, sec. B.

28. United States v. Eugenio Llamera, Case No. 84–167-Cr-Hastings (S.D. Fla. 1984).

29. Florida Stat. Sec. 893.135(3) (1979).

30. Dan Christensen, "Drug Agents Keeping Tabs on Leaders, Stars, Clergy," *Ft. Lauderdale News & Sun-Sentinel*, 3 July 1984, sec. A.

31. Karen Payne, "U.S. List of Small Drug Deals Criticized," *Miami Herald*, 26 March 1985, sec. D.

32. Michael Kranish, "Suspect: I'm Pawn in Drug War," *Miami Herald*, 7 May 1985, sec. A.

33. Editorial, "Heroin Bill's Defeat Unwise," *Ft. Lauderdale News & Sun-Sentinel*, 25 September 1984.

34. Erich Goode, *Drugs in American Society* (New York: Alfred A. Knopf, 1972), p. 191.

35. Webb v. United States, 249 U.S. 96, 99 (1919).

36. United States v. Behrman, 258 U.S. 280, 289 (1922).

37. "Ecstasy—Controlled by DEA," *International Drug Report*, vol. 26, no. 7, July, 1985.

38. Rick Bowers, "Lawmakers Bolster Naval War on Drugs," *Miami Herald*, 27 June 1985, sec. A.

39. Albernaz v. United States, 450 U.S. 333, 343 (1981), quoting Gore v. United States, 357 U.S. 386, 390 (1957).

40. Joel Brinkley, "The War on Narcotics: Can It Be Won?" *New York Times*, 14 September 1984, sec. A.

41. National Commission on Marihuana and Drug Abuse, *Drug Use in America: Problem in Perspective*, p. 229.

42. Karen Payne, "Upset with Court Trends, Top-Rated Nimkoff to Quit," *Miami News*, 4 January 1986, sec. A.

43. Turner v. United States, 396 U.S. 398, 427 (1970).

44. Tom Daray, "Jericho: An American Gulag," *Newsday*, Winter 1982–83, no. 30/3; Ron Sachs, "Clark: Use Armed Might in Drug War," *Miami Herald*, 21 November 1981, sec. B.

45. Representative Ray Liberti, Florida House of Representatives, H.B. 410, A Bill to Be Entitled: *An Act Relating to Drug Abuse; Prohibiting the Sale or Distribution of Certain Printed Matter Encouraging the Consumption, Purchase, or Usage of Any Controlled Substance Enumerated in § 893.03,F.S.*

46. William Flittie, "Proposed Emergency Civil Drug Control Act," in National Commission on Marihuana and Drug Abuse, *Drug Use in America: Problem in Perspective*, 1973, vol. 3, p. 481.

Chapter 8

1. Department of Treasury, IRS, *Estimate of Income Unreported on Individual Income Tax Returns*, September, 1979, table H–3, p. 139.

2. Marcia Chambers, "Cocaine Use by Middle Class Widespread," *New York Times*, 13 December 1982, p. 15.

3. Ibid.

4. *Illegal Narcotics Profits: Hearings Before the Permanent Subcommittee on Investigations of the Senate Committee on Governmental Affairs*, 96th Cong., 1st Sess., 1981, p. 50.

5. Howard Kuhn, "Cocaine: You Can Bank on It," *Esquire*, October, 1983, p. 77.

6. Carl Hiaasen, "Gold Chain Fad Gives Florida a Touch of Sleaze," *Miami Herald*, 21 August 1985, sec. B.

7. *Federal Effort Against Organized Crime, Role of the Private Sector: Hearings Before the Subcommittee on Legal and Monetary Affairs of the House Committee on Government Operations*, 91st Cong., 2d Sess., 1970, p. 96.

8. "U.S. Indicts Attorney for Grandma Mafia," *Miami Herald*, 8 January 1984, sec. A.

9. Edna Buchanan, "Cocaine Wars II," *Rolling Stone*, 3 April 1980, pp. 48–49.

10. Joan Fleischman, "U.S. Cracks Drug Ring at Airport," *Miami Herald*, 13 April 1984, sec. C.

11. Mark Moore, *Buy and Bust: The Effective Regulation of an Illicit Market in Heroin* (Lexington, Mass.: Lexington Books, 1977).

12. New York (City) Commission to Investigate Allegations of Police Corruption and the City's Anticorruption Procedures, *The Knapp Commission's Report on Police Corruption*, 1973, p. 97.

13. People v. Berrios, 270 N.E.2d 709, 714 (N.Y.C.A. 1971). See also Joseph S. Oteri and Charlotte A. Perretta, " 'Dropsy' Evidence and the Viability of the Exclusionary Rule," *Contemporary Drug Problems*, vol. 1, 1971/1972, p. 35.

14. Edward J. Epstein, *Agency of Fear* (New York: G. P. Putnam's Sons, 1977), p. 105.

15. Ibid., p. 106.

16. Arnold Markowitz, "Police Corruption Witness Makes a Dangerous Friend," *Miami Herald*, 2 May 1982, sec. D.

17. Carl Hiaasen, "Greed, Drug Dealers Bring Down Top Federal Agent," *Miami Herald*, 7 May 1983, sec. B.

18. Peter Slevin, "30-Year Customs Agent Convicted in Drug Case," *Miami Herald*, 7 March 1984, sec. D.

19. Peter Slevin, "Ex-Guardsman: I Stole, Sold Drug-Fight Plans," *Miami Herald*, 3 March 1983, sec. D.

20. Miami Herald Wire Service, "Ex-Prosecutor Is Indicted for Bribery in Drug Probe," *Miami Herald*, 27 April 1983.

21. Joan Fleischman and Jim McGee, "Metro Police 'Lost' Drugs Stored in Property Room," *Miami Herald*, 29 August 1982, sec. A.

22. "Supreme Court Removes Judge Leon from Bench," *Florida Bar News*, 1 November 1983.

23. "3 Key West Policemen, Former County Attorney Nabbed on Drug Charges," *Miami Herald*, 30 June 1984, sec. A.

24. Anders Gyllenhall, "Corruption Runneth Over," *Miami Herald*, 29 April 1984, sec. D.

25. Bill Rose, "Drug Money Lures Georgia Police," *Miami Herald*, 8 November 1981, sec. D.

26. Anthony Simpson, *The Literature of Police Corruption* (New York: John Jay Press, 1977), p. 88.

27. *DEA Oversight and Budget Authorization: Hearing Before the Senate Subcommittee on Security and Terrorism Committee of the Judiciary*, 97th Cong., 2d Sess., 1982, p. 2.

28. Simpson, *Police Corruption*, p. 93.

29. Joel Garreau, *The Nine Nations of North America*, (Boston: Houghton Mifflin, 1981).

30. Kurt Anderson, "Crashing on Cocaine," *Time*, 11 April 1983, p. 29.

31. Alice Klement, "FBI Investigates Alleged Plot to Kidnap Judge," *Miami Herald*, 28 August 1982, sec. B.

32. Jennifer L. Sehenker, "Gunmen Murder Mother of Drug Witness," *Miami Herald*, 24 April 1984, sec. D.

33. Benjamin Setien, "The Impact of Cocaine Use and Trafficking on Dade County Community," January, 1982, p. 4. (seminar paper available at Nova Law Center) (interviewing Metro-Dade Detective June Hawkins).

34. Ibid., p. 3.

35. Ibid., p. 5.

36. Leonard Buder, "Almost 25% of Homicides in City in '81 Tied to Drugs," *New York Times*, 18 February 1983, sec. B.

37. Zeta Arocha, "I–95 Shooting Victim Enjoyed Easy Money, Fast Life," *Miami Herald*, 30 April 1983, sec. B.

38. Ellyn Ferguson and Lisa Hoffman, "Police: Bystander Slain as Drug Deal Goes Sour," *Miami Herald*, 20 June 1984, sec. A.

39. D. Lowell Jensen, "We've Begun to Win the War on Drugs," *USA Today*, 2 May 1984, sec. A.

Chapter 9

1. James Brooke, "Bolivia's Arce Gomez: A Trail of Dope and Death," *Miami Herald*, 29 May 1983, sec. A.

2. "Bolivia's Cocaine 'Godfather' Untouched by Crackdown," *Miami Herald*, 27 June 1983, sec. A.

3. Carl Hiaasen and Jim McGee, "A Nation for Sale," *Miami Herald*, 23 September 1984, sec. B.

4. Ibid.

5. Pico Iyer, "Fighting the Cocaine Wars," *Time*, 25 February 1985, pp. 27–28.

6. Ibid., p. 30.

7. Secret diplomatic cable obtained by author through a Freedom of Information Act Request.

8. Guy Gugliotta, "Colombian Underworld Is Changing," *Miami Herald*, 21 May 1984, sec. A.

9. Secretary of State George Shultz, "The Campaign Against Drugs, 'The International Dimension,' " *Current Policy*, no. 611, 14 September 1984.

10. Miami Herald Archives, 1984–85.

11. Rick Bowers, "U.S. Helping Mount Counterattack on Violent Latin Drugs Terrorists," *Miami Herald*, 12 May 1985, sec. A.

12. Ibid.

13. Carl Hiaasen, "Were Drugs Sold to Fund Latin Coup?" *Miami Herald*, 18 February 1984, sec. A.

14. Brian Duffy, "U.S. Prosecutors: Nicaragua Linked to Coke Cartel," *Miami Herald*, 31 July 1985, sec. B.

15. Peter Slevin, "U.S. Indicts 11 in Drug Operation," *Miami Herald*, 29 July 1984, sec. A.

16. Shultz, "Campaign Against Drugs," p. 4.

17. Anders Oppenheimer, "Venezuela Becomes Bridge for Cocaine on U.S. Drug Route," *Miami Herald*, 29 March 1984, sec. A.

18. Iyer, "Fighting the Cocaine Wars," p. 30.

19. Sam Dillon, "Colombia Stumbling on Path to Peace," *Miami Herald*, 11 September 1985, sec. A.

Chapter 10

1. David A. Richards, "Drug Use and the Rights of the Person: A Moral Argument for Decriminalization of Certain Forms of Drug Use," *Rutgers Law Review*, vol. 3, Spring 1982, p. 607. The article was subsequently incorporated into a book, *Sex, Drugs, Death and the Law* (Totowa, N.J.: Rowman and Littlefield, 1984).

2. Office of the Attorney General, *Annual Report on the Organized Crime Drug Enforcement Task Force Program, 1985*, p. 118.

3. Kathy McCarthy, "Dade Police Seize Chance to Make Crime Pay," *Miami Herald*, 22 July 1985, sec. B.

4. Joe Starita, "Drug Dealers Pay in Jail, Out of Wallet," *Miami Herald*, 18 October 1982, sec. A.

5. Jim McGee and Carl Hiaasen, "U.S. Drug Enforcement: The Billion-Dollar Bust," *Miami Herald*, November 1981.

6. Neil Brown, "Local Drug Agents Pan South Florida Task Force," *Miami Herald*, 5 May 1984, sec. A.

7. George Stein, "U.S. Losing Key Drug-War Battles," *Miami Herald*, 28 May 1984, sec. A.

8. Rick Bowers, "Congress Questions Success of Bush Anti-Drug Program," *Miami Herald*, 13 January 1985, sec. A.

9. Joel Brinkley, "Is Drug War Merely a Holding Action?" *New York Times*, 25 November 1984, sec. E.

10. Robert Taylor and Gary Cohn, "The Drug Trade: War Against Narcotics by U.S. Government Isn't Slowing Influx," *Wall Street Journal*, 27 November 1984.

11. Pico Iyer, "Fighting the Cocaine Wars," *Time*, 25 February 1985.

12. Melinda Beck, "Evil Empire," *Newsweek*, 25 February 1985.

13. William F. Buckley, Jr., "After We Admit Drug War's a Failure," *Miami News*, 29 March 1985.

14. "Drug Users Lose Opportunities," *Ft. Lauderdale News & Sun-Sentinel*, 22 August 1984, sec. A.

15. Eileen Ogintz, "Cocaine's Appeal Sifts into the Mainstream," *Miami Herald*, 5 May 1981, sec. B.

16. "Use of Cocaine Grows Among Top Traders in Financial Centers," *Wall Street Journal*, 12 September 1983.

17. "Drug Use in Silicon Valley Is Running Rampant," *Ft. Lauderdale News & Sun-Sentinel*, 8 September 1984, sec. A.

18. Robert Lindsey, "Pervasive Use of Cocaine Is Reported in Hollywood," *New York Times*, 31 October 1982, sec. 1.

19. "Baseball Stars Linked to Drugs," *Miami Herald*, 6 September 1985, sec. A.

20. Francis Flaherty, "Drugs: Crisis for the Bar?—Users and Dealers Abound in the Legal Profession," *National Law Journal*, vol. 5, no. 48, 8 August 1983.

21. Gail Poulton, "Cocaine Crossing Middle-Class Line," *Ft. Lauderdale News & Sun-Sentinel*, 17 June 1984, sec. B.

22. Gail Poulton, "Cocaine Usage Rising Among Women, Minorities," *Ft. Lauderdale News & Sun-Sentinel*, 17 June 1984, sec. B.

23. "12% of Teen-agers Admit They Combine Drugs, Alcohol—Poll," *Ft. Lauderdale News & Sun-Sentinel*, 9 September 1984, sec. A.

24. Roberto Fabricio, "Cocaine Use Among Young Latins Becoming Major Crisis," *Miami Herald*, 22 September 1984, sec. B.

25. Paul Liberatore, "Psychedelic Scene, Sounds Are in Again," *San Francisco Chronicle*, 19 August 1985.

26. Anthony Haden-Guest, "The Young, the Rich and Heroin," *Rolling Stone*, 7 July 1983.

27. Ena Naunton, "Smart Set Stupidly Adopts Heroin," *Miami Herald*, 28 April 1984, sec. C.
28. Glen Collins, "U.S. Tolerance of Drugs Found on Rise," *New York Times*, 21 March 1983, sec. A.
29. National Institute on Drug Abuse, *National Survey on Drugs: Main Findings, 1982*, p. 43.
30. Richard Hofstadter, *Age of Reform: From Bryan to F.D.R.* (New York: Random House, Inc., 1955).
31. David F. Musto, *The American Disease: Origins of Narcotic Control* (New Haven: Yale University Press, 1973), p. 65.
32. Ibid., p. 11.
33. Ibid., p. 65.
34. Ibid., pp. 5–7.
35. United States v. Behrman, 258 U.S. 280, 289 (1922).
36. Jerome Himmelstein, *The Strange Career of Marijuana: Politics and Ideology of Drug Control in America* (Westport, Conn.: Greenwood Press, 1983), p. 60.
37. Edward J. Epstein, *Agency of Fear* (New York: G. P. Putnam's Sons, 1977), p. 33.
38. Ibid., p. 41.
39. Thomas S. Szasz, "The War Against Drugs," *Journal of Drug Issues*, vol. 12, 1982, p. 115.
40. Epstein, *Agency of Fear*, pp. 59–60.
41. Ibid., p. 173.
42. Ibid., p. 179.
43. Ibid., p. 8.
44. Thomas S. Szasz, *Ceremonial Chemistry: The Ritual Persecution of Drugs, Addicts, and Pushers* (Garden City, N.Y.: Anchor Books, 1974), p. ix.
45. Lester Grinspoon and James Bakalar, *Cocaine: A Drug and Its Social Evolution* (New York: Basic Books, 1976), pp. 238–39.
46. Andrew Weil, *The Natural Mind: A New Way of Looking at Drugs and the Higher Consciousness* (Boston: Houghton Mifflin Co., 1972), p. 49.
47. U.S. Department of Health, Education and Welfare, Public Health Service, *Smoking and Health, Report of the Surgeon General*, 1979, pp. 10, 11.
48. "Cigarettes Most Widespread Case of Drug Dependence, U.S. Says," *Miami Herald*, 7 March 1983, sec. A.
49. Russel, "Cigarette Smoking: Natural History of a Dependence Disorder," *British Journal of Medical Psychology*, vol. 44, 1971, pp. 1, 3.
50. Edward M. Brecher and the Editors of Consumer Reports, *Licit and Illicit Drugs: The Consumers Union Report on Narcotics, Stimulants, Depressants, Inhalants, Hallucinogens and Marijuana—Including Caffeine, Nicotine and Alcohol* (Mount Vernon, N.Y.: Consumers Union, 1973), pp. 304–5.
51. National Commission on Marihuana and Drug Abuse, "Control of Marihuana, Alcohol, and Tobacco," in *Marihuana: A Signal of Misunderstanding*, vol. 1, March, 1972, p. 527.
52. Tobacco Institute, *The Tax Burden on Tobacco*, vol. 17, 1982, p. 4.
53. Institute of Medicine, *Alcoholism, Alcohol Abuse and Related Problems: Opportunities for Research* (Washington, D.C.: National Academy Press, 1980), pp. 1, 4, 166.

54. Mike Knepper, "Puff, the Dangerous Drug," *Car and Driver*, June, 1980, p. 43; Steve Thompson, "High Driving," *Car and Driver*, March, 1978. For contrary conclusions, see Ravin v. State, 537 P.2d 494 (Ala. 1975), fn. 3:

Evidence that marijuana has a detrimental effect on driving performance, especially as the dose increases, continues to mount. It has been found to increase both braking and starting times, to adversely affect attention and concentration abilities, and to detract from performance on a divided attention task, all of which are presumably involved in driving. A recent Canadian study of driving ability while marijuana-intoxicated examined drivers' performance under both driving course and actual traffic conditions. A significant decline in performance as measured by several criteria was found in most drivers tested. Based on the accumulated evidence, it seems clear that driving while under the influence of marijuana is ill-advised. Marijuana and Health, Fourth Report to the U.S. Congress from the Secretary of Health, Education, and Welfare 10–11 (1974).

55. Robert Byck, ed., *Cocaine Papers: Sigmund Freud* (New York: New American Library, 1974), p. xxxvi.

56. Szasz, *Ceremonial Chemistry*, p. xv.

57. Joel L. Phillips and Ronald D. Wynne, *Cocaine: The Mystique and the Reality* (New York: Avon Books, 1980), p. 64.

58. Ibid., p. 66.

59. Ibid., p. 65.

60. "The Growing Menace," *New York Times*, 15 April 1926, quoted in Phillips and Wynne, *Cocaine*, p. 69.

61. Itabari Njeri, "The Dark Side of Snow," *Miami Herald*, 22 August 1982, sec. G.

62. Itabari Njeri, "Cocaine and the Quest for Death," *Miami Herald*, 23 August 1982, sec. G.

63. "Cocaine Kills in Many Ways," *Miami Herald*, 22 August 1982, sec. G.

64. Itabari Njeri, "When You're on Coke, Nothing Else Matters, Not Even the Fact That It May Kill You," *Miami Herald*, 22 August 1982, sec. G.

65. Deborah Donnelly, "Cocaine Is Ruining Our Nation, and Nobody Seems to Care," *Miami Herald*, 22 August 1982, sec. D.

66. Al Haas, "Cocaine Causes Panic, Paranoia, Many Users Say," *Miami Herald*, 22 January 1984, sec. G.

67. Ena Naunton, "Habitual Use Can Put Hole in Your Nose," *Miami Herald*, 22 August 1982, sec. C.

68. Itabari Njeri, "Given the Choice, Laboratory Test Animals Get High So Often They Kill Themselves," *Miami Herald*, 23 August 1982, sec. C.

69. National Narcotics Intelligence Consumer Committee, *The Supply of Drugs to the U.S. Illicit Markets from Foreign and Domestic Sources in 1981*, 1981, p. 35.

70. Kurt Anderson, "Crashing on Cocaine," *Time*, 11 April 1983, p. 22.

71. Turner v. United States, 396 U.S. 398, 426 (1979).

72. Robinson v. California, 370 U.S. 661, 673 (1962).

73. Arnold Trebach, *The Heroin Solution* (New Haven: Yale University Press, 1982), p. 292.

74. Norman Zinberg, *Drug, Set, and Setting: The Basis for Controlled Intoxicant Use* (New Haven: Yale University Press, 1984).

75. Burke v. Kansas State Osteopathic Assoc., Inc., 111 F.2d 250, 256 (1940).

76. President Ronald Reagan, Presidential Speech of 2 October 1982.

77. Thomas Kuhn, *The Structure of Scientific Revolutions* (Chicago: University of Chicago Press, 1970), p. 111.

78. Dred Scott v. Sanford, 60 U.S. (19 How.) 393 (1857).

79. Ibid., p. 407.

80. Bradwell v. State, 16 Wall 130 (1872).

81. Ibid., p. 141.

Chapter 11

1. Lester Grinspoon and James Bakalar, *Cocaine: A Drug and Its Social Evolution* (New York: Basic Books, 1976), p. 258.

2. Edward J. Epstein, *Agency of Fear* (New York: G. P. Putnam's Sons, 1977), p. 41.

3. Paul Anderson, "Drug Bill Tough on Smugglers," *Miami Herald*, 26 May 1984, sec. A.

4. Peter Bensinger, "We Can Win the War Against This Cancer," *USA Today*, 26 October 1984, sec. A.

5. Ibid.

6. Andrew Weil, "Altered States of Consciousness, Drugs and Society," quoted in Edward M. Brecher and the Editors of Consumer Reports, *Licit and Illicit Drugs* (Mount Vernon, N.Y.: Consumers Union, 1973), p. 508.

7. Andrew Weil, *The Natural Mind* (Boston: Houghton Mifflin Co., 1972), p. 196.

8. David A. J. Richards, "Drug Use and the Rights of the Person: A Moral Argument for Decriminalization of Certain Forms of Drug Use," *Rutgers Law Review*, vol. 3, Spring 1982, p. 607.

9. Thomas S. Szasz, *Ceremonial Chemistry: The Ritual Persecution of Drugs, Addicts, and Pushers* (Garden City, N.Y.: Anchor Books, 1974), p. 2.

10. Ibid., p. 165.

11. United States v. Moore, 486 F.2d 1139 (D.C. Cir. 1973).

12. Powell v. Texas, 392 U.S. 514 (1968).

13. The Institute of Medicine regards 13.3 million Americans as alcoholics or problem drinkers, out of a total drinking population of 100 million. Institute of Medicine, *Alcoholism, Alcohol Abuse and Related Problems: Opportunities for Research* (Washington, D.C.: National Academy Press, 1980), pp. 1, 165. On heroin addiction, Charles Silberman asserts in *Criminal Violence, Criminal Justice* (New York: Vantage Books, 1978), p. 74, "About 1 heroin user in 10 is an addict, i.e., someone who uses heroin every day—about the same as the ratio of alcoholics to the drinking population." The body of research compiled by Norman E. Zinberg and his associates tends to support this assertion. With respect to cocaine, the recency of the phenomenon makes it difficult to come up with reliable data. The highest estimates of the number of people dependent upon cocaine run in the range of 1–2 million out of a monthly using population of about 10 million, or 10–20 percent.

14. Maure Dolan, "Pushing the Limits of the Impossible," *Miami Herald*, 13 November 1984, sec. B.

15. Ibid.

16. Grinspoon and Bakalar, *Cocaine*, p. 237.

17. Weil, *Natural Mind*, p. 22.

18. Ibid., p. 20.

19. Sigmund Freud, *Civilization and Its Discontents* (New York: W. W. Norton & Co., 1961), p. 13.

20. Ibid., p. 12.

21. Weil, *Natural Mind*, p. 194.

22. Ibid., p. 197.

23. Weil, "Altered States of Consciousness," quoted in Brecher, *Licit and Illicit Drugs*, p. 509.

24. Deena Gross and B. C. Manion, "Officials Disappointed at Sparse Attendance for Chemical People," *Hollywood Sun Tattler*, 3 November 1983, sec. A; Sandra Earley, " 'Chemical People' Suffers from Excess of Dull Talk," *Miami Herald*, 3 November 1983, sec. A.

25. National Academy of Sciences, *Issues in Controlled Substance Use*, 1980, pp. 5 et. seq.

26. Joel Brinkley, "The War on Narcotics: Can It Be Won?" *New York Times*, 14 September 1984, sec. A.

27. National Commission on Marihuana and Drug Abuse, 1973, in Deborah Maloff, "A Review of the Effects of the Decriminalization of Marijuana," *Contemporary Drug Problems*, Fall 1981, p. 132.

28. Drug Abuse Council, Inc., "Survey of Marihuana Use and Attitudes: State of Oregon," News Release, January, 1977. For California statistics, see California State Offices of Narcotics and Drug Abuse, *A First Report of the Impact of California's New Marijuana Law* (SB95), Sacramento, 1976; and San Mateo County, California, *Summary Report: Survey of Student Drug Use*, 1976. For Maine, see Maine Office of Alcoholism and Drug Abuse Prevention, *An Evaluation of the Decriminalization of Marijuana in Maine*, 1978.

Chapter 12

1. Thomas Kuhn, *The Structure of Scientific Revolutions* (Chicago: University of Chicago Press, 1970), pp. 144–45.

2. "Lawmakers Reportedly Tied to Drugs," *Miami Herald*, 28 April 1983, sec. A.

3. John Naisbitt, *Megatrends* (New York: Warner Books, 1982).

4. Ibid., p. 11.

5. Ibid., p. 52.

6. Ibid., p. 51.

7. Ibid., p. 143.

8. Ibid., p. 147.

9. Jane E. Brody, "America Leans to a Healthier Diet," *The New York Times Magazine*, 13 October 1985, p. 32.

10. Naisbitt, *Megatrends*, p. 260.

Appendix 1

The War on Drugs (Cocaine)—An Overview

GOAL: ELIMINATE (REDUCE) SUPPLY OF ILLEGAL DRUGS AND DRUG SUPPLYING SYNDICATES.
METHODS: AGGRESSIVE MULTI-AGENCY ATTACK WITH DOUBLED BUDGET AND NEW ENFORCEMENT PERSONNEL EQUIPPED WITH EXPANDED SEARCH AND SEIZURE POWERS.

THE INDUSTRY	THE WAR
1. PRODUCTION	
Coca leaf: 125,000 + peasant families in Peru, Bolivia grow coca; cultivation spreading to Ecuador, Brazil	State Dept. funds eradication of illicit coca and crop substitution
Conversion to cocaine from paste or base in Colombia (many labs also in Miami)	Seizures in South America by national military and police forces
2. EXPORT (SMUGGLING)	
Colombia to Florida directly; or to Bahamas, Mexico for transshipment to U.S. by private planes and small boats	Interdiction at U.S. borders Coast Guard patrols high seas. Customs:marine, air patrols; cargo inspectors at major ports. Nat'l Narcotics Border Interdiction System-drug perimeter in 6 border cities; uses radar ballons and computers.
3. DISTRIBUTION	
Regional distributors Wholesale: Multi-kilo dealers sell to kilo dealers to pound and ounce dealers ($30,000 per kilo)	DEA/FBI Conspiracy investigations, plus Organized Crime Drug Enforcement Task Forces in 13 core cities focusing on "high level" traffickers
Retail: mostly grams ($60-80) "Rock" houses provide free base in $10 units	Local police sporadically make sweeps of street dealers and base houses. Miami Vice style under-cover work focuses on pound and kilo dealers
4. MONEY LAUNDERING/TAX EVASION	
Smuggling currency for deposit in Caribbean tax havens (secret accounts leave no paper trail) Manipulate U.S. banking system by wire transfers of cash deposits, false CTR's, complex layered transactions, etc.	Treas. enforces Bank Secrecy Act (currency controls) and IRS prosecutes for tax evasion; detection of violations is very difficult
Gross Revenues: $80-100 billion, $30 billion from cocaine; 50-90%=profits [Compare $29 billion in consumer spending for cigarettes, $66 billion for alcoholic beverages]	Asset & currency seizures, civil and criminal, practiced by all agencies Total enforcement budget=$1.2 billion

THE RESULTS	THE MARKET
Only 24 sq. miles needed to grow total U.S. supply	Small plot of coca worth 5 times more than coffee or any other legal crop.
Major quantities seized, e.g., 14 tons in single Colombian seizure.	Huge inventories of cocaine in South America led to falling wholesale prices during 1980's
FY 1985-50,000 lbs. of cocaine interdicted by U.S.	U.S. Supply: (1976) 14-19 Metric Tons (1980) 40-48 Metric Tons (1984) 74-90 Metric Tons (1985) 100 + Metric Tons
± 5,000 arrestees (cocaine)	10-12 million monthly users (1982) ± 1,000,000 "addicts" [Compare: 24,000,000 marijuana smokers, 54 M cigarette smokers, 12-13 M Alcoholics]
Fla. ± 4,000 arrestees cocaine violations (2/3 for possession)	Deaths: 604 (1984) [Compare 360,000 deaths from cigarette smoking, ± 200,000 from alcohol]
Banks fined for currency violations (e.g. $500,000 against Bank of Boston for "laundering" $1.22 billion without filing required reports) ± 400 tax prosecutions of suspected drug dealers	Prices: 1980: kilo/$55,000; gram ± $100 (12% purity) 1985: kilo/$30,000; gram ± $70 (35% purity) Pharmacy: $2.00 gram (100% purity)
± 1/4 billion dollars in drug-related assets seized by U.S. (War on drugs may become self-financing)	

Appendix 2

Chronology of Milestones in the War on Drugs

1914	Harrison Narcotics Act passed by Congress taxes transfers of cocaine and opiates and restricts transfers to medical channels on government forms.
1915	162 IRS agents placed in Miscellaneous Division of Treasury Department to enforce revenue provisions of Harrison Act.
1919–24	25,000 doctors prosecuted for violations of Harrison Act. Addiction maintenance clinics closed by Treasury Agents.
1922	United States v. Behrman decided. Supreme Court denounced doctor's prescription of cocaine for an addict as unlawful "gratification of a diseased appetite for these pernicious drugs."
1930	Federal Bureau of Narcotics established within Department of Treasury.
1937	Marijuana Tax Act passed to restrict marijuana under Harrison Act model.
1956	Narcotics Control Act imposes mandatory prison terms for offenders (later repealed).
1966	Bureau of Drug Abuse Control created with 100 agents to police supply of "dangerous drugs" (amphetamines and barbiturates).
1968	President Johnson submits Reorganization Plan No. 1 to Congress, consolidating FBN and BDAC into Bureau of Narcotics and Dangerous Drugs under authority of Department of Justice. BNDD has a total of 600 agents.
1970	Comprehensive Drug Abuse and Prevention Act passed by Congress, establishing present framework of five drug schedules and import/export controls.

1971 President Nixon sends message to Congress portraying drug abuse as "a national emergency afflicting both the body and soul of America." The same day he creates by executive order the Special Action Office for Drug Abuse Prevention to oversee treatment, rehabilitation, education and research program.

1972 BNDD has 1,361 agents and a budget of $64 million.

By executive order President Nixon creates Office of Drug Abuse Law Enforcement (ODALE), to focus on street "pushers" and Office of National Narcotics Intelligence (ONNI) under FBI authority.

National Commission on Marihuana and Drug Abuse recommends repeal of penalty for private possession of marijuana. In following years, repeal of penalties for private or public possession is endorsed by AMA, ABA, American Public Health Association, National Council of Churches, National Advisory Commission on Criminal Justice Standards and Goals, National Research Council and others.

1973 President Nixon declares "an all-out global war on the drug menace" and submits Reorganization Plan No. 2, consolidating BNDD, ODALE, ONNI and the Customs Service Drug Investigation Unit into the Drug Enforcement Administration (DEA) with 2,000 agents. DEA Budget approaches 1/2 billion dollars.

1976 Supply of cocaine to United States estimated by Government at 14–19 metric tons.

1977 President Carter recommends decriminalization of marijuana.

1979 NIDA household survey reports 9.7 million had used cocaine within the last year, 15.4 million had tried it at least once.

1980 Supply of cocaine to United States estimated by Government at 40–48 metric tons.

Operation Greenback begins to trace money laundering operations. Government indicts 51 defendants and seizes $20,000,000 in currency in first phase.

1981 Posse Comitatus Act—Congress repeals century-old prohibition on military enforcement of civilian laws. Department of Defense administratively implements new statute, with special enlargement of Navy's role in drug interdiction. All branches provide equipment, training and other assistance to Coast Guard, Customs and DEA operations.

Percy amendment (to Foreign Assistance Act of 1961) repealed. Spraying of herbicides on marijuana crops in source countries now encouraged.

1982 Tax Reform Act amended to facilitate disclosure of IRS file information to other enforcement agencies.

"Arctic Penitentiary Act" proposed for federal drug offenders.

CIA brought into War on Drugs by Executive Order.

	IRS intensifies Special Enforcement Program aimed at drug offenders.
	NIDA household survey reports 11.9 million had used cocaine within past year and 21.6 million had tried it at least once.
Jan., 1982	President Reagan announces formation of South Florida Task Force on Crime under direction of Vice President Bush to fulfill federal government's "special responsibility" to control "massive immigration and epidemic drug smuggling."
Feb., 1982	Task Force begins operations under direction of Vice President Bush, with 337 drug agents from DEA and Customs serving as Joint Task Group.
March, 1982	Attorney General orders Director of FBI to assume authority over DEA. FBI given concurrent drug investigative jurisdiction.
Mar. 9, 1982	3,728 pounds of cocaine seized on a Tampa-Colombia cargo jet.
Mar. 12, 1982	Reagan Administration retracts endorsements for stronger health warnings on cigarette packs.
Mar. 15-Dec. 31, 1982	GAO report on Task Force operations shows following results as compared to same period in 1981:
	Marijuana seizures: from 1,074,000 to 1,245,000 pounds.
	Cocaine seizures: from 1,617 to 2,891 pounds.
	Drug arrests: from 742 to 945.
	Price of cocaine drops and purity rises.
	Marijuana smugglers shift routes away from South Florida.
April 18, 1982	U.S. Border Patrol and South Florida Task Force opened a drug and alien checkpoint on U.S. 1, causing a 19-mile traffic jam from Florida City to Key Largo for 6 hours.
May 18, 1982	1,197 pounds of cocaine seized from a four-engine cattle jet.
Sept. 18, 1982	Small plane drops more than 500 pounds of cocaine packed in fiberglass canisters over mountains of North Georgia.
Oct., 1982	President Reagan pledges "unshakable" commitment "to do what is necessary to end the drug menace" and "to cripple the power of the mob in America."
Nov., 1982	President calls South Florida Task Force "unqualified success."
	Carrier *Nimitz* and escort cruiser USS *Mississippi* intercept a tug laden with 30 tons of marijuana.
Dec., 1982	Great American Bank (Miami) indicted for laundering $96 million in cocaine money in 14-month period.
Dec. 4, 1982	Task Force agents seize 680 pounds of 90% pure cocaine worth $20 million (wholesale) from the fuel tanks of a Colombian freighter on the Miami River.

Jan., 1983	Organized Crime Drug Enforcement Task Force program in 13 core cities begins with budget of $127 million. By year's end, OCDETF has staff of agents and 200 prosecutors. Goal is to prosecute members of high level drug trafficking organizations and to destroy their operations.
Jan. 17, 1983	Federal agents confiscated more than 400 pounds of cocaine and arrested 12 Colombians in the largest drug seizure ever on the West Coast.
March, 1983	NNBIS created in 6 border cities to coordinate drug interdiction efforts.
March 7, 1983	Police seize 305 pounds of cocaine from a twin-engine plane, the largest seizure in Martin County, Florida, history.
March 16, 1983	Police find between 600 and 700 pounds of cocaine on an airplane that skidded off a runway in Dothan, Ala.
April, 1983	Contingent of ten marines arrives in South Florida to fly and maintain aircraft in support of United States Customs Service.
April 28, 1983	Customs agents seize 625 pounds of cocaine from small, twin-engine plane that lands in cow pasture, the largest seizure in Hendry County, Florida, history.
May 6, 1983	Cocaine Hotline opens (1–800-COCAINE) and receives 1,000 calls a day.
May 31, 1983	Confidential informant encounters Miami police officers on street and leads them to a boat on the Miami River carrying 1,500–2,000 pounds of cocaine.
June 11, 1983	Customs agents report seizure of $300 million worth of cocaine and 2 tons of marijuana in 5 separate incidents.
Summer 1983	Price of cocaine dips to record low ($15,000-$18,000 per kilo) as result of worldwide glut. (1986 price rises to $35,000 per kilo, about 2/3 of 1981 price.)
July, 1983	USS *Kidd*, a Navy guided missile destroyer, chases and fires upon a marijuana cargo vessel, the first such military/civilian encounter in history.
Nov. 2, 1983	PBS Documentary "The Chemical People" broadcast. Public school officials in Broward County, Florida, report "sparse" attendance.
Dec. 31, 1983	FBI has 1,085 agents working 1,692 "drug-related matters." Its fiscal year 1983 budget allocates $17.8 million for drug enforcement.
Jan. 15, 1984	500 pounds of cocaine seized from beneath deck of a 37-foot sport fishing vessel.
Jan. 31, 1984	United States Customs officers find 965 pounds of cocaine during a routine search of a 33-foot pleasure craft, the largest seizure of its kind.
Feb., 1984	Florida Highway Patrol sets up roadblocks at which drug sniffing dogs check cars.

Feb. 4, 1984	Customs agents seize 910 pounds of cocaine from a sailboat.
Feb. 10, 1984	14 packages of pure cocaine wash up on beaches near Vero Beach, Florida.
Feb. 24, 1984	Big cocaine processing plant discovered in Everglades along with 100 pounds of pure cocaine. Total of 21 drug laboratories seized in United States in 1984.
March, 1984	Attorney General Smith reports on activities of OCDETF, including the biggest drug case in United States history, in which defendants are accused of smuggling over $2 billion worth of cocaine into the United States.
Mar. 21, 1984	Colombian authorities seize 13.8 tons of cocaine and cocaine base from a cocaine "industrial park" in the jungle.
April, 1984	Government concludes three-year investigation by indicting Joe Bonanno family with importing $1.68 billion worth of heroin into the United States. The Attorney General calls it the "most significant case involving heroin trafficking by traditional organized crime that the federal government has ever developed."
Apr. 3, 1984	Coast Guard cutter makes largest ever seizure of cocaine at sea, 2,200 pounds.
June, 1984	The Department of Justice reports a 60 percent increase in the number of wiretaps.
June 16, 1984	2,500 pounds of cocaine found concealed in Panamanian shipment of freezers. As with the 3,700 pound seizure, no arrests were made.
June 19, 1984	1,700 pounds of cocaine discovered in containers of roofing tiles in a Miami warehouse.
July, 1984	DEA reveals that it keeps computer files on 1.5 million persons; only 5 percent are under investigation or suspected.
	Attorney General Smith announces "largest single seizure of cash bank accounts in any drug case in the history of federal law enforcement."
Aug., 1984	3,194 persons indicted and 1,068 convicted in OCDETF cases to date.
Aug. 8, 1984	Florida Department of Law Enforcement announces campaign against marijuana cultivation. Hotline established.
Aug. 13, 1984	Twin-engine plane touches down briefly on unopened section of I–95 in Florida, leaving behind 1,200 pounds of cocaine. No arrests are made.
Aug. 22, 1984	Customs inspectors use detector dogs to uncover 2,754 pounds of cocaine concealed inside 180 large industrial pulleys from Peru.
Sep. 24, 1984	President Reagan signs a proclamation for National Drug Abuse Education and Prevention Week. "We are on the right track," he says.

Sep. 27, 1984	White House Press Release summarizes accomplishments of War on Drugs:
	Arrests of the top-level organizers and financiers of the drug traffic have increased 18 percent, from 195 per month in 1981 to about 231 per month in 1984. Total arrests averaged about 1,000 per month.
	Convictions for all drug law violators have increased 90 percent, from 485 per month in 1981 to about 921 per month in 1984.
	Convictions of top-echelon organizers and financiers have increased 186 percent, from 88 per month in 1981 to about 252 per month in 1984.
	U.S. seizures of cocaine during the first seven months of 1984 are 216 percent greater than cocaine seizures during all of 1981. Heroin seizures are 67 percent greater and marijuana seizures are 8 percent greater for the first seven months of 1984 than in all of 1981.
	In the first half of 1984, over 25 metric tons of cocaine were seized in the United States and Latin America, compared to approximately 3.7 metric tons in 1981.
	(Not mentioned: Imports of cocaine to U.S. reach 74–90 metric tons.)
Oct., 1984	Comprehensive Crime Control Act of 1984 passed by Congress authorizes pretrial detention, lengthens drug sentences to 20 years, and increases use of criminal forfeitures.
Oct. 4, 1984	Federal agents seized 650 pounds of cocaine from a twin-engine Piper Navajo at Fort Lauderdale airport, the largest in Broward County history.
Nov. 24, 1984	Operation Hat Trick, a joint Navy–Coast Guard interdiction of unprecedented scope in the Caribbean, produces ordinary seizure. To date, 108 tons of marijuana, the same as the year before, have been seized.
Dec., 1984	Miami News reports that $3.5 billion per year in cash is deposited in Florida banks. Most of it is believed to be drug money.
Dec. 1, 1984	A Piper Seneca enters United States air space from the Bahamas without filing flight plan. It carries 15 duffel bags stuffed with 1,000 pounds of cocaine.
1985	350,000 people die from effects of cigarette smoking.
	NORML estimates that marijuana is largest United States cash crop, worth about 14 billion per year. In one 3-day sweep, DEA agents sight over 3000 illegal plots of marijuana.
Feb. 7, 1985	Bank of Boston pleads guilty to felony charge of failing to report $1.22 billion in cash transactions with 9 foreign banks. $500,000 fine assessed.

Feb. 12, 1985	Metro-Dade Organized Crime Commander says South Florida cocaine traffic is worse than ever.
March, 1985	IRS reports that United States financial institutions launder about $80 billion per year in drug money.
March 13, 1985	Federal prosecutors arrest "El Gordo," a 32-year old Colombian, charging him to be kingpin of drug syndicate that ships 200 kilos of cocaine per month from Miami to New Jersey.
Apr. 20, 1985	$1.3 million in small bills seized from Piper Navajo at Fort Lauderdale Airport.
May 8, 1985	A local police officer in Everglades City, Florida, stops a Winnebago Camper because it rides very low on its suspension. He discovers one ton of cocaine.
May 10, 1985	Department of Justice won 704 motions for pretrial detention (and lost 185) under CCC Act of 1984.
June, 1985	Congress expands military role in War on Drugs.
June 27, 1985	Ten persons arrested and one ton of cocaine seized in Palm Beach County's largest cocaine seizure.
July 1, 1985	DEA uses emergency powers to place MDMA ("Ecstasy") on Schedule I ("no legitimate medical use"). Previously, DEA had made a similar emergency ban of methyl fentanyl ("China White").
July 12, 1985	*Miami Herald* reports that federal agents stand guard over ten tons of seized cocaine at a secret location in Florida.
July 17, 1985	Blue Lightning Task Force announced in Miami. Operation to include radar balloons and 60-knot interceptor boats tied into high-tech computerized command post. 1–800-BE-ALERT hotline established for citizen tips.
July 18, 1985	Customs agents find 1,000 pounds of cocaine concealed in a 40,000 pound sesame seed shipment from Guatemala.
Aug. 21, 1985	Dept. of Treasury fines Crocker National Bank of San Francisco record fine of $2.25 million for failing to report $3.88 billion in cash transactions during 1980–84 period.
Sept. 27, 1985	Miami police open a drug house in Liberty City. They sell drugs and arrest 83 unwitting customers.
Dec. 1985	DEA reports appearance of "crack," prepared cocaine freebase pellets, in New York City and other markets.
Dec. 31, 1985	United States Marshall's Service reports it has $313 million in seized cash and property in its custody.
Jan., 1986	United States Magistrate Peter Nimkoff resigns in partial protest over governmental abuses of power in War on Drugs.
Jan. 14, 1986	DEA announces mandatory drug tests for all staff and agents.
Feb., 1986	Florida Marine Patrol makes its largest cocaine seizure ever—935 pounds.

	The Department of Justice announced the largest seizure of cash ($11.6 million) in a single drug trafficking case in the history of federal law enforcement.
	DEA reports wide spread of high potency black tar heroin throughout the United States.
	President Reagan's budget message urges Congress to allow United States to spend an additional $181 million in the War on Drugs in fiscal year 1987.
March 3, 1986	President's Commission on Organized Crime calls for mandatory drug testing of all federal employees and workers hired by federal contractors; intensified military action also urged.
Apr. 18, 1986	Nova Law Center sponsors Symposium "War on Drugs: In Search of a Breakthrough."

Afterword: An Agenda for Study and Action

The contemporary drug scene is so dynamic that my subject seemed to change before I could finish writing about it. As the manuscript was being prepared for printing, new developments emerged to challenge its central thesis—that the only principled and effective source of drug regulation is the informed individual. The challenge arose from reports of a national "epidemic" of crack cocaine and the apparent increase in sensational overdoses and deaths from all types of cocaine.

Crack (or "rock")—pre-pared, ready-to-smoke cocaine freebase—has been around for a while, but during 1986 it achieved wide distribution and special prominence in the media. Dr. Arnold Washton, director of research for the National Cocaine Hotline, publicly called crack the most addictive of all forms of cocaine. Other authorities emphasize its potential to induce heart attack or respiratory failure.

Among the many accounts of injuries resulting from overdoses of cocaine are some bizarre incidents. In Miami a woman and her six-year-old daughter jumped from the fifth story window of a housing project in order to escape a pistol-wielding friend who went "beserk" from smoking cocaine. The little girl broke her back. A 34-year-old lawyer was seen hiding naked in the bushes of a stranger's house. When the police arrived, he put up fierce resistance, in an apparent psychotic state. His body temperature reached 104.4 degrees, and he died that evening of a cocaine overdose. On the national level, sports figures Len Bias and Don Rogers died of cocaine overdoses within a few days of each other. Surely, the argument goes, these events expose a fatal weakness in the notion of relying upon the common sense and responsibility of the individual to stay out of trouble; however, the answer is no.

The fundamental point is that these tragedies occurred under the *present* regime of prohibition. Where is the protection offered by the War on Drugs? Where is its contribution to the national security and well-being? Why do these destructive events increase so rapidly in number and severity in the teeth of an aggressively enforced policy designed to prevent them?

As I have argued above, the War on Drugs is premised on the ignorance and foolishness of the individual. Indeed, the War on Drugs maximizes ignorance, both of the medical community (which lacks experience in dispensing controlled doses of heroin, cocaine or marijuana to patients) and the drug-using population, which is kept in the dark about product quality or the line between safe and lethal doses. Drug users have no way of knowing the purity of the cocaine they snort or inject. No one at DEA or NIDA has tried to save the lives of crack smokers by warning them that smoking x number of pellets in y number of hours will put them in the danger zone; nor have they publicized antidotes or emergency treatment procedures. So, of course, we have rising numbers of overdoses and deaths; they are the predictable casualties of the War on Drugs. The ignorance of drug users coupled with a more potent delivery system for cocaine—what is experientially a new drug—is a prescription for havoc. Indeed, our contemporary situation with cocaine (and especially with crack) resembles in many respects the disruption that resulted when the White Man brought liquor to the Indian tribes of North America. Lacking cultural experience with the drug, native societies were especially vulnerable to its destructive potential. Similarly, as long as current government policy treats people as ignorant and foolish, we can expect them to fulfill the prophecy by hurting themselves and others.

The War on Drugs' fanatic insistence on total abstinence rather than reasonable regulation has endangered the lives of those who defy the law's command, as well as those of innocent bystanders; note that the "lust for rock" is blamed by local police in many cities as the motive for a sudden upsurge in burglaries and robberies. So, horror stories in the media do not change the fundamental analysis. On the contrary, they show that the public health and safety is endangered by the War on Drugs.

The prospect of changing this policy is understandably threatening. The American people fear they have a tiger by the tail and cannot let go. Predictably, the President's Commission on Organized Crime issued a shallow report adding an unconvincing "demand reduction" component to its basic call for . . . more of the same: stricter enforcement, mandatory urine testing for federal employees (and federal contractors' employees) and an enlarged role for the military. On April 8, 1986, President Reagan issued a national security directive designating drug trafficking as a national security concern in order to encourage local military commanders to more freely lend assistance to DEA or Coast Guard. The Department of Justice has taken under consideration plans costing up to $400 million to finance expanded military operations. In July, United States Army helicopters and troops participated in Bolivian raids against cocaine traffickers. And according to the *New York Times*, "Washington is in a frenzy over drugs," with Democrats and Republicans racing to "outperform" one another. In August, the House of Representatives was putting together "a hastily drafted multibillion dollar antidrug bill." Thus, the War on Drugs will soon escalate to even higher levels of conflict. Yet, if the War on Drugs incorporated as a private venture and issued stock to the public—with profits to be determined by its success in controlling drug abuse—who would invest in it?

As for the future, it is foolish to speculate. On the one hand, political forces make it difficult to forsee any end to this drug enforcement madness. On the other hand, it is equally difficult to believe that the War on Drugs can survive into the twenty-first century. Since its dynamic is one of inexorable expansion, a continuation of present policy almost certainly means gradual evolution into a soft-core police state: a massive drug enforcement bureaucracy funded at $50 billion a year or more, widespread arrests of drug users, full-scale involvement of the National Guard and other military forces, and the end of many rights of personal privacy. Will Americans really give up their legacy of personal freedom for the illusion of security from drugs? Or will the lessons of National Prohibition and Vietnam come to dominate public debate?

Things will almost certainly get worse before they get better. When, finally, the timing is right for policy reform, the search for new directions should begin by convening a commission of the best and brightest to plan the gradual transition to a regime of drug regulation premised on the centrality of individual responsibility and accountability. The regulatory approach would pursue two specific goals:

1. to deflate the profits of the black market in drugs in order to shrivel the size and scope of destructive black market pathologies.
2. to discourage the use of drugs, licit and illicit, and to promote moderation among those who take them, as a means of promoting other specifically identified social goals.

The commission's agenda should include study of the following matters:

1. Articulation of the specific societal objectives sought to be achieved by drug regulation. Since most drug taking occurs without lasting personal or social impact, drug use per se should not be the target of control. The only legitimate and practical basis of drug regulation is not as an end in itself but as a means to pursue other goals, e.g., public order, traffic safety, workplace security, etc. In short, "the drug problem" should be redefined out of existence.
2. Repeal of (or moratorium on) enforcement of most small-scale drug offenses to free up wasted resources and improve public safety. Currently, about three-quarters of a million persons per year are arrested at the state and local levels

for drug offenses at a cost of billions of dollars. Most of them are cases of simple possession or petty sales. This constitutes a massive diversion of scarce resources from the policing of real crimes—murder, rape, robbery, assault, burglary and predatory white collar crimes.

3. Exploration of now unthinkable regulatory alternatives to prohibition, including controlled substance ID cards or licenses issued after health and competency testing: preventive pairing of drugs (such as stimulants and depressants) and dispensing of antidotes; ration coupons; day-of-the-week restrictions; and the integration of legal and illegal drugs of abuse into a consolidated framework of taxation and regulation.
4. A plan for policing the time, place and manner of drug consumption and distribution to achieve the maintenance of drug-free zones such as schools, parks, hospitals, stadiums, and public institutions and places of business. In this regard, the use of zoning laws modelled after pornography "red light" districts should be explored.
5. A plan to achieve maximum possible protection of minors from access to the drug supply. A realistic and effective program of drug education should be designed for high schools and junior high schools to instill a sense of right relationship to the drug issue, by locating it in a broader context of citizenship. The program should be premised on the connectedness of life on the planet, as a basis of moral responsibility and social duty. It should embrace the union of mind and body, teaching that the body is the temple of the soul. It should emphasize the role of spirituality in wellness and teach natural techniques for altering consciousness. It should acknowledge the differences between adults and minors. It should *not* be an anti-drug propaganda campaign.
6. A plan to implement a major shift of drug enforcement resources away from the glamorous but ineffective focus of the OCDETFS on high-level drug trafficking organizations. Regulation in place of prohibition requires policing of unauthorized low-level street sales, drug markets and the like to ensure compliance with zoning, licensing, and age restrictions. The relationship between federal/state/local enforcement agencies needs to be restructured and funded accordingly.
7. A plan for generous funding of addiction treatment clinics, which should be authorized to prescribe maintenance doses of the drugs "needed" by patients to avoid commission of street crimes to pay for drugs. Clinics (and perhaps other sources) should be authorized to offer "softer" alternatives to powder drugs (cocaine, heroin, etc.) such as marijuana and coca leaves to those who insist on taking some drug.
8. Market research should precede implementation of any of the foregoing changes to estimate the elasticity of the demand for particular drugs, i.e., the size of the population that will begin to take illegal drugs or to increase consumption of them under the new system. Instead of building policy on fearful speculation (such as Dr. Pollin's fear of 100 million cocaine users), let's test the proposition—ask the people and find out. Actual implementation of new regulatory programs should first "test the waters" with marijuana, where the risks of miscalculation are *de minimis*.

9. Develop some index or measurement of national well-being. A bare statement of the number of drug overdoses or deaths standing alone has no policy significance. The drug related harms that occur need to be integrated into a complete picture of public health and safety, taking into account competing sources of injury and mortality (cigarettes, alcohol, motorcycles, swimming pools, etc.) in the social environment. The number of additional injuries or deaths that might result from increased drug use must be balanced against the savings in crimes not committed by desperate addicts and the decline in black market pathologies.
10. A plan for a regulatory climate that encourages employers to use appropriate tests to minimize on-the-job impairment and to regulate the imposition of sanctions. The ability to confine or channel drug use to weekends and holidays will go a long way toward minimizing the overall level of drug use. Drug tests that measure *present* impairment, as opposed to "historical" traces in the urine are needed. The invasion of employees' privacy is a substantial concern; but as an *alternative* it represents the lesser evil compared to police wiretaps, surveillance, roadblocks, dog sniffs, etc. At least the employee is given a choice whether to submit. Further, a single incident of impairment should rarely be grounds for dismissal.
11. A plan for encouraging participation (and possibly funding) of the private sector through community organizations—tenants associations, civic groups, Guardian Angels, etc. Private sector discipline should be preferred whenever possible to police action.

CONCLUSION

Perhaps in an ideal world there would be no drugs. But the genie is out of the bottle; and our existential predicament requires us to choose among options that all include an abundance of drugs. We can choose wisely and well among our options, to improve the quality of life in the United States, or we can cling to an irrational standard—no drugs (except alcohol or tobacco)—that has served the national interest badly and promises worse in the future.

Perhaps I am utopian, but I refuse to believe that the human mind that devised the oldest continuous system of representative democracy, the most dynamic free enterprise system in the West, the computer revolution, and a popular culture that captivates the imagination of the world is not up to the challenge of devising a principled and effective response to what is now conceived of as "the drug problem." The paradox is that regulation offers more real control and gains in public health and safety than outright prohibition. Charting a new course is always risky, and does not offer a panacea. But given the proven failures of the War on Drugs, it's the right thing to do. There simply has to be a better way.

Bibliography

Books

Alexander, Herbert E., and Gerald E. Caiden, eds. *The Politics and Economics of Organized Crime* (Toronto: Lexington Books, 1985).

Ashley, Richard. *Cocaine: Its History, Uses and Effects* (New York: Warner Books, 1975).

Bakalar, James B., and Lester Grinspoon. *Drug Control in a Free Society* (Cambridge, England: Cambridge University Press, 1984).

Blum, Richard H. *Offshore Haven Banks, Trusts and Companies* (New York: Praeger, 1984).

Bonnie, Richard J. *Marijuana Use and Criminal Sanctions* (Charlottesville, Va.: Michie, 1980).

Brecher, Edward M., and the Editors of Consumer Reports. *Licit and Illicit Drugs: The Consumers Union Report on Narcotics, Stimulants, Depressants, Inhalants, Hallucinogens and Marijuana—Including Caffeine, Nicotine and Alcohol* (Mount Vernon, N.Y.: Consumers Union, 1972).

Byck, Robert, ed. *Cocaine Papers: Sigmund Freud* (New York: New American Library, 1974).

Chaterjee, S. K. *Legal Aspects of International Drug Control* (London: Martin Nijhoff, 1981).

Devlin, Patrick. *The Enforcement of Morals* (New York: Oxford University Press, 1965).

DuPont, Robert I., Avram Goldstein, and John O'Donnell. *Handbook on Drug Abuse* (Washington: D.C.: U.S. Government Printing Office, 1979).

Duster, Troy. *The Legislation of Morality: Laws, Drugs, and Moral Judgement* (New York: Free Press, 1972).

Epstein, Edward J. *Agency of Fear* (New York: G. P. Putnam's Sons, 1977).

Freud, Sigmund. *Civilization and Its Discontents* (New York: W. W. Norton & Co., 1961).

Garreau, Joel. *The Nine Nations of North America* (Boston: Houghton Mifflin, 1981).

Goode, Erich. *Drugs in American Society* (New York: Alfred A. Knopf, 1972).

Grinspoon, Lester, and James Bakalar. *Cocaine: A Drug and Its Social Evolution* (New York: Basic Books, 1976).

Grinspoon, Lester, and Peter Hedlom. *The Speed Culture: Amphetamine Use and Abuse in America* (Cambridge, Mass.: Harvard University Press, 1975).

Hart, H. L. *Law, Liberty and Morality* (Stanford: Stanford University Press, 1963).

Hellman, Arthur D. *Laws Against Marijuana: The Price We Pay* (Chicago: University of Illinois Press, 1975).

Himmelstein, Jerome. *The Strange Career of Marijuana: Politics and Ideology of Drug Control in America* (Westport, Conn.: Greenwood Press, 1983).

Hofstadter, Richard. *Age of Reform: From Bryan to F.D.R.* (New York: Random House, Inc., 1955).

Jeri, F. R., ed. *Cocaine 1980* (Lima, Peru: Pacific Press, 1980).

Kaplan, John. *Marijuana—The New Prohibition* (New York: World Publishing Co., 1970).

Kaplan, John. *The Hardest Drug: Heroin and Public Policy* (Chicago: University of Chicago Press, 1983).

Kruger, Henrick. *The Great Heroin Coup* (Boston: South End Press, 1980).

Kuhn, Thomas. *The Structure of Scientific Revolutions* (Chicago: University of Chicago Press, 1970).

Kurian, George, ed. *The Yearbook of World Rankings* (New York: Facts on File, 1979).

Latimer, Dean, and Jeff Goldberg. *Flowers in the Blood: The Story of Opium* (New York: Franklin Watts, 1981).

Lee, David. *Cocaine Handbook: An Essential Reference* (Berkeley, Calif.: And/Or Press, 1980).

Messick, Hank. *Of Grass and Snow: The Secret Criminal Elite* (Englewood Cliffs, N.J.: Prentice-Hall, 1979).

Moore, Mark. *Buy and Bust: The Effective Regulation of an Illicit Market in Heroin* (Lexington, Mass.: Lexington Books, 1977).

Musto, David F. *The American Disease: Origins of Narcotic Control* (New Haven: Yale University Press, 1973).

Naisbitt, John. *Megatrends* (New York: Warner Books, 1982).

New York (City) Commission to Investigate Allegations of Police Corruption and the City's AntiCorruption Procedures, *The Knapp Commission's Report on Police Corruption* (New York: G. Braziller, 1973).

Packer, Herbert. *The Limits of the Criminal Sanction* (Stanford: Stanford University Press, 1968).

Phillips, Joel L., and Ronald D. Wynne. *Cocaine: The Mystique and the Reality* (New York: Avon Books, 1980).

Pike, Frederick B. *The United States and the Andean Republics: Peru, Bolivia and Ecuador* (Cambridge, Mass.: Harvard University Press, 1977).

Polich, J. Michael, et al. *Strategies for Controlling Adolescent Drug Use* (Santa Monica: Rand Corp., 1984).

Reuter, Peter. *Disorganized Crime* (Cambridge, Mass.: M.I.T. Press, 1983).

Richards, David. *Sex, Drugs, Death and the Law* (Totowa, N.J.: Rowman and Littlefield, 1984).

Sabbag, Robert. *Snowblind: A Brief Career in the Cocaine Trade* (New York: Avon Books, 1976).

Samuelson, Paul. *Economics* 11th ed. (New York: McGraw-Hill, 1980).

Satinder, K. Paul. *Drug Use: Criminal, Sick or Cultural?* (New York: Libra Publishers, Inc., 1980).

Silberman, Charles. *Criminal Violence, Criminal Justice* (New York: Vantage Books, 1978).

Simpson, Anthony. *The Literature of Police Corruption* (New York: John Jay Press, 1977).

Szasz, Thomas S. *Ceremonial Chemistry: The Ritual Persecution of Drugs, Addicts, and Pushers* (Garden City, N.Y.: Anchor Books, 1974).

Tanzi, Vito, ed. *The Underground Economy in the United States and Abroad* (Lexington, Mass.: Lexington Books, 1982).

Trebach, Arnold. *The Heroin Solution* (New Haven: Yale University Press, 1982).

Uelmen, Gerald, and Victor Haddox. *Drug Abuse and the Law* (New York: Clark Boardman Co., 1983).

Weil, Andrew. *The Natural Mind: A New Way of Looking at Drugs and the Higher Consciousness* (Boston: Houghton Mifflin Co., 1972).

Williams, Jay, Lawrence Redlinger, and Peter Manning. *Police Narcotics Control: Patterns and Strategies, 1979* (Washington, D.C.: U.S. Government Printing Office, 1979).

Zinberg, Norman. *Drug, Set, and Setting: The Basis for Controlled Intoxicant Use* (New Haven: Yale University Press, 1984).

Articles

Allen, Francis A. "Majorities, Minorities, and Morals: Penal Policy and Consensual Behavior," *Northern Kentucky Law Review*, vol. 9, no. 1, 1982.

Andenaes, J. "General Prevention—Illusion or Reality," *Journal of Criminal Law, Criminology and Police Science*, vol. 43, 1952.

Anderson, Kurt. "Crashing on Cocaine," *Time*, 11 April 1983.

Bassouni, Chariff. "The International Narcotics Control System: A Proposal," *St. John's Law Review*, vol. 46, 1972.

Bayer, Ronald. "Heroin Decriminalization and the Ideology of Tolerance," *Law and Sociology Review*, vol. 12, 1978.

Beck, Melinda. "Evil Empire," *Newsweek*, 25 February 1985.

Becker, Gary. "Crime and Punishment: An Economic Approach," *Journal of Political Economy*, vol. 76, 1968.

Brody, Jane E. "America Leans to a Healthier Diet," *The New York Times Magazine*, 13 October 1985.

Cabranes, Jose. "International Law and Control of the Drug Traffic," *International Lawyer*, vol. 7, 1973.

Caffrey, Ronald. "The Strategy of Enforcement," *Drug Enforcement*, Fall 1982.

Cazalas, Mary. "Addiction in the United States: A Medical Legal History," *Loyola Law Review*, vol. 28, 1972, p. 1.

Cohrssen, John, and Lawrence Hoover. "The International Control of Dangerous Drugs," *Journal of International Law and Economics*, vol. 9, 1974, p. 81.

Demarest, Michael. "Cocaine: Middle Class High," *Time*, 6 July 1981.

DiCarlo, Dominick L. "International Initiatives to Control Coca Production and Cocaine Trafficking," *Drug Enforcement*, Fall 1982.

diGenova, Joseph E., and Constance L. Belfure. "An Overview of the Comprehensive Crime Control Act 1984—The Prosecutor's Perspective," *American Criminal Law Review*, vol. 22, no. 4, Spring 1985.

Drug Abuse Council, Inc. "Survey of Marihuana Use and Attitudes: State of Oregon," News Release, January, 1977.

"The Economics of Heroin: Key to Optimizing the Legal Response," *Georgia Law Review*, vol. 10, 1976.

Flittie, William. "Proposed Emergency Civil Drug Control Act," in National Commission on Marihuana and Drug Abuse, *Drug Use in America: Problem in Perspective*, vol. 3, 1973.

Greenberg, David. "Drug Courier Profiles, Mendenhall and Reid: Analyzing Police Intrusions on Less Than Probable Cause," *American Criminal Law Review*, vol. 19, 1981, p. 49.

Haden-Guest, Anthony. "The Young, the Rich and Heroin," *Rolling Stone*, 7 July 1983.

Heller, J. Dean. "The Attempt to Prevent Illicit Drug Supply," in National Commission on Marihuana and Drug Use, *Drug Use in America: Problem in Perspective*, vol. 3, 1973.

Hiassen, Carl. "The Drug Lawyers," *Miami Herald*, 28 June 1981.

———. " 'Killer': The Life and Death of a Cocaine Cowboy," *Miami Herald*, 3 January 1982.

Kadish, Sanford. "The Crisis of Overcriminalization," *Annals of American Political Science*, vol. 374.

Katz, David. "The Paradoxical Role of Informers within the Criminal System: A Unique Perspective," *University of Dayton Law Review*, vol. 7, 1981.

Kennedy, Edward M. "Foreword," *American Criminal Law Review*, vol. 22, no. 4, Spring 1985.

Knepper, Mike. "Puff, the Dangerous Drug," *Car and Driver*, June, 1980.

Krieger, Albert J., and Susan W. Van Dusen. "The Lawyer, the Client and the New Law," *American Criminal Law Review*, vol. 22, no. 4, Spring 1985.

Kuhn, Howard. "Cocaine: You Can Bank on It," *Esquire*, October, 1983.

Leen, Jeff. "The Selling of Ecstasy: How a Sarasota College Student Became the Timothy Leary of the '80s" *Miami Herald*, 1 September 1985.

Mandel, Jerry. "Problems with Official Drug Statistics," *Stanford Law Review*, vol. 21, 1969.

McGee, Jim, and Carl Hiassen. "U.S. Drug Enforcement: The Billion-Dollar Bust," *Miami Herald*, November 1981.

McLaughlin, Gerald T. "Cocaine: The History and Regulation of a Dangerous Drug," *Cornell Law Review*, vol. 58, 1973.

Moore, Mark. "Limiting Supplies of Drugs to Illicit Markets," *Journal of Drug Issues*, vol. 8, 1979.

Nagel, Stuart. "Tradeoffs in Crime Reduction Among Certainty, Severity, and Crime Benefits," *Rutgers Law Review*, vol. 3, 1982.

Richards, David A. J. "Drug Use and the Rights of the Person: A Moral Argument for Decriminalization of Certain Forms of Drug Use," *Rutgers Law Review*, vol. 3, Spring 1982.

Rivier, L., and J. G. Burns. "Analysis of Alkaloids in Leaves of Cultivated Erythroxylum and Characterization of Alkaline Substances Used During Coca Chewing," *Journal of Ethno-Pharmacology*, vol. 3, 1981.

Robinson, Timothy, and Ruth Simon. "Report Urges Unorthodox Crackdown on Tax Evaders," *National Law Journal*, 30 August 1982, sec. A.

Rosenthal, Barry. "International Control of Narcotic Drugs: An Examination of Supply Reduction Strategies," *Contemporary Drug Problems*, vol. 8, 1979.

Rosenthal, Michael. "Partial Prohibition of Nonmedical Use of Mind Altering Drug," *Houston Law Review*, vol. 16, 1979.

Rothchild, John. "The Informant," *Harper's*, January, 1982.

Speisser, Stuart. "Abolish Paper Money and Eliminate Most Crime," *American Bar Association Journal*, vol. 61, 1975.

Szasz, Thomas S. "The War Against Drugs," *Journal of Drug Issues*, vol. 12, Winter 1982.

Thompson, Steve. "High Driving," *Car and Driver*, March, 1978.

Timmer, Doug. "The Productivity of Crime in the U.S.: Drugs and Capital Accumulation," *Journal of Drug Issues*, vol. 12, Fall 1982.

Voboril, Mary. "Drug Money Is Touchy Topic Among Bankers," *Miami Herald*, 19 October 1981, sec. B.

Wasserstrom, Silas. "The Incredible Shrinking Fourth Amendment," *American Criminal Law Review*, vol. 21, no. 3, Winter 1984.

Whitefield, Mimi. "Cash and a Flood of Customers Mark Miami Federal Reserve Unit," *Miami Herald*, 19 October 1981, sec. A.

Yeager, Matthew. "The Political Economy of Illicit Drugs," *Contemporary Drug Problems*, vol. 4, 1978.

Zarefsky, David. "Government Statistics: The Case for Independent Regulation—A New Legislative Proposal," *Texas Law Review*, vol. 59, 1981.

Government Documents

Congressional Documents

Amendment to the Single Convention on Narcotic Drugs of 1961, 25 March 1972, 26 U.S.T. 1439, T.I.A.S. No. 8118, *Single Convention on Narcotic Drugs*, 30 March 1961, 18 U.S.T. 1407, T.I.A.S. No. 6298.

Annual Report of Activities for Year 1981, Select House Committee on Narcotics Abuse and Control, 97th Cong., 1st Sess., March, 1982.

Cocaine: A Major Drug Issue of the Seventies: Hearings Before the House Select Committee on Narcotics Abuse and Control, 96th Cong., 1st Sess., 1979.

Crime and Secrecy: The Use of Offshore Banks and Companies, Hearings Before the Permanent Subcommittee on Investigation, Senate Committee on Governmental Affairs, 98th Cong., 1st Sess., 1983.

DEA Oversight and Budget Authorization: Hearing Before the Senate Subcommittee on Security and Terrorism Committee of the Judiciary, 97th Cong., 2d Sess., 1982.

Federal Effort Against Organized Crime, Role of the Private Sector: Hearings Before the Subcommittee on Legal and Monetary Affairs of the House Committee on Government Operations, 91st Cong., 2d Sess., 1970.

Financial Investigation of Drug Trafficking: Hearing Before the House Select Committee on Narcotics Abuse and Control, 97th Cong., 1st Sess., 1981.

Foreign Assistance Legislation for Fiscal Year 1982 (Part 7): Hearings and Mark-up Before the Subcommittee on Inter-American Affairs of the House Committee on Foreign Affairs, 97th Cong., 1st Sess., 1981.

Hearings Before the Committee on Foreign Affairs (International Narcotics Control), House of Representatives, 97th Cong., 2d Sess., 1982.

Hearings Before the Permanent Senate Subcommittee on Investigations: Illicit Traffic in Weapons and Drugs Across the United States-Mexican Border, 95th Cong., 1st Sess., 1977.

Hearings Before the Permanent Subcommittee on Investigations of the Committee on Governmental Affairs, U.S. Senate, 98th Cong., 1st Sess., 1983.

Hearings Before the Permanent Subcommittee on Investigations of the Committee on Governmental Affairs: International Narcotics Trafficking, U.S. Senate, 97th Cong., 1st Sess., 10 November 1981.

Hearings Before the Senate Select Committee on Narcotics Abuse and Control: Community Action to Combat Drug Use, 97th Cong., 1st Sess., 22 April 1981.

Hearings Before the Select Committee on Narcotics Abuse and Control: Community Efforts in Drug Abuse Prevention and Early Intervention, House of Representatives, 97th Cong., 1st Sess., 14 September 1981.

Hearings Before the House Select Committee on Narcotics Abuse and Control: Federal Drug Law Enforcement Coordination, House of Representatives, 97th Cong., 2nd Sess., 1982.

Hearings Before the Select Committee on Narcotics Abuse and Control: Financial Investigations of Drug Trafficking, House of Representatives, 97th Cong., 1st Sess., 1981.

Hearing Before the Subcommittee on Alcoholism and Drug Abuse: Health and Educational Effects of Marijuana on Youth, Senate, 97th Cong., 1st Sess., 21 October 1981.

Hearings Before a Subcommittee of the House Committee on Governmental Operations: Review of the Administration's Drug Interdiction Efforts, 98th Cong., 1st Sess., 1983.

Hearings Before the Subcommittee on Crime of the House Committee on the Judiciary: Posse Comitatus Act, 97th Cong., 1st Sess., 1981.

Hearings Before the Subcommittee of the Senate Committee on the Judiciary to Investigate the Administration of the Internal Security Act and Other Internal Security Laws, World Drug Traffic and Its Impact on U.S. Security, 92d Cong., 2d Sess., 1972.

Hearings Before the Subcommittee on Oversight of the House Committee on Ways and Means: Underground Economy, 96th Cong., 1st Sess., 1979.

House of Representatives, Select Committee on Narcotics Abuse and Control, "International Study Missions" (Summary Report), 97th Cong., 1st Sess., 1984.

Illegal Narcotics Profits: Hearings Before the Permanent Subcommittee on Investigations of the Senate Committee on Governmental Affairs, 96th Cong., 1st Sess., 1979.

International Narcotics Control: Hearings Before the House Committee on Foreign Affairs, 97th Cong., 2d Sess., 1982.

International Narcotics Control Study Missions: A Report of the Select Committee on Narcotics Abuse and Control, 98th Cong., 2d Sess., August, 1984.

International Narcotics Trafficking: Hearings Before the Permanent Subcommittee on In-

vestigations of the Senate Committee on Governmental Affairs, 97th Cong., 1st Sess., 1981.

International Security Assistance and Arms Export Control Act of 1976, Public Law No. 94–329, sec. 504(b), Codified at *United States Code*, vol. 22, sec. 2291(c)(1), 1982.

Joint Hearing Before the Subcommittee on Security and Terrorism: The Cuban Government's Involvement in Facilitating International Drug Traffic, 98th Cong., 1st Sess., 1983.

Report of the Committee on Governmental Affairs: Illegal Narcotics Profits, U.S. Senate, 96th Cong., 2d Sess., 1980.

Report of the Select Committee on Narcotics Abuse and Control: Congressional Resource Guide to Federal Effort on Narcotics Abuse and Control, 1969–76, 95th Cong., 2d sess., 1978.

Senate Hearing Before the Committee on Appropriations, Drug Interdiction on the Gulf Coast, 98th Cong., 1st Sess., 1984.

Staff of Subcommittee on International Development Institution and Finance of the House Committee on Banking, Finance and Urban Affairs, *Oversight on Illegal Drug Trafficking from Bolivia and U.S. Application of the Rangel Amendment*, 97th Cong., 1st Sess., 1981.

State, Justice, Commerce, the Judiciary, and Related Agencies Appropriations, Fiscal Year 1983: Hearings Before a Subcommittee of the Senate Committee on Appropriations, 97th Cong., 2d Sess., 1982.

U.S. Congress, *Oversight Hearings on Federal Drug Strategy 1979: House Select Committee on Narcotics Abuse and Control*, 96th Cong., 1st Sess., 1979.

Institutional Government Agency Reports and Research Monographs

DEA, Offender Based Transaction System. *Case Level Arrests by Drug* (1982).

Department of Treasury, IRS. *Estimate of Income Unreported on Individual Income Tax Returns*, September, 1979.

Drug Abuse Policy Office. *1984 National Strategy for Prevention of Drug Abuse and Drug Trafficking* (Washington, D.C.: U.S. Government Printing Office, 1984) (annual).

U.S. Justice, FBI. *Crime in the United States*, 1982.

Florida Department of Law Enforcement. *Uniform Crime Report for 1982* (annual).

Institute of Medicine. *Alcoholism, Alcohol Abuse and Related Problems: Opportunities for Research* (Washington, D.C.: National Academy Press, 1980).

National Academy of Sciences. *Deterrence and Incapacitation: Estimating the Effects of Criminal Sanctions on Crime Rates*, 1978.

———. *Issues in Controlled Substance Use*, 1980.

National Commission on Marihuana and Drug Abuse. *Marihuana: A Signal of Misunderstanding* (New York: New American Library, 1972); Appendix One, *The Technical Papers of the First Report of the National Commission on Marihuana and Drug Abuse*, 2 vols. (1972); Appendix Two, *Drug Use in America: Problem in Perspective*, 4 vols. (1973).

National Institute on Drug Abuse. *Cocaine 1977* (Washington, D.C.: U.S. Government Printing Office, 1977).

———. *Cocaine Use in America: Epidemiologic and Clinical Perspectives* (Washington, D.C.: U.S. Government Printing Office, 1985).

———. *Drugs and the Class of '78: Behaviors, Attitudes, and Recent National Trends*, 1979.

———. *National Survey on Drug Abuse: Main Findings, 1979.*

———. *National Survey on Drug Abuse: Main Findings, 1982.*

———. *Statistical Series, Annual Data: Data from the Client Oriented Data Acquisition Process (CODAP)* (Series E).

———. *Statistical Series, Annual Data: Data from the Drug Abuse Warning Network (DAWN)* (Series I).

———. *Student Drug Use in America, 1975–1980.*

National Narcotics Intelligence Consumers Committee. *The Supply of Drugs to the U.S. Illicit Market from Foreign and Domestic Sources* (Washington, D.C.: U.S. Government Printing Office) (annual).

Office of the Attorney General. *Organized Crime Drug Enforcement Task Force Program Annual Report* (annual).

President's Commission on Organized Crime. *The Cash Connection: Organized Crime, Financial Institutions, and Money Laundering*, October, 1984.

State Department, Bureau of International Narcotics Matters. Satellite Survey of Bolivia Coca Fields Done By Earth Satellite Corporation, 15 April 1981.

Tobacco Institute. *The Tax Burden on Tobacco*, 1982.

United Nations. *Report of the International Narcotics Control Board for 1984* (New York: United Nations, 1984).

United States Attorney's Manual, 11 September 1979, sec. 9–7.160.

U.S. Department of Health, Education and Welfare. *Research Issues 15, Cocaine—Summary of Psychological Research* (Rockville, Md.: National Institute on Drug Abuse, 1976).

———. *Research Issues 16: The Lifestyles of Nine American Cocaine Users* (Washington, D.C.: U.S. Government Printing Office, 1976).

U.S. Department of Justice. *Attorney General's Task Force on Violent Crime Final Report*, 17 August 1981.

———. *Drug Enforcement Administration: A Profile*, July, 1981.

———. *Drug Enforcement Statistical Report*, 1980.

———. *Handbook on the Comprehensive Crime Control Act of 1984 and Other Criminal Statutes Enacted by the 98th Congress*, December, 1984.

———. *The National Crime Survey: Working Papers*, vol. 1, December, 1981.

———. *Report to the Nation on Crime and Justice: The Data*, October, 1983.

General Accounting Office Reports

GAO. *FBI-DEA Task Forces: An Unsuccessful Attempt at Joint Operations*, 26 March 1982.

———. *Reported Federal Drug Abuse Expenditures—Fiscal Years 1981 to 1985*, 3 June 1985.

———. Report by the Comptroller General. *Asset Forfeiture—A Seldom Used Tool in Combatting Drug Trafficking*, 10 April 1981.

———. Report by the Comptroller General. *The Coast Guard's Role in Drug Interdiction—How Much Is Enough?*, 12 February 1979.

———. Report by the Comptroller General. *Disclosure and Summons Provisions of 1976 Tax Reform Act—An Analysis of Proposed Legislative Changes*, 1980.

———. Report by the Comptroller General. *Disclosure and Summons Provisions of 1976 Tax Reform Act—Privacy Gains with Unknown Law Enforcement Effects*, 12 March 1979.

———. Report by the Comptroller General. *Drug Control in South America Having Limited Success—Some Progress but Problems Are Formidable*, 1978.

———. Report by the Comptroller General. *Federal Drug Interdiction Efforts Need Strong Central Oversight*, 13 June 1983.

———. Report by the Comptroller General. *Improved Planning for Developing and Selecting IRS Criminal Tax Cases Can Strengthen Enforcement of Federal Tax Laws*, 6 November 1979.

———. Report to the Attorney General. *Heroin Statistics Can Be Made More Reliable*, 30 July 1980.

———. Report to the Chairman, Subcommittee on Government Information, Justice and Agriculture Committee on Government Operations, House of Representatives. *Coordination of Federal Drug Interdiction Efforts*, 15 July 1985.

———. Report to the Chairman, Subcommittee on Government Information, Justice and Agriculture Committee on Government Operations, House of Representatives. *Customs Service's Participation in Followup Investigations on Drug Smuggling Interdictions in South Florida*, 18 July 1984.

———. Report to the Congress. *Problems in Slowing the Flow of Cocaine and Heroin from and Through South America*, 30 March 1975.

———. Report to the Congress of the United States. *Bank Secrecy Act Reporting Requirements Have Not Yet Met Expectations, Suggesting Need for Amendment*, 23 July 1981.

———. Report to the Congress of the United States. *Stronger Crackdown Needed on Clandestine Laboratories Manufacturing Dangerous Drugs*, 6 November 1981.

———. Report to the Congress of the United States by the Comptroller General. *Gains Made in Controlling Illegal Drugs, Yet the Drug Trade Flourishes*, 15 October 1979.

———. Report to the Congress of the United States by the Comptroller General. *Reducing Federal Judicial Sentencing and Prosecuting Disparities: A Systematic Approach Needed*, 19 March 1979.

———. Report to the Congress of the United States by the Comptroller General. *Retail Diversion of Legal Drugs—A Major Problem with No Easy Solution*, 10 March 1978.

———. Report to the Hon. Joseph R. Biden, U.S. Senate. *Organized Crime Drug Enforcement Task Forces: Status and Observations*, 9 December 1983.

———. Report to the Hon. Joseph R. Biden, U.S. Senate. *Investigations of Major Drug Trafficking Organizations*, 5 March 1984.

Index

Addiction, 24–30, 204–9; concept of, 26, 204–8; and thievery, 142; examples of, 190
Air Force, 92–93. *See also* Interdiction network
Alcohol: behavioral effects, 18–19; withdrawal, 26; death toll, 29, 187; advertising, 188; addiction, 202; *Powell v. Texas*, 206
Alliance between drug trade and guerrillas, 162–67
Anslinger, Harry S., 181–82
Arctic Penitentiary Act, 120
Arrest statistics, 77
Ashley, Richard, 23–24
Assault on justice: perceived leniency of the system, 118–19; congressional proposals and reforms, 119–21, 125; constitutional rights, 121–25
Assets: seizure and forfeiture, 79–81; statistics on, 80; effect on industry profits, 80
Attitudes, 184–96; role of media, 189–91; transformation of, 195–96, 213
Attorney General, 12, 35, 66–67, 74–75, 80, 89, 106, 135, 175; William French Smith, 99–100, 113, 137, 150; Organized Crime Drug Enforcement Task Force Report, 101–2, 104
Bahamas, 44, 64, 93; money laundering, 47; Prime Minister Pindling, 72, 86; as tax haven, 85–86; corruption in, 158–60; Robert Vesco, 159
Bank Secrecy Act, 68, 81, 90, 119, 123; investigations under, 81–87
Betancur, Belisario, 72, 161–63
Big Brotherism, 117; wiretapping, 126–27; stopping cars on highways, 127–28; monitoring students and schools, 129–30; abusive enforcement, 130–32; keeping tabs on citizens by computers, 132–33; stigmatizing, 133; extradition of U.S. citizens, 133–34; obstructing medical practice, 134–35; militarizing drug enforcement, 135–39
Bill of Rights, 117–18, 120, 130. *See also* Civil liberties
Black, Hugo, 138, 192, 200
Black market in drugs, 12–17, 217; supply and demand, 31–36, 77; expansion of, 49, 55, 106; alternatives, 52–53; revenues in, 80, 112–13, 142; corruption of foreign governments by, 155–62; narco-terrorist connection with, 162–65; financing of law enforcement, 174–75

Black market pathologies, 166, 194, 213–14; values jeopardized by, 117–18; derivative crimes, 141–54
Bolivia, 12, 37, 75, 153, 156; areas under cultivation of coca, 40–41; Roberto Suarez, 43, 55, 75, 157–58; failure of crop control in, 50–51, 57; crop substitution program, 53; Herman Siles Zuazo, 53, 57, 157; history of coca in, 54–56; *campesinos*, politics of, 55–56; Yungas, 55; Chapare region, 55, 58; media and Catholic Church criticism of U.S., 56; Black Eagles, 56, 157–58; export of cocaine, 56; corruption in government, 56, 72; political and economic climate in, 55–60; Culumani massacre, 58; "Cocaine Coup," 156–57
Bonilla, Lara, 72, 161, 163
Bureau of Narcotics and Dangerous Drugs (BNDD): corruption in, 146–47; manpower, 183
Bush, George, as head of South Florida Task Force, 91–92, 98
Buy and bust, 69–70, 78. *See also* Law enforcement, case making techniques
Byck, Robert, 20, 26–29, 36–38, 42–43, 188, 208

Cayman Islands: money laundering, 47; as tax haven, 85–86
Central Intelligence Agency (CIA), 61, 92, 162
Cigarette smoking, addiction, 186; advertising, 187; death, 187; protection by United States government, 187
Civil liberties, 117–20; courts' failure to protect, 124; as fatality in war on drugs, 130
Coast Guard, 12, 61, 136; funding of, 61; and South Florida Task Force, 92–94, 97; and NNBIS, 98
Coca, cultivation of leaf, 12; species of, 37–40; in Bolivia, 40–53; in Colombia, 40; in Peru, 40–53; control of, 49–50; crop substitution, 52; leaf chewing in Andean culture, 54–55; Single Convention outlawing by 1986, 54; as a cash crop, 55; dependence of *campesinos* on, 56; eradication of, 58; spread of cultivation to Brazil and Ecuador, 169
Cocaine: medical uses, 9–11, 20, 67, 134–35; health problems, 10–11, 14, 67; addicts or users, 12–14, 189, 216; consumption, 12–15; black market in, 12–17, 31–36, 49, 106, 153; production, 12, 37–41; purity of, 14–16; deaths, 14, 29, 189; effects, 17–30; physical responses, 18, 20–21, 24; psychosis, 23–24; addiction, 24–30; crack (rock) and freebase, 28–29, 45, 134; price, 31–32, 35–36, 41, 73, 91–96, 117, 153; profits in, 32, 44–46; penalties, 32–33, 67–68; arrests, 32, 46, 68, 77–78; seizures, 40, 43, 51–52, 63–64, 72–73, 95–97, 104, 153; laboratories, 40–41; importation and distribution, 41–47; ports of entry, 44–45; adulteration or cutting practices, 45–46; marketing practices, 45–47; U.S. foreign policy, 48–50; Single Convention on Narcotic Drugs, 50–51; withholding funds, 51; interdicting, 61–65; techniques for arrest, 69–72; South Florida Task Forces, 91–99; business, 108–9; media abuse, 189–91
Cocaine Industry: production, 37, 40–41; importation and distribution, 41–47; structure of, 72–73
Colombia, 12, 34, 37, 40, 43, 64, 72, 153, 158, 161–62, 169; areas of cultivation, 40; Colombian syndicates, 43; interdiction, 52; amnesty on illegal income, 58; as base for traffickers, 72; political climate, 72–73; extradition, 72, 133–34; murder of Lara Bonilla, 72, 161, 163; Belisario Bentancur, 72–73; *coqueros*, 72–73; "The Code," 150–51; corruption, 161–62; narco-

terrorism (guerrilla–drug traffickers alliance), 162–69; M–19, 163–64, 169
Communist subversion, tied to drug trafficking, 181–82
Comprehensive Crime Control Act of 1984, 79, 81, 123, 125, 128; denial of bail, 120; sentencing provisions, 121
Computers, 100, 166. *See also* Big Brotherism
Congressional reforms, 119–21, 125. *See also* Assault on justice
Conspiracy, investigations of, 69–71
Continuing Criminal Enterprise Act (CCE), 121, 123; penalities under, 33, 68; arrests under, 68; indictments under, 78, 101–2
Controlled Substances Act, 67, 120
Corruption of public officials, 145–50; Knapp Commission, 146; in foreign governments, 156–62. *See also* Black market pathologies, derivative crimes
Counterattack against narco-terrorism, 165–69
Crime tariff, 34–36
Criminal justice system, 117; assault on Justice, 118; preventive detention, 120–21; attorney-client relationship, 123; disrespect for, 153; heritage of, 201; principle of individual responsibility, 205–9
Crowley, Aleister, 17, 22, 191
Cuba, 155, 163, 184; involvement in drug trade, 163–64, 167–68
Currency and Monetary Instrument Report, 81, 85
Currency Transaction Report, 81, 84
Customs Service, 11, 12, 119, 153; methods of smuggling, 43, 63–65; funding, 61; interdiction at borders, 61, 63; functions, 63; manpower, 63; seizures, 63; South Florida Task Force, 91, 93, 98; NNBIS, 98; "paying its own way," 175

Dealing drugs: deterrence of, 110; as entrepreneurship, 110; benefits of, 111
Defense lawyers: forfeiture of fees, 121–22; subpoenaed as witnesses, 123; reporting of cash fees, 123
Deficit Reduction Act of 1984, 123, 193
Demand, elasticity of. *See* Economics
Department of Defense, 61, 92–93, 95
Destabilization of foreign governments by trade in drugs, 155–62
Deterrence, 106–15
Disrespect for law, 153–54. *See also* Black market pathologies, derivative crimes
Dogs as drug detectors, 41, 63–64, 124, 128
Douglas, William O., 192–93, 200
Drug Abuse Warning Network (DAWN), 14, 29, 189, 216
Drug Control: individual choice, 198; positive potential of drugs, 201–2; refusal to accept, 202–3; moratorium on possessory offenses, 203, 215; successful drug users, 203–5; user as a victim, 205; user in control, 206–7; schooling and training, 212–13; redefining the drug problem, 213–14
Drug Enforcement Agency (DEA), 12, 14–16, 22, 29, 32, 34–36, 41, 43–47, 49, 74–78, 85–86, 119, 130, 135, 145–46, 167–68, 183, 185, 200; history of, 65–67; manpower, 66; arrest techniques, 68–71; clearance rate, 69; limited by privacy, 73; use of informants, 74; arrests, 77–78; payment of rewards, 80–81; and South Florida Task Force, 91, 95; computer files, 132–33; value of seized assets, 175; as profitable, 178
Drug investigation techniques, 74–76
Drug laws, 67–68; public disregard of, 178–79
Drug seizures, 11, 40, 43, 51–52, 57, 63–64, 72–73, 95

Eastern Airlines, 64, 91
Eastern Europe, drugs in, 178
Economics: supply and demand of cocaine, 32, 34–36, 77, 105, 112–14;

prohibition of cocaine as affecting supply and demand, 32–33
Effects of cocaine, 17–30
Eighth Amendment, 121, 193
Entrapment. *See* Sell and bust
Escobar, Pablo, 72–73
Extradition of drug offenders to U.S., 72, 161; from U.S., 133–34. *See also* Big Brotherism

Federal Bureau of Investigation (FBI), 12, 61, 149, 151, 153; role in drug enforcement, 66–69; manpower, 66–67; wiretapping, 126
Federal Reserve System, 82, 84
Financial controls: seizure and forfeiture of assets, 79–81; effect on drug industry, 80; Financial Law Enforcement Center, 83
Financial crimes: emphasis on, 47–48; Bank Secrecy Act investigations, 81–87; Internal Revenue Code investigations, 87–90
Florida, 32–33, 43–46, 131–32, 188; arrests in, 32, 46, 78; penalties in, 33; trafficking laws in, 132; Federal Reserve Banks in, 142
Foreign policy: effects of War on Drugs in Guatemala, 166; El Salvador, 166; Honduras, 167; Venezuela, 169
Fourth Amendment, 124–25, 129
Freud, Sigmund, 21–22, 27, 135, 199, 202. Works: "Uber Coca," 9; *Civilization and its Discontents*, 210–11

Garcia, Meza, 72, 156–57
General Accounting Office (GAO), 53, 95–98, 105
Gold chain fad, 144–45
Gomez, Arce, 156–57
Grinspoon, Lester, 28, 209

Harrison Narcotics Act, 10–11, 24, 32, 65, 106, 135, 179, 181, 189
Heroin: experiences of U.S. soldiers in Vietnam, 27, 203; addiction, 29; importation of, 104; seizures of, 105; supply of, 105–6; medical use of, 134; "French Connection," 147; status of, 177; *Robinson v. California*, 193; *U.S. v. Moore*, 205–6; "China White" synthetic, 221
History of drug enforcement, 65–66, 179–82
Homicide, 150–53; Colombians, 150–52; Cocaine Cowboys, 152
House Select Committee on Narcotics Abuse and Control, 17, 58–59, 76–78

Informants: confidential, 74–75; rewards paid to, 80–81; amateur, 131–32
Informer system, 131–32
Interdiction: methods of avoiding, 43, 63–65; at the source, 51–52; effect on U.S. market price, 52; at the borders of United States, 61–65; by the Customs Service, 61–65; rate of, 65–68
Interdiction network: South Florida Task Force, 91–99; Posse Comitatus Act, 92–94; tracking, 93; problems with, 94–95; seizures, 95–97; arrests, 95–96; NNBIS, 98–99
Internal Revenue Service (IRS), 12, 46, 61, 65, 79, 81, 123; study of drug profit margins, 80; Currency Transaction Report, 81; estimates of money laundering, 83; Criminal Investigation Division of (CID), 87–89; underground economy, 90, 142
International law, 50–51, 54

Justice, Department of, 67–68, 167, 183; proceeds of forfeited assets, 80; South Florida Task Force, 98; wiretapping, 126; War on Drugs "paying its own way," 175

Knapp Commission Report, 146
Kuhn, Thomas, *The Structure of Scientific Revolution*, 194–95, 219

Law Enforcement: goals, 31–36; supply reduction, 31, 49, 61; priorities in

arrest, 32, 46–47; in foreign countries, 51; Mansfield Amendment, 51; funding of, 61, 106; history of, 65–69; rivalries between agencies, 67; case-making techniques, 69–72; drug investigation techniques, 74–75; role of state and local agencies, 78; impact on foreign nations, 167–68
Laws: Pure Food and Drug Act of 1906, 10; Harrison Narcotics Act, 10, 17, 106; Continuing Criminal Enterprise Act, 33, 68; Controlled Substances Act, 66–67, 79; Bank Secrecy Act, 68, 71, 79, 81, 87, 90, 119; Omnibus Crime Control and Safe Streets Act, 75; Comprehensive Crime Control Act, 79, 81; Right to Financial Privacy Act, 86; Tax Reform Act, 86–89, 120; Marijuana Tax Act, 181
Lehder, Carlos, 55, 72
Liddy, G. Gordon, 66, 183
Lopez, Michelsen Alfonso, 72–73
LSD, 177, 223

Mafia, 45, 67, 76, 104, 152
Marijuana: seizures of, 95–97; supply of, 95–96; Operation Grouper, 104; cost of, 151; decriminalization of, 174, 178, 194, 215; number of smokers of, 185; federal law against, 181; varieties of, 221
Media: treatment of cocaine, 11, 14, 24–27; exaggeration and distortion by, 24–25, 189–191; contribution to demise of Wars on Drugs, 175–77
Medical practice, laws obstructing, 134–35. *See also* Big Brotherism
Medical research, 18–20; animal experiments, 24–25
Medical uses of cocaine. *See* Cocaine
Miami, 40–41, 43–44, 74–75, 82, 93, 143, 168; laundering of drug money in, 47; as port of entry, 44–45, 63–64
Miami Herald, 91, 106, 118, 130, 159, 166, 169, 175–77, 189
Money laundering, 47–48, 81–87; Operation Greenback, 47; weighing currency, 47; tax haven, 47–48; by banks, 82–84; to avoid IRS investigations, 89–90
Monitoring of students and school personnel, 129–30; tipster program, 129–30. *See also* Big Brotherism
Musto, David, *The American Disease*, 179

Narco-terrorism: Colombia, 162–64; Cuba, 163–64, 167; Nicaragua, 163, 167–68; Peru, 164–65; El Salvador, 166; Counterattack on, 165
Narcotics and Dangerous Drug Information System (NADDIS), 132–33. *See also* Big Brotherism
National Commission on Marihuana and Drug Abuse, 135–37, 173–74, 192, 194, 213
National Institute on Drug Abuse (NIDA), 12–14, 20, 22, 177–78, 215
National Intelligence Estimate (NIE), 12–14, 17, 40, 43, 55
National Narcotics Border Interdiction System (NNBIS), 91, 98–100
Navy, 92–94, 135–36. *See also* Interdiction network
Nicaragua, 155, 163; as safe haven for traffickers, 167–68; Sandinistas, 167
Nimkoff, Peter, 130–31, 137–38
Nixon, Richard, 3, 61, 65–66, 173, 182–83

Ochoa Family, 55, 72–73
Omnibus Crime Control and Safe Streets Act, 75, 126–27
Organized Crime Drug Enforcement Task Forces (OCDETFs), 99–115; manpower, 99; budget, 99; format, 99–100; coordination problems, 100; objectives, 100–101; successes, 101–2, 104; effect on supply, 104; stratagems, 112

Panama, as tax haven, 47, 84–85; role in drug trade, 169
Peru, 12, 37, 40–41, 43, 64, 153, 156;

areas under cultivation, 40–41; failure of crop control, 50–51, 57; and coca, 52–55; crop substitution program, 52–53, 58 (*see also* Tingo Maria); political and economic climate in, 54, 57–60; Shining Path, 60, 164–65; (*see also* Narco-terrorism)
Pindling, Lyndon O. *See* Bahamas
Politics of the drug issue, 181–84
Posse Comitatus Act, 92–93, 120; 1981 amendments to, 135

Racketeer Influenced Corrupt Organization (RICO), 67–68, 78, 101, 121
Radar. *See* Interdiction network
Reagan, Ronald, 91, 92, 95, 99, 118, 173, 194
Reagan Administration, 17, 155, 165, 167–68, 187, 194, 214
Reverse sting. *See* Law enforcement, case-making techniques
Right to Financial Privacy Act, 86
Risk: to drug dealers, 109–15; as premium in price of drugs, 34, 41, 64–65, 77, 105; and transaction costs, 86; and revenues, 113
Rockefeller, Nelson, 182, 199

Sale of Cocaine, 14, 17, 31–32, 45–46. *See also* Cocaine
Schools and students. *See* Big Brotherism
Sell and bust, 70–71. *See also* Law enforcement, case-making techniques
Shining Path (*Sendero Luminoso*). *See* Peru
Shultz, George, 163–64, 167–68
Siegel, Ronald, 22–24, 29
Single Convention on Narcotic Drugs, 68–70; 1972 Amendment, 50–51. *See also* Cocaine
Smuggling, 63–65; technology and, 63; cargo concealment, 64. *See also* Interdiction, methods of avoiding
South Florida Task Force, as prototype, 91; manpower, 91–92; tracking of planes and boats, 93; costs, 93; seizures by, 95–97; arrests, 95–96; effect on black market, 96
State Department, 12, 165; funding of crop substitution program, 49–50, 52; Bureau of International Narcotics Matter (INM), 52–53; pressure on tax haven countries, 85–86
Suarez, Roberto, 43, 55, 57, 72, 75, 157–58. *See also* Bolivia
Suarez, Roberto, Jr., 75, 151
Supreme Court, 129, 136, 181; decisions affecting constitutional rights of drug defendants, 121–25; interpretation of Harrison Act, 135; *Dred Scott v. Sanford*, 195; *Bradwell v. State*, 195–96; *Powell v. Texas*, 205–6
Surgeon General, 67, 135, 186–87
Surveillance, 75
Szasz, Thomas, *Ceremonial Chemistry*, 33, 184–85, 188, 198, 203, 205–6, 220

Tax evasion, 141–42. *See also* Black market pathology, derivative crimes
Tax havens, 47–48; money laundering, 85–87, 89; Bahamas, 85; Cayman Islands, 85; Panama, 85; Pacific, 87
Tax Reform Act, 86–89. *See also* Laws
Tingo Maria, 52, 58, 59, 164. *See also* Peru
Treasury Department, 47, 65, 81
Trebach, Arnold, *The Heroin Solution*, 193

Undercover investigations, 74
United States Code, Title 21 (Controlled Substances), 67
United States dependence on drug enforcement revenues, 174–75; dangers of "partnership" in crime, 175

Vesco, Robert, 72, 160
Vietnam, 27, 203; role of media in, 175
Violence, crimes of, 150–53, 214. *See also* Black market pathologies, derivative crimes

War on Drugs, 17, 36, 47, 63, 65, 195, 198, 214, 215–22; arrests under, 32; increase in manpower of agencies, 66; growth of cocaine under, 78; banking prosecutions under, 82; central strategy of, 91; South Florida Task Force, 91–99; interagency rivalries, 98–100; OCDETF, 99–115; deterrence, 106–13; assault on justice under, 118–26; growth of Big Brotherism under, 126–39; derivative crimes under, 141–54; destabilization of foreign governments under, 155–69; lack of realistic objectives, 173–74; immunization from criticism, 174–75; "paying its own way," 175; erosion of public support for, 178–79; history of, 179–84; politics of, 182–84; shift to new context, 197–206

Weil, Andrew, *The Natural Mind*, 19, 185–86, 198, 202, 208–11, 220–21

Wiretapping, 75–76, 126–27

Work ethic, 142–45. *See also* Black market pathologies, derivative crimes

Zinberg, Norman, 19, 26; *Drug, Set, and Setting*, 193

About the Author

STEVEN WISOTSKY, Professor of Law, Nova University Law Center, is editor of the proceedings of the recent War on Drugs Symposium. His research on the effects of the War on Drugs has attracted wide attention.